Microsoft

Microsoft®

Small Business Server 2000

W9-CNA-949

Resource Kit

IT Professional

PUBLISHED BY
Microsoft Press
A Division of Microsoft Corporation
One Microsoft Way
Redmond, Washington 98052-6399

Library of Congress Cataloging-in-Publication Data
Microsoft Small Business Server Resource Kit / Microsoft Corporation.
     p. cm.
   ISBN 0-7356-1252-8
   1. Client/server computing.   2. Microsoft Small Business Server (Computer file).   I.
Microsoft Corporation.
QA76.9.C55 M5318   2000
005.7'13769--dc21   00-051109

Printed and bound in the United States of America.

1 2 3 4 5 6 7 8 9   QWT   6 5 4 3 2 1

Distributed in Canada by Penguin Books Canada Limited.

A CIP catalogue record for this book is available from the British Library.

Microsoft Press books are available through booksellers and distributors worldwide. For further information about international editions, contact your local Microsoft Corporation office or contact Microsoft Press International directly at fax (425) 936-7329. Visit our Web site at mspress.microsoft.com. Send comments to *rkinput@microsoft.com*.

Active Directory, ActiveX, BackOffice, BizTalk, FrontPage, Hotmail, IntelliMirror, Microsoft, Microsoft Press, MS-DOS, MSN, NetMeeting, NetShow, Outlook, Visual Basic, Visual Studio, Win32, Windows, Windows Media, and Windows NT are either registered trademarks or trademarks of Microsoft Corporation in the United States and/or other countries. Other product and company names mentioned herein may be the trademarks of their respective owners.

Unless otherwise noted, the example companies, organizations, products, people, and events depicted herein are fictitious. No association with any real company, organization, product, person, or event is intended or should be inferred.

Acquisitions Editor: Juliana Aldous
Project Editor: Maureen Williams Zimmerman

Thank you to those who contributed to this book:

Documentation Manager

Amy Michaels

Project Manager/Lead Technical Editor

Liz Halverson

Lead Technical Writer

Steve Holland

Technical Writer

Harry M. Brelsford, NetHealthMon.com

Technical Editors

Mary Harris, Deborah Annan, Karin Roberts

Copy Editors

Carolyn Emory, Lead

Nan Pardew, Gina Craig, Kristin Elko

Technical Consultants

Erin Bourke-Dunphy, Charles Anthe, Lingan Satkunanathan, Lisa Butler, Sam Kim, Dean Paron,
Brian Strully, Sears Young, Roy D. Riley, Jr., Tracy Daugherty, Paul Fitzgerald, Scott Walker,
David Copeland, Chris Avis, Patricio F. Oliva J., Gerard Linck, Kristin Thomas,
Jesse Vurgason-Graham, Terry McKinney, Dave Forrest, and Beth Harmon

Production Lead

Mike Birch

Production Specialist

Theano Petersen

Graphic Designer

David Hose

Indexers

Lee Ross, Tony Ross

Contents

CHAPTER 2 Continued

CHAPTER 5 Continued

CHAPTER 7 Continued

CHAPTER 11 Continued

CHAPTER 11 Continued

CHAPTER 14 Continued

CHAPTER 18 Continued

CHAPTER 18 Continued

CHAPTER 22 Continued

APPENDIX D   Continued

Figures and Tables

FIGURES

TABLES

Procedures

CHAPTER 13

CHAPTER 15

CHAPTER 18 Continued

CHAPTER 19

CHAPTER 21

About The Resource Kit

Welcome to the Microsoft® Small Business Server 2000 Resource Kit. This resource kit contains one copy of the Microsoft Small Business Server Resource Guide, and a single compact disc with Small Business Server software tools, Online Help, various utilities, and an online (HTML) version of this book.

The resource guide provides detailed information for Small Business Server 2000 and its associated applications. The in-depth information is a technical supplement to the Small Business Server 2000 core documentation, which includes the Getting Started guide and the Online Guide. The resource guide is not intended to replace the core documentation as a source for learning how to use the product features and programs.

About The Small Business Server Resource Guide

This resource guide contains the following information:

About The Resource Kit

- Outlines the contents of the resource guide.
- Describes the Microsoft Small Business Server Resource Kit Disc.
- Describes the support policy for the Microsoft Small Business Server Resource Kit.

Chapters 1-3, Introductory Information for the Technology Consultant

Introduces Small Business Server 2000 to the technology consultant, and also may be used as customer presentation material. The following information is provided:

- Customer profile.
- Design philosophy.
- Ease-of-setup, management, and use.
- Communication in new and more efficient ways.
- Everything needed to run a small business.
- Benefits of using Small Business Server for the technology consultant.
- Solution development.
- Other resources.

Chapters 4-7, Planning

Addresses the issues that arise when planning for the deployment of Small Business Server 2000 in a small business organization. The following topics are discussed:

- Small Business Server network characteristics.
- Client and server computer requirements.
- Backup system configuration planning.
- Disaster recovery planning.
- Planning for an Internet presence.
- Planning for remote access users and virtual private network connectivity.
- Planning for Microsoft Shared Fax Service and Shared Modem Service.
- Planning for Internet Security and Acceleration (ISA) Server 2000.
- Planning for Exchange 2000 Server.

Chapter 8-14, Deployment

Outlines factors and conditions that should be considered when customizing the deployment of Small Business Server 2000 in a small business organization. The following topics are covered:

- Installing Small Business Server on new machines.
- Upgrading from Small Business Server 4.5 to Small Business Server 2000.
- Installing Small Business Server in existing environments, such as Novell NetWare.
- Setup issues.
- Using the Add User Wizard and the Set Up Computer Wizard.
- Internet service provider (ISP) connectivity tasks.
- Setting up remote client computers.
- Installing virtual private network capabilities in the small business network.
- Underlying Windows 2000 Server configurations and tools such as Group Policy.

Chapters 15-18, Administering and Maintaining

Describes administration of Small Business Server tools, applications, and components. The following topics are covered:

- Small Business Server wizard processes, including background configuration of applications performed by the console wizards.

- Administrative tools such as remote administration with NetMeeting®, Policy Editor, Server Status, Fax/Internet Reporting, Performance Monitor, and the Task Scheduler.

- Administering Small Business Server components including Shared Fax Service 2000, Shared Modem Service 2000, Exchange 2000 Server, ISA Server 2000, and SQL Server™ 2000.

- How the overall performance of Small Business Server is maximized.

- How server applications are performance-optimized on a single server platform.

- Why the default configuration of Small Business Server is optimal for the small business.

- Administrative tips.

Chapters 19-20, Integration and Interaction

Topics discussed include:

- E-mail and Internet connectivity alternatives, including Web browsing, Post Office Protocol 3 (POP3), Simple Mail Transport Protocol (SMTP), and Web hosting strategies.

- Client interaction with the server, including Windows NT®, Windows® Me, 95, 98, Windows 3.1, MS-DOS, and Macintosh® client interactions with Small Business Server.

- Cross platform interoperability, including NetWare, UNIX®, and Macintosh client compatibilities with Small Business Server.

Chapters 21-23, Security

Discusses the Small Business Server 2000 features that provide network security, including:

- ISA Server 2000 overview, managed network access, and key security features with security architecture.

- Windows 2000 Server and computer security.

- Internet Information Server (IIS) 5.0 security model.

Chapters 24-25, Migration and Upgrade

Topics discussed include:

- Licensing requirements for expanding the Small Business Server user base.

- Client access licenses and the installation of client add packs.

- Migrating an Access database to SQL Server 2000.

Chapter 26, Disaster Recovery

Provides disaster recovery information, with strategic planning considerations and recovery scenarios for a small business network.

Appendix A, Networking Basics

Provides an introduction to computer networks and fault-tolerant disk configurations.

Appendix B, Migrating from Netware

Includes specific planning, testing, and implementation steps to migrate successfully from an existing NetWare network to a Small Business Server 2000 network using tools such as Gateway Services for NetWare (GSNW).

Appendix C, Customization and Extensibility Options

Describes how Small Business Server functionalities can be extended or enhanced by:

- Architectural background, mechanisms, and procedural information for extending the Small Business Server consoles.

- Extending the Set Up Computer Wizard.

Appendix D, Office 2000 Deployments

Describes efficient and effective ways to deploy Office 2000 on a Small Business Server 2000 network, including:

- Enhancing Office 2000 functionality.

- Office 2000 Customer Manager.

Appendix E, TAPI Solutions for Small Businesses

Introduces Telephony Applications Programming Interface (TAPI) solutions for Small Business Server 2000.

Appendix F, Small Business Server 2000 Resource Kit Installation and Access

Describes how to install the Microsoft Small Business Server 2000 Resource Kit Disc on your server and how to access the Small Business Server tools. Descriptions of the numerous tools are included.

Glossary

Contains definitions of terms used in the Microsoft Small Business Server Resource Guide.

Index

Provides a topic index to the resource guide.

Resource Kit Compact Disc

The compact disc that accompanies the Microsoft Small Business Server Resource Guide contains the following:

- Software tools specifically developed for Small Business Server 2000.
- Online (HTML) Help for Small Business Server tool use.
- HTML version of this resource guide.

After installing the *Microsoft Small Business Server 2000 Resource Kit*, please refer immediately to the Release Notes.

Resource Kit Tools

The *Microsoft Small Business Server 2000 Resource Kit* contains a wide variety of tools and utilities to help you work more efficiently with Small Business Server 2000.

The compact disc contains tools for:

- Computer Management
- Deployment
- Desktop
- Diagnostics and troubleshooting
- Security
- Internet Information Server
- Internet Explorer
- Network management
- Scripting
- Autorun menu for linking to the resources on the disc
- A setup program to install the HTML version of the resource guide, Small Business Server tools, and associated Help files

For detailed descriptions of the tools and how to access them, refer to Appendix F of this resource guide.

Resource Kit Support Policy

The SOFTWARE supplied in the *Microsoft Small Business Server 2000 Resource Kit* is not officially supported. Microsoft does not guarantee the performance of the resource kit tools, response times for answering questions, or bug fixes for the tools. However, we do provide a way for customers who purchase the Microsoft Small Business Server Resource Kit to report bugs and possibly receive fixes for their issues. You can do this by sending e-mail to RKInput@microsoft.com.

The SOFTWARE (including instructions for its use, all printed documentation, and Online Help) is provided "AS IS" without warranty of any kind. Microsoft further disclaims all implied warranties, including, without limitation, any implied warranties of merchantability or of fitness for a particular purpose. The entire risk arising out of the use or performance of the SOFTWARE and documentation remains with you.

In no event shall Microsoft, its authors, or anyone else involved in the creation, production, or delivery of the SOFTWARE be liable for any damages whatsoever (including, without limitations, damages for loss of business information, or other monetary loss) arising out of the use of, or inability to use, the SOFTWARE or documentation, even if Microsoft has been advised of the possibility of such damages.

Small Business Server Design Philosophy

Small business owners constantly search for a simpler way to run their businesses. Microsoft® Small Business Server 2000 provides a complete business solution for the small business owner at a reasonable price, based on a single-server operating environment. By using Small Business Server, small business owners can share files and printers, secure company information, communicate with business partners and customers, connect to the Internet, and run business-critical applications.

Small Business Server is designed for companies that operate from a single location and use a maximum of 50 client computers. Because most businesses of this size have a limited number of employees and resources, they typically cannot employ a full-time Information System (IS) professional on staff. Instead, they routinely rely on their accountants or office administrators to set up and manage their networks. This presents a unique challenge, because although these individuals have some experience with computers, they usually have little or no experience dealing with networks, making network setup and management a difficult and overwhelming task.

A Complete Business Solution

Despite not having onsite IS professionals, small businesses still need a complete business solution to manage their companies. They are looking for programs and products designed to help them take advantage of the business benefits of current information technology. They also want to stay on the leading edge by keeping in touch with their customers and peers through e-mail and the Web.

Due to limited resources, the focus of most small businesses is on job completion. Although they may want to move toward a technical business solution, the time or personnel to implement and maintain a complex network is rarely available.

The idea of buying a network—or upgrading poorly performing peer-to-peer networks—intimidates many small business customers. The idea of reducing overall costs by investing in technology, however, is often compelling. In fact, one of the primary reasons that purchasing Small Business Server is preferable to alternatives, such as purchasing each server component separately, is cost savings from technology.

A Single, Integrated Package

Today, small businesses looking for computer solutions face many separate and complicated issues. They must either purchase separate components from multiple vendors and then contract with a reseller to install and configure them, or learn the technology to implement their own systems. Small Business Server addresses these issues for the small business customer, making it easier for small business owners to concentrate on growing and managing their companies.

Small Business Server contains a suite of server products that allow companies to share information and resources, access the Internet, communicate with customers and partners, and run business-critical applications. Essentially, Small Business Server provides all the services that small business customers want in a single integrated package. It is simple and intuitive, and easy to set up, manage, and use. Small Business Server provides a solid information system foundation for today's needs. In addition, Small Business Server accommodates organizational growth in the future—even allowing upgrades to the full Microsoft BackOffice® Server 2000 suite.

Advantages of a Client/Server Network

Many growing companies find that the limitations of peer-to-peer networking restrict the expansion of their business. Peer-to-peer network users benefit by upgrading to a robust and reliable business solution that uses a client/server network for the following reasons:

- Better network performance

- Line-of-business applications

- Accommodation of remote users (because peer-to-peer networks will not support them)

- Secure and controlled shared access to the Internet and intranet

- Integrated external and internal e-mail system

- Centralized file sharing and backup

Peer-to-peer networks are adequate for basic file and printer sharing. When it comes to getting the most out of a network, however, a client/server model network handles issues such as performance, security, group e-mail, and scheduling better. Small Business Server provides these capabilities and offers additional features that are not standard in peer-to-peer networks.

A "Best Practices" Deployment of Windows 2000 Server

Microsoft designed Small Business Server to enable the customer to implement the underlying operating system, Microsoft Windows® 2000 Server, according to recommended "best practices" with ease. Small Business Server installs and configures Windows 2000 Server in accordance with its best practices guidelines. For example, during Small Business Server Setup, Microsoft Active Directory™ directory service is installed and configured optimally for small business use. Setup creates an Organizational Unit and several security groups to manage the small business according to Windows 2000 Server best practices.

Upgrading from a NetWare Network

Small Business Server is a complete and integrated business solution. Small business customers using NetWare 3.x, 4.x, 5.x, or IntranetWare who upgrade to Small Business Server will not have to acquire pieces and parts to create an application-rich solution. In order to get the same high level of functionality as Small Business Server, current NetWare users must purchase and install separate servers for their database, Web, and firewall capabilities, and possibly for e-mail and fax as well. Small Business Server provides all this functionality in one box.

Small Business Server Design Goals

Several key design concepts were adopted to allow a satisfying and productive computing experience for the small business customer.

Easy to Use

The most important aspect of Small Business Server is that it is easy to use. Tasks are clearly defined, so administrators and users avoid the confusion of needing to identify the next step in the process. For example, the Small Business Server consoles and wizards guide administrators and users through the required steps necessary to complete each task simply. Each choice is supported with enough information to enable the user to make an informed decision.

It is also easy for technology consultants to teach their Small Business Server customers how to perform various tasks, and there is consistency between sites.

Clear and Consistent Setup Decisions

Small business customers are generally inexperienced in dealing with network, setup, and application problems. Time constraints do not permit them to research all the issues and alternatives in enough detail to make informed decisions. As a result, they usually rely on a technology consultant to install and configure their networking environments. For this reason, Small Business Server was designed so the technology consultant can easily provide the appropriate configuration and avoid presenting the small business customer with complex network decisions. During setup, the technology consultant is presented with the most appropriate choices, eliminating confusion and work for the customer and reducing the likelihood of mistakes.

Clear and consistent setup decisions result in a network configuration that efficiently addresses small business customer needs and is easy to maintain. For example, during the Windows 2000 Server operating system portion of Small Business Server Setup, the server is promoted to a domain controller, Domain Name System (DNS), and Dynamic Host Configuration Protocol (DHCP) is automatically configured.

> **Note**   The Windows 2000 Server installation under Small Business Server 2000 has been simplified to not display the Workgroup or Computer Domain page and the Licensing Modes page, because Small Business Server makes these decisions automatically.

With clear and consistent setup decisions, Small Business Server eliminates difficulties and avoids unnecessary or less-than-ideal configurations. This feature further benefits the technology consultant by producing consistent Small Business Server configurations that support ease of management.

Designed for Success

Technology consultant and customer success is very important. Frequently, technology consultants and power users (users with strong computer skills) set out to perform a task and become frustrated by its complexity and the time it takes to finish the task. Sometimes they wonder if they actually completed the task. It is important that these individuals find out how to do things quickly, easily, and completely. Small Business Server is designed to make it easy for technology consultants and power users to succeed in the tasks they want to perform.

Small Business Server promotes task-oriented success through two consoles:

- **Small Business Server Administrator Console.** An advanced, sophisticated console used by the technology consultant to manage Small Business Server. Nearly all tasks performed by the technology consultant may be done from this console.

- **Small Business Server Personal Console.** Although this console presents fewer options, it is ideal for those power users who help manage Small Business Server. These users are typically employees at the customer site who supplement the technology consultant's efforts from this console.

The consoles benefit the technology consultant, because training small business customers to perform simple tasks is easy and such training reduces excessive support calls. Technology consultants may also modify each console to add important tasks.

Increased Stability

Small Business Server benefits in many ways from having Windows 2000 Server as its underlying operating system. Windows 2000 Server provides increased stability compared with earlier operating systems. Both the small business customer and technology consultant benefit from increased system availability. Windows 2000 Server significantly reduces the need for restarts, thereby increasing network availability. The number of actions that force a restart of the system have also been significantly decreased. For example, when implementing or modifying network protocols, it is unnecessary to restart Small Business Server.

Business-Class Computing Power

Small Business Server is a business-class networking solution. Small business customers will not notice any limitations with respect to business computer performance. Small Business Server can run on powerful servers, including multi-processor models, and can execute business application instructions at high levels of performance. Common business applications that function with Small Business Server include:

- Independent software vendor (ISV) accounting programs.

- Large databases (such as Microsoft SQL Server™ 2000, included in Small Business Server).

- Computer-aided design (CAD) applications.

- Vertical market applications (such as legal and medical document management or time and billing solutions).

- Custom applications developed by the small business customer (for example, programming solutions such as Microsoft Visual Studio®).

Small Business Server does not compromise the ability of a small business to run the most powerful business applications.

Tools for Remote Administration

The small business customer and the technology consultant develop a long-term relationship. Small Business Server includes network management tools to facilitate this relationship and enable an administrator or technology consultant working remotely to monitor the performance and health of the small business customer's network. These tools include:

- Periodic reporting through Server Status Reports (an automatic reporting tool).

- Health Monitor 2.1 (a network health monitor).

- Terminal Services, a new feature in Windows 2000 Server enabled by default in Small Business Server 2000 Remote Administration mode.

Remote administration typically results in faster response time and quicker resolution of network problems.

Keeping Things Simple

Small Business Server achieves both ease of use and user success by keeping things simple. Because most network setup and management decisions are made automatically for the customer, tasks are inherently simple. There are times, however, when the user must make decisions. In these instances, a clear and concise Small Business Server interface asks the user to perform one task at a time, and only the information necessary for completing the task is presented.

The simplicity of Small Business Server makes it easy for users to comprehend the scope of each task, which ultimately enhances their confidence levels and success rates, and thus helps the technology consultant engage the small business customer in performing tasks.

Securing the Information Infrastructure

Small Business Server provides robust network security, utilizing both Windows 2000 Server and Microsoft Internet Security and Acceleration (ISA) Server 2000 (a successor to Proxy Server). ISA Server enhances Windows 2000 Server's native security by providing advanced firewall configurations difficult for intruders to penetrate. With Small Business Server, small businesses have the same level of network security as larger enterprises, including the following elements:

- File-level encryption

- Secure virtual private network (VPN)

- Internet Protocol Security (IPSec)

- Public Key Infrastructure (PKI)

- Packet filtering and port management using ISA Server

- Secure Network Address Translation (NAT) using ISA Server

   ☑ **Note**   If the small business is using Windows 2000 Professional clients, Kerberos-based security is available.

As small businesses depend more and more on networks to store business-critical information, run business applications, and allow Internet access, this feature of Small Business Server becomes more important for—and more appreciated by—small business customers.

   ☑ **Note**   For further discussion on Small Business Server security, refer to Chapter 21, "Firewall Security and Web Caching With ISA Server."

Summary

Small Business Server 2000 provides a cost-effective small business networking solution for businesses with 50 computers or less, with both an internal local area network and a secure connection to the Internet. Based on the traditional client/server networking architecture, Small Business Server is the infrastructure needed by many small businesses to run applications such as small business accounting systems. Both the technology consultant and the small business customer benefit from the simplified administration of Small Business Server.

CHAPTER 2

Component Feature Summary

Microsoft® Small Business Server has everything needed to run a small business network. It integrates server applications from Microsoft to provide a solution for sharing files, databases, printers, e-mail, fax services, applications, Internet connection services, and other resources such as supporting independent software vendors (ISVs) and custom business applications. Small Business Server provides a complete array of services to enable communication with anyone, anywhere, at any time.

Small Business Server combines Microsoft server products, including:

- Microsoft Windows® 2000 Server operating system including Internet Information Services (IIS) 5.0.

- Microsoft Internet Security and Acceleration (ISA) Server 2000.

- Microsoft Exchange 2000 Server.

- Microsoft SQL Server™ 2000.

- Shared Fax Service.

- Shared Modem Service.

- Small Business Server consoles using Microsoft Management Console (MMC).

- Wizard-based Internet connectivity providing shared access to the Internet.

A summary of Microsoft server products, components, and features contained in Small Business Server 2000 follows.

Components Providing File, Print, Application, and Security Services

The components outlined in this section provide file, print, application, and security services to Small Business Server 2000.

Windows 2000 Server

Windows 2000 Server is a secure, reliable operating system on which small businesses can easily share files, manage users and computers, back up critical company information, share equipment such as printers and modems, and run business applications reliably. The following features enable these capabilities:

- Server Operating System
- Active Directory™ directory service
- Terminal Services
- Group Policy (with Windows 2000 Professional clients)
- Microsoft Management Console
- Disk Quotas
- Microsoft IntelliMirror® (with Windows 2000 Professional clients)
- Remote Installation Services (RIS) (Windows 2000 Professional clients only)

Server Operating System

Windows 2000 Server offers the small business customer a robust 32-bit server operating system that provides resource sharing, application services, and security. Resource sharing enables small businesses to share files and printers easily.

> ☑ **Note** Small Business Server restricts Windows 2000 Server to the root of the domain forest, as well as 50 connected personal computers. Trust relationships are not possible.

Active Directory

One of the most powerful features in Windows 2000 Server is Active Directory, a state-of-the-art directory services solution. Active Directory manages all Small Business Server network objects, including:

- **Users**. You can set up and administer user accounts.

- **Groups**. You can create and manage e-mail distribution and security groups.

- **Computers**. You can add and modify computer accounts.

- **Organizational units**. You can create and manage organizational units, which are containers that typically reflect the departments in a small business (for example, Marketing), locations (East), or projects (Project#1). Users and computers are typically placed in organizational units and can be a member of only one organizational unit at a time.

    ☑ **Note**   Small Business Server creates an organizational unit called MyBusiness to store the distribution and security groups that administrators create from the Small Business Server console.

- **Printers**. You can manage shared network printers.

- **Mailboxes**. You can create user mailboxes (assuming that Microsoft Exchange 2000 Server is installed).

- **Shared folders**. You can publish shared folders to Active Directory as objects.

Active Directory Tools

Active Directory can be managed directly through MMC tools. The most popular tool for technology consultants managing Small Business Server is Active Directory Users and Computers. It is used to manage Active Directory objects, including users, groups, computers, organizational units, printers, contacts, and Active Directory published shared folders.

☑ **Note**   Two additional Active Directory tools designed for use at the enterprise-level include:

- **Active Directory Domains and Trusts**. Enterprises use this tool to manage multiple domains and trust relationships. This tool has no practical use in Small Business Server, because Small Business Server creates only one domain, and trusts are not possible.

- **Active Directory Sites and Services**. This tool is used to manage the physical network infrastructure, typically defined as sites based on locations or Internet Protocol subnetworks. This tool also manages services, including network services, public key services, and Routing and Remote Access Services.

Active Directory Standards and Interfaces

Active Directory is based on published and widely accepted directory services standards such as X.500, Lightweight Directory Access Protocol (LDAP), and Microsoft enhancements such as Active Directory Services Interfaces.

X.500

An underlying standard that forms the framework for nearly all directory services is X.500. This standard defines the basic structure of directory services, starting at the highest-level object (country) and proceeding to greater levels of detail, including organizational units and ending with common names. Active Directory is X.500 compatible. This makes Active Directory compatible with other directory services but also allows for Microsoft-based directory services enhancements, such as Active Directory Services Interface.

Lightweight Directory Access Protocol

LDAP, a widely accepted directory services standard, is the foundation for Active Directory. LDAP enables Active Directory to interact with other directory services and applications—this is part of Microsoft's directory services unification strategy. Because it is LDAP-based, Active Directory can pass user logon authentication credentials to other systems. This enables the user to enjoy a single sign-on experience.

Active Directory Services Interface

Active Directory Services Interface (ADSI) is an application programming interface (API) that enables ISV developers to extend Active Directory to accommodate new features and functionality. For example, a software developer can create custom objects in the Active Directory schema for the developer's application.

Terminal Services

Small Business Server installs Terminal Services in remote administration mode as part of the
Windows 2000 Server Setup. Terminal Services supports multi-session computing, better known
as remote sessions. Terminal Services enables an administrator or technology consultant to access
and manage Small Business Server remotely from other workstations or locations, as shown in
Figure 2.1.

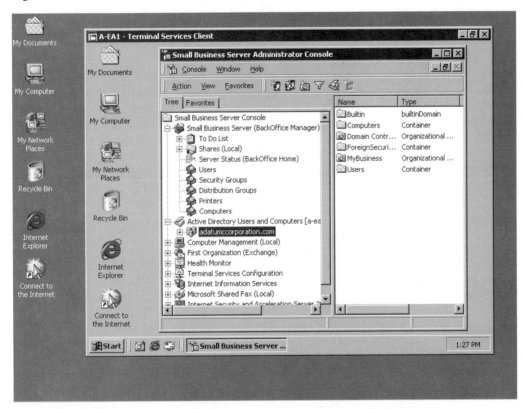

**Figure 2.1   Remote administration facilitated by a Terminal Services session from other
workstations or locations**

In Figure 2.1, notice that the inner session is a Terminal Services session running the Small
Business Server Administrator Console. The outer window is the local computer session. For more
information on Terminal Services, refer to Chapter 16, "Terminal Services and Group Policy
Administration."

Group Policy

Group Policy facilitates centralized management of Windows 2000 Server and Windows 2000 Professional computers. This simplifies tasks for the Small Business Server administrator or technology consultant, who can apply Group Policy to computers to enable or restrict specific features, capabilities, settings, and security. You can also apply Group Policy to users to extend or restrict the user experience, including features, capabilities, settings, and security. For example, using Group Policy, desktop and Start menu settings can be specified for a given group of users. Group Policy supports roaming user profiles and provides the ability to deploy software to client computers with ease. Group Policy may be applied at the domain, site, or organizational-unit level.

Microsoft Management Console

Microsoft Management Console (MMC) is the standard tool-set interface in Windows 2000 Server. Small Business Server administrators and technology consultants have a consistent interface and user experience when using Windows 2000 Server. MMC standardizes the way in which Windows 2000 administration is performed, so that the server-level tools no longer have different appearances and behaviors.

Disk Quotas

Windows 2000 Server implements disk quotas at the volume level, enabling the Small Business Server administrator or technology consultant to set storage limits on a per-user basis. Quota management enables the issuance of both warnings and quota limits based on storage values set by the administrator.

IntelliMirror

Windows 2000 Server provides IntelliMirror as a built-in feature. IntelliMirror enables users to work from various computers and have their personal settings and data follow them. IntelliMirror has three core features: user data management, software installation and maintenance, and user settings management. IntelliMirror automatically synchronizes local folders and server-based folders, enabling users to work online or offline.

☑ **Note**   IntelliMirror requires Windows 2000 Professional clients.

Remote Installation Services

Windows 2000 Server supports efficient installation of Windows 2000 Professional clients through Remote Installation Services (RIS). Client computers do not need to be identical, which is a significant improvement over other installation tools.

Improvements over Windows NT Server 4.0

Windows 2000 Server has improved on Microsoft Windows NT® Server 4.0 in both stability and security. Windows 2000 Server requires the administrator or technology consultant to restart the operating system fewer times as part of the day-to-day administration of Small Business Server 2000. For example, when a new network protocol is added, a restart is not required to bind the new protocol. Security is stronger, with Active Directory and new security implementations provided by logon authentication (Kerberos, Public Key Infrastructure), share-level permissions, NTFS file system permissions, Internet Protocol Security (IPSec), TCP/IP packet filtering, smart card support and file- and folder-level encryption.

Windows 2000 Professional

Windows 2000 Professional is the desktop operating system in the Windows 2000 family, replacing Windows NT Workstation version 4.0. For the highest performance on a Small Business Server network, it is recommended that users working at desktop computers run Windows 2000 Professional, enabling them to experience full Windows 2000 network functionality and features, including:

- Group Policy participation.

- IntelliMirror technologies.

- Windows file protection, which protects core system files from being overwritten.

- Driver certification to ensure that users are installing Windows 2000 tested and compliant drivers.

- Kerberos security and other security enhancements, such as Encrypting File System (EFS).

- Offline files and folders with Synchronization Manager, for file and folder management away from the office network.

- Device Manager with Plug and Play hardware support.

SQL Server 2000

SQL Server 2000 provides a powerful, secure, relational database for running business applications. When compared with previous versions, SQL Server 2000 has overall increased performance, reliability, and availability. Support of the XML format improves the storage and retrieval of data. SQL Server 2000 improves data access to the Internet by providing an easier way to present database information on dynamic Web pages that are hosted on the Small Business Server using IIS 5.0.

Many third-party ISVs, such as accounting software vendors, have applications that use the features of SQL Server. For example, several accounting software vendors offer packages that have higher reliability and availability using SQL Server, because of the transaction logging function of SQL Server. Before accounting transactions are committed in SQL Server, the transaction is first written to a transaction log. This provides greater accounting software reliability if, for some reason, the transaction is not correctly written to the database. With SQL Server, transaction logs enable administrators to rebuild the accounting database from the point of failure.

Components Providing Powerful Communications Services

The components outlined in this section provide communication services in Small Business Server 2000.

Exchange 2000 Server

Microsoft Exchange 2000 Server, an Internet mail and collaboration server, includes business solutions to help get customers connected and coordinated; it provides a solid foundation built on Internet and other open standards.

Outlook 2000

Microsoft Outlook® 2000, a desktop information manager, helps users manage their messages, appointments, contacts, and tasks, as well as track activities, open and view documents, and share information.

With the Exchange Server and Outlook combination, the small business can build a community through rich electronic messaging, discussion groups, list services, and other groupware capabilities. The small business can communicate immediately with internal and external customers and suppliers, right from the desktop.

Outlook Web Access

Small Business Server supports Microsoft Outlook Web Access, a feature of Exchange 2000 Server. The Outlook Web Access enables users to access their Exchange Server mailboxes from any computer platform-based Web browser, such as Internet Explorer, through the Internet. The client computer requires no additional configuration. Outlook Web Access supports multiple operating systems, such as UNIX and Macintosh-based Web browsers. Users can read and reply to e-mails, look up contact information, set appointments, and manage tasks while out of the office.

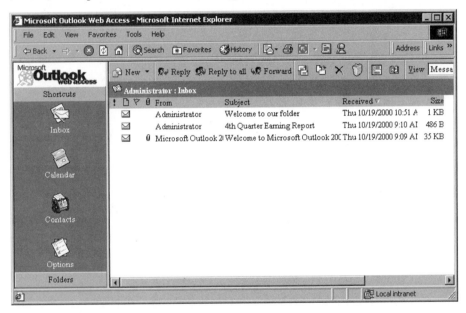

Figure 2.2   Microsoft Outlook Web Access gives users full Outlook functionality when they are away from the Small Business Server local area network

Figure 2.2 illustrates the Exchange Web Client interface, which offers the same features as Outlook 2000. For example, the icons for Inbox, Calendar, and Contacts are displayed in the far left column, as in Outlook 2000. Also, the **New** message and **Reply** buttons are displayed above the Inbox, and e-mail messages are displayed in the Inbox.

Outlook Team Folders

The Outlook Team Folder is a new team collaboration tool that blends the flexibility of public folders with the intuitiveness of the Web. To create a location for shared information, users can easily create a Team Folder and select the users who can access the folder. Team Folders enable small businesses to easily share information and enjoy the benefits of Web-based collaboration.

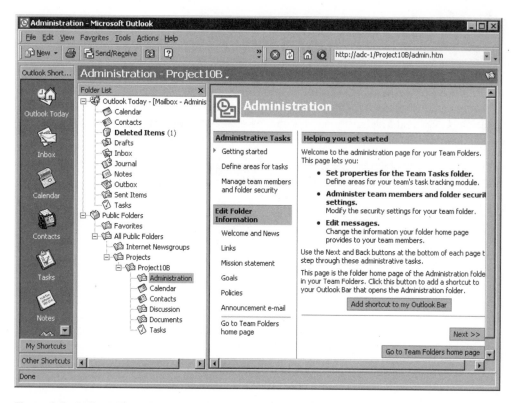

Figure 2.3 Outlook Team Folders are used by small businesses to improve employee and vendor communications

In Figure 2.3, a Team Folder Home Page is displayed. From here, team members can read project news under Top News. In addition to participating in discussion threads, team members can also check the Team Calendar, see Team Tasks, and look up information in Team Contacts.

Instant Messaging Service

Instant Messaging Service enables one user to chat over the Internet with another user, in a real-time, point-to-point chat mode. This is a popular feature in organizations with dispersed users that require real-time communications, and it typically extends traditional e-mail communications. The use of Instant Messaging Service enables small businesses to avoid long-distance telephone charges because it uses the Internet connection. Instant Messaging Service can also be used internally in the business. For example, workers on the phone can simultaneously answer questions by using instant messaging on the computer.

Chat Service

Exchange 2000 Server provides a multi-user chat system that enables people to convene for conversations on channels (also known as chat rooms). Users can join live, real-time discussion forums that cover a broad range of topics. Chat Service is based on Internet Relay Chat (IRC), a client-server protocol that supports real-time conversation between two or more users over a TCP/IP network (including the Internet).

Exchange Multimedia Control

Exchange Multimedia Control is a feature of both Outlook 2000 and the Exchange Web Client. It enables the e-mail sender to embed rich multimedia content, such as voice recordings, into an e-mail message. This feature is configured from the Option button on Exchange Web Client. You can download and install the latest version of the Exchange Multimedia Control from the Small Business Server 2000 server computer.

Web Storage System

Microsoft Web Storage System enables businesses to create Exchange public folders that appear as native Windows 2000 folders on the network. Documents stored in these folders are accessed on the network by using native Windows 2000 file browsing tools, such as My Network Places.

Shared Fax Service

Shared Fax Service enables businesses to communicate by fax more efficiently with fewer telephone lines. From their desktops, users can fax any document created in any program, as well as receive faxes, route faxes through e-mail, and manage fax devices. Small businesses can control who can view and send faxes and determine how faxes are distributed within their companies. Small Business Server 2000 has improved faxing capability from previous versions and can accommodate additional modems, fax boards, and Integrated Services Digital Network (ISDN) cards.

Shared Modem Service

Shared Modem Service enables small businesses to share modems installed on their servers, eliminating the need for a modem and telephone line for each workstation. In addition, Shared Modem Service reduces wait times because the server automatically uses the next available modem in the pool to handle dial-in or dial-out requests.

NetMeeting

Microsoft NetMeeting® enables small businesses to conduct live audio and video conferences and work collaboratively. NetMeeting provides both internal LAN and external Internet conferencing and collaboration capabilities, including one-on-one video conferencing, desktop sharing (for both support and collaboration), whiteboard capabilities, and multiple-user chat room capabilities. NetMeeting requires a low-cost computer video camera, placed on the user's desk or computer monitor, to send video images. No camera is required to receive video images.

Figure 2.4   A popular use of NetMeeting with Small Business Server sites is video conferencing

In Figure 2.4, a user displays video in the NetMeeting video window. This user could also chat, share the desktop, transfer files, and use the white board capabilities of NetMeeting.

Components Supporting Internet Access

The components outlined in this section provide Internet access to Small Business Server 2000.

Small Business Server Internet Connection Wizard

The Small Business Server Internet Connection Wizard makes it easy for small businesses to connect to the Internet and work with an existing Internet service provider (ISP). It automatically configures Internet Security and Acceleration (ISA) Server and configures Exchange Server to send and receive e-mail across the Internet. The Small Business Server Internet Connection Wizard even helps small businesses that want to keep using existing Post Office Protocol 3 (POP3) e-mail accounts that are maintained by an ISP. For example, the customer may want to retain a long-time e-mail address that is a POP3 account with the domain name of a local ISP in their community. Typically, POP3 accounts are retained to maintain a long-standing identity, with the belief that closing the account would result in lost communications, and thus lost business. Small Business Server accommodates these needs with its POP3 gateway, which effectively reroutes inbound POP3 e-mail to the appropriate Exchange 2000 Server e-mail account.

The improved Small Business Server Internet Connection Wizard supports connections to virtually any ISP, regardless of the connection type—broadband, router, ISDN, or analog modem.

Microsoft Internet Information Services 5.0

IIS 5.0, a secure Web server integrated with Windows 2000 Server, is designed to deliver a wide range of Internet and intranet server capabilities. IIS provides small businesses with all the tools they need to create powerful and professional Web sites. IIS also provides a comprehensive foundation for building a new generation of Web applications. For example, a small business can use IIS 5.0 to create professional-quality policies and procedures manuals on the small business's intranet for all employees to access.

Internet Security and Acceleration Server 2000

ISA Server 2000 creates a single, secure, and cost-effective gateway to the Internet, eliminating the need a connection at each workstation. The Auto-dial feature is configured through the Small Business Server Internet Connection Wizard, providing seamless Web browsing for all clients in a dial-up scenario. Web browsing is accelerated through caching, which stores the most frequently accessed Web sites on the Small Business Server. The cache periodically updates the data, based on either a default or administrator-set caching schedule. A new virtual private network (VPN) wizard, Local ISA Server VPN Configuration Wizard, enables the technology consultant to configure a secure VPN easily so that mobile workers can connect to the Small Business Server network over the Internet, without needing to dial directly into the server. VPNs can save companies telephone charges by providing a way for workers outside the local telephone area to use their local Internet connections to connect with the Small Business Server network.

Internet Explorer 5.0

Microsoft Internet Explorer 5.0 provides the best Internet browser for Windows clients, providing a rich user experience in navigating intranets or the Internet.

Routing and Remote Access Service

Routing and Remote Access Service (RRAS) enables home and mobile users to work as if they were in the office. These users can securely access files, run programs, send and receive e-mail, fax documents, and print files to an office printer just as they would in the office. RRAS is set up and configured by selecting Configure Remote Access from the To Do List.

Features Providing Easy Setup, Management, and Use

Small Business Server has gained a reputation in the small business community as a comprehensive business network solution that is integrated from the operating system-level through the configuration and management of key applications, such as Exchange 2000 Server e-mail.

Integrated Server Setup

Integrated Server Setup minimizes the input needed to install Windows 2000 Server and the Small Business Server tools and server applications. Setup configuration flexibility is an important design characteristic of Small Business Server. Server applications may be installed together or separately, during setup or at a future date. Setup minimizes user input into configuring applications; typically, the administrator is asked to confirm default server and application installation settings, which helps to ensure a successful and consistent Small Business Server setup.

To Do List

The To Do List takes the technology consultant through the steps of connecting printers and workstations, creating user accounts, and connecting to the Internet, which ensures that the small business has a complete network.

    ☑ **Note** The To Do List contains all the items needed to prepare your server for a favorable operational state.

Set Up Computer Wizard

The Set Up Computer Wizard provides the simplest way to add new computers to a network. The Set Up Computer Wizard makes it easy to connect client computers running Windows 2000 Professional, Windows Me, Windows NT Workstation 4.0, Windows 98, or Windows 95 operating systems to Small Business Server. The wizard configures the network settings, installs the appropriate protocol, adds the appropriate client applications for the user, and creates shortcuts to shared folders on the server from the user's desktop, thus increasing the success rate of getting the client up and running. Refer to Chapters 12, 15, and Appendix C for more information about the Set Up Computer Wizard.

Small Business Server Consoles

Small Business Server consoles offer a centralized, easy-to-use interface that places all the common management tasks in one location. This simplified user interface is task-based and provides centralized and integrated management of Small Business Server network components. Commands executed at a Small Business Server console typically launch wizards that use clear language to efficiently guide the technology consultant through the key tasks of managing users, peripherals, and devices on the server. Task-based administration saves time and results in more tasks being done correctly. Technology consultants enjoy standardized administration of tasks from site to site, a lower learning curve, and faster development of Small Business Server administration expertise.

> ☑ **Note**   There are two consoles in Small Business Server 2000, as follows:

- Small Business Server Administrator Console, for technology consultants performing nearly all tasks relating to Small Business Server 2000.

- Small Business Server Personal Console, for power users who have been selected by the technology consultant to perform common Small Business Server 2000 tasks.

Online Guide

Online Guide provides training to the technology consultant or the small business administrator. It includes tutorials, comprehensive Help, checklists, recommended best practices, and troubleshooting tips, along with a fast Search feature to ensure that help is available when needed.

Client User Guide

Client User Guide provides just-in-time training to the users connected to Small Business Server. Users can obtain Help, comprehensive tours, and troubleshooting tips on topics such as printing, e-mail, and the Internet to help them become productive more quickly.

Upgrading

Small Business Server accommodates growth in the small business and its computing needs. When the small business expands beyond 50 client computers, Small Business Sever can be upgraded to Microsoft BackOffice® Server 2000, a product designed for larger enterprises. The technology consultant should carefully assess a customer's needs to determine if installing BackOffice Server 2000 is a better fit than Small Business Server 2000. If the business is approaching a 50-client computer limit and growing rapidly, BackOffice Server 2000 may be a better solution.

> ☑ **Note** Because Small Business Server 2000 is optimized for small business customers, functionality specific to large enterprises, such as Systems Management Server (SMS) and Host Integration Server 2000 (formerly SNA Server), are not included.

Features Facilitating Solution Development and Administration

A primary design goal in Small Business Server 2000 is to make both the technology consultant and the customer successful. This includes providing a platform for solution development, as well as efficient administration.

Small Business Server Consoles

Small Business Server consoles are designed so that technology consultants can customize and deliver solutions tailored for the small business application.

Client Application Integration

Client Application Integration enables ISV applications to be integrated into the Set Up Computer Wizard so that they can be installed at the same time that workstations are being configured for the network. Using the Client Setup Extensibility Wizard, technology consultants or administrators can edit and configure applications for automatic setup, which will then run from the Set Up Computer Wizard. This capability enables the small business to get up and running much faster, because client software must only be installed once. For more information, refer to Chapter 15 and Appendix C.

Consistent Solution

Technology consultants appreciate the consistent installation and management approach of Small Business Server 2000, because it provides an easily replicated solution where everything is integrated and optimized to work together. With few exceptions, Small Business Server 2000 customer sites are set up at the same time, which enables the technology consultants to minimize the time spent learning on the job at the customer site. The consistency of Small Business Server 2000 networks enables technology consultants to leverage past learning experiences for higher productivity. If a technology consultant has solved a problem at one Small Business Server 2000 site, the solution can be replicated at other sites.

Remote Server Administration

Remote Server Administration enables the technology consultant to administer and manage Small Business Server remotely through a Windows-based Terminal Services session running on a Terminal Services client, or by using MyConsole with a Web browser. The Terminal Services client may be installed on 32-bit and 16-bit Microsoft desktop operating systems. Using Terminal Services-based remote administration eliminates the need for a technology consultant to be onsite and thus facilitates quicker problem resolution.

Server Status View, Server Status Report, and Health Monitor 2.1

Server Status View, Server Status Report, and Health Monitor 2.1 enable the Small Business Server technology consultant to transmit logs and system data in order to monitor the server's health. The log files enable technology consultants to track specific system activities that can be used for diagnostic purposes, enabling the consultants to determine in advance whether small business customers will encounter any problems with their servers. The Server Status View, Server Status Report, and Health Monitor are extensible, which enables the technology consultant to add other application logs to the server reporting list, including those created by an ISV.

Summary

Small Business Server has enjoyed success as a small business networking solution in large part because of its integrated components. These integrated components include the Windows 2000 Server operating system and applications and management and reporting tools.

CHAPTER 3

Technology Consultants

Small businesses represent the fastest-growing customer segment of the economy today. According to IDC/Link, 74.6 percent of small businesses in 1998 had one computer or more, and yet only 29.9 percent were networked. The number of networked computers is expected to rise to 40.9 percent by the year 2001. This will dramatically increase the need for computer professionals who focus on setting up networking systems for small business customers. As a result, a significant number of Small Business Server 2000 implementation opportunities exist for technology consultants.

Microsoft® Small Business Server 2000 is an integrated network operating system designed to meet the needs of the small business. The benefits that Small Business Server provides to the technology consultant are discussed in this chapter.

An Integrated and Optimized Solution

Small Business Server 2000 provides a solution in which all the essential services, including file, print and applications services, e-mail and fax, and Internet connection services, have been integrated and optimized to work together. The integration and deployment of independent software vendor (ISV) applications on Small Business Server is simplified by the ability to add applications to the client installation. This enables technology consultants to have a consistent solution that is easily replicated for multiple customers.

Because the complexity of piecing together applications has been removed, it is easier for the technology consultant to install and support more customers in a more cost-effective manner. The technology consultant can focus on customization, configuration, and application integration rather than the chore of making pieces fit together. Because Small Business Server contains everything needed to run a small business from a networking infrastructure viewpoint, technology consultants can focus on selling customer-specific solutions to their small business customers rather than just installing networks.

Better Customer Service and Reduced Support Cost

With Small Business Server, technology consultants can provide customers with a complete small business solution that is easy to manage and use. Small Business Server offers users an integrated operating system that has all the core services needed from an application development perspective—a robust and reliable database, a complete messaging system, and Web services. The technology consultant can also present and address the need for an integrated solution to manage small businesses and accommodate for their expansion.

Remote Management

Small Business Server simplifies common administrative tasks. After the customer is trained, they will be able to handle basic tasks like adding a user, so the technology consultant can focus on other value-added services. Should a problem arise that the customer cannot resolve, the technology consultant can easily manage Small Business Server by accessing the console from a remote location.

Remote management can be done from any computer with Microsoft Windows® 2000 Terminal Services installed and that runs any of the following operating systems: Windows 2000 Server, Windows 2000 Professional, Windows Me, Microsoft Windows NT® Server, Windows NT Workstation 4.0, Windows 95, or Windows 98. The technology consultant uses these platforms to gain access to the small business customer's server console from a Windows-based Terminal session. Internally, such a connection is made over the local area network (LAN). Externally, such a connection is typically made through a virtual private network over the Internet to the Small Business Server 2000 computer. Thus, customers are serviced more cost effectively, avoiding expensive on-site visits to resolve basic issues. Access to the server from a remote location also enables the technology consultant to diagnose and resolve problems.

> **Note** The technology consultant needs to install Terminal Services client on the remote computer in order to log on and use Terminal Services on the Small Business Server 2000 computer. Alternatively, it is possible to use the Web Console feature of Small Business Server 2000, where a Terminal Services session runs inside a Microsoft Internet Explorer Web browser through a Microsoft ActiveX® control. For more information, refer to Chapter 16, "Terminal Services and Group Policy Administration."

Server Status View and Health Monitor 2.1

The technology consultant can monitor the health of the server from a remote location by using the Server Status View and Health Monitor 2.1. The technology consultant can upload logs and system data to provide a record of system activities in order to troubleshoot a problem, and then use this information to determine whether the Small Business Server customer may encounter future problems.

The Server Status View is preconfigured to send application logs and reports to the technology consultant by e-mail or fax. The Server Status View can be extended to include reports for other Small Business Server applications, including those created by an independent software vendor (ISV).

With the addition of Health Monitor in Small Business Server, a comprehensive set of alerts and performance indicators can be monitored directly on the server or by a scheduled e-mail message sent to the technology consultant or onsite administrator.

Money-Saving Features for Small Businesses

Small Business Server provides or works with many excellent value-added features, including Microsoft Outlook® Team Folders, Microsoft NetMeeting®, Instant Messaging, console customizations, the Small Business Server Internet Connection Wizard (enabling Web site design and management), and the Set Up Computer Wizard (enabling integration and management of ISV-based applications).

Outlook Team Folders

Small businesses can greatly benefit from the technology consultant's suggestions for how to best utilize their Small Business Server network. The use of Outlook Team Folders is one such suggestion that has been well received by small businesses. Many small businesses work on projects or perform custom work. This means that many tasks are complex and performed infrequently, and they require high levels of communication among project team members, including clients, vendors, and employees of the small business. Outlook Team Folders facilitate complex communications in a single forum.

> ☑ **Note** Although Outlook Team Folders are not installed as part of Small Business Server, they can be downloaded from the Microsoft Web site at: www.microsoft.com/outlook/.

NetMeeting

Many small businesses use NetMeeting to facilitate better communications with clients and workers at remote sites. NetMeeting provides live audio and video conferencing, multiple user chat forums, remote desktop sharing, and white-board capabilities. In particular, NetMeeting facilitates a robust video conferencing solution at far less cost than traditional charge-by-the-hour corporate video conferencing centers.

> **Note** Although NetMeeting is not installed as part of Small Business Server 2000, it can be downloaded from the Microsoft Web site at: www.microsoft.com/netmeeting/.

Instant Messaging Service

Instant Messaging Service enables one user to chat over the Internet or internally with another user, in a real-time, point-to-point chat mode. Instant Messaging Service is a good tool for resolving queries quickly. For example, if an employee of a small business receives a call from an unknown person who wants to do business with their company, the employee can put the caller on hold and then send an instant message to a coworker, asking if they have previously done business with the person calling. The employee could get an "instant" reply from their coworker, helping them determine how to handle the call.

The Instant Messaging Service is installed as a service in Microsoft Exchange 2000 Server by using the Small Business Server Setup Wizard.

Set Up Computer Wizard

The Set Up Computer Wizard facilitates the easy installation of additional ISV applications during Small Business Server Setup. The applications can be installed at the same time client workstations are being configured for the network, or later as part of Small Business Server network administration.

Console Customizations

The Small Business Server console can be customized to accommodate ISV-based snap-ins. It is common for ISV-based snap-ins to be added to existing Microsoft Management Consoles. An example might be a Small Business Server 2000 specific snap-in application, such as an ISV virus-detection program. Note that it is also possible for the technology consultant to customize a management console to start executable programs.

> ☑ **Note** By default, both Small Business Server consoles are run in full-access user mode, providing users full access to all Windows management commands and to the Console Tree. This mode does prevent users from adding or removing snap-ins, or changing console properties. To modify the consoles with a snap-in, you must change the console mode to Author mode. For more information, refer to Appendix C, "Customization and Extensibility Options."

Small Business Server Internet Connection Wizard

The Small Business Server Internet Connection Wizard enables small business customers to set up and use Internet access services, to learn about Internet services, and use e-mail with unprecedented ease. After small businesses see how the Internet can help them enhance their customer service and expand their business, we anticipate that they will seek connectivity, Web design and hosting, and other services.

Leveraging One Set of Skills and Solutions

Small Business Server is built with Microsoft server products, including Windows 2000 Server, Microsoft Internet Information Services (IIS), Microsoft Exchange Server, Internet Security and Acceleration (ISA) Server 2000, and Microsoft SQL Server™. This enables the technology consultant to make a single training investment in learning these products, which can then be applied across a broad spectrum of small to large businesses. The technology consultant can develop solutions that rely on Microsoft server products with the knowledge that all businesses will be able to use their solutions. Also, as small businesses grow, they can upgrade to Microsoft BackOffice® Server, and the technology consultant's solutions remain viable.

Other Resources

Technology consultants can use the following resources to plan, deploy, and administer Small Business Server:

- **Small Business Server Web site**. Located at: http://www.microsoft.com/smallbusinessserver/.

- **Microsoft Direct Access Web site**. Includes product guides, sales tools, training, and a Small Business Server newsgroup. The site is located at: http://www.microsoft.com/directaccess/.

  Registration for the Microsoft Direct Access Web site. The site is located at: http://premium.microsoft.com/directaccess/.

- **Microsoft Product Support Services**. The site is located at: http://support.microsoft.com.

- **Microsoft TechNet**. A subscription service that includes more than 200,000 pages of technical content from the Microsoft Knowledge Base, evaluation and deployment guides, white papers, third-party integration information, case studies, training materials, and Microsoft Resource Kits.

  The Technical Information compact disc is one of 15-plus compact discs included with a subscription to TechNet. A TechNet trial compact disc, which is a fully functional version of the monthly Technical Information compact disc, is located at: http://www.microsoft.com/technet.

- **Small Business Server newsgroup**. A subscription-based, Microsoft-supported public newsgroup. By using a newsgroup reader, technology consultants can visit the newsgroup at: microsoft.public.backoffice.smallbiz/.

  The newsgroup is also available from the Web at: http://support.microsoft.com/support/news/rules.asp.

- **Private Small Business Server Web site**. A privately maintained Small Business Server Web site on the Internet is located at: http://www.smallbizserver.com.

- **Small Business Server news list**. A subscription-based, privately maintained news list, or listserv. To sign up on the listserv, technology consultants can visit: http://www.egroups.com/group/sbs2k/.

  Note Small business owners can find Small Business Server technology consultants by contacting the nearest Microsoft sales office (located in major cities) and attending Direct Access and TechNet events, which many technology consultants attend. Also, by using the Search feature on the Microsoft Network Web site (http://www.msn.com) and by typing such terms as "small business server," a list of Web sites of technology consultants dedicated to working with small businesses will display.

Summary

Small Business Server 2000 is designed to make life easier for both the technology consultant and small business customer. Typically, small business customers do not have in-house networking technical expertise, and so they rely heavily on the technology consultant to assist them with networking decisions—to implement and maintain their network. Many Small Business Server features support the technology consultant's ability to provide efficient, quality service to the small business customer.

Planning a Small Business Server Network

When planning for the deployment of Microsoft® Small Business Server 2000, the technology consultant must first understand the characteristics of the small business network and the general requirements of the server computer. This chapter provides this baseline information to help the technology consultant effectively plan for the small business server network environment. Included are minimum hardware requirements for the Small Business Server network.

Business Needs Analysis

All successful network implementations start with a planning cycle that includes a business needs analysis, which traditionally includes a review of how the business operated in the past, how it currently operates, and how it intends to operate in the future. When this analysis is complete, it is relatively easy to identify the business needs of the organization and how Small Business Server satisfies these needs.

Past

Observing the small business's past provides a rich source of information that enables the technology consultant to forecast better how the firm might behave in the future. Questions for the technology consultant to consider include:

- Does the small business have a long history of embracing technology?

- How has the small business managed the technology that it deployed?

- Is the small business an early or late adopter of technology solutions?

- Has the small business had a bad experience with the implementation of a technology, such as a computer network?

- Have employees embraced technology solutions as a tool of empowerment, enabling work to be completed more efficiently and at a higher quality level?

- Have employees resisted incorporating technology into their work, causing solutions such as computer networks to be a disabling technology that actually decreases worker productivity?

Answering these questions enables the technology consultant (1) to assess how much the small business has accepted technology and (2) to successfully match Small Business Server capabilities with the current needs of the small business.

Present

Another way of ensuring a successful implementation of Small Business Server is to observe the small business's present operations. Questions for the technology consultant to consider include:

- How is the firm using technology, particularly computer networks, today?

- Does the firm provide products or services that create a standardized, or perhaps redundant, flow of information?

- Does the firm have the sufficient financial resources and adequate time to successfully deploy Small Business Server?

- What are the main benefits of using Small Business Server for the small business (for example, e-mail communications, business applications, or data security)?

- What other applications does the small business rely on (for example, desktop applications, custom applications, or narrow vertical market solutions)?

- In general, are employees embracing or resisting the use of technology?

Future

A competent technology consultant will not recommend a business networking solution such as Small Business Server unless it also meets foreseeable technology needs. Questions for the technology consultant to consider include:

- Does the suggested hardware and software (including software licensing) enable the small business to operate in the near future without having to undergo a significant upgrade?

- Will the firm exceed the limit of 50 client computers in the near future?

- If the small business will exceed the limit of 50 client computers, is the firm prepared to upgrade to the full Microsoft BackOffice® Server 2000 product?

- Will the firm's operation grow to include branch offices, thus necessitating an upgrade to BackOffice Server 2000?

Small Business Server Goals

When the business needs analysis is complete, the technology consultant can match the small business's needs with the capabilities of Small Business Server to determine if they are a good fit. In most cases, because Small Business Server provides a range of infrastructure solutions—from Microsoft Windows® 2000 Server to Microsoft Servers applications—the technology consultant selects Small Business Server as the networking solution for the small business.

Microsoft developed Small Business Server to specifically address the needs of small businesses with less than 50 client computers with the following design features:

- **Private local area network (LAN)**. Small Business Server provides a single LAN based on the TCP/IP networking protocol. Small Business Server, by default, provides the server computer a static, nonroutable Internet protocol (IP) address. The Dynamic Host Configuration Protocol (DHCP) Service is installed by default with a scope of private network nonroutable IP addresses that matches the IP address of the server. The underlying Windows 2000 Server operating system provides robust storage management, security, data protection, and support for business applications. Small Business Server Tools provide easy-to-use network management and reporting capabilities.

- **Internet connectivity and electronic commerce**. Small Business Server provides a secure and robust way for the small business to connect to the Internet and conduct electronic commerce, such as interacting with customers, suppliers, and vendors. Small Business Server also enables the small business to connect over the Internet to an application services provider (ASP) to run a business application, such as an accounting program.

- **Remote users**. Small Business Server provides remote connectivity services ranging from basic dial-up connections to more complex virtual private network (VPN) solutions that use the Point-to-Point Tunneling Protocol (PPTP).

- **Shared Modem Service and Shared Fax Service**. Small businesses can use Small Business Server to handle a large volume of inbound and outbound fax and modem activity—up to four fax modems are supported.

- **Electronic Mail with Microsoft Exchange 2000 Server**. Few small businesses can function today without robust and reliable e-mail capabilities. Small Business Server meets this need with Exchange 2000 Server.

- **Security with Microsoft Internet Security and Acceleration (ISA) Server 2000**. All small businesses have concerns about computer security, especially as full-time Internet connections become the norm. ISA Server 2000 provides firewall security for Small Business Server.

- **Remote Administration with Terminal Services**. Windows 2000 Server Terminal Services enables the technology consultant to remotely manage the Small Business Server network. Remote management capabilities make administration of the network easier and lower support costs.

- **Capacity planning**. Small Business Server can grow with the small business in two ways. First, up to four additional processors, additional RAM memory, and hard disk storage can be added to the server computer as the small business's computing needs demand. The addition of processors and memory requires no additional setup because new elements will be recognized and used by the existing Small Business Server network automatically.

- **Support for Business Processes with Microsoft server applications**. Small Business Server offers popular applications for the small business, including the most applicable Microsoft server applications. Microsoft SQL Server™ 2000 database application is an example of a Small Business Server feature used by many business applications, such as accounting programs.

Small Business Office Network Characteristics

Small Business Server supports the typical small business network configuration.

Network Configuration

The Small Business Server network requires Ethernet connections, consisting of network interface cards, cabling, and hubs between computers. Appropriate configurations and equipment requirements depend on the size of the small business office. Figure 4.1 shows a high-level view, appropriate for a businessperson, of a typical configuration for a small business network that uses Small Business Server 2000.

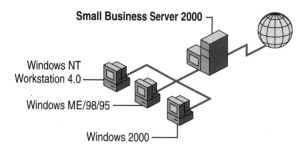

Figure 4.1   Simplified view of a typical Small Business Server network configuration

Figure 4.2 shows a more complex view, appropriate for the technology consultant. The illustration displays the main server applications of Small Business Server in relation to the LAN and Internet connectivity, which gives the technology consultant a conceptual view of the network, along with the components used in a typical small business implementation. Components may vary slightly, as when Microsoft Access 2000 is used for the small business database instead of SQL Server 2000 or when a dedicated connection to the Internet is used instead of a modem, but the general configuration is still valid.

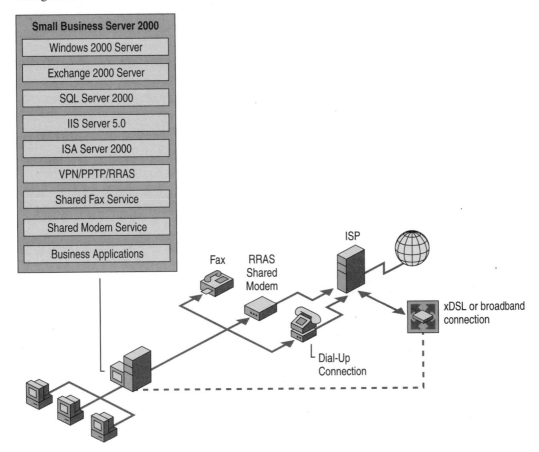

Figure 4.2   A typical Small Business Server network configuration

In Figure 4.2, all the major Small Business Server 2000 features are highlighted in the box at the top left. Faxing/modem-based capabilities are displayed for fax, Routing and Remote Access Service (RRAS) modem, and dial-up connections. Also, a broadband-type connection to an Internet service provider (ISP) is shown. This is representative of the typical Small Business Server 2000 network. For more information about network configuration, refer to Appendix A, "Networking and Storage Basics."

Small Business Server Requirements and Recommendations

Small Business Server 2000 requires the minimum computer configuration described in the paragraphs that follow.

Server Computer Hardware Requirements

The following is the minimum equipment required by Small Business Server 2000. As the user base and server use expands, the processor, memory, and disk configurations should be modified in accordance with the recommendations in Chapter 7, "Planning for Small Business Server Applications."

- **Intel Pentium II 300 microprocessor**.

- **128 megabytes (MB) of RAM**. The RAM requirement should increase to 256 MB of RAM or more for heavy workloads such as Internet activity involving CPU-intensive sessions and processing load attributable to the use of Terminal Services for remote administration purposes. Small Business Server 2000 cannot be installed on a computer with less than 128 MB of RAM.

- **4 gigabytes (GB) of hard disk space**.

- **3.5-inch high-density disk drive**. This drive must be configured as drive A.

- **Super VGA (SVGA) monitor and video adapter, 800x600 or higher resolution, 256 colors**.

- **Compact disc read-only memory (CD-ROM) drive**.

- **Modem**. One or more supported modems are required to use Shared Modem Service, Shared Fax Service, Dial-Up Networking (DUN), and modem-based Internet access. All modems must be the same brand and model to take advantage of Shared Modem Service. It is recommended that at least one modem be dedicated to each service that uses modems. To use the Shared Fax Service, a dedicated Class 1 fax modem is required. For heavy fax use, a business-quality fax board is recommended.

- **Network adapter card**. The network adapter card must be selected from among those listed in the Windows 2000 Hardware Compatibility List (HCL). The HCL is continuously updated on Microsoft's Small Business Server Web site at: http://www.microsoft.com/hcl/.

Internet Connection Hardware

A Small Business Server connection to the Internet requires one of the following hardware solutions:

- **Modem**. A modem for a dial-up connection to an ISP. This inexpensive solution provides satisfactory performance for up to three users.

- **Broadband connection**. Options include a Digital Subscriber Line (xDSL) , a cable modem, or an Integrated Services Digital Network (ISDN) service with an ISP. Broadband Internet connection solutions typically require a second network adapter card.

- **Router**. Establishes either dial-on demand or full-time Internet connections. A router can be connected to the LAN, where it acts as a default gateway for all client computers by forwarding requests outside the LAN as appropriate.

Other Hardware Recommendations

The following hardware is recommended for use with Small Business Server 2000:

- **A tape or other backup system**.

- **Two phone lines**. One dedicated to Shared Fax Service, and the other dedicated to Dial-Up Networking.

- **An uninterruptible power supply**.

- **Additional hard disks**. For file storage or disk mirroring, a dynamically updated duplicate of the computer's information.

  Note   Redundant Array of Independent Disks (RAID) Level-5 storage solutions are highly recommended. Storage configurations are provided in Appendix A, "Networking and Storage Basics."

Client Computer Requirements and Recommendations

Client computers connected to a Small Business Server network must meet the following minimum hardware and software requirements.

Client Computer Hardware Requirements

For a client computer on the Small Business Server network, the following hardware is recommended:

- **Pentium 90 megahertz (MHz) processor**.
- **32 MB of RAM**.
- **3.5-inch high-density disk drive**.
- **300 MB of free hard disk space**.
- **Ethernet network adapter supported by the operating system**.
- **VGA or higher resolution monitor and video adapter**.
- **Microsoft mouse or compatible pointing device**.

Dial-Up Networking Server Access

Small Business Server DUN access requires the following hardware solutions:

- **Modem**.
- **Microsoft DUN**. DUN comes with the Microsoft client operating systems discussed in the next section. The latest version of DUN is available on the Microsoft Web site at: http://www.microsoft.com/.
- **TCP/IP and Point-to-Point Protocol (PPP) installed**.

  Note Remote clients may also connect to Small Business Server over the Internet backbone. PPTP is configured on the server and installed and configured on client computers to facilitate secure virtual private networking. Also, PPTP must be enabled when the Small Business Server Internet Connection Wizard is running.

Recommended Operating System Software

Users can gain access to all the features of Small Business Server 2000 from computers running the following operating systems:

- Microsoft Windows 2000 Professional
- Microsoft Windows Me
- Microsoft Windows 98
- Microsoft Windows 95
- Microsoft Windows NT® Workstation version 4.0

Other Operating System Compatibilities

With manual configuration of the client computer, the following operating systems can use the Small Business Server file and print services:

- Microsoft Windows NT Workstation version 3.x
- Microsoft Windows for Workgroups
- MS-DOS®
- Apple Macintosh
- Various versions of UNIX

Small Business Server Limitations

Managing expectations is important when planning and deploying Small Business Server as the infrastructure of a small business network. Part of managing expectations is understanding the limitations of Small Business Server. The known Small Business Server 2000 limitations are as follows:

- **One domain**. There can only be one domain on a Small Business Server 2000 network. In addition, Small Business Server 2000 must be the root of the forest.

- **No trust relationships**. Because only one domain is supported on a Small Business Server 2000 network, there can be no trust relationships with other domains. This restriction on trust relationships includes parent-child trust relationships. There can, however, be other domain controllers on the network.

- **A maximum of 50 client computers**. Only 50 client computers can be connected to a Small Business Server, assuming that the appropriate client access licenses are in place. Client access licenses are enforced in Small Business Server 2000.

Backup and Disaster System Planning

Protecting company data on Small Business Server 2000 is a critical consideration. The small business may have a fault-tolerant disk configuration that provides limited immunity from hardware failure. However, this method alone will not protect crucial company data from fire or other natural disasters. Two additional methods of protecting company data are making backups and having a disaster plan. Disaster recovery planning for Small Business Server encompasses both reducing the potential for problems to occur and developing the necessary plans and procedures to handle failure recovery.

☑ **Note** For more information about making backups, refer to Appendix A, "Networking and Storage Basics." For more information about disaster system planning, refer to Chapter 26, "Disaster Recovery."

Windows 2000 Server Backup Utility

The Windows 2000 Server component of Small Business Server has a comprehensive backup utility that permits the technology consultant to back up critical company data to tape media. The scheduling capability found in the Windows 2000 Backup utility provides data backup on the server itself and for workstations in the small business network. This includes security information, file and share permissions, and registry data. For data security, only a user from the administrator or backup operator group should back up data to tape. Individual files and directories or the entire server can be restored by using the Windows 2000 Backup utility.

The Windows 2000 Backup utility in Small Business Server requires that the tape backup device be connected to a compatible small computer system interface (SCSI) or non-SCSI controller card. The controller card must be properly installed and functional. Windows 2000 Server automates the installation of a controller card because Device Manager detects new hardware at system startup and automatically installs the appropriate drivers.

Choosing a Backup Scheme

Selecting a tape backup rotation scheme that ensures data protection in case a tape is lost or malfunctions is recommended. A popular tape rotation scheme is grandparent-parent-child:

- The tape used for backup on the last Friday of each month is called the grandparent tape. This tape is stored off-site.

- The tape used for backup every Friday (except the last Friday of the month) is called the parent tape. This tape is also stored off-site.

- The tapes used for backup on Monday, Tuesday, Wednesday, and Thursday are called children tapes. Often all children tapes are stored on-site except for the tape from the preceding day.

The following backup options are available:

- **Normal**. Backs up all selected files and marks the files as backed up.

- **Copy**. Backs up all selected files but does not mark the files as backed up.

- **Differential**. Backs up selected files only if they have not been previously backed up or have been changed since the last backup, but does not mark the files as backed up.

- **Incremental**. Backs up selected files only if they have not been previously backed up or have been changed since the last backup, and marks the files as backed up.

- **Daily**. Backs up only files that have been changed today and marks them as backed up.

Because small businesses typically do not have technology professionals on staff, a Normal backup, performed daily and according to the suggested grandparent-parent-child backup scheme, is recommended as part of the small business's backup and disaster recovery plan.

System State Data Backup

The Windows 2000 Backup utility also can back up System State data. System State data includes the Active Directory™ directory service, boot files, the Component Services Class Registration database, the registry, and SysVol. Possible backup locations for System State data include floppy disks, a hard disk, removable media, recordable compact discs, and tapes.

Exchange 2000 Server Backup

The Windows 2000 Backup utility can back up the Exchange 2000 Server information store and directory services. Because Exchange 2000 Server is backed up at the post office–level, it is not possible to restore an individual mailbox or individual piece of e-mail by using the Windows 2000 Backup utility. Some third-party tape backup applications have the ability to restore at the individual mailbox level. For more information about Exchange 2000 Server disaster planning, refer to the *Microsoft Exchange 2000 Server Resource Kit*.

SQL Server 2000 Backup

The Windows 2000 Backup utility cannot back up online SQL Server databases. Use the SQL Server 2000 Enterprise Manager to create a backup of the SQL Server databases. Thereafter, a backup job can be run from the Windows 2000 Backup utility to include database backups created by SQL Server 2000 Enterprise Manager. You would schedule the backup routing in SQL Server 2000 Enterprise Manager to run first, followed by a backup job run in the Windows 2000 Backup utility. For more information about SQL Server backups, refer to Chapter 26, "Disaster Recovery," and the SQL Server 2000 Books Online, available from the SQL Server Web site at: http://www.microsoft.com/sql/.

Using Windows 2000 Backup Utility

To perform a backup by using the Windows 2000 Backup utility

1. Click **Start**, point to **Programs**, point to **Accessories**, and then click **System Tools**.

2. In the **System Tools** program group, click **Backup**. The **Backup** box appears.

3. Click **Backup Wizard**. Follow the on-screen instructions to complete the wizard.

To restore data from a backup by using the Windows 2000 Backup utility

1. Click **Start**, point to **Programs**, point to **Accessories**, and then click **System Tools**.

2. In the **System Tools** program group, click **Backup**. The **Backup** box appears.

3. Click **Restore Wizard**. Follow the on-screen instructions to complete the wizard.

   ☑ **Note**   For more information about disaster planning, refer to the "Improving Your Disaster Recovery Capabilities" section of Chapter 19, "Determining Windows 2000 Storage Management Strategies," in the *Windows 2000 Server Deployment Planning Guide* in the Windows 2000 Server Resource Kit.

Summary

This chapter outlined critical Small Business Server 2000 network planning tasks that need to be considered before setting up a network, including a business needs analysis, the goals for your network, hardware and software requirements, and planning for data backup and disaster recovery.

Planning for an Internet Presence

Businesses today require a presence on the Internet to be competitive and to reach their customers, suppliers, and vendors effectively. Microsoft® Small Business Server 2000 takes full advantage of the Internet with specific focus on benefits for a small business. With an Internet connection in place, a small business can realize the full potential of Small Business Server through Microsoft Exchange 2000 Server, Microsoft Internet Security and Acceleration (ISA) Server 2000, Microsoft Internet Information Services (IIS) 5.0, Point-To-Point Tunneling Protocol (PPTP), virtual private networking (VPN), Terminal Services, Instant Messaging Service, Microsoft NetMeeting®, and other capabilities.

Connecting to the Internet means opening an account with an Internet service provider (ISP). An ISP provides a wide range of services to the small business, including browsing access to the World Wide Web, e-mail, and Web site hosting. Establishing these services helps the small business create a stronger profile and greater visibility in the marketplace.

It is a simple matter to establish an Internet connection by using the Small Business Server Internet Connection Wizard. However, before implementing the Internet connection, the technology consultant should consider several issues involved in creating a comprehensive Internet proposal for a small business customer. These issues, which are discussed in this chapter, are as follows:

- ISP capabilities and services
- Internet connection types
- Web site development and hosting
- Bandwidth requirements
- Intranet considerations
- Impact of Internet access on server hardware
- Web site testing
- Location of an ISP
- Sign-up process
- Types of ISP services
- Required ISP connection information
- Domain naming issues

Internet Access Proposal to the Small Business

When the technology consultant is given approval to plan for small business Internet access, a proposal should be made to the small business owner. This proposal should help the small business owner understand the requirements that the firm must meet and the services that it must have in order to implement a cost-effective Internet solution. Information related to Web site hosting and World Wide Web access should be specified as appropriate. The proposal should include specifications on ISPs, site capacity, and required computer hardware. More specifically, a comprehensive proposal prepared by the technology consultant will:

- Recommend an ISP and its services.

- Ascertain the performance of various connectivity options on the basis of number of users, speed of data transmission, and other performance-related parameters.

- Identify the necessary connection hardware, estimate maximum bandwidth, and specify the appropriate connectivity methods.

- Determine the best approach to Web site development, site hosting options, and the advantages of having an intranet.

- Recommend the minimum hardware requirements for the server computer, including RAM, hard disk space, and CPU architecture, with respect to the operating parameters for the small business Web site.

- Identify the Internet connection process and related connectivity issues.

- Recommend any applicable security features the small business may require. Refer to Chapter 21, "Firewall Security and Web Caching With ISA Server" in this guide, for information about Internet-related security features that may be used with Small Business Server.

The following table may be useful when making decisions about connection types and relative cost. When making calculations and recommendations, the technology consultant should keep in mind the peak hours and the intended purpose of the small business site. The sections that follow this table discuss Internet connection specifications in detail.

Table 5.1 Internet Proposal Factors for the Small Business

Type connection	Bandwidth	Cost relative to other connection types
Leased line (analog)	56 kilobytes per second (KBps)	1
xDSL	256 KBps – 1.5 megabytes per second (MBps)	2
Cable modem	256 KBps–10 MBps	2
ISDN	128 KBps	4
T1 (DS1)	1.5 MBps	10

✔ **Note**   Table 5.1 applies primarily to conditions observed in the United States. International locations may or may not have the same relative cost relationships.

Internet Connection Types

The connection types described in the following table represent typical levels of service for full Internet connections in the United States. The services offered by ISPs vary by area. The number of simultaneous users supported may vary because of other factors, such as the size of Web pages or the number of downloads.

Table 5.2 Internet Connection Types and User Capacity

Connection	Simultaneous site users supported
Modem	5-10
xDSL	10-500
Cable modem	10-500
ISDN	10-500
T1 and fractional T1	50-500

A dial-up modem connection may be used if the small business server is to handle only light traffic. However, a server handling medium traffic should probably use a Digital Subscriber Line (xDSL), a cable modem, an Integrated Services Digital Network (ISDN), a T1 line, or some fraction of a T1 line.

Dial-up Modem Connections

Modem connections to the Internet are available but are typically only used on client computers. Modem connections are usually not recommended for servers. Nevertheless, a connection to the Internet using a telephone line and modem can serve up to 10 simultaneous users. Modem connections are often considered slow links because data is transmitted at the speed of the modem, typically from 14,400 through 56,000 kilobytes per second (KBps).

Digital Subscriber Line

xDSL services are one of the most exciting telecommunication advances and popular Internet connection options available for Small Business Server networks. xDSL, a broadband solution, uses the same copper telephone cable as a Public Switched Telephone Network (PSTN) and Plain Old Telephone System (POTS). xDSL is offered by telecommunications firms (which are frequently also ISPs) as a service to connect to the ISP. As a broadband service, xDSL is always online and connected to the ISP.

Charges are assessed to the small business based on the speed commitment (256 KBps, 512 KBps, up to 1.5 MBps) and the amount of data downloaded. Charges are not a function of connect time, as is often the case with dial-up connections and ISDN.

The benefits of xDSL include stability, low cost relative to performance, and guaranteed bandwidth. The drawbacks to xDSL are twofold. First, the small business that requests xDSL service must be within a certain distance of the telecommunications firm's central office. This requirement ensures that the small business will receive an xDSL signal of sufficient strength. Second, due to demand for xDSL service, the wait to receive xDSL service may often exceed several weeks or even months.

> **Note**   xDSL quality and timing of service vary by area.

Figure 5.1 displays a typical xDSL connection to the Internet.

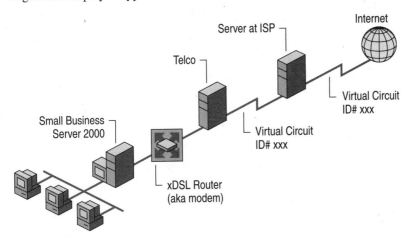

Figure 5.1 xDSL scenario

Cable Modems

Cable modems are another Internet connection option gaining popularity with small businesses. Cable television companies can provide Internet connection over the same cable that feeds a television signal to a site. The benefits of cable modems include no location restrictions (as with xDSL), relatively low cost, stability, and potential high speed transmission of data. The drawbacks include restrictions on Web and File Transfer Protocol (FTP) site hosting typically imposed by the cable television company, restriction on choosing an ISP (the cable television company must typically be the ISP), and signal degradation, which occurs as the number of users on the cable segment increases.

Figure 5.2 displays a typical cable modem connection to the Internet.

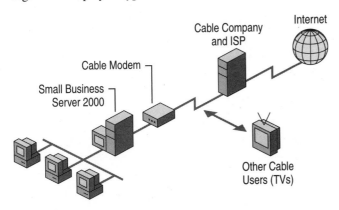

Figure 5.2 Cable modem scenario

Integrated Services Digital Network

ISDN is a telecommunications service that integrates data, voice, and video onto a digital telephone line. It is available in two different bandwidths: basic rate interface (BRI) and primary rate interface (PRI). Figure 5.3 shows how Small Business Server connects to the ISP through an ISDN interface.

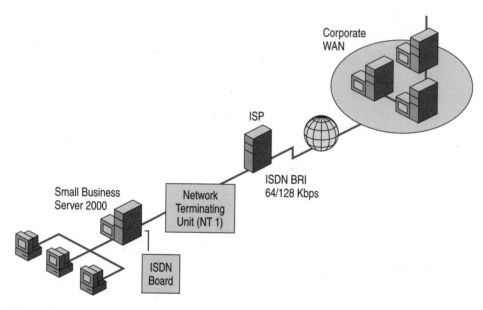

Figure 5.3 ISDN scenario

Basic Rate Interface

The BRI is the most common ISDN bandwidth available. It uses the telephone company's twisted-pair local loop and divides it into three channels. The first two channels, running at 64 KBps, are the B channels, which carry voice and data. The third channel, or the D channel, runs at 16 KBps and carries signaling and low-speed packet data. BRI is sometimes called 2B+D.

Primary Rate Interface

The PRI is functionally similar to BRI except that 23 data B channels are provided and the D channel is upgraded to 64 KBps (this varies by country or region). This is the functional equivalent of moving data at T1 speeds. In Europe, PRI has 30 B channels and one 64 KBps D channel. These are also known as 23B+D and 30B+D, respectively.

ISDN Connections

ISDN BRI can connect Small Business Server using an NT1 (network terminating) unit. The NT1 box conditions the signal and is attached with an ISDN card inside the computer. ISDN BRI connects the small business LAN by using an ISDN bridge. The ISDN bridge enables the computers that plug into it to use standard Ethernet cards.

ISDN PRI uses the same CSU/DSU equipment that a T1 dedicated digital line uses. Special PRI bridges and adapters are also available from a variety of manufacturers.

T1

High-speed T1 connections are typically considered by larger businesses seeking dedicated Internet access when other, lower-cost solutions such as xDSL are not available. A T1-based solution is typically more costly than xDSL and the other options discussed in Table 5.2, but it is sometimes the only solution available. Businesses seeking to link multiple offices through a secure and stable private wide area network (WAN) typically require T1 service. Small Business Server will accept and work very well with a T1 Internet connection.

Web Site Development

Small Business Server acts as a Web site staging area. Here, a Web site can be developed or edited using Microsoft FrontPage® prior to being posted to the ISP. For best performance, the small business's Web site should be hosted by an ISP rather than on the client computer, for two reasons. First, ISPs have larger bandwidth connections to the Internet, providing faster Web site access than is available for small businesses hosting their Web sites directly. Second, the ISP typically has back-up power to stay up and running in the event of a power outage. This results in the increased availability of an ISP Web site.

When an ISP hosts the Web site, the small business needs an alternative means of notification for responding to inquiry traffic on the site. In this scenario, the simplest solution may be for the ISP (or an ISV) to develop a script to send an e-mail to the small business in response to Web site inquiries automatically. This solution is a minimum configuration that may work well for lower-volume sites.

Small Business Web Site Hosting with Internet Information Services 5.0

The small business may host its own Web site using the Internet Information Services application in Small Business Server, even though such an approach is not recommended. FrontPage may be used to develop and maintain the Web site. When IIS is used to host the Web site, access speed for customers browsing the Web becomes an important consideration. The section that follows discusses several methods for estimating the bandwidth needed for quick access to the small business Web site. This estimate will have an impact on the modem configuration required to support the determined bandwidth. Generally, a higher-volume site requires more bandwidth and, as a result, needs more modems (or a faster connection type, such as XDSL, cable modem, ISDN, or T1) to handle the traffic.

Internet Information Services 5.0

When an Internet site is being designed, a careful analysis of the services planned needs to be made. For example, if only Hypertext Transport Protocol (HTTP) is offered, FTP services should not be installed on Small Business Server.

The use of inbound FTP may be necessary for the small business that needs a Web site hosted. The FTP service is commonly used to transfer large file transfers between a professional and a small business (for example, an architect transferring large drawing files to a client computer at the small business) when such files are too large to transport as e-mail attachments. FTP services are supplied with Small Business Server 2000 but not installed by default. ISA Server must also be configured to handle this protocol.

Internet Access Protocols and Services

The following table describes the features available with several basic Internet access protocols. This information can be used to determine the type of site access that most benefits the small business.

Table 5.3 IIS Service Features

Feature	HTTP	FTP
Download files	Yes	Yes
Upload files	No	Yes
Command-line user interface	No	Yes
Menu user interface	Yes	No
Graphical user interface	Yes	No
WAIS interface	Yes	No
Security	Yes	No
Unlimited possibilities for page design	Yes	No
SQL Server or Microsoft Access database interface	Yes	No
CGI interface	Yes	No
Active Server Pages interface	Yes	No

Web Site Development Resources

For more in-depth technical information and tools that assist in creating, testing, and deploying Web pages for small businesses, refer to the *Microsoft Internet Information Server Resource Kit,* available from Microsoft Press.

Estimating Bandwidth

When the type of connection for a Web site hosted by the small business is being determined, the current *and* future bandwidth of the site must be estimated correctly. Bandwidth is determined by the number of bits transferred per second (bps). Bandwidth is commonly noted in kilobytes per second (KBps) or megabytes per second (MBps). Sufficient bandwidth is required for quick access to resources on the small business Web site.

One of the best sources for determining current and future bandwidth needs is the ISP. Their experience is invaluable when estimating initial and future needs. Historical data from other Web sites may also be used to estimate bandwidth. The number of bytes transferred is a commonly recorded statistic on Web sites. Once the site is up and running, the technology consultant can gather statistics on bytes transferred by using the performance counters of ISA Server. Refer to ISA Server administration in Chapter 18, "Administering Small Business Server Components," for setting up ISA Server performance monitors.

Calculating Bandwidth, Using Bytes Transferred

Bandwidth needs can be estimated by converting bytes to bits by multiplying the number of bytes by 12 (there are 8 bits per byte, plus 4 bits of overhead data).The results need to be expressed in terms of seconds in order to have the proper specification. So, if the data transfer statistic obtained is specified as bytes per hour, the number of hours must be multiplied by 3,600 (60 minutes per hour x 60 seconds per minute).

If a hypothetical Web site transfers approximately 250,000,000 bytes in an average 12-hour period, the following formula can be used to calculate the type of connection required for a small business Web site with a similar profile:

(Bytes x 12) / (Hours x 3,600 s/hr) = bits/sec
250,000,000 x (8 bits data + 4 bits overhead) / (12 hours x 60 minutes x 60 seconds)

which is equivalent to

3,000,000,000 bits / (43,200 seconds x 1,024 bits) = 67.8 KBps

A Web site would require at least two 56-KBps high-speed modems or one ISDN connection to accommodate this estimated use level.

Calculating Bandwidth, Using Connections and Document Size

Another bandwidth calculation method is to use the estimated number of connections and the average size of documents transferred. The following formula can be used to estimate bandwidth with this data:

(Average connections per day / Number of seconds per day) x (Average document size in kilobytes x (8 bits data + 4 bits overhead))

Substituting the following criteria

86,400 seconds in one day

8 bits in a byte

4 bits overhead per byte of data

yields

(Avg. daily connections / 86,400) x (Avg. document size in KB x 12)

For example, if 3,000 connections per day are predicted, and the average file size is 85 KB, the equation would look like this:

(3,000 / 86,400) x (85 x 1,024 x (8+4)) = 36.3 KBps

For performance to be maintained at or above an average bandwidth of 36.3 KBps, at least one 56 KBps leased line must be installed. Bandwidth requirements can change monthly, weekly, daily, and even hourly. The preceding formula can be used as a starting point, and adjustments can be made according to the load on the server.

Advantages of an Intranet

The technology consultant's proposal to the small business owner should discuss the advantages of having an intranet. Intranets are a convenient way to share information and data within an organization. Common uses include human resource information, company newsletters, schedules (such as company picnics and parties), photo galleries, and general announcements. Technically, an intranet is a network within an organization that uses Internet protocols and technologies for data transfer. An intranet site requires the same software and hardware as an Internet site, with the exception of connections to an ISP.

Intranet Site

Figure 5.4 shows the relationship between a small business IIS-hosted intranet site and an ISP-hosted Internet site.

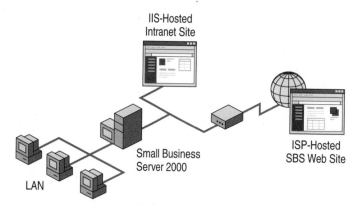

Figure 5.4   Intranet and Internet relationship

Intranet Security Precautions

The small business should always take security precautions when establishing an intranet site. The information that goes on the Internet server and the information that goes on the intranet server must be separated. Certain documents that may be legal to distribute on the intranet site may violate copyright, trademark, and export laws if they are placed on the Internet server. Care should also be exercised to protect the proprietary information of the organization. An organization should never place sensitive or proprietary research material on the Internet site instead of its intranet site.

Impact of Internet Connectivity on Server Computer Hardware

When a personal computer is used as the Small Business Server, the type of CPU chosen and amount of RAM available can affect performance. For example, a fast processor should be used to facilitate CPU-intensive sessions involving HTML files. The amount of RAM needed is affected by several factors, including the number of services running.

CPU Architecture

The number of simultaneous users that may be accommodated varies according to the type of sessions that are open. Small Business Server should be able to accommodate more site users when running sessions that are not CPU-intensive, such as e-mail, Telnet, and FTP. Sessions that are CPU-intensive include those running common gateway interface (CGI) scripts, making database queries, and downloading HTML files.

RAM Requirements May Vary

The requirements for a small business server discussed in the "Server Computer Hardware Requirements" section of Chapter 4, "Planning a Small Business Server Network," should suffice for the general small business application. However, the variables described in the following list affect the amount of RAM required and depend on the level of Internet activity to be supported.

- Number of simultaneous users

- Number of HTTP users versus FTP users

- Amount of RAM used for caching

- Size of swap file

- Free disk space

- Amount of system RAM used for video

- Networked IIS versus stand-alone IIS

- Number of services running

- CPU type

- SQL Server database searches

A general guideline is to have about 256 KB of RAM for each simultaneous user, in addition to the recommended minimum hardware requirements for the Small Business Server 2000 computer.

Web Site Testing

Whether the Web site is hosted by the small business or the ISP, the design should be tested before the site is published on the Internet. The following is a checklist for things to consider when doing Web site testing:

- Security breaches

- Proper permissions set on downloadable files

- Functional links on all pages

- Proper display of graphics and text at different resolutions and color depth

- Proper operation of scripts

Also, the following conditions must be met:

- FTP files can be downloaded and function properly.

- Different Web browsers can access the Web site and activate the site links.

- Simultaneous connections to the server are supported.

Internet Connection Process

Small Business Server 2000 helps the technology consultant simplify the process of connecting the small business customer to the Internet by providing a step-by-step configuration tool—the Small Business Server Internet Connection Wizard. This wizard configures new or existing ISP relationships. An existing ISP relationship already has configuration information for the customer, which the technology consultant can use. For example, the technology consultant might type the existing static IP address information on the appropriate Internet Connection Wizard page. See Chapter 11, "ISP Connectivity Tasks," for a detailed discussion of the Small Business Server Internet Connection Wizard.

Connectivity Issues with Existing ISPs

Although the Small Business Server Internet Connection Wizard automates most tasks necessary to configure an Internet connection, the wizard requires accurate information from the existing ISP to complete the configuration. The following section describes the information needed from the existing ISP and addresses other connection issues.

ISP Functions Required for Small Business Server Compliance

The primary functions an ISP should supply in order to support Small Business Server are as follows. These are the minimum functions required to support current and future needs of the small business using Small Business Server.

- Electronic mail routing and queuing

- Internet access

- Web hosting

The existing ISP handling the Small Business Server customer may provide some or all of the functions listed.

Types of Existing ISP Services

A small business can have several types of ISP accounts and relationships. The information that follows describes the various types of ISP accounts available and the appropriate recommendations for Small Business Server connectivity in each case.

Full-time Internet Connection

The small business may have an existing full-time connection to the Internet through a modem or leased line. Most small businesses do not need a full-time connection to the Internet, although Small Business Server does make it possible for the small business to have a full-time Internet presence while maintaining only a demand-dial Internet account. This may be implemented if the ISP is able to host the customer's Web site and receive and store its mail during offline periods. Small Business Server and ISPs work together to provide these services securely and reliably.

If the small business wishes to retain the full-time connection to its existing ISP, the technology consultant must make sure that the ISP fully supports the services planned for Small Business Server. Also, the technology consultant must configure Exchange 2000 Server, ISA Server, and the Web site information by using the Internet Connection Wizard, as described in Chapter 11, "ISP Connectivity Tasks."

Dial-up E-mail Accounts

Dial-up accounts, as well as national, regional, and local ISPs, are used by small businesses primarily to send and receive POP3-based e-mail on individual desktops. Dial-up accounts provide a way for a small business to use Internet e-mail, but such accounts require that everyone who wants an e-mail account have a separate account with the ISP. This is a one-to-one ratio between user and ISP, which, after just a few users, can become costly. In contrast, Small Business Server provides a more cost-effective solution. By using Exchange 2000 Server, the small business customer has a full mail solution for the entire company, using a single ISP account and a single phone line.

For a small business that already uses dial-up accounts, an ISP that supports mail queuing, Web hosting, and dial-up connectivity for ISA Server should be enlisted. The small business customer can then set up its account with an ISP through the Small Business Server Internet Connection Wizard or through another supported configuration process.

> ☑ **Note** You can retain a small business's individual POP3 accounts if necessary (if the addresses are already printed on business cards, for example), or you can slowly migrate e-mail being sent to those accounts over to the Small Business Server account. Customers choosing to maintain POP3-based e-mail accounts can use the POP3 gateway (developed by the same team that created Small Business Server 2000), enabling Exchange 2000 Server to reroute incoming POP3-based to directory-based e-mail accounts.

Web Hosting Services

The small business customer may have an existing ISP that hosts its Internet Web pages. In this arrangement, small businesses can take advantage of the benefits of the ISP's higher bandwidth connection and availability. The only drawback might be real-time electronic commerce activity, such as when the ISP e-mails customer orders to the small business. For example, if a customer places an order for products from the small business's Web site (hosted by the ISP) and the order information is then e-mailed to the small business for fulfillment, a delay is common. This is usually because the ISP doesn't have the ability to fulfill customer orders, but only to forward the order information. ISPs are typically very efficient in forwarding e-mail-based orders. The burden is then placed on the small business to read its e-mail and fulfill the order. Such fulfillment activities may take a few minutes or days, depending on the customer service capabilities of the small business.

> ☑ **Note** Many ISPs support Microsoft SQL Server™. An ISP can create SQL Server-based tables to accept Web input from customers. The tables are copied to the Small Business Server regularly to update the SQL Server database on the Small Business Server 2000 computer.

Simple Mail Transfer Protocol Dial-up Mail

Some ISPs support the dial-up connection of a Simple Mail Transfer Protocol (SMTP) server such as Exchange 2000 Server. If this is the case for the existing ISP, the technology consultant must configure Exchange 2000 Server accordingly, using the Internet Connection Wizard, as described in Chapter 11, "ISP Connectivity Tasks." The technology consultant should be aware that the ISP must support enhanced TURN (ETRN) or TURN after Authentication (TURN) for the small business to have a suitable mail de-queuing method.

Dedicated Internet Connections

A dedicated Internet connection may use the following device types:

- xDSL
- Cable modem
- ISDN router
- ISDN terminal adapter

If the small business customer has any of these devices, or other dedicated WAN connection devices, the Small Business Server Internet Connection Wizard can complete its tasks only if the routing device has been properly configured. Refer to the device manufacturer's documentation for configuration procedures.

> **Note** Small Business Server 2000 does not configure routing devices; it configures only the server computer to interact with the devices.

Existing Small Business POP Accounts

If the small business has existing POP3 mail accounts and wants to retain them, the Exchange 2000 Server and Microsoft Outlook® 2000 clients can be manually configured to send and receive POP3 mail. This occurs through the Small Business Server 2000 POP3 gateway for Exchange 2000 Server.

Information Required from an Existing ISP

This section covers the information required from the small business customer's existing ISP for configuring a new Small Business Server Internet connection.

Connection Information

The following connection requirements are based on the assumption that a modem is being used to connect to the ISP. The configuration requirements of dedicated or high-bandwidth connections are described in the section "Internet Connection Types" earlier in this chapter. The following are needed from the ISP:

- A dial-in phone number for the modem connection.

- A user ID and password to authenticate the small business connection.

- The Internet domain name (or IP address) for Small Business Server.

- Dial-up networking configuration information (optional).

DNS Configuration

To communicate on the Internet, the small business must obtain an Internet domain name from the ISP for Small Business Server. This name identifies the location of the small business network server and will be part of the company's Internet e-mail address. The formats for these are as follows:

- user@InternetDomainName.xxx (e-mail)

- www.InternetDomainName.xxx (URL for a Web site)

The ISP plays a critical role in the Domain Name System (DNS) configuration. For e-mail-related DNS name resolution, the ISP creates a Mail Exchange (MX) record that is propagated across the Internet to other DNS servers. This enables e-mail to be routed correctly. For Web site-related DNS name resolution, the ISP creates a general (A) resource record that is propagated across the Internet to other DNS servers.

Internet Domain Name Levels

A company can choose from two levels of Internet domain names:

- **Second-level**. A second-level Internet domain name contains the name by which the small business chooses to be known: @YourCompanyName.xxx

- **Third-level**. A third-level Internet domain name contains the ISP name in addition to the name by which the small business chooses to be known: @YourCompanyName.ISPcompany.xxx

E-mail Information

In addition to the DNS issues described next, the technology consultant needs to find out the DNS name and IP address of the ISP's mail host. In some cases, the ISP may have separate hosts for inbound and outbound mail. The DNS name of both hosts is needed in order to configure Exchange 2000 Server. This information is readily available from the ISP and is typically posted on the ISP's Web page.

Domain Naming Service Configuration Issues

During the Internet connection process, some minor issues may arise regarding the registration of domain names for the small business organization. These issues are discussed in the paragraphs that follow; the technology consultant needs to be aware of them before deploying Small Business Server.

Registering a Second-Level Domain Name

Before the small business can register a second-level domain name, the Small Business Server Internet Connection Wizard must gather information for the ISP DNS. This wizard executes all the necessary commands to ensure that e-mail is delivered to the correct accounts and that Web posting and hosting work correctly. The technology consultant should be aware that the small business ISP must support the creation and use of second-level domain names in order for the Small Business Server Internet Connection Wizard to complete these tasks.

Configuring Small Business Server to Use an Existing Second-Level Domain Name

A small business may already have the rights to a second-level domain name and may want to configure Small Business Server to work with this domain name. To do this, the technology consultant must contact the ISP to change any third-level domain name entries to the second-level domain name. For more information, refer to Chapter 11, "ISP Connectivity Tasks," in this guide.

ISP DNS Tasks

The technology consultant typically lists the ISP that hosts the domain as the technical contact when registering a domain name. In addition, the ISP's DNS servers are listed in the domain registration record. The ISP must make resource record entries in its DNS tables. The technology consultant should consult with the ISP regarding these tasks.

Summary

One of the most popular uses of Small Business Server 2000 is to connect to the Internet. This chapter outlined the planning issues involved in creating an Internet presence for the small business, including domain naming, e-mail, Web hosting, and connection types and hardware.

CHAPTER 6

Planning for Remote Access Users

Providing employee access to small business network resources from distant locations is becoming a competitive necessity. A suitable remote access solution enables people to work as productively at home or while traveling as they do in the office.

Windows 2000 Routing and Remote Access Service

Microsoft® Windows® 2000 Server, integrated in Microsoft Small Business Server 2000, includes a powerful set of services that deliver the easiest, most cost-effective way to implement remote network access. With Small Business Server, a small business can extend the reach of its office network to remote users through secure, high-performance access. Remote users can either dial directly into the small business network server or connect across the Internet backbone with a virtual private network (VPN). Because Windows 2000 Server is an open, extensible platform based on industry standards, the Small Business Server customer has not only superior remote access flexibility but also cost savings. The Routing and Remote Access Service (RRAS) feature of Windows 2000 Server provides access to the small business network from a remote location.

Key Features of RRAS

RRAS is a robust solution and has several key features, including:

- **Authentication**. Windows 2000 Server provides a choice of secure authentication mechanisms for direct-dial and VPN connections based on industry standard Challenge Handshake Authentication Protocol (CHAP), MS-CHAP (including the new MS-CHAP version 2), and Password Authentication Protocol (PAP) protocols. Authentication services include mutual client/server authentication to ensure that intruders cannot intercept passwords and information.

- **Secure encryption**. Windows 2000 Server also provides secure encryption for both direct-dial and VPN access through either 128-bit or 40-bit encryption keys. These services include random and changing encryption keys to protect sensitive data. Other important security enhancements are also available for remote access, such as digital certificates.

- **Scalability**. Windows 2000 Server routing and remote access technologies provide high performance with room to grow. Windows 2000 Server provides up to 256 concurrent connections for direct-dial and VPN connections.

- **Multi-link**. Windows 2000 Server supports multi-link Point-to-Point Protocol (PPP). This industry standard enables the combination of multiple physical remote access links into a single logical link to accelerate data transfers and reduce communications and connect-time costs.

- **Compression**. Windows 2000 Server supports Microsoft Point-to-Point Compression for an accelerated remote user connectivity experience. This can double or quadruple data transfer throughput across a remote connection. Other enhancements available for VPN dramatically improve performance over difficult, high-loss network connections.

- **Superior connectivity options**. Windows 2000 Server enables remote access through any type of WAN connectivity—including dial-up Public Switched Telephone Network (PSTN), Digital Subscriber Line technologies (xDSL), Integrated Services Digital Network (ISDN), wireless, leased line, frame relay—and enables any type of local area network (LAN) connectivity, including Ethernet, Fiber Distributed Data Interface (FDDI), asynchronous transfer mode (ATM), and Token Ring.

- **Broad protocol support**. Windows 2000 Server supports a wide variety of networking protocols, including PPP, multi-link PPP, TCP/IP, Internetwork Packet Exchange/Sequenced Packet Exchange (IPX/SPX), NetBIOS Enhanced User Interface (NetBEUI), and Point-to-Point Tunneling Protocol (PPTP). The technology consultant can choose the options that provide the small business the most flexibility and investment preservation.

- **Broad client support**. Routing and Remote Access Service with Windows 2000 Server supports a broad variety of client operating systems, including Windows 2000 Professional, Windows 98, Windows 95, Microsoft Windows NT® Workstation, Macintosh, and UNIX.

- **Open, extensible platform**. Microsoft publishes a rich set of Application Programming Interfaces (APIs) for remote access and other operating system services. These APIs enable independent software vendors (ISVs) to build commercial or custom remote access and communications solutions in a variety of forms—all based on Windows 2000 Server.

- **Low-cost hardware and systems**. By applying a PC-industry business model to communications and networking, small business customers are offered unparalleled choice and innovation. Open platforms drive volume, competition, and innovation, yielding lower prices for applications, hardware, and services while reducing risk of obsolescence.

RRAS Management Features

Management features of RRAS include:

- **Direct dial and VPN—with the same client**. Windows 2000 Server provides a consistent client experience for both VPN and direct-dial access to minimize user training requirements and costs. The Dial-Up Networking client interface also provides a straightforward, end-user managed method of defining connections and phonebook entries on the client computer for direct dial and VPN connections.

- **Integrated management and administration**. Windows 2000 Server enables the technology consultant to manage remote client connections as well as other network-to-network connections from a unified management environment. The technology consultant can use either an easy, intuitive graphical interface, or a scriptable command-line interface—both options enable local or remote management. The standard administrator interface reduces training and the expense required to manage networks.

- **Wizard-based setup**. Wizards for both client and server features make the process of setting up a remote access system fast and easy for the technology consultant and end users.

- **Central phonebook services**. Connection Point Services enables the technology consultant to manage one of the most expensive and troublesome aspects of supporting a group of remote access users: keeping users up to date with remote access dial-up phone numbers. With Windows 2000 Server, these centralized phonebooks store remote access dial-up numbers and update remote client computers automatically. You install Connection Point Services by using the Connection Manager Administration Kit, which is discussed in the Windows 2000 Server Help system.

- **Support for ISV tools**. Windows 2000 Server enables numerous ISVs to provide management, reporting, and accounting applications that integrate with the server's communications features. The server's APIs, support of Simple Network Management Protocol (SNMP), and other extensibility features enable easy integration of ISV applications.

Point-to-Point Tunneling Protocol Versus Analog Routing and Remote Access Service

RRAS can be configured in two ways to enable users to gain remote access to the Small Business Server network. The first way is to configure the built-in Point-to-Point Tunneling Protocol (PPTP) in Windows 2000 Server by creating VPN ports for remote users. To connect to the VPN port, the remote user first establishes an Internet connection and then configures the desktop Dial Up Network connection to "dial" an IP address across the Internet.

The other method to enable remote users to gain remote access to the Small Business Server network is to configure RRAS for analog modem dial-up calls. This method is the same as configuring dial-up remote access in Windows NT with Remote Access Service. A user places an analog modem call to a telephone number used by Small Business Server for inbound RRAS connections. The server answers the call and starts an RRAS session with logon authentication.

Requirements for Implementing RRAS

Basic remote dial-up and VPN server support is part of Windows 2000 Server; it can be set up and turned on immediately. Basic Dial-Up Networking also is included with each of the client Windows operating systems—Windows 2000 Professional, Windows NT Workstation 4.0, Windows 98, and Windows 95. The following table lists the components needed for RRAS.

Table 6.1 RRAS Required Components

What is needed	Where to get it
Routing and Remote Access Service (on the server computer).	Included with Windows 2000 Server.
Dial-Up Networking (on the client computer).	Included with Windows 2000 Professional, Windows Me, Windows 98, and Windows NT 4.0. With Windows 95, you will need to install Dial-Up Networking (DUN) 1.2 or later.

Remote Access to Small Business Server

Small Business Server can be accessed through a direct point-to-point connection with a standard dial-up modem link connecting to RAS across the PSTN, or by establishing a VPN on the Internet backbone by using RRAS and PPTP. These two scenarios are shown in Figure 6.1. The Internet Security and Acceleration (ISA) Server 2000 firewall from the Small Business Server Internet Connection Wizard must be configured before these settings can be used.

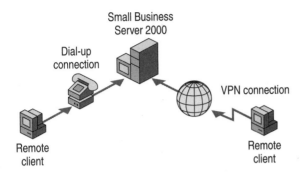

Figure 6.1   Remote access scenarios

In Figure 6.1, the dial-up connection to the Small Business Server computer (top) is illustrated on the left. The Internet-based VPN connection is illustrated on the right.

VPN for Secure Remote Access

When a remote client gains access to Small Business Server across the Internet, protecting organizational information is an issue. A VPN running PPTP must be used for the secure transfer of data between Small Business Server and the remote user. The paragraphs that follow provide some planning issues to consider before implementing PPTP. A brief description of a VPN and its features are included. For more information about installing and configuring a VPN, refer to Chapter 13, "Remote Connectivity."

Defining Virtual Private Networks

A VPN is an on-demand connection between two computers in different locations. It consists of the two computers (one computer at each end of the connection) and a route, or *tunnel*, over a public or private network. To ensure privacy and secure communication, data transmitted between the two computers is encrypted by the remote access protocol known as Point-to Point Tunneling Protocol (PPTP). The data is then routed over a dial-up or LAN connection by a VPN device.

Advantages of a Virtual Private Network

One of the primary advantages of a VPN is that it eliminates the need of owning and maintaining dedicated telecommunication equipment to support remote and mobile users who need to connect to the small business network. A VPN enables the secure use of public telecommunication networks and reduces the costs of supporting remote access.

Defining Point-to-Point Tunneling Protocol

PPTP is a network protocol that enables the secure transfer of data from a remote client to a private server by creating a VPN within a TCP/IP-based data network. PPTP supports multiple network protocols (IP, IPX, and NetBEUI) and can be used for virtual private networking over public and private networks.

PPTP can be used to provide secure, on-demand, virtual networks by using dial-up lines, LANs, WANs, the Internet, and other public TCP/IP-based networks. PPTP uses the VPN device to establish and maintain private, secure communication between computers.

VPN Key Features

The key features of VPN provided with Small Business Server include:

- User authentication integrated with Windows 2000 security. This enables ease of use and simple management while also providing for security.

- Information and privacy secured through robust data encryption and key management.

- Productivity of the small business client ensured by easy-to-use features.

- Management across all services made easy through integrated administration.

- Economical and manageable network connectivity enabled by dynamic address assignment.

Small Business Server has secure 128-bit encryption, Dynamic Host Configuration Protocol (DHCP) support, simple and customizable clients, directory integration, and remote administration. These features enable the small business organization to do the following tasks:

- Use existing public infrastructure to reduce communication transmission costs.

- Outsource remote access to reduce capital expenditures for hardware and software.

- Reduce administrative and support costs through a familiar user interface and common management tools.

- Minimize investment risk through open systems and a programmable networking infrastructure.

- Take advantage of rich network application advancements.

    Note 128-bit encryption is available only in North America; all other locations use 56-bit encryption.

Virtual Private Network Usage

For Small Business Server, the technology consultant can use a VPN to provide secure and encrypted communication when remote users are connecting to the small business network by using Dial-Up Networking and an ISP connection to the Internet. Remote access through Dial-Up Networking connects the remote client to the ISP's PPTP-enabled network access server, sometimes referred to as a front-end processor (FEP).

Figure 6.2 shows a remote VPN client with PPTP installed. The remote client dials up an ISP server configured as a *VPN client* and establishes a PPP session. The remote client dials a second time, concurrent with the PPP session. The ISP server then connects to a PPTP tunnel that goes from the ISP, and over the Internet, to RRAS on Small Business Server (configured as a *PPTP server*). PPP packets are then tunneled through the virtual connection, and the client becomes a virtual node on the small business LAN, from across the Internet. Small Business Server handles all validation and can require that data be encrypted in both directions.

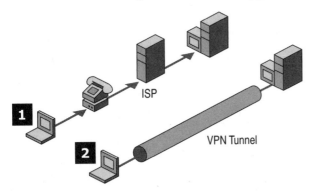

Figure 6.2   Remote access with PPTP tunneling

Figure 6.2 illustrates the first call to an ISP as a simple dial-up connection (left side, callout 1). The VPN tunnel is established to the Small Business Server computer (right side, callout 2).

Network Protocols on the Small Business Network

PPTP enables the use of virtual private networking over public TCP/IP networks while retaining existing network protocols, network node addresses, and naming schemes on the small business network. By using PPTP to tunnel across the Internet or other TCP/IP-based public networks, no changes to existing network configurations and to network-based applications are required. For example, IPX or NetBEUI clients can continue to run applications that require these protocols.

In addition, name resolution methods—such as Windows Internet Naming Service (WINS) for NetBIOS computers, Domain Name System (DNS) for TCP/IP host names, and Service Advertisement Protocol (SAP) for IPX networking—do not need to be changed. IP addresses that are not valid on the Internet can be used on the private network.

The address and name resolution schemes on the small business network must be correctly configured. If not, the VPN remote client cannot communicate with computers on the small business network.

Requirements for a VPN Client

The minimum configuration for a VPN client is dependent on the operating system. A VPN client can be a computer configured with any of the following operating systems:

*   Windows 2000 Professional

*   Windows 2000 Server

*   Windows Me

*   Windows NT Workstation 4.0 (with PPTP installed)

*   Windows NT Server 4.0 (with PPTP installed)

*   Windows 98

*   Windows 95 with Dial-Up Networking (DUN), version 1.2 or later

The hardware requirements for computers running any of these operating systems can be found in Chapter 4, "Planning a Small Business Server Network."

Summary of Virtual Private Network Deployment Considerations

Deployment considerations for VPNs include:

*   VPN functionality uses the Microsoft implementation of RRAS and PPTP to establish connections with remote computers by using dial-up lines or Internet-based network connections. PPTP provides remote-user authentication and data encryption between the VPN client and the VPN server. Dial-Up Networking (DUN) must be installed and configured on both the VPN clients, so that the client can establish a VPN session with the Small Business Server 2000 computer.

*   Because a VPN and PPTP requires RRAS and a PPP protocol, a PPP account with an ISP must be established in order to use PPTP over an ISP connection to the Internet.

- When configuring PPTP, the technology consultant must install and configure VPNs in RRAS, just as if they were physical devices, such as modems.

- PPTP is installed and configured on VPN clients and servers only. Computers on the route between the VPN client and server do not require PPTP installation.

- A VPN server is placed behind a firewall on the small business network, which ensures that traffic in and out of the private network is secured by the ISA Server firewall.

  > **Note** Use the Small Business Server Internet Connection Wizard to configure the ISA Server firewall settings, enabling outbound VPN traffic through port openings. In addition, it enables a Small Business Server client computer to create a VPN connection to a remote network. The Small Business Server Internet Connection Wizard will not, however, configure Small Business Server to support inbound VPN traffic.
  >
  > Configure inbound VPN traffic by using the ISA Server VPN Wizard and not the Routing and Remote Access Service (RRAS) VPN Wizard.

- To ensure network security, VPN client users must be authenticated (just like any other remote user using RRAS and DUN) in order to connect to the small business network.

- Using the Internet to establish a connection between a VPN client and server means that the VPN server must have a valid, Internet-sanctioned IP address. However, the encapsulated IPX, NetBEUI, or TCP/IP packets sent between the VPN client and server can be addressed to computers on the small business network by using private network addressing or naming schemes. The VPN server disassembles the PPTP packet from the VPN client and forwards the packet to the correct computer on the small business network.

Other Resources

White papers on VPNs can be downloaded from the Windows NT Server Web site at: http://www.microsoft.com/Windows2000/

Refer to Chapter 9, "Virtual Private Networking" in the *Windows 2000 Server Resource Kit Internetworking Guide*, or Chapter 13, "Remote Connectivity," in this guide.

Summary

This chapter presented the remote access planning issues the technology consultant needs to consider as part of a Small Business Server 2000 implementation, including defining and managing RRAS and VPN planning and connection scenarios.

CHAPTER 7

Planning for Small Business Server Applications

After the basics of the Microsoft® Small Business Server 2000 network are planned, the next step is planning for applications. Applications are typically implemented and used after the core Small Business Server network is in service. This chapter discusses the following applications:

- Shared Fax Service
- Shared Modem Service
- Microsoft Internet Security and Acceleration (ISA) Server 2000
- Microsoft Exchange 2000 Server
- Microsoft SQL Server™ 2000

Planning for Shared Fax Service and Shared Modem Service

The information on Shared Fax Service and Shared Modem Service provided in this section is intended to help the technology consultant and small business owner decide how these services are best implemented in the small business network.

Scenario

A small business seeks to cut costs by reducing the number of extra telephone lines used in the organization for dial-out operations and faxing. Currently, the small business provides an additional telephone line to each employee who requires modem dial-up access to the Internet. Although they need Internet access, employees have little need to dial out to locations that are not Internet connections—for example, a credit bureau that does not transmit credit information over the Internet. In addition, the small business has several telephone lines for fax machines used primarily for outbound faxing. Inbound faxes can pose other problems for the small business, including the occasional misplacement of a fax because of volume or other demands on the workspace surrounding the main inbound fax machine.

Recommendation

The small business just described can benefit from using Shared Fax Service and Shared Modem Service. By centralizing dial-out modem activity, the small business can reduce the total number of telephone lines needed. Shared Modem Service, in conjunction with ISA Server, allows the user to access the Internet with fewer dial-up connections. Shared Fax Service allows the small business to centralize its inbound and outbound faxing process, eliminating the need for fax machines and decreasing additional telephone lines. Shared Fax Service enables the small business to save faxes and recover lost or misplaced faxes.

Benefits

Benefits to deploying Shared Fax Service and Shared Modem Service include:

- **Cost savings**. Centralizing fax and modem processes results in overall cost savings to the small business because the number of additional telephone lines is reduced. Additional cost savings result from lower maintenance costs—a fax modem does not require the amount of maintenance that a plain-paper fax machine does.

- **Better management**. Centralized fax and modem processes are easier to manage than dispersed fax machines and modems.

- **Reporting and archives**. Centralized fax and modem processes enable the technology consultant to monitor fax and dial-up activity and to assess the usage of these services. Shared Fax Service enables incoming faxes to be stored in electronic mail folders. In addition, faxes can be saved in a folder on the Small Business Server computer and printed on a network printer.

- **Security**. Deploying analog lines in employee offices poses a security risk when modems are connected to individual computers because they may be used by external parties to illegally gain access to the internal computer network.

  ☑ **Note** When the small business has a high-speed Internet connection, Small Business Server customers who have historically used dial-up modems to access certain services, such as banking, should investigate whether such modem-based transactions can be conducted over the Internet.

Pre-Deployment Considerations

Before installing Shared Fax Service and Shared Modem Service, the technology consultant should determine the number and type of modems required, based on the following considerations:

- If users need to dial out frequently, one or more modems on lines dedicated to dialing out should be used to ensure that outgoing calls do not block incoming data or fax calls.

- For optimal performance, Shared Fax Service and Shared Modem Service must each have at least one dedicated modem. It is not recommended that the services use the same modem.

- If modem use is essential to productivity, the cost of extra modems and phone lines should be weighed against the following:

  - If more than 10 users regularly use any one service, such as faxing, a second modem dedicated to that service should be installed.

  - Shared Modem Service and Shared Fax Service can each handle a maximum of four modems.

- When more than one modem is being purchased, it is recommended that they are the same brand and model so they can be shared by using Shared Modem Service.

- It is not recommended that Peripheral Component Interconnect (PCI)–based or universal serial bus (USB)–based modems be used with Small Business Server. Although these modems are advertised as being easily configured and less expensive, they have proved problematic in real-world conditions with Small Business Server.

- It is recommended that you purchase external modems, which feature status lights during troubleshooting sessions. In addition, external modems can be reset externally, whereas internal modems require that the Small Business Server network be shut down before the modem can be reset.

  ☑ **Note** The technology consultant should frequently review the Microsoft Windows® 2000 Hardware Compatibility List (HCL) posted on Microsoft's Web site at: http://www.microsoft.com/windows2000/.

  This list is periodically updated.

Modem Planning Considerations

Small Business Server no longer requires a modem during setup. However, at least one modem must be installed and detected before you can configure modem-dependent server applications, such as:

- Routing and Remote Access Service (RRAS)

- Shared Modem Service

- Shared Fax Service (requires a Class 1 modem to install properly)

On a moderately busy day, more than 10 users can easily overload a one-modem configuration for Small Business Server. If the small business is using modem-based services with 10 or more users on the network, installing more than one modem is strongly suggested to distribute the load.

Separate modems are required if multiple services are to be facilitated efficiently. Otherwise, services may be disrupted if only one modem is available on the server and it is occupied with other tasks.

Multiple Usage Scenarios

Shared Fax Service and Shared Modem Service can each handle a maximum of four modems. However, to support multiple usage scenarios with improved network access and stability, modems must be dedicated to the specific services, as discussed earlier in the chapter.

For example, if there are four modems or modem lines and the small business receives and sends a moderate number of faxes, has RRAS needs, and is frequently connected to the Internet, a possible configuration is as follows:

- Shared Modem Service is set up to use two non-fax modems for outbound Dial-Up Networking (DUN) and Internet service provider (ISP) connections.

- A Class 1 fax modem is dedicated to faxing.

- One non-fax modem is dedicated to inbound RRAS.

Figure 7.1 illustrates the configuration.

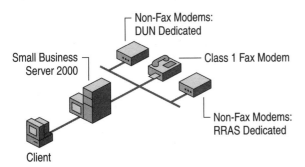

Figure 7.1 Typical Small Business Server modem configuration

Another option is to install a dedicated or leased line for outbound services and leave the dial-up modems for inbound RRAS. Modem scenario solution sets vary depending on the unique needs of the small business.

RRAS Modem Requirements

Remote users can gain access to Small Business Server by using RRAS. Remote access users can either dial directly into Small Business Server by using DUN or connect across the Internet with virtual private networking. If the small business plans to support multiple dial-up connections for remote access users, the technology consultant should consider using a multiport serial device with Small Business Server.

Because most microcomputers have only two physical serial ports for supporting modems, and at least one of these ports is used for a mouse or uninterruptible power supply (UPS) monitoring cable, this leaves only one port for an external modem. Adding a multiport serial card resolves this problem and provides an effective solution for remote access users.

Fax Service Modem Requirements

If the small business sends and receives many faxes, a dedicated business-class fax modem is recommended. The fax modem dedicated to faxing should not be assigned to the modem pool. That way, it will not be used for outbound DUN.

☑ **Note** As a general rule, modems that work with Windows 2000 Server work with Small Business Server 2000.

Modem Communication Standards

Two standards for high-speed modem technology (rates of 33 kilobytes per second [KBps] or higher) exist today: x2 from companies such as US Robotics/3Com Corporation and K56Flex products from Motorola. The ISP must support the small business's modem technology to attain maximum access speed to the Internet. Modem technology used for RRAS clients should also match these criteria.

Shared Fax Service Planning Considerations

Shared Fax Service is optimized and tested for up to 50 users. Much development work went into Shared Fax Service for Small Business Server 2000, resulting in significant improvement over previous versions of Shared Fax Service.

When planning for Shared Fax Service, the technology consultant should consider the following:

- Shared Fax Service allows network users to send and receive fax documents with any fax device capable of handling Group 3 fax calls. The Group 3 standard is the successor to Group 2 and contains additional AT modem commands.

- Network clients do not need a separate fax modem attached to their desktop, thereby reducing small business hardware costs and phone line usage.

- When a Small Business Server client setup disk is created for Microsoft Windows 2000 Professional, Microsoft Windows 95, Microsoft Window 98, or Microsoft Windows NT® Workstation client computers, Shared Fax Service client software can be conveniently included on the disk by using the Set Up Computer Wizard.

Planning for Internet Security and Acceleration Server

Small Business Server 2000 uses ISA Server to provide Internet connectivity network security and Web page caching for the entire small business network. Also, Windows 2000 Professional, Microsoft Windows Me, Windows 98, Windows 95, or Windows NT Workstation remote users are protected by ISA Server security features when they access the Internet through the Small Business Server network.

Scenario

Small businesses need to effectively compete with larger enterprises. Small Business Server helps them compete by establishing a strong Internet presence. Also, small businesses demand the same type of Internet security experienced by larger enterprises.

Recommendation

The small business in this scenario can have a strong, secure, and high performance Internet presence by implementing ISA Server. ISA Server enables an office network with less than 50 clients to use a single security policy that applies to all clients. ISA Server provides maximum network security with the following features:

- Credential authentication
- User permissions
- Protocol definitions
- Domain filtering
- Caching
- Packet filtering
- Secure Network Address Translation (NAT)
- Published Rules (Server, Web publishing)

With these features, the small business network can maintain security and retain appropriate flexibility for Internet access.

ISA Server Configuration for Dial-Up Internet Connectivity

ISA Server makes a dial-on-demand connection to the Internet by using an existing dial-up connection. If the Small Business Server network has dial-up connectivity to the Internet, ISA Server uses it to start an Internet session as needed.

Web Caching Minimizes Demand Dialing

In a typical small business office network configuration, caching should be enabled and configured to minimize the occurrence of demand dialing to the Internet and improve the network user's Internet experience. Web caching lowers costs for the small business, improves performance of the network, and contributes to minimizing security risks. Caching can be used to store a local copy of the most frequented URLs in dedicated disk drive volumes. A feature known as Active Caching can be used to automatically retrieve the most popular URLs without client initiation. This feature is disabled by default in Small Business Server 2000 to reduce the load on the server, but can easily be enabled by the technology consultant. For more information about Active Caching, refer to Chapter 21, "Firewall Security and Web Caching with ISA Server."

> ☑ **Note** Active Caching can cause excessive dialing activity on Small Business Server computers with a dial-up connection to the Internet, because the feature forces calls to keep the cached Web pages as current as possible.

Other Planning Resources for ISA Server

The extensive online documentation supplied with ISA Server is useful when planning a Small Business Server 2000 deployment. This documentation can be used in conjunction with the configuration of ISA Server described in Chapter 18 and Chapter 21 of this guide to assist in the development of a security solution for the Small Business Server 2000 customer. Chapter 21, "Firewall Security and Web Caching with ISA Server," describes the services and architecture of ISA Server and presents security configuration scenarios.

> ☑ **Note** A default configuration for ISA Server Internet connectivity is set up by the Small Business Server Internet Connection Wizard, as described in Chapter 21.

Planning for Exchange 2000 Server

Because Small Business Server 2000 automatically configures Exchange 2000 Server, little planning is required. One important planning issue is the selection of names for electronic mail services. This is discussed in the following sections.

Scenario

A small business seeks to improve its internal and external communications and also to promote its Internet identity by providing each employee with a dot-com e-mail address.

Recommendation and Benefits

Exchange Server, included with Small Business Server, requires minimal configuration to work well for the small business. It provides the e-mail capabilities to improve communications that the small business in the scenario seeks. More importantly, Exchange Server accommodates naming strategies that enable the firm to display a dot-com e-mail address to external parties.

> ☑ **Note** If there is excessive e-mail traffic, the hardware level of the Small Business Server computer may need to be boosted. For example, more RAM, a second processor, and more hard disk space may be needed.

Naming Standards

Each object in the Exchange Directory is uniquely identified by a name—the distinguished name. Distinguished names are a directory services concept. In Small Business Server, the organization name defaults to First Organization. The server name in Exchange Server is the same as the Windows 2000 Server network basic input/output system (NetBIOS) computer name.

> ☑ **Note** The server naming restrictions in Windows 2000 Server accommodate the name restrictions needed for a proper Exchange 2000 Server computer name. Non-standard characters (for example, symbols) are not supported in the naming convention.

Mailbox Names

Mailbox names should be easy to identify. They could be based on existing standards for phone and address books. If the existing naming standards are too cryptic, they can be changed at this time. Mailbox naming standards could be coordinated with the naming scheme used for Small Business Server or other types of existing user accounts. The fields described in Table 7.1 can be specified in a mailbox name.

Table 7.1 Fields in the Mailbox Name

Field	Guideline	Restrictions
First Name	The user's first name.	Up to 64 characters. Can be changed.
Last Name	The user's last name.	Up to 64 characters. Can be changed.
Display Name	The mailbox name as it will appear in the From field of an outgoing message and in the address lists.	Up to 256 characters. Can be changed.
Alias Name	This is an alternative name that can be displayed for e-mail purposes.	Up to 256 characters. Can be changed.

SMTP Considerations

When Exchange Server is connected to the Internet or other Simple Mail Transfer Protocol (SMTP) systems, the technology consultant should consider the character restrictions that SMTP imposes on its addressing scheme. This includes restrictions on the use of certain symbols (such as the @ character) and not allowing spaces between names.

✍ **Note** The SMTP address is created on the basis of the registered Internet domain name information provided during the setup of Windows 2000 Server and Small Business Server 2000.

Other Resources

For additional information about Exchange Server, refer to the *Microsoft Exchange 2000 Server Resource Kit*.

Microsoft Connector for POP3 Mailboxes

Small Business Server 2000 provides the Microsoft Connector for Post Office Protocol 3 (POP3) Mailboxes for Exchange 2000 Server, which acts as a gateway for routing POP3-based e-mail to internal Exchange 2000 Server mailboxes. This is configured from the Small Business Server Internet Connection Wizard. The Microsoft Connector for POP3 Mailboxes is discussed in later chapters.

Planning for SQL Server 2000

SQL Server 2000 is a powerful relational database that is included with Small Business Server 2000. SQL Server 2000 can be used for custom programming or to install and integrate third-party applications, such as accounting programs.

Scenario

A small business seeks more powerful reporting capabilities than its off-the-shelf accounting software can provide. A technology consultant recommends a package that requires SQL Server as the underlying database engine.

Recommendation

SQL Server can be easily installed as part of the Small Business Server Setup. It is ready for use after completing only a few configuration screens. Third-party applications, such as the accounting system in the preceding scenario, then can be installed.

> ☑ **Note** SQL Server is not installed by default in Small Business Server 2000. To install it, select it and its applicable subcomponents on the **Components** page of the Small Business Server Setup Wizard.

Benefits

The preceding scenario illustrates two major benefits to implementing SQL Server. The first benefit is lower cost for the small business. Because SQL Server is included with Small Business Server, no additional expenditures are necessary for the small business to implement the third-party accounting system. The second benefit is the power of SQL Server. This small business not only can run the new accounting software but also can develop powerful custom applications based on SQL Server.

Note Few drawbacks exist for implementing SQL Server. One possible drawback is that smaller firms might not have the technical expertise to develop custom SQL Server applications.

SQL Server and Third-Party Applications

Small businesses that use SQL Server do so at the recommendation of the technology consultant and to be able to implement a third-party application. Many third-party software vendors support SQL Server, including most major accounting packages. Typically, the technology consultant that installs Small Business Server, including SQL Server, does not install specialized third-party applications because the Small Business Server technology consultant rarely has the third-party application expertise required. For example, the technology consultant must have an accounting background to be able to implement one major accounting program correctly. Similarly, a consultant working for a third-party software firm rarely has the expertise to correctly implement Small Business Server.

At a minimum, the Small Business Server technology consultant and the third-party software consultant should coordinate the implementation of SQL Server.

Other Resources

One of the best resources for SQL Server is the online documentation, which is included with Small Business Server.

Extending Small Business Server 2000

When Small Business Server 2000 is installed, it serves as a powerful information infrastructure to implement additional Microsoft solutions. Two of these solutions are included with Small Business Server 2000: Exchange Instant Messaging and Microsoft NetMeeting®. A third solution, Microsoft Digital Dashboard, can be downloaded from the Microsoft Web site at: http://www.microsoft.com/.

Instant Messaging

Instant Messaging, included with Exchange 2000 Server, allows users to communicate quickly with other users on the Small Business Server network or across the Internet through chat sessions. Instant Messaging is better than e-mail for quick back-and-forth communications, such as a telephone call or two-way radio conversation. In fact, Instant Messaging can often replace costly long-distance telephone calls.

Chat Service

Exchange 2000 Server provides a multi-user chat system that enables people to convene for conversations on channels (commonly known as chat rooms). Users can join live, real-time discussion forums that cover a broad range of topics. Chat Service is based on Internet Relay Chat (IRC), which is a client/server protocol that supports real-time conversation between two or more users over a TCP/IP network (including the Internet).

Outlook Web Access

Small Business Server supports Outlook Web Access (OWA), a feature of Exchange 2000 Server. OWA enables users to access their Exchange Server mailboxes from any computer-based Web browser through the Internet. The client computer requires no additional configuration. OWA supports multiple operating systems such as UNIX and Macintosh-based Web browsers. Users can read and reply to e-mails, look up contact information, set appointments, and manage tasks while away from the office.

Exchange Multimedia Control

Exchange Multimedia Control, found in Microsoft Outlook® 2000 and the Exchange Web Client, enables the e-mail sender to embed rich multimedia content—such as voice recordings—into an e-mail message. When the e-mail client (Outlook 2000 or OWA) is configured for the Exchange Multimedia Control, the latest version of the Exchange Multimedia Control is downloaded and installed from the Small Business Server 2000 computer.

NetMeeting

NetMeeting is installed as part of Microsoft Internet Explorer 5.0. NetMeeting enables desktop sharing, chat conferencing (including the ability to save chat transcripts,) communication through the white board collaboration feature, and real-time audio and videoconferencing. NetMeeting is a popular business communication application that assists in collaboration.

Digital Dashboard

Small business managers and owners place a premium on obtaining and reviewing information that affects their business. Information is typically processed in a business application and presented as a report. Digital Dashboard enables the technology consultant to present relevant business information to decision makers in a simplified format. For example, financial information could be presented by using a traffic light metaphor of red light (unfavorable), yellow light (caution), and green light (favorable). A small business owner could decide on needed actions based on this information. Digital Dashboard is similar to the Executive Information System (EIS) tools used by larger enterprises. Digital Dashboard can be downloaded from the Microsoft Web site at: http://www.microsoft.com/.

Summary

This chapter discussed planning for several Small Business Server 2000 applications, including Shared Fax Service, Shared Modem Service, ISA Server, Exchange 2000 Server, and SQL Server 2000.

Installing Small Business Server on New Computers

This chapter describes installation and deployment of Microsoft® Small Business Server 2000 on a new computer. The installation process consists of the following steps:

- Ensuring minimum server requirements are met and checking hardware against the Microsoft Windows® 2000 Server Hardware Compatibility List.

- Gathering disks, compact discs, and other required materials for installing Small Business Server 2000 on a new computer.

- Installing Small Business Server.

Server Requirements and Hardware Compatibility

Before deploying Small Business Server, verify computer requirements and hardware compatibility. Devices such as a network adapter, serial adapter, disk controller, and fax modems have the highest chance of being detected correctly by Small Business Server during setup if they appear on the Windows 2000 Server Hardware Compatibility List. Otherwise, the hardware manufacturer must be contacted and must provide the drivers.

Computer Requirements

Requirements for Small Business Server and client computers are provided in Chapter 4, "Planning a Small Business Server Network."

Hardware Compatibility

In general, all hardware compatible with Windows 2000 Server is compatible with Small Business Server 2000. The Hardware Compatibility List can be found at: http://www.microsoft.com/hcl/.

Network Adapter Cards

Small Business Server requires a network adapter card to configure the network. Cards that can be used with Small Business Server are identified on the Windows 2000 Server Hardware Compatibility List. Cards that are used with client computers must be identified as compatible with specific operating systems.

If your network adapter is not detected or not on the Hardware Compatibility List, refer to Chapter 10, "Advanced Setup."

Modems

There are several considerations to be aware of with modems in Small Business Server 2000:

- A modem is not required for installation of Small Business Server 2000. This is a change from the previous version, Small Business Server 4.5, which required a modem. For Shared Fax Service to work properly, however, a Class 1 fax modem is required.

- For high-volume fax use (more than 100 faxes per day), a business-class fax modem is strongly recommended. Business-class modems are identified in the Hardware Compatibility List on the Small Business Server Web site.

- An external modem is preferred over an internal modem for ease-of-management purposes such as powering off and powering on the modem.

- Peripheral Component Interconnect (PCI) and universal serial bus (USB-based) modems should not be used with Small Business Server 2000.

  ☑ **Note** Modems used with Small Business Server should only perform one function. For example, a fax modem dedicated to the Shared Fax Service should not be used by the Shared Modem Service.

Multiport Serial Adapter Boards

Multiport boards supported by Small Business Server Shared Modem Service are identified in the Windows 2000 Server Hardware Compatibility List.

  ☑ **Note** For information about upgrading existing computers to Small Business Server 2000, refer to Chapter 9, "Installing Small Business Server in Existing Environments," and Chapter 24, "Small Business Server Licensing and Upgrades."

Requirements for Installing Small Business Server 2000 on a New Computer

Before beginning installation, record settings for future reference. The following items are needed to install Small Business Server 2000 on a new computer:

- Small Business Server 2000 setup boot disks 1, 2, 3, and 4. Running the Makeboot.exe program in the Bootdisk folder on Disc 1 can create these. Note that these setup disks must be for Small Business Server 2000 and not Windows 2000 Server.

  Note Small Business Server Disc 1 is for computers that have a disc drive that supports startup media, in which case the four Windows 2000 Server setup boot disks are not needed.

- Small Business Server Discs 1, 2, 3, and 4.

- Blank disks (for Emergency Repair Disk and the client setup disk).

- Drivers for network adapters, mass storage devices, modems, and video adapters.

  Note The Quick Start Card included with Small Business Server 2000 provides fill-in-the-blank forms to assist with setup.

Installing Small Business Server

There are several steps to installing Small Business Server software on a new computer. The steps are performed in the following order:

- Creating Small Business Server 2000 setup boot disks (if needed).

- Windows 2000 Server Text Mode is set.

- Windows 2000 Server Graphical User Interface (GUI) mode is set.

- Windows 2000 Server is configured and server applications are installed by the Small Business Server Setup Wizard.

Anticipated Number of Restarts

Setup requires you to restart the system at least five times during installation, including after the following steps:

- Text-based setup of Microsoft Windows 2000 Server.

- Graphical user interface-based (GUI-based) setup of Windows 2000 Server.

- Computer name is changed in the Small Business Server Setup Wizard (optional).

- Microsoft Active Directory™ directory service is installed or Small Business Server completes the Windows 2000 configuration.

- Small Business Server 2000 Setup is finished.

Setup Boot Disks

Small Business Server Disc 1 is used to create setup boot disks. These are required only if the hardware does not support booting directly from the disc drive.

Creating Setup Boot Disks

The four setup boot disks can be created on a Windows 2000 computer, per the following steps.

To create setup boot disks

1. Insert Disc 1 into the disc drive. Insert the first disk into the floppy disk drive on the server computer.

2. Open a command window or prompt.

3. From the command window or prompt, you may need to change the drive letter to your disc drive.

4. Type *cd bootdisk* at the prompt, and then press ENTER.

5. Type *makeboot*, and then press ENTER.

6. Follow the onscreen instructions, inserting floppy disks as files are copied. Number and label the disks.

Installing Small Business Server

The next step is to install Small Business Server by beginning the Windows 2000 Server Text Mode portion of setup, as described in the next section.

☑ Note   If you boot directly to Small Business Server Disc 1 to start setup not all of the steps (such as inserting setup disks) will apply to you.

Stage One: Windows 2000 Server Text Mode

During the Windows 2000 Server Text Mode portion of setup, drivers are loaded and storage devices are detected in order to initialize and prepare the computer. The following steps make up the first stage of Windows 2000 Server installation.

To begin Small Business Server installation in the Windows 2000 Server Text mode

1. Insert setup boot disk 1 into your floppy disk drive and start the computer.

2. Setup starts a minimal version of Windows 2000 that runs an initial Windows 2000 setup program.

3. Follow the onscreen instructions to insert boot disks 2, 3, and 4 in the floppy disk drive when asked.

4. Setup loads drivers and detects the mass storage devices, such as Small Computer System Interface (SCSI) controllers.

5. When asked, type the appropriate installation information for the license agreement.

6. Setup continues and completes the following:

    - Enables the user to partition the hard disk.

    - Enables the user to format the partition as NTFS file system or file allocation table (FAT). NTFS is recommended and Small Business Server requires at least one NTFS drive to complete setup.

    - Copies necessary files.

    - Restarts the computer.

Stage Two: Windows 2000 Server GUI Mode

During the GUI mode, the Windows 2000 Server is installed. The following steps make up the second stage of this installation.

To continue Small Business Server installation in the Windows 2000 Server GUI Mode

1. A **Welcome** page appears. Click **Next**.

2. When asked by the Windows 2000 Server Setup Wizard, accept or reject the **Regional Settings**, and then click **Next**.

3. When asked, enter the following information:

    • *Name*. The licensee name is required to define the name of the person to whom Small Business Server is licensed.

    • *Organization*. Setup uses the first eight characters in the company name to generate part of the suggested computer name.

4. When asked, type the **Small Business Server Product-Key**, and then click **Next**.

5. When asked, accept or change the computer name.

    ⚠ **Caution** Computer names must be composed of standard characters (A-Z, a-z, 0-9, hyphen). Although the computer name can be changed during the Small Business Server 2000 installation (see the next stage), name changes thereafter are restricted.

6. Type an Administrator password, and then click **Next**.

7. On the **Windows 2000 Components** page, select the components you want to install, and then click **Next**.

    ☑ **Note** It is recommended that you select Typical networking settings as Small Business Server Setup will configure networking later. This strategy minimizes the amount of troubleshooting required if the installation fails.

8. Accept or change the date and time settings, and then click **Next**. Setup installs the networking components.

9. When asked at the **Network Setting** page, click either the **Typical** (the default) or the **Custom** setting. Click **Next**.

    ☑ **Note** It is recommended that the selected default components be accepted. You can install additional components after completing Small Business Server 2000 Setup. This strategy minimizes the amount of troubleshooting required if the installation fails.

10. Setup automatically completes the following actions:

    - Copies files.

    - Performs final tasks.

    - Installs Start menu times.

    - Registers components.

    - Saves settings.

    - Removes any temporary files used.

11. When the **Completing the Windows 2000 Setup Wizard** appears, click **Finish**. The computer restarts.

     > ✒ **Note** Up to this point, Small Business Server 2000 Setup has been identical to Windows 2000 Server Setup except that neither a Workgroup or Computer Domain page nor a Licensing Modes page appears. This is because Small Business Server 2000 promotes the computer to a domain controller and then the licensing is enforced. As a result, these pages were removed to avoid confusion.

12. When asked, log on to the computer.

Stage Three: Installing Small Business Server Applications

After the Windows 2000 Server GUI Mode portion of setup is complete, logging on to the computer is the next step. The Small Business Server Setup Wizard starts to gather organizational information and to configure Windows 2000 Server, and also to install server applications, additional Small Business Server files, and installation files for the client applications. The following steps make up stage 3. Small Business Server Disc 1 may have to be inserted if it was removed.

To continue installation with the Small Business Server Setup Wizard

1. When the **Autorun** page appears, click **Set Up Small Business Server** to start the Small Business Server Setup Wizard.

2. On the **Welcome** page, click **Next**.

   > ✒ **Note** If the major Small Business Server 2000 requirements have not been met, a Suite Requirements page appears and states any conditions that must be fixed before continuing. For example, if the display resolution is too low, the warning error message, "Display resolution should be at least 800x600" will appear. Other messages, such as inadequate disk space, are blocking messages that prevent setup from continuing. For further information on how to correct the error, select the message and click Details.

3. Read and agree to the Small Business Server 2000 License Agreement, and then click **Next**.

4. On the **Product Identification** page, confirm the Name, Organization, and Computer Name, type the Small Business Server and Microsoft Outlook® Product keys, and then click **Next**.

   ☑ **Note**   After this step, the computer name cannot be changed again.

5. On the **Automatic Logon Information** page, type the administrator's password in the **Automatically log on** field, or click **Manually log on**, and then click **Next**.

6. On the **Company Information** page, type the address, city, state/province, and zip/postal code information, and then click **Next**.

7. On the **Telephony Information** page, type the business telephone, fax, and dialing information, and then click **Next**.

8. If you are installing multiple network adapter cards, you will be asked on the **Network Card Information** page to select your server (LAN) network adapter card. Once selected (or if you only have one network adapter card) you will be asked for your networking configuration on the **Server Network Card Information** page. On this page, accept either the default IP address configuration of 192.168.16.2 with a Subnet Mask of 255.255.255.0 for the internal network card, or specify your own IP addressing. When finished, click **Next**.

   ☑ **Note**   If you select a routable address, the Client Networking Configuration page appears, enabling you to specify how your client computers will receive IP addresses. (The default selection is for client computers to use static IP addresses.) Once you specify this, click Next. If you select a non-routable address, Dynamic Host Configuration Protocol (DHCP) and Windows Internet Naming Service (WINS) will automatically be installed and configured according to the network configuration of the server network card.

9. On the **New Domain Information** page, type the full Domain Name Server (DNS) name and network basic input/output system (NetBIOS) domain name, and then click **Next**.

   ▼ **Important**   Carefully select the domain names, as you will have to reinstall Small Business Server if you want to change these names. Click the **More Information** button for details on selecting a domain name. Refer to Chapter 11, "ISP Connectivity Tasks" and Chapter 19, "E-mail and Internet Connectivity Alternatives" for more information on Internet domain naming.

10. On the **Directory Services Restore Mode Administrator Password** page, type the administrator password in the **Password** field, and then click **Next**.

11. On the **Scenario Baseline** page, review the Windows 2000-related setup information, and then click **Next**.

12. Setup installs Windows 2000 Server applications, including Terminal Services. The computer restarts, and if you specified automatic logon, you are automatically logged on to the computer.

13. On the **Component Selection** page in the Small Business Server Setup Wizard, select the Small Business Server components you want to install, and then click **Next**. The default setting selects the recommended Small Business Server 2000 components (all components except Microsoft SQL Server™ 2000).

Installing SQL Server 2000

If you chose to install SQL Server 2000, complete the following steps.

To install SQL Server

☑ **Note**   It is recommended that only advanced users change any of these settings, as default settings are adequate for most SQL applications.

- **Collation settings**. The default selections for this page include:

  - SQL Collations

  - Dictionary order, not case-sensitive for use with a 1,252 character set

- **Network libraries**. The default selections for this page include:

  - Named Pipes with name \\. \pipe\sql\query

  - TCP/IP Sockets, port number 1433

Installing ISA Server

If you chose to install Internet Security and Acceleration (ISA) Server 2000, complete the following steps.

To install ISA Server

1. On the **ISA Server Cache Drives** page, set the cache size and then click **Next**.

2. The **ISA Server Construct Local Address Table** page appears. Specify your local address table (LAT) settings. You may select the network adapter card(s) for ISA Server to query in constructing the LAT. Click **Next**, and then the LAT is constructed.

3. When the **ISA Server Local Address Table Configuration** page appears, displaying the suggested LAT address ranges, review the ranges for correctness, and then click **Next**. You will return to the core Small Business Server 2000 setup process.

Completing the Small Business Server 2000 Installation

Assuming you have made your installation decisions and completed the applicable installation pages for SQL Server 2000 and ISA Server, you return to the core Small Business Server 2000 Setup to complete several remaining steps. These steps are a continuation of the preceding steps.

1. On the **Data Folders** page, specify the location of the data folders, and then click **Next**.

    ☑ **Note** If you elected to install SQL Server 2000, the Service Accounts page appears. Select the logon service account and type a password, and then click Next.

2. On the **Installation Summary** page, review the information and make any configuration changes.

3. Click **Next**.

    ☑ **Note** If you elected to install Microsoft Exchange 2000 Server a message may appear indicating the Windows 2000 Server Directory Schema must be modified. Click **OK**, which enables the Active Directory schema to be customized. At this point, all of the selected Small Business Server 2000 components are installed in the following order:

    *   Windows 2000 Optional Components

    *   SQL Server 2000

    *   ISA Server 2000

    *   Shared Fax Service

    *   Shared Modem Service

    *   Microsoft Exchange 2000 Server

    *   Small Business Server

    *   Service Packs (for Windows 2000 compatibility)

4. When asked, switch discs. When the **Completing the Microsoft Small Business Server 2000** page appears, click **Finish**. You have now successfully installed Small Business Server 2000.

5. Restart the computer.

Completing Setup by Using the To Do List

Small Business Server installation and configuration are automatic, except for a few items that require user input in the To Do List. The To Do List includes the following selections. Although these tasks can be completed in any order after server setup, the tasks are listed in the suggested completion order.

- **Welcome**. This is a welcome notice.

- **Add client licenses**. You can add client licenses to your Small Business Server 2000 computer so additional users can log on. License packs can be purchased separately.

- **Define client applications**. You can configure client computers for use on the Small Business Server network by specifying software applications to be installed on the client computers. For more information, refer to Chapter 12, "Small Business Server Client Setup."

- **Add user**. You can add a user to the Small Business Server 2000 network.

- **Add printer**. You can add a printer to the Small Business Server network.

- **Configure Internet Information Services**. You must secure IIS when it runs on a computer that also runs ISA Server 2000. To complete this task, you will need the IP address of your local (internal) network adapter card.

- **Enable network interfaces**. You must re-enable all disabled network interfaces on the server computer after the Small Business Server 2000 setup is complete. Perform this setup before you establish any Internet connection to your Small Business Server, using either the Small Business Server Internet Connection Wizard or manual configuration.

- **Internet Connection Wizard**. You can configure the Small Business Server network connection to the Internet. For more information, refer to Chapter 11, "ISP Connectivity Tasks."

- **Configure remote access**. You can configure Routing and Remote Access (RRAS) on the Small Business Server 2000 computer. For more information, refer to Chapter 13, "Remote Connectivity."

- **Configure modems**. You can read useful information on a Help page about verifying the installation and configuration of fax devices, configuring incoming and outgoing fax routing methods, and configuring modem-related security options (permissions allocation).

- **Configure access for Terminal Services**. You can configure Terminal Services for administrative use on the Small Business Server 2000 computer. For more information, refer to Chapter 16, "Terminal Services and Group Policy Administration."

- **Configure Exchange management**. You can configure Exchange 2000 Server. For more information, refer to Chapter 19, "E-mail and Internet Connectivity Alternatives."

- **Configure server status report**. You can configure server status reports. These reports can be e-mailed or faxed to the technology consultant for analysis.

- **Getting started**. From here, you can start a Small Business Server 2000 tour.

Each To Do List selection starts a wizard that is completed in a step-by-step fashion. For more information about any of these features, consult the *Microsoft Small Business Server Planning and Installation* guide that accompanies Small Business Server 2000, in addition to the specific chapters in this book just referenced.

Summary

This chapter described the Small Business Server setup process, focusing specifically on:

- Learning about Small Business Server Setup requirements.

- Determining if your hardware is Windows 2000 Server-compatible.

- Gathering materials needed for Small Business Server setup—for example, media.

- Performing Small Business Server Setup in phases.

- Completing Small Business Server Setup, using the To Do List.

Installing Small Business Server in Existing Environments

Microsoft® Small Business Server 2000 is installed on a new computer according to the procedures in Chapter 8, "Installing Small Business Server on New Computers." However, it can also be deployed in other environments, which are described in this chapter.

New Installation

- Microsoft Windows NT® 4.0 servers

- Microsoft Windows® client operating systems

- 16-bit operating systems

  Note In the new installation scenario with the above operating systems, Small Business Server should be installed to a different partition.

Supported Upgrades

- Windows 2000 Server

- Small Business Server 4.5

  Note With Small Business Server 4.0, you must install Small Business Server 2000 to a new machine or upgrade to Small Business Server 4.5 first.

  Important If you plan to upgrade Small Business Server 4.5 to Small Business Server 2000 *on a new computer*, refer the white paper, "Small Business Server 2000 Migration Upgrade," located in the **\upgrade** folder on Small Business Server 2000 Resource Kit compact disc.

Migration and Integration

- Migration and integration with a NetWare environment

The technology consultant will find that many Small Business Server 2000 installations involve existing server environments. Many small businesses already have a networking solution in place and migrate to Small Business Server 2000. Installing Small Business Server 2000 in an existing server environment is different from installing to a new computer, which was discussed in Chapter 8.

☑ **Note** It is important to remember the Small Business Server installation phases discussed in Chapter 8 as you read this chapter. First, Windows 2000 Server is installed in a manner consistent with any Windows 2000 Server installation. The Windows 2000 Server installation has text mode and graphical user interface (GUI) mode phases. Small Business Server 2000 Setup is run to configure Windows 2000, and applications are installed. Keeping these installation phases in mind will help you understand the following existing environment installation scenarios for Small Business Server 2000.

Upgrading Windows Client Operating Systems

While Small Business Server 2000 does not upgrade to Microsoft Windows® Millennium Edition, Windows 95, Windows 98, or Microsoft Windows NT® Workstation 4.0, these operating systems can coexist on the same computer with Small Business Server. The two must be installed on different hard disk partitions, however. Small Business Server must be on an NTFS file system partition, as it cannot be installed on the either a FAT32 or FAT16 partition.

Installing Small Business Server on a computer with Windows client operating systems is similar to a new installation of Small Business Server.

To install Small Business Server on a computer with a Windows client operating system

1. Insert Small Business Server Disc 1 (or the Small Business Server 2000 installation [DVD]) into the disc drive.

2. On the **Auto Run** page, click **Set Up Small Business Server**.

3. After the **Welcome** page, the **Suite Baseline** page appears, informing you that you need to install Windows 2000 Server. Click **Next** to start the Windows 2000 Setup Wizard.

    ☑ **Note** The **Suite Requirements** page could appear after the **Welcome** page if setup detects issues with the existing computer settings that must be remedied before continuing with setup.

Upgrading Windows NT Server 4.0

The upgrade from Windows NT Server 4.0 to Small Business Server 2000 is not supported. You must first install Windows 2000 Server and then upgrade to Small Business Server 2000. For more information about this installation, after Windows 2000 Server is installed, refer to the *Small Business Server Planning and Installation* guide.

Other Windows NT Versions

You can install Small Business Server 2000 over the other Windows NT versions listed below. Note that, in all cases, Windows 2000 Server must be installed prior to running Small Business Server Setup.

- Windows NT Server 4.0 Enterprise Edition

- Windows NT Server 4.0 Terminal Server Edition

- Windows NT Server 3.51

- Window NT Workstation 3.51 (this is a migration, not an upgrade)

You cannot upgrade to Small Business Server 2000 from Windows NT Server 3.51 with Citrix software. For complete upgrading information, visit the following Microsoft Web site: http://www.microsoft.com/windows2000/upgrade/.

Upgrading Small Business Server 4.5

Small Business Server 2000 provides several key improvements from earlier versions of Small Business Server, including:

- **Improved stability and performance**. All the Microsoft server applications have been updated to ensure better stability, fewer restarts, and better performance than Small Business Server 4.5.

- **Improved setup and hardware detection**. With Windows 2000-based Plug and Play support, most new hardware devices are detected, installed, and configured with no user intervention.

- **Improved remote server management**. Remote users, including technology consultants, when authorized, can dial in to the Small Business Server computer and manage the server by using Windows 2000-based Terminal Services. You can access this feature by installing Terminal Services Client software on a supported workstation or by connecting to a Web page that enables a remote Terminal Services session from a browser.

- **Improved Add User Wizard**. The new Add User Wizard enables you to create new user accounts either individually or by using a template user account. Template user accounts enable you to preset common information—such as company name, phone number, and various group permissions—for user groups, so that you do not need to type this information every time you add a user. You can quickly change or add templates.

- **Improved server monitoring**. With the addition of Health Monitor 2.1, Server Status View, and Server Status Report, the new Small Business Server provides a more comprehensive set of alerts and performance monitoring features. The Small Business Server network can be monitored locally or remotely, customized alerts can be sent in response to set performance thresholds, and scheduled e-mail messages summarizing server performance can be sent to technology consultants or a power user on the network.

Before You Begin

Before you begin the upgrade to Small Business Server 2000, you must perform the following steps to complete setup successfully:

- Ensure that the existing server meets the hardware and resource requirements for installing Small Business Server 2000.

- If you are connected to the Internet, disable the external network adapter card.

- Log on by using the built-in administrator account.

- Verify that all fax and e-mail queues are cleared and that no one is accessing the Small Business Server computer.

  Note   If you are running a version of Small Business Server 4.5 that has Microsoft Exchange Server 5.5 installed and Microsoft Exchange Internet Mail Connector (IMC) configured to dial out and retrieve mail for the domain, ensure that all queued IMC messages are delivered before the upgrade.

  Tip   Before you begin, it is recommended that you perform a complete system backup, and then verify that the backup was successful by performing a test data restore.

Configuration Issues

The following is an additional list of configuration issues that you should be aware of when upgrading to Small Business Server 2000. For further information, refer to the Small Business Server 2000 Release Notes, located on setup disc 1.

- If you had a connection in Exchange Server 5.5 that was configured to use TURN after Authentication (TURN) or enhanced TURN (ETRN), the server name and ETRN domain will be lost in the upgrade. When the upgrade is complete, you must manually re-enter the e-mail server name of the Internet service provider (ISP) to send the TURN or ETRN signals.

- After the upgrade, Exchange message size restrictions are lost.

- If you used Webpost to transfer your Web site files to your ISP, you will need to determine an alternative method of transferring files to your ISP after the upgrade is complete.

- If you had any custom Proxy Server 2.0 packet filtering settings, the Small Business Server Internet Connection Wizard will disable them. You will have to reset these manually on the Small Business Server 2000 computer's Internet Security and Acceleration (ISA) Server 2000 firewall.

Anticipated Number of Restarts

Setup requires you to restart the system at least four times during installation, including after:

1. Windows 2000 Server temporary file copy is created.

2. GUI-based setup of Windows 2000 Server.

3. Microsoft Active Directory™ directory service is installed.

4. Completion of the Small Business Server 2000 installation.

Upgrading to Small Business Server 2000

When you insert Small Business Server 2000 Disc 1 (or the Small Business Server 2000 installation DVD) into the disc drive, the following four options appear on the **Auto Run** page:

- **Plan your Installation**. This option starts an online tour providing a high-level overview of the installation process.

- **Set up Small Business Server**. This option starts Small Business Server Setup.

- **Read Release Notes**. This option opens Small Business Server 2000 release notes.

- **Browse this Disc**. This option enables you to browse the contents of Small Business Server 2000 Disc 1.

To begin the upgrade, click **Setup Small Business Server**. When the **Welcome** page appears, click **Next**.

Upgrading to Windows 2000 Server

The **Suite Requirements** page alerts you to potential issues that setup has detected with existing applications or computer settings.

⚠ Indicates that setup will continue, but that it may have problems.

✖ Indicates that setup is blocked. You must exit setup, resolve the problem, and then restart setup.

Select the suite requirements, and then click **Details** to view specific information for each alert and instructions for resolving the problem. After resolving all blocking issues, rerun setup. Some system deficiencies that could cause setup problems include insufficient memory or insufficient disk space.

The **Suite Baseline** page outlines those items that must be installed for Small Business Server 2000, such as Service Pack 3 for Exchange Server 5.5 and Windows 2000 Server. Setup automatically installs these items when you click **Next**.

The **Upgrade Message** page outlines the tasks that you must complete before upgrading. For instance, if you have not backed up the system, you must cancel out of setup, perform a full system backup, and then rerun setup.

When the **License Agreement** page appears, read it carefully. To accept the terms of the Small Business Server 2000 End User License Agreement, click **I Agree**, and then click **Next**.

On the **Product Identification** page, provide the following information:

- Your name

- The name of your organization

- Your 25-digit Small Business Server Product Key

- Your 25-digit Microsoft Outlook® 2000 Product Key

On the **Automatic Logon Information** page, decide whether to log on automatically or manually after the system restarts. If you choose to log on automatically, the password is stored in an encrypted registry key and will be removed after installation or if setup is stopped for any reason.

Click **Next** to begin upgrading the operating system to Windows 2000 Server. The **Component Progress** page, which provides a progress summary, appears.

> ☑ **Note** After the upgrade to Windows 2000 Server, you receive numerous errors from services, such as Net Logon, that are unable to start. This is normal and expected because the domain is not fully functional until after the Windows 2000 configuration phase of setup.

Windows 2000 Configuration

After restarting, Small Business Server Setup automatically continues and configures Windows 2000.

On the **Company Information** page, type the company's address. On the **Telephony Information** page, type the telephone and fax information. By default, these pages should be prepopulated with information from the previous Small Business Server installation.

The **Network Card Information** page does not appear during an upgrade unless there is a configuration problem.

On the **New Domain Information** page, type the name of the new Small Business Server domain. The domain network basic input/output system (NetBIOS) name will be displayed on this page, but it cannot be changed.

> ☑ **Note** Click **More Information** for information on choosing a domain name.

On the **Directory Services Restore Mode Administrator Password** page, specify a password to be used when starting the Small Business Server computer in directory services restore mode. Use a strong password that consists of uppercase and lowercase letters, numbers, and punctuation.

> ☑ **Note** You may want to write this password down and keep it in a secure location.

The **Scenario Baseline** page shows that setup will configure networking, install Windows 2000-based Terminal Services in remote administration mode, and install Active Directory.

The **Component Progress** page shows the progress of the installation. When the configuration is complete, you automatically move to the component selection phase of setup.

Upgrading Small Business Server Components

On the **Component Selection** page, the install action for default applications is set to **Install**.

For each nondefault application or service that you want to install, set its install action to **Install**. If you do not want to install an individual application or service, set its install action to **None**. If a server application has an expandable node (indicated by a "+" sign), you have the option of customizing its installed application subcomponents. To do so, expand the node to reveal the subcomponents and then set each install action appropriately.

For example, when you install the Small Business Server Component (value-added features), setup enables you to choose from the five subcomponents in the following list:

- Administration
- Monitoring
- Connectivity
- Client Setup
- Documentation

In addition, many subcomponents have subcomponents that you can customize. For example, Monitoring includes Health Monitor 2.1, Server Status View, Server Status Report, and Monitoring Troubleshooting.

Setting the install action of a server application to **Install** does not automatically set the install action to any of its subcomponents. You must do so separately for each subcomponent, which provides you with flexibility in customizing the Small Business Server installation. For example, you can set the install action of the Small Business Server Component to **Install**, the Monitoring subcomponent to **Install**, Health Monitor to **Install**, and Server Status View to **None**.

Applications Upgraded by Default

The following applications are upgraded by default:

- ISA Server 2000
- Exchange 2000 Server
- Shared Fax Service
- Shared Modem Service
- Small Business Server Component (value-added features)

Service Packs

After you have made the application selections, a message appears if setup detects that Microsoft SQL Server™ 6.5 is installed. To ensure that it runs on Windows 2000 Server, setup installs Service Pack 5 for SQL Server 6.5.

Individual Component Installation

After you select the applications that you want to install, you must provide application-specific information for each.

This section discusses the information that you must provide to install Small Business Server applications. The pages that appear during setup depend on the applications and subcomponents that you selected on the Component Selection page. The pages for each application that you select appear consecutively while Small Business Server Setup collects the information, and then Small Business Server Setup installs the applications.

Internet Security and Acceleration Server 2000

Three setup pages appear during installation of the ISA Server, including:

- **Server Cache Drives**. This page allows you to enable caching, select which NTFS drive to use, and select the maximum size of the cache. By default, caching is enabled at 100 megabytes (MB).

- **Construct Local Address Table**. This page enables you to define the internal address space for the network adapters that will be on the internal network.

- **Configure Local Address Table**. This page enables you to select Internet Protocol (IP) addresses for the *internal* network. You can add or remove IP address ranges that span the internal network address space.

Remaining Applications

No pages should appear while you are upgrading to:

- SQL Server 2000
- Exchange 2000 Server

    ☑ **Note** If you had a connection in Exchange Server 5.5 configured to use TURN or ETRN, the server name will be lost during the upgrade. When the upgrade is complete, you must manually re-enter the mail server name of the ISP to send the TURN or ETRN signals.

    ☑ **Note** The Exchange message size restrictions are lost during the upgrade from Exchange Server 5.5 to Exchange 2000 Server. If you want to limit the size of e-mail messages, you must set it manually. For more information, refer to Exchange 2000 Server documentation.

- Shared Fax Service
- Shared Modem Service
- Small Business Server Component (value-added features)

Data Folders

After you select Small Business Server applications, services, and features, a list of default folder locations for data storage appears on the Data Folders page. You can accept these locations or change them according to your needs.

Service Accounts

If you are upgrading Exchange Server 5.5, you will be asked for the Exchange 5.5 service account information. Enter the account name and password.

Installation Summary

After you select applications and provide application-specific installation information, the **Installation Summary** page appears, with a summary of your installation choices. Examine this page carefully to make sure that you install all the applications, services, and subcomponents that you need. If you want to add or change your choices, click **Back**.

Extend Schema Warning

Depending on the Small Business Server applications and services that you select to install, a message may appear that states that setup must extend the Windows 2000 schema. One application that extends the Active Directory schema is Microsoft Exchange 2000 Server. Click **Yes** to authorize Small Business Server Setup to add object classes and definitions to Active Directory.

Note Extending the Active Directory schema can take time.

Component Progress

The Component Progress page appears with a list of the Small Business Server applications and services that you selected to install. Items on the list appear in installation order. A black triangle appears to the left of the application or service when Small Business Server is installing it. A green check mark replaces the black triangle after an application or service is successfully installed.

The bottom of the Component Progress page displays two progress bars. The top bar shows the installation progress of each individual application or service and the bottom bar shows the progress of the entire installation.

You should not need to interact with setup again until the end, except to provide additional setup discs when required.

Setup files for each Small Business Server application and service are located on the setup discs, in the following order:

- **Disc 1**. Microsoft Windows 2000 Server, Service Pack 1 for Windows 2000, Small Business Server Setup

- **Disc 2**. SQL Server 2000, Shared Fax Service, Shared Modem Service, Internet Security and Acceleration Server 2000

- **Disc 3**. Exchange 2000 Server, Health Monitor 2.1, Small Business Server component

- **Disc 4**. Microsoft Outlook 2000 Service Release 1

- **Disc 5**. Service Pack 3 for Exchange 5.5, Service Pack 5 for SQL Server 6.5

When the **Completing the Small Business Server 2000 Setup Wizard** page appears, click **Finish**. This completes the Small Business Server installation. The computer restarts.

Upgrading Client Access Licenses

After the upgrade from Small Business Server 4.5 to Small Business Server 2000 is complete, the available Client Access Licenses (CALs) are limited to five. You must purchase additional CALs for each client computer connected to the Small Business Server computer.

Contact an independent software reseller to obtain additional licenses. For information about software resellers in your area, or for licensing information, refer to the following Web site: http://www.microsoft.com/sbserver/.

▨ **Note**   CALs can be added from the post-installation To Do List.

Upgrading Windows 2000 Server

You might have a small business customer that already has installed Windows 2000 Server. In this situation, the small business purchased Windows 2000 Server without knowing about Small Business Server 2000. This type of installation is straightforward as long as you first meet the upgrade criteria.

Upgrade Criteria

The upgrade criteria include the following elements:

- **Root of Active Directory forest**. The existing Windows 2000 Server to be upgraded must be the root of the existing Active Directory forest. This role, once defined, cannot be revoked without losing account information. Small Business Server requires that its server computer be the root of the Active Directory forest. The existing Windows 2000 Server can have no trust relationships with other domain controllers as a condition for upgrading to Small Business Server. The first server computer installed as a domain controller in Windows 2000 is, by definition, the root of the Active Directory forest. For more information, see Part 3, "Active Directory Infrastructure," in the *Windows 2000 Server Resource Kit Deployment Guide*.

- **Increased hardware requirements**. Upgrading from an existing Windows 2000 Server to Small Business Server is much more than an operating system upgrade. Small Business Server includes a suite of applications that is much richer than that offered by Windows 2000 Server alone. Recommended hardware requirements for Small Business Server include more RAM memory (256 megabytes [MB] of RAM), additional hard disk storage (4 gigabytes [GB] hard disk space), and a more powerful processor (300 megahertz [MHz]). These recommended hardware requirements exceed the requirements for Windows 2000 Server and might require the customer to upgrade the server.

- **Client Access Licenses**. Windows 2000 Server must be configured with exactly five CALs to match the number of CALs that come with Small Business Server 2000.

- **Additional considerations**. Installing Small Business Server on an existing Windows 2000 Server typically requires additional planning by both the technology consultant and the customer. Necessary planning includes procuring an Internet connection account from an ISP, arranging for additional communication services from the telephone company, and purchasing and installing a business-class fax modem on the server. Technology consultants should review the planning topics in this resource kit and plan the installation of Small Business Server on an existing Windows 2000 Server computer as they would plan installation on a new computer.

Upgrade Process

After you have met the upgrade criteria, installing Small Business Server on an existing Windows 2000 Server computer is simple. Small Business Server Setup assesses the underlying Windows 2000 Server operating system for its fitness to host Small Business Server. Without user intervention, Small Business Server Setup enhances the underlying Windows 2000 Server operating system to ensure that it meets the Small Business Server setup requirements. Such modifications typically include:

- **Licensing**. Small Business Server Setup installs licensing capabilities on the Windows 2000 Server operating system to comply with the Small Business Server licensing model, enabling up to 50 connected client computers on the network.

- **Installation of Terminal Services**. Small Business Server Setup installs Terminal Services in remote administrative mode. If the existing Windows 2000 Server computer is running Terminal Services in application sharing mode, a warning message appears, stating that it is not recommended to install Small Business Server 2000 on a Terminal Services computer in application sharing mode.

   Note   For the latest information on Small Business Server compatibility with Terminal Services in application sharing mode, please refer to the following Web site: http://www.microsoft.com/sbserver/.

- **Service Packs**. Small Business Server Setup installs Windows 2000 Server Service Pack 1, if needed.

- **Additional modifications**. Depending on the current status of the existing Windows 2000 Server, Small Business Server Setup performs the following tasks:

  - Promotes server computer to domain controller (DC) status, which installs and configures Active Directory and Domain Name Service (DNS).

  - Ensures that the networking configuration is valid and installs and configures DHCP if necessary.

After these processes are complete, applications are installed starting with Stage Three, which is outlined in Chapter 8 in a section entitled "Stage Three: Installing Small Business Server Applications."

Existing Users, Data, and Applications

Upgrading from an existing Windows 2000 Server computer to Small Business Server and then using the Migrate User Wizard migrates existing Windows 2000 users to become Small Business Server users. Data is migrated seamlessly. Prior to the upgrade, it is recommended that the technology consultant make a verified backup of the existing Windows 2000 Server system state, including Active Directory, Registry settings, and data.

Applications installed and running on the existing Windows 2000 Server computer typically operate correctly after Small Business Server is installed. The existing application settings are not modified during the Small Business Server 2000 installation.

Installing Small Business Server Over a 16-Bit Operating System

Similar to Windows 95 and Windows 98, DOS and Windows 3.x operating systems will only run with the FAT file system. If you want to preserve these installations, install Small Business Server on a different partition. There is no direct upgrade path from Windows 3.x to Small Business Server 2000.

🍃 **Important** Always back up important files or information before installing Small Business Server. Multiple verified backups are recommended.

Integrating Small Business Server with a NetWare Network

The following key components enable Small Business Server to perform seamlessly with Novell NetWare operating system.

NWLink IPX/SPX Protocol

The first component providing NetWare interoperability with Small Business Server is NWLink IPX/SPX protocol. IPX/SPX is the default protocol supported by Novell NetWare, and NWLink IPX/SPX is Microsoft's implementation of the IPX/SPX protocol. Windows 2000 requires NWLink IPX/SPX for compatibility with NetWare IPX/SPX protocol. Although NWLink IPX/SPX by itself does not provide a high degree of connectivity to NetWare servers, it is the core component that enables a Windows 2000-based computer to communicate with a NetWare client or server. This communication occurs at the middle layers of the Open Standards Interconnection (OSI) model. The NWLink IPX/SPX protocol must be installed on Small Business Server in order to enable communication and support for the tools that enable interoperability with NetWare.

To install the NWLink Protocol

1. Log on to your Small Business Server computer as an administrator.

2. Right-click **My Network Places** on your desktop, and then click **Properties**. The **Network and Dial-up Connections** dialog box appears.

3. Right-click **Local Area Connection**, and then click **Properties**. The **Local Area Connections Properties** dialog box appears.

4. Click **Install**.

5. Select **Protocol**, and then click **Add**.

6. Select **NWLink IPX/SPX/NetBIOS Compatible Transport Protocol**, and then click **OK**. The NWLink IPX/SPX protocol is installed.

7. After the system is finished copying files, click **Close**. You do not need to restart the computer.

Gateway Service for NetWare

Gateway Service for NetWare (GSNW) enables the Windows 2000 Server to function as a NetWare client. Once GSNW is installed—in addition to the Microsoft servers that appear in the Windows Explorer's Network Neighborhood browse list—any NetWare Servers configured for the same frame type and the same internal network number as the Windows 2000 Server appear in their list. You can configure the frame type and network number from the property page for the NWLink IPX/SPX/NetBIOS Compatible Transport Protocol. GSNW is required for NetWare-to-Windows 2000 Server functionality.

GSNW enables the migration of data from a NetWare server to a Small Business Server 2000 computer.

A Gateway to NetWare Resources

A second feature of GSNW is the Windows 2000 Server to NetWare gateway, which provides Small Business Server network clients with access to NetWare resources. The connection to NetWare resources is transparent to the client. It appears that they are seamlessly connected to a standard Microsoft server resource.

One of the practical uses of GSNW for the small business organization is that Small Business Server and connected client computers can be enabled to access file and print resources on a NetWare server.

For example, a Small Business Server can connect to a NetWare file server's directory using GSNW, just as if the directory were on the Small Business Server itself. Small Business Server network clients can then access the directory on the NetWare server by connecting to the share created on the Small Business Server.

> **Note** GSNW is not intended to function as a full-service router for NetWare services. It is designed for occasional access to NetWare servers, or to serve as a migration path. Network performance degrades if it is used for unlimited server access, because all clients are receiving services through the one connection. In addition, all users have access to the NetWare server based on the gateway account, not based on the individual user's account settings.

Providing a Preferred NetWare Server

During installation, you will be asked to identify a preferred NetWare server. This is the default NetWare server that a user logs onto from the Windows 2000 Server. If Windows 2000 Server is unable to find the selected "preferred" server, check the following items:

- Verify that the Novell server is physically on the network and that it is currently running. This server must be version 2.x, 3.x, or 4.x, and must be running in bindery emulation mode.

- You may select a default NetWare Directory Services (NDS) tree and context instead of a preferred server for NetWare servers running NDS. NDS is a directory services solution from Novell that is similar to Microsoft's Active Directory. Note that GSNW is not a full NDS client.

- Verify that there is not an unmatched frame type between the Windows 2000 Server and the Novell server. Information about how to check the frame type is provided in Step 8 of the next procedure.

GSNW Installation

GSNW is a powerful utility for accessing NetWare file and print resources from any Small Business Server client.

Before installing GSNW, create duplicate administrator names on both the Windows 2000 Server domain and the NetWare server. You can do any of the following:

- Add an Administrator account to the NetWare server, and give it the same rights as the NetWare Supervisor account.

- Add a Supervisor account to the Windows 2000 Server domain, and make it a member of the Domain Admins group.

- Pick a neutral name and create an account (with appropriate Administrator group memberships in Windows 2000 Server and Supervisor in NetWare) such as "MockAdmin" on both the Windows 2000 Server domain and the NetWare server.

To install GSNW

1. Click **Start**, point to **Settings**, and then click **Network and Dial-up Connections**.

2. Right-click **Local Area Connection**, and select **Properties** from the shortcut menu.

3. Select **Install**.

4. Select **Client**, and then click **Add**.

5. From the list that appears, select Gateway (and Client) Services for NetWare, and then click **OK**.

6. Provide a **Preferred Server** name or select a **Default Tree and Context**, and then click **OK**.

7. When the system is finished copying files, click **Yes** to restart the computer.

8. If the preferred server name was not found, check the NWLink IPX/SPX frame type on the Small Business Server through the property page for the NWLink IPX/SPX protocol. If the settings between the NetWare server and Small Business Server do not match, select **Auto Frame Type Detection**, click **Apply**, and then click **OK**.

9. Restart the computer. If the NetWare server name is still not found, return to the NWLink IPX/SPX protocol **Properties** page and set the frame type to match exactly what appears on the NetWare server. Click **Apply**, click **OK**, and then restart the computer.

10. At this point, if the connection is still not found, check the network cables on both computers and make sure the hub indicator lights are showing active connections to the cables from each of the computers.

To verify that Gateway Service for NetWare has been installed

1. Click **Start**, point to **Settings**, and then click **Control Panel**. A new **GSNW** icon appears.

2. Start **GSNW**, and make sure a dialog box appears to change the preferred server and print options.

   ☑ **Note**   Users needing robust access to a NetWare server on a regular basis should locally install a NetWare networking client and IPX/SPX protocol. Using the gateway capabilities of GSNW on a Windows 2000 Server for continuous client access is not recommended and will provide unsatisfactory performance.

To create a NetWare Gateway User Account

1. Start the **NWAdmin** utility from the **sys** volume from a NetWare client.

2. Go to **User Information** on the NetWare server, and then press ENTER.

3. Press INSERT to create a new user.

4. Enter a user name for the gateway account, and then press ENTER (a good name choice might be "gatewayuser"). Press ENTER again to accept the default home directory path.

5. Click **Yes** to verify creation of new directory, and then press ENTER. Press ESC if you want to return to the main menu.

6. Create a group called "NTGATEWAY". From **NWAdmin**, select **Group Information**, and then press ENTER. Type the group name, and then press ENTER.

7. Make the user name of the new Gateway User Account a member of the NTGATEWAY group.

8. From **NWAdmin**, click **Select User Information**, and then choose the user name you created. Press ENTER.

9. In the new menu that appears, select **Groups Belonged To**, and then press ENTER.

10. Press INSERT, highlight the **NTGATEWAY** group in the **Groups Not Belonged To** menu, and then press ENTER. Exit **NWAdmin**.

To configure the Small Business Server portion of GSNW

1. Click **GSNW** in **Control Panel**, and then click **Gateway**.

2. Select **Enable Gateway**, and then type the Gateway User Account and password in the appropriate text boxes. Retype the password in the **Confirm Password** box.

3. Click **Add** to add a Small Business Server shared folder to the NetWare volume. To do this, specify a name for the share, the network path to the NetWare volume to be mapped, and a drive letter.

    Note The network path must be specified in a syntax known as the Uniform Naming Convention (UNC). For this syntax, the computer name and the directory name are specified in the format *computername**directoryname*. For example, to map a drive letter to the **sys** volume of a NetWare server called "netware," type *netware**sys* for the UNC name.

4. Click **OK** on all the open windows when finished to save your changes and quit **GSNW**.

To test the functionality of the GSNW installation

1. On the Small Business Server desktop, double-click **My Network Places**, and then the Small Business Server computer name.

2. Select the share created in the earlier section (refer to the previous procedure, "To configure the Small Business Server portion of GSNW"), and then click **Map Network Drive** on the **Tool** menu.

3. Select a drive letter from the drop-down box, and then click **OK**.

4. Click **Start**, point to **Programs**, point to **Accessories**, and then click **Command Prompt**. At the prompt, type the following (press ENTER after each line; and for N, substitute the selected drive letter):

   N:

   cd\public

   NWAdmin

5. Make sure **NWAdmin** is open on the NetWare server. This verifies successful installation of GSNW.

6. Press ESC to quit **NWAdmin**.

To check access to NetWare resources from the Small Business Server client

1. From the client desktop, double-click **My Network Places** (Windows 2000) or **Network Neighborhood** (Windows 98 or Windows 95) and select the name of the Small Business Server computer.

2. Double-click the name of the share you created in GSNW. Open one of the folders until a list of files appears.

3. Try copying a file to the desktop by clicking it and dragging it to the desktop. If this is successful, the gateway feature of GSNW is functioning.

Summary

This chapter provided information about installing Small Business Server in existing networking environments, including:

- Supported upgrades for Small Business Server 2000.

- New installations of Small Business Server 2000 over existing operating systems.

- Integrating Small Business Server into a NetWare environment.

CHAPTER 10

Advanced Setup

Microsoft® Small Business Server 2000 was designed to be easy to install. However, this ease disguises the complexity of Small Business Server Setup. To provide a full range of services while also providing simplicity to the small business customer, the different applications and components that Small Business Server comprises must work together in ways that are transparent to the user. To accomplish this, setup applies several default settings and makes performance optimization decisions. As a result, several issues concerning hardware compatibility, detection, or reconfiguration might arise.

The following issues are discussed in this chapter:

- The move away from the unattended installation
- Network adapter detection
- Modem detection issues
- Performance optimizations
- Management optimizations

Setup Conditions

This section discusses the move away from the unattended file during the operating system installation and default installation settings.

Move from Unattended File

Compared to Small Business Server 4.x, however, the amount of interaction with the operating system installation in Small Business Server 2000 is much greater because of the move away from the unattended file during the operating system setup. One reason for this is to allow for correct hardware detection of newer hardware during setup. This move away from the unattend file reflects the reality that technology consultants who work with Small Business Server work on a wide range of hardware offerings and newer hardware and drivers.

In Small Business Server 4.x, the underlying setup of Microsoft Windows NT® Server 4.0 was almost completely automated because of the use of an unattended file, which eliminated unnecessary input from the user. The result was a much simpler operating system installation. Although Small Business Server 2000 allows you to interact more with the underlying Microsoft Windows® 2000 Server installation, the goal of simplifying the operating system installation has been maintained. To achieve this goal, the Windows 2000 Server installation limits user interaction by not displaying unnecessary setup pages, such as the Workgroup or Computer Domain or the Licensing Modes page. This provides the technology consultants the flexibility of the native Windows 2000 setup for hardware selection, yet avoids the need to make unnecessary selections.

With the move away from unattended setup for Small Business Server 2000, the Small Business Server-specific setup information file (.sif) file from Small Business Server Disc 1 has been removed. The .sif file drove the unattended installation by providing the setup information used during the installation of the operating system. With Small Business Server 2000, the standard Windows 2000 Server .sif file is included in the \I386 directory of Small Business Server Disc 1.

 Note   A .sif file is the unattended file that provides setup information used during the installation of the underlying Windows 2000 Server operating system.

If you want to automate the Windows 2000 Server installation, there are ways to do so. Windows 2000 Server supports a number of automatic installation methods, including:

- Syspart
- Sysprep

For more information about these automatic installation methods, refer to Chapter 13, "Automatic Server Installation and Upgrade" of the *Windows 2000 Server Resource Kit Deployment Planning Guide*.

 Note   If a technology consultant has a large number of Small Business Server 2000 installations that use identical hardware, it is possible to create an unattended file by using the Setup Manager tool that comes with Windows 2000 Server. This file can be used to make the Windows 2000 Server portion of the Small Business Server installation more efficient. This approach, however, is not officially supported by the Small Business Server 2000 Product Support team at Microsoft.

Hardware Detection Problems

Because Small Business Server 2000 supports many common hardware components, setup issues can arise concerning hardware compatibility, detection, and configuration of these components. The most common setup issues occur during the detection and configuration of network adapters and modems.

Before installing Small Business Server 2000, consult the Windows 2000 Hardware Compatibility List at the Microsoft's Web site located at: www.microsoft.com/hcl/.

For more information on hardware detection issues, refer to the Small Business Server 2000 Release Notes located on Small Business Server Disc 1. If hardware problems arise during setup, consult the information in the sections that follow.

> ☑ **Note**   A history of Small Business Server Setup events can be viewed in your Small Business Server log file (Setup.log) in the \%SystemDrive%\Program Files\Microsoft Integration\Microsoft Small Business Server 2000\Logs folder. This log file reports both setup successes and errors. Log files can be sent to the technology consultant or referenced for further information during a product support call.

Mass Storage Devices Not Detected

During the text mode of Windows 2000 Server installation phase, the mass storage device controller card might not be detected. This typically occurs with newer controller cards that are not supported natively by Windows 2000 Server. To resolve this problem, obtain the Windows 2000 Server driver from the hardware manufacturer for your mass storage device controller card and install it when asked to specify a controller card during the text mode of Windows 2000 Server installation.

Network Adapter Card Not Detected

Depending on the model of the network adapter, Windows 2000 Server setup might not detect the network adapter correctly. During the hardware detection process, setup does one of the following:

- Windows 2000 Server stops the setup process, allowing you to provide a suitable network adapter card driver.

- Small Business Server Setup displays a blocking message at the start of the setup process. At this point, you can begin manually installing the network adapter card. For further information on how to do so, select the message and click **Details**.

> ☑ **Note**   An autosensing network adapter card has to be connected to an active computer networking hub, or the blocking message appears.

Modem Issues

In previous versions of Small Business Server, it was necessary to have a modem detected and installed for the Remote Access Server (RAS), Shared Modem Service, and Shared Fax Service to install correctly. This is not the case with Small Business Server 2000, where no modem is required during setup.

If an external modem is connected to the Small Business Server computer, however, make sure it is plugged in, turned on, and connected to the correct Component Object Model (COM) port. For modem-dependant services in Small Business Server 2000 to run properly with all supported modem features, it is essential that the correct driver be used for your modem. You should obtain the latest modem drivers before attempting to install your modem.

> ☑ **Note** It is recommended that you dedicate specific modems to specific services in Small Business Server. For example, while a modem might be used by the Shared Fax Service, the same modem should not be used by the Shared Modem Service. For more information, refer to the **Configure Modems** link available from the Small Business Server To Do List.

Video Cards Not Detected

When a video card is not properly detected, the default video graphics adapter (VGA) driver will be used. You will typically receive an error message from the Small Business Server Setup Wizard relating to unacceptable video resolution. To resolve the problem, obtain a Windows 2000 video driver from the manufacturer of your video card and install it by using the steps that follow.

To install a Windows 2000 video driver

1. Log on to your Small Business Server 2000 machine as an Administrator.

2. Click **Start**, point to **Settings**, and then click **Control Panel**.

3. Double-click **Add/Remove Hardware**.

4. The Add/Remove Hardware Wizard appears. Click **Next**.

5. Select **Add/Troubleshoot a device** and click **Next**. A new hardware detection process begins.

6. If your video card was not detected, on the **Choose a Hardware Device** page, select **Add a new device**, and then click **Next**.

7. On the **Find Hardware** page, select **No, I want to select hardware from a list**. Click **Next**.

8. On the **Hardware Type** page, select **Display adapters**, and then click **Next**.

9. On the **Select a Device Driver** page, select **Have Disk**.

10. Insert a disk into the floppy drive that contains the Windows 2000 video card driver(s) that you obtained from the hardware manufacturer.

11. In the **Install From Disk** dialog box, click **OK**.

12. Click **Finish**, and then restart your machine.

Server Installation Defaults

The items described in the sections that follow are created by default during the installation process. The automatic configuration of these optimizes Small Business Server Setup.

Shared Folders

Table 10.1 describes the folders that are set up by default during installation of Small Business Server.

Table 10.1 Default Shared Folders

Folder name and description	Share name	Location
Company Shared Folder. This folder contains company-wide data that is shared.	Company	User specifies during setup. The default is: %systemdrive%\Company Shared Folders
User Shared Folders. These folders contain user-specific data.	Users	User specifies during setup. The default is: %systemdrive%\Users Shared Folders
Clients. This folder contains specific client configuration files.	Clients	%systemdrive%\Program Files\ Microsoft BackOffice\ClientSetup\Clients
ClientApps5. This folder contains Small Business Server client applications.	ClientApps5	User specifies during setup. The default is: %systemdrive%\ClientApps5

Note The Clients share must exist in the installed locations in order for the Add User Wizard and Set Up Client Computer Wizard to function correctly.

Default Permissions

During installation of Small Business Server, default permissions are applied to the user, groups, Small Business Server templates, and built-in accounts as described in Tables 10.2 and 10.3.

Table 10.2 Default permissions

Account	Permission level/description
Administrator	Full
Creator/owner	Full
Server operators	Change
System	Full
Small Business Server Administrator	Full. This template can be used to create other users.
Small Business Server User	Users have access to all printers, shared folders, fax devices, and Internet connections by default. This template can be used to create other user accounts.
Small Business Server Power User	All Small Business Server User rights. Can also manage users, groups, printers, shared folders, and faxes. Can log on to the system from a remote computer. This template can be used to create other users.
Microsoft BackOffice® Fax Operators	Members of this group can manage fax devices.
BackOffice Folder Operators	Members of the group can manage shared folders.
BackOffice Internet Users	Members of this group can use the Internet connection.
BackOffice Mail Operators	Members of the group can perform low-level administration of Exchange 2000 Server, such as creating mailboxes for users.
BackOffice Template Users	This group contains three template accounts: Small Business Server Administrator, Small Business Server Power User, and Small Business Server User.

Note Administrators have the permissions necessary to run the Small Business Server Administrator Console. Power Users have the permissions necessary to run the Small Business Server Personal Console.

In addition, the following default permissions are applied to folders, as shown in Table 10.3.

Table 10.3 Default Permissions Applied to Shared Folders

Folder name (Share Name)	Access control lists (ACLs)	Contents
Company Shared Folder (Company)	Domain Users = Read and Change, Administrators = Full Control	For use by end users.
User Shared Folders (Users)	Domain Users = Read and Change, Administrators = Full Control	Contains the shared folders for each user.
Clients (Clients)	Administrators = Full Control, Users = Modify	BackOffice client applications setup components.
ClientApps (ClientApps)	Everyone = Full Control	BackOffice client applications

Favorites

The Internet Explorer browser favorites described in the following table are set up during the installation process.

Table 10.4 Default Favorites

Favorite name	Address
Small Business Server Web site	http://www.Microsoft.com/SmallBusinessServer/
Bcentral	http://www.bcentral.com
Small Business Server User Guide	http://LocalHost/Intranet/SBSClientHelp/

Default Internet

The installation of Internet Explorer 5.x configures a default Internet site, the Microsoft Network (MSN). The location of the MSN Internet page is: www.msn.com.

Implementation of Performance Optimizations

Small Business Server 2000, along with its server applications, is designed to run on a single server computer. In the past, Microsoft has specifically recommended that the server applications run on separate, dedicated computers in order to achieve optimum performance and reliability. With Small Business Server, this has changed—although some limitations are inherent to this configuration. This section describes how the server applications were optimized on the Small Business Server 2000 platform along with the engineering techniques that enable Small Business Server 2000 to run multiple services on a single computer while achieving enterprise-level performance.

Server Applications Optimized on a Single Platform

For enterprise server applications to work well together on a single platform, several modifications were made to achieve successful integration, as follows:

- Code was optimized to reduce memory consumption—each server application is tuned to use a limited amount of memory. This enables the entire platform of applications to work well together, and uses only 256 megabytes (MB) of random access memory (RAM).

- Other limitations were placed on user applications (refer to the later section entitled, "User Limitations on Applications").

- In Small Business Server 2000, all server applications support a silent and scriptable setup with minimal setup input required. This enables the technology consultant to successfully deploy Microsoft server applications without having significant expertise in those applications.

- All server applications use the client access licenses (CALs) shipped with Small Business Server 2000.

Reduction of Application Memory Consumption

In Small Business Server, the native server applications are self-optimizing to conserve memory usage while still delivering optimal performance. For example, Exchange Server and Microsoft SQL Server™ dynamically allocate memory, allowing the full-featured versions of these and other applications to work well in a Small Business Server environment (see the following section to learn about user limitations).

User Limitations on Applications

Microsoft imposed user limits on applications for Small Business Server to ensure that the server can support all services running on a single 128 MB of RAM computer. Limitations include:

- **50-user limit**. The technology consultant can create an unlimited number of user accounts, but the actual number of connected computers is limited to 50 to ensure acceptable performance levels for all users. Client licenses are added by using the Client Add Packs, not License Manager.

- **Single domain**. Small Business Server supports a single domain. The Small Business Server must be installed as the root of the Microsoft Active Directory™ directory service forest. Additional domain controllers can be installed on a peer level. This optimization not only minimizes performance overhead on the Small Business Server computer, but also confines Microsoft Exchange 2000 Server to a single domain because it is confined to a single forest.

- **Disabled trusts**. Trusts, which are used to segment the administration of large numbers of users and machines, are intended for businesses with more than one physical network location. This is not applicable to most small business network scenarios. By disabling trusts, Small Business Server reduces the administrative overhead associated with managing trust relationships and the amount of memory and processor overhead required by the server domain controller processes.

- **Fax limited to four modems**. The maximum number of modems that can be assigned to Shared Fax Service is four.

- **Modem Sharing limit is four modems**. The maximum number of modems that can be assigned to the Shared Modem Service is four.

Management Optimizations

Management of Small Business Server 2000 is optimized by using consoles, which consolidate and automate most server administration tasks. Microsoft improved the usability features of Small Business Server 2000 to create business network-level functionality in the small business environment without the need for a dedicated information technology staff. These features include:

- **Single setup process**. Small Business Server 2000 consolidates the entire setup process into a single wizard. Information entered in the wizard during setup is used to perform behind-the-scenes configuration across all server applications.

- **Small Business Server consoles**. Small Business Server 2000 has two consoles. The Small Business Server Personal Console is used by power users to perform low-level basic administration. The Small Business Server Administrator Console is for use by administrators. These Microsoft Management Consoles (MMCs) consolidate all the common administration tasks into an MMC user interface.

- **Preconfigured shared folders**. The Small Business Server Set Up Computer Wizard creates a company shared folder and user folders automatically. When the Set Up Computer Wizard adds a workstation to the domain, it also creates desktop shortcuts to the company shared folder and to a user's personal folder. The technology consultant can also enable additional shares by using the console.

- **Configuration wizards**. Small Business Server 2000 configuration wizards can be used for most administration tasks. These wizards enable the technology consultant to confidently and accurately configure and deploy server applications. A few of the key wizards in Small Business Server 2000 include:

  - *Internet Connection Wizard*. This wizard takes the technology consultant through the process of signing up the small business customer with an Internet service provider (ISP) and configures Windows 2000 Server, Exchange 2000 Server, and Internet Security and Acceleration (ISA) Server.

  - *Add User Wizard*. This wizard creates users and configures Exchange mailboxes and distribution list memberships. In addition, the Add User Wizard configures Terminal Services, RRAS, and firewall and virtual private networking permissions and settings. You can model users after existing users by using preconfigured templates.

  - *Set Up Computer Wizard*. This wizard enables Small Business Server client applications to be selected for installation. A setup disk for client computers is created. The setup disk configures network settings, installs client applications, and configures user settings. One setup disk supports the configuration of the entire Small Business Server network.

Summary

This chapter addressed Small Business Server setup issues that the technology consultant may encounter. Specific topics discussed include:

- How Small Business Server Setup is more interactive without the unattended setup file.
- Hardware detection problems, such as network adapter card and modem problems.
- Defaults for a server installation, such as shared folders and default permissions.
- Specific performance optimizations, such as the use of a single domain.
- Ease-of-management functionality, such as the Small Business Server consoles.

CHAPTER 11

ISP Connectivity Tasks

This chapter discusses specific tasks that configure Microsoft® Small Business Server 2000 for Internet service provider (ISP) connectivity. These tasks are applicable whether the small business customer selects a new Internet connection or uses an existing ISP account. The chapter also provides a Small Business Server Internet Connection Wizard walk-through, describing the Small Business Server Internet connection process. This chapter's information is presented as follows:

- Internet connection basics

- Internet connection issues

- Small Business Server Internet Connection Wizard walk-through

Internet connectivity is a key feature for small- and medium-sized businesses. International Data Corporation (IDC) in Framington, Massachusetts, estimates that Internet access drives computer sales faster than LAN connectivity. One might extrapolate from this research that businesses buy computers to be able to access the Web and that deployment of a LAN is secondary. IDC now estimates that 85 percent of businesses with 100 or fewer employees have computers.

Broadband Internet access is exploding, as are the connectivity services for those broadband connections. "By 2005, more than 35 million small and medium businesses, residential consumers and small office/home office customers will be using some form of broadband access, according to the NxGen Data Research report [by New Paradigm Resources Group]. DSL will represent about 13 million of those lines in service, while cable modems, terrestrial microwave and satellite access methods will claim significant market share, as well." –PRNewswire, July 1999.

Internet Connection Basics

Small Business Server 2000 supports Internet connectivity primarily through the Small Business Server Internet Connection Wizard. The Small Business Server Internet Connection Wizard helps you configure Microsoft Windows® 2000 Server, Microsoft Exchange 2000 Server, and Microsoft Internet Security and Acceleration (ISA) Server 2000 for an Internet connection. The wizard relies on the Windows 2000 Routing and Remote Access Service (RRAS) for network or dial-on-demand modem connectivity. After network connectivity has been established with RRAS, the wizard configures Exchange 2000 Server and ISA Server accordingly.

Internet Connection Topologies

Before starting the Small Business Server Internet Connection Wizard, you might want to review how Small Business Server connects to the Internet. For overall network topology diagrams, including Digital Subscriber Line/Asynchronous Digital Subscriber Line (xDSL), cable modem, Integrated Services Digital Network (ISDN), and dial-up, refer to Chapter 5, "Planning for an Internet Presence."

Internet Connection Types

Small Business Server supports many types of connectivity hardware, which can be grouped into two categories: dial-up and non-dial-up.

- **Dial up**. Dial-up connection hardware establishes an Internet connection by using the Network and Dial-up Connections feature. The dial-up connection hardware includes analog modems and ISDN terminal adapters. These devices are connected to Small Business Server through a serial port, multiport serial board, or an internal card and can be configured with the Phone and Modem Options utility in Control Panel.

  > **☑ Note**   Small Business Server 2000 has much stronger modem support than previous versions of Small Business Server. Small Business Server 2000 supports any Windows 2000 Server–compatible modem and automatically detects the modem with Device Manager.

  ISDN dial-up connections are beneficial in areas not served by other high-speed Internet connection alternatives. In general, ISDN is more expensive that the non-dial-up Internet connection alternatives discussed later in this section. One benefit of an ISDN connection is that you can dial other ISDN telephone numbers if your primary connection fails. You can also dial other ISDN-based communications servers (for example, a customer site) and use RRAS to transfer files, use a remote network, and so on. More information on ISDN connections is provided later in this section.

- **Non-dial up**. Non-dial-up Internet connections consist of full-time broadband connections and routers. There are two popular full-time connections that use broadband devices:

  - xDSL modems or routers
  - Cable modems

xDSL Modems or Routers

Establishing an Internet connection by using an xDSL modem or router requires an internal adapter and a second network adapter. The default gateway is configured on the second network adapter, causing all Internet connections to be filtered by ISA Server. xDSL connections are typically configured to be "always on" from the time the Small Business Server computer starts. A static Internet Protocol (IP) address is recommend for this configuration and is obtained from the ISP, and it should be applied to the device's external network adapter (WAN port). However, you can have either a registered Internet IP address or dynamic IP address assigned to the xDSL by the ISP. An xDSL modem or router solution might accrue additional service charges for the small business if you exceed a certain level of downloads during a billing period.

> **Note** When the hardware device used to connect the Small Business Server network to xDSL service is running in bridging mode (Layer Two of the Open Standards Interconnection model), it is typically referred to as an xDSL modem. When the same device is running in Point-to-Point Protocol (PPP) mode (Layer Three of the Open Standards Interconnection model), the device is known as an xDSL router. ISPs vary on whether you connect in bridging mode or PPP mode, but PPP mode has emerged as the preferred connectivity approach for xDSL.

Cable Modems

With the advent of cable technology that enables information to flow two ways, cable companies started providing Internet connectivity services to homes and businesses. The cable company serves as both the telecommunications company providing communications services and the ISP company providing Internet connectivity.

Cable connections are initiated at the time the Small Business Server computer starts and are maintained while the computer is on. The default gateway is configured on the second network adapter, causing all Internet connections to be filtered by ISA Server. Cable modems typically receive a dynamic IP from the ISP to discourage the user from running an external Web server. Cable companies discourage this practice because the bandwidth for a cable modem is multiplexed for everyone on that cable segment. If one user consumes a large amount of the available bandwidth, all cable modem users on that segment experience decreased performance. However, cable companies do offer business-level Internet connection packages that allow for the acquisition and use of static IP addresses. Cable companies typically charge a flat fee, regardless of download volumes.

Routers

A routing device establishes either dial-on-demand or full-time Internet connections. A router can be connected to the LAN, where it acts as a default gateway for all client computers, forwarding requests outside the LAN as appropriate.

Another router configuration supported by Small Business Server requires two network adapters—an internal adapter for the LAN and a second network adapter attached to a router connected to the Internet. The default gateway is configured on the second network adapter, causing all Internet connections to be filtered by ISA Server.

Other Connections

Companies with demanding connectivity needs or lack of lower-priced alternatives often pursue Internet connections based on leased lines and private networks. These solutions include dedicated frame-relay solutions that use fractional or full T1. This type of solution also enables you to combine a WAN (for example, with a small branch office) with a powerful Internet connection.

For more information about Internet connection configurations, refer to Chapter 5, "Planning for an Internet Presence."

ISDN Connections

How you install an ISDN device depends on the type of hardware purchased. ISDN devices are available as Industry Standard Architecture (ISA) or Peripheral Component Interconnect (PCI) cards that can be installed inside the computer just like an internal modem. These are typically called ISDN terminal adapters or ISDN modems. ISDN devices are also available as external devices, sometimes called dial-on-demand routers.

Both internal and external ISDN devices can be operated in one of two modes—dial-up or dedicated. The dial-up mode is the most common because of the cost advantage. In the dedicated configuration, the line is up all the time and has the same characteristics as the leased-line solutions (discussed later in the chapter), with bandwidths of either 64 kilobytes (KB) or 128 KB.

ISDN Terminal Adapters

Internal ISDN terminal adapter cards are available with a variety of features from several vendors. Some are installed as network cards through the Network Dial-up Connections utility in Control Panel, and others are installed as modems.

ISDN Routers

ISDN routers are often used in a dial-on-demand configuration. This is possible because the call setup times for ISDN are extremely fast compared to standard analog modems (2-3 seconds versus 20-30 seconds). In this configuration, Small Business Server is configured with two network interface cards (NICs)—one for the internal network and one for the external network that connects to the ISDN router. Whenever there is outbound traffic from Small Business Server, the router automatically raises the connection to the ISP. To the clients on the Small Business Server network (and to the Small Business Server), it appears as if there is a full-time connection.

This configuration is unique. From the perspective of the ISP host, it appears as a normal dial-up connection.

Leased Line Connections

Leased line connections typically range from 56 KB to 1.544 megabytes (MB) (T-1) lines. These are all dedicated connections and are available all the time. Like dedicated modems or ISDN lines, leased line connections have some special configuration issues—primarily with Exchange Server. Leased line connections require a router for operation. For security purposes, Small Business Server should be configured with two NICs for these connections—one for the internal LAN and one for the external connection with the leased line router.

Internet Connection Issues

This section describes several configuration issues and provides information the technology consultant needs when connecting Small Business Server 2000 to the Internet. This information is presented as follows:

- Information required for the Small Business Server Internet Connection Wizard.
- Registering a second-level domain name.
- Configuring Small Business Server to use an existing second-level domain name.
- Exchange Server and domain name changes.
- Configuring the ISP Domain Name Server.
- Dynamic IP addressing and Internet mail issues.
- Web hosting information (optional).

Information Required for the Small Business Server Internet Connection Wizard

Before using the Small Business Server Internet Connection Wizard, obtain the information outlined in the following subsections from the ISP for the type of Internet connection you are using. Print out and use "Small Business Server ISP Information Forms" from the Online Guide to record the information.

☑ **Note**   You can also use the appropriate configuration form—modem, router, or full time—that is available when you click **Form** on the **Configure Hardware** page of the Small Business Server Internet Connection Wizard.

Dial-Up Connection

For a modem connection or any dial-up connection that uses a phonebook entry to dial, the following information is required:

- **Account name**. The User ID required to dial in to the ISP.

- **Account password**. The password associated with the account name.

- **Mail type used**. The type of mail you will use, either Exchange (SMTP) Server or POP3.

  For Exchange (SMTP) mail, you need the host name or IP address of the ISP's Simple Mail Transfer Protocol (SMTP) server. If the ISP is queuing mail for your dial-up connection, obtain the appropriate signaling (de-queuing) command.

  For POP3 mail, obtain the host name or IP address of the ISP's POP3 and SMTP servers.

- **Internet domain name**. The Small Business Server Internet domain name.

- **Static IP address**. The static IP address for your dial-up account, if necessary.

Router Connection

For a router connection, the following information is required, in addition to the information listed in the previous "Dial-Up Connection" section:

- **ISP DNS server name(s)**. The name or IP address of the ISP's Domain Name Service (DNS) host(s).

- **IP address of the router**. Use a static IP address if your router connection is full time.

- **Subnet mask and default gateway addresses**. When using a second network adapter with the router, these are the IP addresses that identify the small business LAN on the Internet and the default gateway address of the adapter.

    ☑ **Note** If you want to use the security features of ISA Server with a router connection, you must use a second network adapter on Small Business Server to interconnect ISA Server and the router. Use the Network and Dial-up Connections utility in Control Panel to configure the second network adapter with the correct IP address and protocol information.

- **Mail type used**. The type of mail you will use, either Exchange (SMTP) Server or POP3.

    For Exchange (SMTP) mail, you need the host name or IP address of the ISP's SMTP server. If the ISP is queuing mail for your dial-up connection, obtain the appropriate signaling (de-queuing) command.

    For POP3 mail, obtain the host name or IP address of the ISP's POP3 and SMTP servers.

- **Internet domain name**. The Small Business Server Internet domain name.

Full-Time Connection/Broadband Device

For a full-time connection/broadband device, the following information is required, in addition to the information listed in the "Dial-Up Connection" section earlier in this chapter.

- **ISP DNS server name(s)**. The name or IP address of the ISP's DNS host(s).

- **Static IP address for the device's external network adapter**. The Internet-routable IP address to be bound to the external network adapter connected to the Internet. Note that this information is not required if you obtained the IP address dynamically.

- **Subnet mask address**. An IP address assigned to the second network adapter, identifying the address space of the small business LAN on the Internet.

- **Default gateway address**. The IP address that identifies the default gateway to the Internet.

  ☑ **Note** For a full-time connection/broadband device, a second network adapter is needed to interconnect ISA Server and the device. Use the Network and Dial-up Connections utility in Control Panel to configure the second network adapter with the correct IP address and protocol information.

- **Mail type used**. The type of mail you will use, either Exchange (SMTP) Server or POP3.

  For Exchange (SMTP) mail, you need the host name or IP address of the ISP's SMTP server. If the ISP is queuing mail for your dial-up connection, obtain the appropriate signaling (de-queuing) command.

  For POP3 mail, obtain the host name or IP address of the ISP's POP3 and SMTP servers.

- **Internet domain name**. The Small Business Server Internet domain name.

Registering a Second-Level Domain Name

To register a second-level domain name, the technology consultant must contact the ISP. The name to be registered must be checked against the Internet Corporation for Assigned Names and Numbers (ICANN) database to see if it is presently being used. You can find the ICANN database at the following Web site:
http://www.icann.com/

☑ **Note** The ISP might complete registration for you.

Configuring Small Business Server to Use an Existing Second-Level Domain

If the small business customer already has a second-level domain name, configure Small Business Server to work with it by using the Small Business Server Internet Connection Wizard. Contact the ISP and have them change any existing small business third-level domain name entries to the second-level domain name, as follows:

- Create an appropriate DNS record to map the second-level domain name to the existing third-level domain name.

- Change the third-level domain name to the new second-level name in all records.

Exchange Server and Domain Name Changes

Exchange Server must have the proper domain name configured for each e-mail address to be able to send and receive messages properly. If the small business customer asks their ISP to change their domain name from *yourcompany.isp.com* to *yourcompany.com*, Exchange can be configured to recognize the new name by using the Small Business Server Internet Connection Wizard. The configuration can also be performed manually. You will need to change the administrator name and start of authority (SOA) record in the DNS tables. For more information, refer to "Configuring Exchange 2000 Server" later in this chapter.

Configuring the ISP Domain Name Server

The ISP must make entries in their DNS table for the small business customer running Small Business Server. For Internet-based e-mail to function, there should be two DNS Mail eXchange (MX) records for the small business domain and a DNS Address (A) record for your host server computer.

Dynamic IP Addressing and Internet Mail Issues

Small Business Server is configured by default with static IP addresses for the internal network adapter card. The second network adapter card in a Small Business Server, typically denoted as the external network adapter card, can have either a static or dynamic IP address. SMTP mail delivery typically requires a static or dedicated IP address—the result of the mechanisms used to route and deliver mail on the Internet.

SMTP mail relies on DNS MX records to direct mail for a domain (the part of the address to the right of the "@" sign) to a client destination. The Internet standards for mail require that the MX record point to a host name that has a DNS A record. The A record maps the host name to an IP address. This configuration relies on the ISP allocating a fixed IP address to the small business Dial-Up Networking (DUN) session. With a fixed or static IP address, the same IP address is used for the Small Business Server every time the ISP is dialed.

> ☑ **Note**   Some ISPs have reportedly developed alternative solutions to the dynamic IP addressing issue. Check with your ISP for more information.

Web Hosting Information

Microsoft FrontPage® can be purchased separately from Small Business Server and can be used for creating Web pages. After your Web pages are created with FrontPage and tested, use the File Transfer Protocol (FTP) capabilities in FrontPage to publish your Web pages to the ISP that hosts the small business Web site. To facilitate publishing your Web site, the ISP must support FrontPage extensions and provide you with the following information:

- **Web posting URL**. The FTP address where the initial data and updates for the small business Web site are located. If the small business Web site URL is http://www.*yourcompany.internetserviceprovider*.tld, the Web posting URL might look like this: ftp://ftp.*yourcompany.internetserviceprovider*.tld, where .tld refers to a top-level domain such as .com, .edu, .net, and so on.

- **Web posting account name and password**. The account name and password required for making changes to the Web site at the FTP address.

- **Web site URL**. The Web page URL publicly available on the Internet.

Configuring Internet Security and Acceleration Server

The Small Business Server Internet Connection Wizard configures the ISA Server. Several things are accomplished here, including:

- Configuring firewall packet filtering to allow network traffic for primary Small Business Server 2000 traffic, which includes Outlook Web Access (OWA) and Exchange-based Internet e-mail (both SMTP and POP3).

- Granting Internet browsing rights to members of the BackOffice Internet Users security group.

ISA Server configures and tunes network settings on a case-by-case basis, accounting for differences in server machine configurations such as the IP addresses that are assigned to the local and external network adapter cards.

> ☑ **Note** The ISA Server Local Address Table (LAT) must be configured to differentiate the internal and external networks whenever the base IP address is changed on Small Business Server. This is done automatically as part of Small Business Server Setup on the ISA Construct Local Address Table page. For information about LAT configuration procedures, refer to Chapter 18, "Administering Small Business Server Components."

Configuring Exchange 2000 Server

When configuring Exchange 2000 Server, note that the ranges of high-speed Internet connections available in the following two scenarios.

Scenario 1: Dial-Up Networking

In this scenario, Exchange Server can send outbound mail immediately, but the Internet connection must be established to receive mail. While the Internet connection is down, mail will be queued on the ISP's mail host. Exchange Server and most ISPs now support the SMTP extension, defined in RFC1985 (called ETRN).

Exchange Server's ETRN capability forces mail to de-queue from the ISP every time outbound mail is sent from Small Business Server. This delivery rate may not be acceptable for small business inbound mail delivery requirements. You can define the schedule for mail delivery frequency in the Small Business Server Internet Connection Wizard.

If the small business ISP does not support ETRN, the technology consultant and the ISP need to develop a suitable de-queuing method. Alternatively, the technology consultant could advise the Small Business Server customer to change to an ISP that offers supported e-mail methods.

Scenario 2: Leased Line or Dedicated Connection

With the components described in the preceding scenario, Exchange Server can always send and receive mail immediately.

POP Mail

Post Office Protocol (POP) is a commonly used messaging protocol. The most widely used implementation of this protocol is POP3. POP3 is a retrieval protocol, used to retrieve mail messages from a POP server. (Note that POP2 is no longer used.) E-mail messages received by the POP server are delivered to a server mailbox, and messages reside there until an individual with a POP mail client retrieves them. Depending on the POP mail client used, users can choose to:

- Download all of the messages that are queued on the POP server and then remove the messages from the server.

- Download all messages or all new messages and then leave a copy on the POP server.

- Download just the message headers and then mark the messages they want to download. (This feature is not found in all POP mail clients).

Because POP3 is a messaging protocol designed for retrieval only, it must work in conjunction with a protocol capable of sending messages, such as SMTP.

SMTP

SMTP is the standard protocol for mail transfer over the Internet. It defines how a message is formatted for delivery and also provides the delivery mechanism over connection-based protocols, such as TCP/IP.

The Exchange Server uses SMTP to send and receive mail. In addition, POP clients use SMTP to send messages to SMTP hosts to route and deliver over the Internet.

Differences Between POP and SMTP

POP3 protocol is only capable of retrieving mail from a POP3 host and is therefore dependent on the SMTP protocol to deliver outbound messages. The SMTP protocol is a more robust transport protocol, capable of two-way communication with other SMTP hosts.

Benefits of Using an SMTP Server

Exchange 2000 Server is a server application that provides not only messaging capabilities between users on a local network, but also messaging capabilities over the Internet. Exchange 2000 Server is configured with the SMTP protocol to send and receive messages over the Internet, therefore making it an SMTP server. The advantages of using an SMTP server over a POP mail client are many.

Limitations of a POP mail client include:

- Messages are not received in real time.

- Messages cannot be viewed from multiple clients after download.

- Storage increases because multiple message copies are stored by multiple recipients.

- Online backups are difficult to perform.

- There is no transactional integrity of the message store (client-side files).

- ISP POP accounts require additional user ID and password maintenance.

Advantages of Exchange 2000 Server include:

- There is single-instance storage for messages addressed to multiple recipients.

- Online backups can be made.

- There is transactional integrity of the message flow.

- Message size limits can be imposed.

- Users have access to Exchange Public Folders.

- Powerful offline capabilities exist.

- Server-based rules exist that control how the server handles messages on reception.

- Security is integrated with Small Business Server security.

Advantages of the Exchange-based client include:

- Messages are received in real time.

Additional Resource for ISP Connectivity

A good source of additional information for the technology consultant, ISP, and small business customer is the Microsoft Small Business Server Web site at: http://www.microsoft.com/smallbusinessserver/.

This site is particularly useful in relation to ISP connectivity issues.

Configuring Exchange E-mail Clients

When Small Business Server is installed, Exchange 2000 Server is typically also installed. Exchange Server's support for receiving and delivering your Internet-based SMTP-based e-mail is automatically installed during setup. The Microsoft Connector for POP3 Mailboxes is installed by default as well. Both the SMTP-based support and POP3 e-mail support are configured when the Small Business Server Internet Connection Wizard is run with your specific Internet e-mail information.

Configuring Outlook 2000 and Outlook Express Clients for POP3 Mail Exchange

If you want Small Business Server users with the Microsoft Outlook® Express e-mail client to send and receive POP3 mail by using Exchange Server, configure Exchange 2000 Server by using the Small Business Server Internet Connection Wizard.

Small Business Server Internet Connection Wizard Walk-Through

This section contains a Small Business Server Internet Connection Wizard walk-through to assist the technology consultant in gathering the necessary information for configuring Small Business Server 2000 Internet connectivity settings. The walk-through also serves as a guide to explain the configurations made by the wizard, thus ensuring that settings are correctly made for the network environment.

Running the Small Business Server Internet Connection Wizard

Start the Small Business Server Internet Connection Wizard for the first time from the Small Business Server Administrator Console as follows:

- Click the **Small Business Server Internet Connection Wizard** on the To Do List.

When the wizard starts, click **Next** on the **Welcome** page. The Small Business Server Internet Connection Wizard helps you perform the following tasks:

- Configure Hardware.
- Set Up Modem Connection to ISP.
    - Set Up Router Connection to ISP.
    - Set Up Full-time Broadband Connection.
- Configure Internet Mail Settings.
- Configure Internet Domain Name.
- Configure SMTP Server Address.
- Receive Exchange Mail.
- Set Up Authentication.
- Mail Delivery Frequency.
- Configure Firewall Settings.

The sections that follow describe each of these tasks in detail.

Configure Hardware

The Small Business Server Internet Connection Wizard displays the Configure Hardware page, as shown in Figure 11.1.

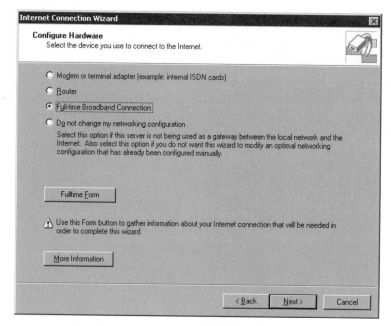

Figure 11.1 Select a device on the Configure Hardware page

Select Internet communications hardware options for the ISP connection as follows:

- **Modem or terminal adapter**. Use when you have an analog modem or ISDN terminal adapter accessed through DUN or RRAS. Selecting this option causes the wizard to display the Set Up Modem Connection to ISP page, described later in this section.

  Install these devices by using the Phone and Modem Options utility in Control Panel prior to using the Small Business Server Internet Connection Wizard.

- **Router**. Use when an xDSL, ISDN, frame relay, or cable router is used to connect to the Internet. Selecting this option causes the wizard to display the Set Up Router Connection to ISP page, described later in this section.

  If a second network adapter is attached to the router, configure it with a valid IP address prior to using the Small Business Server Internet Connection Wizard by using the Network and Dial-up Connections utility in Control Panel. Refer to the manufacturer's documentation for router configuration procedures.

  > **Note** If you use a router to connect to the Internet, it must do network address translation to ensure delivery of SMTP mail.

- **Full-time Broadband Connection**. Use for a full-time, high-speed connection to the ISP (for example, when using cable modems or an xDSL modem or router). Requires a second network adapter. Selecting this option causes the wizard to display the Network Interface Card Configuration page, described later in this section.

  You must configure a static IP address on at least one of the network adapter cards prior to using the Small Business Server Internet Connection Wizard by using the Network and Dial-up Connections utility in Control Panel. Refer to the manufacturer's documentation for device configuration procedures.

- **Do not change my networking configuration**. Use if the server is not functioning as a gateway between the private network and the Internet. Also use to preserve existing network settings. This selection will eliminate the display of wizard pages that have previously been configured.

  ☑ **Note** If you run the Internet Connection Wizard an additional time, your original hardware settings are retained from the first time the wizard was run.

Setup Forms

Depending on the hardware configuration selected in the last step, one of three pages appears. The Setup Form page is mapped to the hardware configuration selection, as shown in Table 11.1. The other pages column of the table lists pages that either precede or follow the Setup Form page for the specified form. In all cases, the Small Business Server Internet Connection Wizard displays the Configure Internet Mail Settings page after the setup (and dependent) forms are completed.

Table 11.1 Setup Forms

Hardware configuration	Setup page	Other pages
Modem or terminal adapter	Set Up Modem Connection to ISP	N/A
Router	Set Up Router Connection to ISP	The Configure Network Adapter page will follow if you select the **My router is connected to the server via a second network adapter** check box.
Full-time broadband connection	Set Up Full-time Broadband Connection to ISP	The Configure Network Adapter page will precede the setup form.
Do not change my networking configuration	No setup page. Proceeds directly to the Configure Internet Mail Settings page.	N/A

Set Up Modem Connection to ISP

If you selected **Modem or terminal adapter** on the Configure Hardware page, the Set Up Modem Connection to ISP page appears. Enter your ISP credentials information as follows:

- **Dial-up Connection**. The dial-up network connection entry used to connect to the ISP. If an entry was previously created, select it. If not, click **New** to create a new dial-up network connection.

  Note You will be asked to enter the telephone number to connect to your ISP and use the dialing rules. Refer to the Small Business Server Help for information about creating dialing rules.

- **ISP account name**. The name of the account assigned by the ISP to Small Business Server.

- **Password**. The password for your account, obtained from your ISP.

- **Confirm password**. Confirmation of the account password.

- **I have a static IP address from my ISP with this connection**. If you select this check box, you must provide an IP address in the **IP address** field and complete the **Primary DNS Server Address** field.

  Note Click **More Information** to display Help on setting up a modem connection to the ISP.

Set Up Router Connection to ISP

If you selected **Router** on the Configure Hardware page, the Set Up Router Connection to ISP page appears. Provide the information used to configure the Small Business Server Internet connection with a router as follows:

- **Router address**. Enables TCP/IP connectivity from the Small Business Server network to the Internet. In the default gateway configuration, use an IP address on the same subnet as the second network adapter.

- **My router is connected to the Small Business Server via a second network adapter**. Select this option if you are using Small Business Server as the default gateway to the Internet and you want to use the security features of ISA Server. This causes the Network Interface Card Configuration page to appear for configuring network adapter use.

- **Primary DNS server address**. Use the primary DNS server IP address provided by the ISP.

- **Secondary DNS server address**. Use the secondary DNS server IP address, if available from the ISP.

  Note Click **More Information** to display Help on setting up a router connection to the ISP.

Set Up Full-time Broadband Connection to ISP

If you selected **Full-time Broadband Connection** on the Configure Hardware page, the Configure Network Adapter page appears (described later in the following section). Next, the Set Up Full-time Broadband Connection page appears. Provide the information used to configure the Small Business Server Internet broadband connection as follows:

- **External Network Adapter**. Specify the IP address, subnet mask, and default gateway information for the second network adapter.

- **Primary DNS server address**. Use the primary DNS server IP address provided by the ISP.

- **Secondary DNS server address**. Use the secondary DNS server IP address, if available from the ISP.

> ✍ **Note** Click **More Information** to display Help on setting up a full-time broadband connection to the ISP.

Network Interface Card Configuration

The Network Interface Card Configuration page appears if you selected either of the following:

- **My router is connected to the Small Business Server via a second network adapter** (on the Set Up Router Connection to ISP page).

- **Full-time Broadband Connection** (on the Configure Hardware page).

This page appears when Small Business Server is configured as the default gateway to the Internet. In this configuration, a second network adapter is used to connect Small Business Server and the Internet communications device (router, asymmetric digital subscriber line [ADSL] modem, and so on). The page identifies all configured network adapters, as follows:

- **Select the network card you want to use for your LAN**. Select which network adapter to use for the LAN. Make sure the internal network adapter is configured with the base IP address of Small Business Server and that the ISA Server LAT configuration includes it. This network adapter card must have a static IP address.

- **Select the network card you want to use to connect to the Internet**. Select the second network adapter used for Internet communications. Make sure the second network adapter IP address is not in the internal address space of the ISA Server LAT configuration.

Configure Internet Mail Settings

When configuring Internet mail settings by using the Small Business Server Internet Connection Wizard, the Configure Internet Mail Settings page appears, as shown in Figure 11.2.

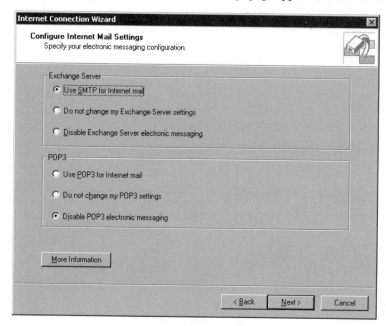

Figure 11.2 Configure Internet mail settings

Provide the information used to configure Small Business Server for Internet e-mail exchange as follows:

- **Use SMTP for Internet Mail**. Select this option any time you want to use Exchange Server to send and receive Internet-based e-mail.

    ☑ **Note** If in the future you run the Small Business Server Internet Connection Wizard again and select the **Use SMTP for Internet Mail** option, your original SMTP settings will be overwritten. This effectively updates your SMTP settings, but it also overrides any custom settings you have created.

- **Do not change my Exchange Server settings**. This prevents Exchange Server settings from being overwritten by the wizard configuration. Select this option if Exchange Server settings are already configured and you want to retain them.

- **Disable Exchange Server electronic messaging**. Select this option when you want to disable Internet mail through Exchange Server. Note that this will delete Small Business Server–specific Internet e-mail settings created by the Small Business Server Internet Connection Wizard. If you manually created Internet e-mail settings instead of using the Small Business Server Internet Connection Wizard, these settings will be retained. This option enables continued e-mail exchange between LAN recipients.

- **Use POP3 for Internet Mail**. Enables retrieval of e-mail from an ISP POP3 mail server instead of an SMTP server. Select **Do not change my POP3 settings** to preserve any existing POP3 e-mail settings. You can disable POP3 e-mail by selecting **Disable POP3 electronic messaging**.

   ✓ **Note**   Click **More Information** to display Help on configuring Internet mail settings.

Configure Internet Domain Name

When configuring your Internet domain name by using the Small Business Server Internet Connection Wizard, the Configure Internet Domain Name page appears. If you have an Internet domain name or use the Exchange Server for SMTP mail, you must enter the domain name information as follows:

- **Your Internet domain name**. Configures the reply address for recipients appearing in the Active Directory™ directory service (as shown on the Exchange-related tab on a user property sheet in the Active Directory Users and Computers snap-in). The domain name must be registered with a Domain Name Registry service on the Internet or provided to you by the ISP. Click **More Information** to display Help on configuring the Internet domain name.

   ✓ **Note**   Exchange 2000 Server contains recipient policies, allowing an organization to receive e-mail sent to multiple Internet domains and, as a result, small businesses to have multiple Internet identities.

   If a new recipient policy, with a new Internet domain name used for e-mail, is introduced to Exchange 2000 Server in the future, subsequent users added to the Small Business Server network will have only the new Internet domain name for their e-mail. Refer to Small Business Server Help for more information about recipient policies.

Configure SMTP Server Address

If you selected **Use Exchange Server for Internet mail** on the Configure Internet Mail Settings page, the Configure SMTP Server Address page appears. Provide the necessary information as follows:

- **Forward all mail to host**. Sets Exchange Server to forward all messages to an ISP SMTP relay host. Select this option if you have an Internet connection that is not full time, such as a dial-up modem or dial-on-demand router connection.

- **Use domain name system (DNS) for mail delivery**. Enables DNS resolution of Internet e-mail addresses. Select this option if you have a full-time Internet connection (for example, with a router or broadband device).

☑ **Note**   Click **More Information** to display Help on configuring SMTP server addressing.

Receive Exchange Mail

If Exchange Server is used for SMTP mail, the Receive Exchange Mail page appears next.

Provide the information used to configure mail retrieval options. Obtain the appropriate configuration information from the ISP for the mail de-queuing method in use. Table 11.2 describes some common mail de-queuing configurations compatible with Small Business Server.

Table 11.2   De-queuing Configurations for Mail Retrieval

IP address type	Full-time connection	Dial-up connection	Demand-dial router connection
Fixed	Do not send a signal	ETRN	ETRN
Dynamic	TURN	TURN	TURN

☑ **Note**   TURN refers to TURN after authentication.

Mail retrieval options are configured on the Receive Exchange Mail page as follows:

- **Send a signal**. Configures Exchange Server to send a signal or command to the ISP's SMTP server to de-queue messages destined for the Small Business Server domain. Select this option to retrieve mail queued at the ISP only if you have a dial-up or dial-on-demand Internet connection (such as an ISDN service).

- **ETRN command**. The most common command used for de-queuing mail from an ISP, supported by most major e-mail implementations.

   If the ETRN command is chosen for a dial-up connection, the ISP must configure a DNS MX record and a DNS A record to point directly to Small Business Server. In addition, the ISP must add another MX record with a preference number pointing to the ISP SMTP server—the lower the preference number, the higher the priority. The ISP must have a higher cost value to become the second preference. This enables the ISP to queue mail until Small Business Server connects with the ISP and sends the de-queuing command. Mail then flows directly to the Small Business Server domain with minimum delay.

   > **Note**   ETRN is the most likely scenario for Internet connections that use demand-dial routers with static IP addresses. If a static IP address is not used, ETRN does not work.

- **Receive Mail from a different host**. If your ISP sends SMTP mail back to you through a different mail server, you will need to enter the name or IP address of that server.

- **Issue TURN after authentication**. A mail de-queuing command that may be used if the ISP specifically supports Exchange 2000 Server TURN.

- **Do not send a signal**. Prevents Exchange Server from sending a de-queuing signal to the ISP. Select this option if you are using a full-time Internet connection and hosting SMTP mail for the Small Business Server domain. Note that some ISPs have their own solution for detecting when Small Business Server is connected.

A full-time Internet connection does not require ISP mail queuing. This type of connection does require that the MX and A records for the Small Business Server domain point directly to the Exchange Server. Because static A records are needed, a full-time connection also requires a static IP address.

Mail Delivery Frequency Page

The Small Business Server Internet Connection Wizard's Mail Deliver Frequency page enables you to select the frequency at which Exchange 2000 Server will contact the ISP to send and check for new mail. This may be configured for hours and minutes. The most frequent setting is to send and check for e-mail every 15 minutes.

TURN Authentication Page

On the Small Business Server Internet Connection Wizard's Receive Exchange Mail page, if you selected **Issue TURN after Authentication**, the Setup Authentication page appears, enabling you to select the Secure Socket Layer (SSL) security mechanism and provide an ISP account name and password.

Review POP3 Mailboxes

If you selected **Use POP3 for Internet mail** on the Configure Internet Mail Settings page, you will need to configure the Review POP3 Mailboxes page with individual POP3 e-mail account information. This information is used to configure the connector for POP3 Mail in Exchange 2000 Server.

Configure Exchange 2000 Server to download mail from the ISP for POP3 mailboxes by using the following steps.

To configure POP3 mailboxes

1. On the **Review POP3 Mailboxes** page in the Small Business Server Internet Connection Wizard, click **Add**. The **Create POP3 Account** dialog box appears.

2. In the **Create POP3 Account** dialog box, in the **Mail Server**, **Login name**, **Password**, **Authentication,** and **Exchange user** fields, type the required information.

3. Click **OK** to close the dialog box.

4. Click **Add** to create more POP3 mailboxes.

Configure Firewall Settings

When configuring firewall settings by using the Small Business Server Internet Connection Wizard, the Configure Firewall Settings page appears. On this page you can provide security for the LAN through an ISA Server firewall as follows:

- **Enable ISA Server firewall**. Enables packet filtering so that LAN users have Internet access through the Web Proxy or Winsock Proxy service. The following packet filters are installed by default:

  - Dynamic Host Configuration Protocol (DHCP) Client

  - Internet Control Message Protocol (ICMP) Ping Echo

  - ICMP Ping Response

  - ICMP Source Quench

  - ICMP Timeout

  - ICMP Unreachable

  - ICMP Outbound

  - DNS Lookup

  - IdentD

If you select **Enable ISA Server firewall** without also selecting any of the Small Business Server services described in the following list, LAN users will be able to use the services outbound to the Internet, but inbound requests for these services will be denied. Enable specific services for inbound Internet requests by selecting from the following:

- **My Mail Server (Exchange Server)**. Enables Transmission Control Protocol (TCP) port 25 (SMTP) on Small Business Server for mail exchange with the ISP's SMTP server. If you want to receive Internet e-mail, this selection is necessary.

- **My Web Server**. Permits your Web site hosted by Small Business Server to be accessible on the Internet. Enables Small Business Server to listen for Internet requests on TCP ports 80 (Hypertext Transfer Protocol [HTTP]) and 443 Hypertext Transport Protocol Secure (HTTPS), to serve Web pages from Microsoft Internet Information Services (IIS). The **My Web-based Mail Server** option provides access to Exchange Server's Web Client.

- **Virtual Private Networking (PPTP client access)**. Enables remote clients to connect to Small Business Server over the Internet through Point-to-Point Tunneling Protocol (PPTP). Opens the PPTP call and receive filters (TCP port 1723) so that remote clients can connect to the LAN through a secure tunnel.

- **POP3**. Enables Small Business Server to listen to POP3 requests from the Internet on TCP port 110.

- **FTP**. Enables Internet users to access the FTP service of Small Business Server by enabling the server to listen on TCP ports 20 and 21 for FTP and FTP data, respectively.

- **Terminal Services**. Enables Internet users to access Small Business Server Terminal Services.

- **Disable ISA Server firewall**. Disables ISA Server protection of LAN security.

- **Do not change firewall settings**. Select this item if you have previously configured ISA Server settings that you do not want changed by the wizard configuration. Retains the existing ISA firewall settings.

    ☑ **Note** Click **More Information** to display Help on configuring the firewall settings.

Finishing the Small Business Server Internet Connection Wizard

The Small Business Server Internet Connection Wizard Completion page appears when the information-gathering phase of configuration is complete. Review the information presented on the Completion page because it is your chance to review your selection before committing the changes. Click **Back** if you want to make any changes. Click **Finish** to start the automatic configuration process of Small Business Server applications. A Status page appears, showing you the overall progress of the configuration.

> ☑ **Note** Scripts to automatically configure a Small Business Server computer to use a specific ISP can modify the Small Business Server Internet Connection Wizard. An ISP that offers automatic Internet configurations for its Small Business Server customers might best use this capability.

Summary

This chapter provided a detailed discussion of ISP connectivity tasks, including:

- Internet connection methods, including xDSL, cable, routers, and modems.
- Internet connection by using the Small Business Server Internet Connection Wizard.
- Comparison of SMTP and POP3 e-mail.

CHAPTER 12

Small Business Server Client Setup

Microsoft® Small Business Server 2000 includes the Set Up Computer Wizard, which enables the technology consultant to accomplish the following tasks easily:

- Configure the server for the client.
- Configure the client's networking.
- Install applications on the client.

This chapter discusses the background processes that the Set Up Computer Wizard uses to accomplish these tasks. For information about extending the Set Up Computer Wizard, refer to Chapter 15, "Small Business Server Wizard Processes" and Appendix C, "Customization and Extensibility Options."

Configure Server for Client Computer

The first step is to configure the Small Business Server computer for the client computer. This section outlines the process, starting with the Set Up Computer Wizard.

Set Up Computer Wizard

The Set Up Computer Wizard initiates the client computer setup from the server. The SCW.exe file starts the Set Up Computer Wizard, which uses the wizard scripting engine (WSE) developed for Small Business Server 2000.

Computer Account

The Set Up Computer Wizard creates a computer account for the client if one does not already exist. Setup does not distinguish between Microsoft Windows® 2000 Professional, Microsoft Windows Millennium Edition (Me), Windows 95, Windows 98, and Windows NT® Workstation client computers, even though Windows Me, Windows 95, and Windows 98 clients do not require a computer account to access a Windows NT domain.

Configuring the Client's Networking

Creating the Networking Setup Disk configures client computer networking components. The disk contains the following five files:

- Setup.exe

- IpDetect.exe

- Ipd2000.exe

- Ipdx86.exe

- Netparam.ini

    ☑ **Note**   With Small Business Server 2000, you need to create only one Networking Setup Disk to be used on all network client computers. This is a change from Small Business Server 4.5, in which each network client computer had its own client configuration floppy disk.

On the client computer, run Setup.exe from the floppy disk. Data will be read from Netparam.ini on the floppy disk. Setup.exe creates a setup log on the client computer, found at:

    %windir%\support\ClientNetworkSetup.log

Setup.exe displays three pages for user input:

- **Computers**. This page displays a list of known computers, obtained from the Netparam.ini file. You can select a computer name or enter a new computer name. If you enter a new computer name, it must be an existing computer in the Microsoft Active Directory™ directory service.

- **Users**. This page enables you to add users to the Windows NT 4.0 or Windows 2000 local administration group. These users then have permission to install applications. You can select multiple users at once from a list of known users, obtained from the Netparam.ini file. You can also type in the name of existing user accounts that do not appear as a selection option but exist in Active Directory. This page is not displayed for Windows Me, Windows 95, or Windows 98 client computers.

- **Admin credentials**. This page enables you to enter a user name and password with the authority for the client computer to join the domain. This page is only displayed for Windows 2000 client computers.

At the end of the setup process, the Netparam.ini file is updated with the selected computer name and user names. Setup.exe then runs IpDetect.exe for Windows Me and Windows 95 and Windows 98 clients, Ipdx86.exe for Windows NT 4.0 clients, and Ipd2000.exe for Windows 2000 clients.

IpDetect.exe

IpDetect.exe, Ipd2000.exe, and Ipdx86.exe provide similar functions for different client operating systems. IpDetect.exe reads the computer name and domain information from the Netparam.ini file. The client computer is renamed, and the workgroup name is changed to the Small Business Server domain name. IpDetect.exe performs the following actions:

- Installs TCP/IP networking protocol.

- Installs client for Microsoft Networking.

- Changes the workgroup name for Windows Me, Windows 95, and Windows 98 client computers.

- Installs file and print sharing.

- Configures TCP/IP to access a Dynamic Host Configuration Protocol (DHCP) server so that the client computer obtains all of its DHCP options (such as Domain Name Service (DNS) Internet Protocol (IP) address and default gateway) from the DHCP Server service in Small Business Server 2000.

- Binds TCP/IP to the network adapter card.

- Sets the client to log on to the Small Business Server 2000 domain.

- Sets user-level desktop and Start menu preferences.

IpDetect.exe writes information to the following log on the client machine:

%systemdrive%/IPDETECT.log

Ipdx86.exe

Ipdx86.exe reads the computer name from the Netparam.ini file and joins Windows NT client computers to the Small Business Server domain. Ipdx86.exe does the following tasks, as necessary:

- Verifies that there is only one network adapter card. If more than one network adapter card is present, an error message appears.

- Installs the TCP/IP protocol networking protocol.

- Installs the Client for Microsoft Networking.

- Configures file and print sharing.

- Configures TCP/IP to access a DHCP server so that the client computer obtains all of its DHCP options (such as DNS IP address and default gateway) from the DHCP Server service in Small Business Server 2000.

- Binds TCP/IP to the network adapter card.

- Changes the computer network basic input/output system (NetBIOS) name and domain.

- Adds the computer to the Small Business Server 2000 domain.

Ipdx86.exe does not create a log file. One update in Ipdx86.exe for Small Business Server 2000 is that the ADMINS key is read from Netparam.ini and that all its users are added to the Windows NT local administration group.

> **Note** The client computer name account must already exist on the Small Business Server computer before Ipdx86.exe can be used to join the domain. In addition, the client computer name cannot have been used before—there is no recycling of computer names. This can be a problem if a client computer is replaced with a new computer and the user wants to retain the same computer name.

Former Windows NT Workstation client computers might require an intermediate restart in order to fully configure their network, so Ipdx86.exe might create **RunOnce** entries to handle the continuation of setup.

Ipd2000.exe

The Ipd2000.exe file configures networking on a Windows 2000 computer by completing the following:

- Verifies that there is only one network adapter card. If more than one network adapter card is present, an error message appears.

- Installs the TCP/IP networking protocol.

- Sets TCP/IP to gain access to a DHCP server.

- Binds TCP/IP to the network interface card (NIC).

- Joins the domain.

- Installs client for Microsoft Networking.

- Installs file and print sharing.

- Authentication is passed on the command line.

- Joins the domain. Verifies that the computer name is unique and not already in use.

- Adds users to the local administration group. Reads the ADMINS key from the Netparam.ini file.

- Changes the computer name. Reads the computer name from Netparam.ini.

Netparam.ini

The Netparam.ini file is a snapshot in time of users and computers on the Small Business Server network. The Netparam.ini file is updated only when you create a new computer account with the Setup Computer Wizard and then update a Networking Setup Disk that contains the most recent Netparam.ini file.

> ☑ **Note** To save time, the technology consultant could add all the users and client computers to the Small Business Server network, deferring creation of the Networking Setup Disk until the last user and client computer have been added. This disk, created after the last user is added, will have the most current Netparam.ini file. It will reflect all users and client machines added to the network, and prevent the time-consuming disk creation read/write activity as each user and computer are added. For example, say the technology consultant adds 25 users to the Small Business Server network. The technology consultant does not create a Networking Setup Disk until the twenty-fifth user is added. The Netparam.ini file on that disk will reflect all 25 users and associated client computers.

Installing Applications on the Client

This section discusses the files that are part of the client computer application installation process.

- **SBSClnt.exe**. This file replaces the Startcli.exe in previous versions of Small Business Server. This program, also known as Application Launcher (and App Launcher), performs the following tasks:

    a. Verifies that the computer is not a Small Business Server server computer.

    b. Searches for a response directory for the computer and the Apps.ini file. If either is missing, Application Launcher quits.

    c. Checks for applications that need to be installed, including verifying that any of the applications are already installed. If the client computer does not need applications to be installed, Application Launcher quits.

    d. Verifies that the user is a member of the local administration group. This only applies to Windows 2000 or Windows NT 4.0 client computers and is not performed for Windows Me, Windows 95, and Windows 98 client computers.

    e. Asks you to click **Start Now** or **Postpone**. Click **Postpone** if you are working across a slow link or do not want to install applications at this time. This dialog box will appear each time a user logs on from the client computer, until he or she installs the applications.

    f. If the client computer requires applications to be installed, SBSClnt.exe checks whether the computer receiving the installed applications is running as a Windows 2000 Terminal Services server machine. If so, the computer is automatically placed in Terminal Services application installation mode. The client computer is changed back to remote administration mode after the installation process completes.

    g. If the client machine is Windows NT-based, SBSClnt.exe asks you to select either a manual logon or auto logon when the computer restarts. Selecting auto logon will save you time. After the client computer applications are installed, the auto logon is disabled.

    h. Verifies and creates as necessary numerous registry entries for user information, user and company shortcut creation, Microsoft Internet Explorer 5.01 configuration settings, and Microsoft Outlook® 2000 configuration settings. These entries are located under: HKEY_LOCAL_MACHINE\Software\Microsoft\Small Business.

    i. Copies and modifies the Outlook.prf and Default.prf. These files are used to set up Outlook for each user on the client computer.

The file SBSClnt.exe resides on the Small Business Server server computer and runs (or executes) on the client machine. When the SBS_LOGIN_SCRIPT.BAT login script is started, the SBSClnt.exe program runs on the client computer.

- **SBSOSUpd.exe**. This program applies Windows NT 4.0 Service Pack 6. The file ensures that the service pack is applied only once and checks the operating system. The file works only with Windows NT-based clients. Other client operating systems are ignored. A log file is created on the client computer at: %windir%\support\SBSOSUpdate.log.

Add a User to an Existing Client

You can assign multiple users to one client computer on a Small Business Server network. This is done so that the assigned users are added to the local administration group on a Windows 2000 Professional or Windows NT Workstation 4.0 client computer. When a user is a member of the local administration group and is logged on at the client computer, this user has the explicit permissions necessary to install Small Business Server client applications locally. You can add users to existing client computers by using the Networking Setup Disk on the client computer either during the initial setup or at a future date. The Specify User page enables you to select a name from the Users list and move it to the Assigned Users list for the existing client computer. Once Users are added to the Assigned User list they will be able to log on to the local computer as local administrators. This gives the added user rights to add Small Business Server software to the computer, with full administrative rights to the local machine.

> ✔ **Note** It is not necessary to add a user to an existing client in order for the user to log on to the Small Business Server 2000 network. That is because the user logon to the network occurs at the domain level, not at the local computer level.

Add Software to an Existing Client

Small Business Server enables you to add software to an existing client computer easily. To do so, perform the following steps.

To add software to an existing client

1. From the Small Business Server Administrator Console, click **Favorites**, **Small Business Server Tips**.

2. Click **Add Software to Computer**.

3. The Set Up Computer Wizard starts, enabling you to add software to existing client computers. Complete each page as directed by the onscreen instructions.

4. Click **Finish** after completing the pages of the Set Up Computer Wizard.

   The next time the user logs onto the client computer, App Launcher will ask the user to start installation of the new software.

To remove applications from a client computer

- Use the Add/Remove Programs utility in Control Panel.

Remove a Computer from Your Network

You can remove computers from the Small Business Server network by performing the following steps.

To remove a computer from your network

1. From the Small Business Server Administrator Console, click **Favorites**, **Management Shortcuts**.

2. Click **Computers**.

3. Right-click the computer you want to remove in the Details Pane, and then select **Remove Client Computer** from the secondary menu.

4. Complete the onscreen instructions in the Setup Computer Wizard to remove the computer.

Client Application Optimizations

To optimize client setup, client applications and components are, by default, set to a typical configuration for Small Business Server users, including the following components described in this section.

*   Fax

*   Microsoft Internet Explorer 5.0

*   Outlook 2000

*   Outlook client profile updates with Modprof utility

*   Microsoft Shared Modem Service Client

*   Firewall Client

Small Business Server Version

During client setup, the following registry key is set to indicate the version of Small Business Server 2000:

HKLM\SOFTWARE\Microsoft\SmallBusiness, *Version, 0, 5.0.*

Fax Client

By default, faxing is available from applications when you select the fax device from the **Printer** dialog box. In effect, you *print* to the fax device to send a fax. However, sending a fax as part of the Outlook *send mail* function is different.

To make faxing from Outlook available to Small Business Server users, the fax transport must be added to the profile by using the following steps.

Adding faxing capabilities in Outlook 2000

1. Click **Start**, point to **Programs**, and then click **Microsoft Outlook**.

2. On the **Tools** menu, click **Services**.

3. Click **Add**, select the **Fax Mail Transport**, and then click **OK**.

4. Click **OK** to close **Services**.

Internet Explorer 5.01

During client setup, Internet Explorer 5.01 is configured for each user as detailed in the following sections.

Install.ins

Internet Explorer 5.0 enables configuration of several settings in the Install.ins file during client application installation. These settings in Install.ins are applied to each new user profile after the initial Internet Explorer 5.0 installation computer restart. Before the restart, this file is copied into <ie install dir>\signup on the client computer. The following settings are added to Install.ins:

- **Favorites**. Favorites are added into [FavoritesEx] section.

- **Proxy settings**. The following section is added to Install.ins:

  [Proxy]

  HTTP_Proxy_Server=http://SBSServer:8080

  FTP_Proxy_Server=http://SBSServer:8080

  Secure_Proxy_Server=http://SBSServer:8080

  Socks_Proxy_Server=http://SBSServer:8080

  Use_Same_Proxy=1

  Proxy_Enable=1

  Proxy_Override= "<local>"

  Note Although Microsoft Proxy Server has been updated and renamed Microsoft Internet Security and Acceleration (ISA) Server, Internet Explorer stills makes references to Microsoft Proxy Server.

Set Favorites

Favorites are set up as described in Table 12.1

Table 12.1   Small Business Server Favorites Setup

Title	URL
Microsoft Small Business Server Web site	**http://www.microsoft.com/SmallBusinessserver**
Microsoft Small Business Internet Services	**http://www.bcentral.com**
My E-mail	**http://%sbsserver%/exchange/**
Small Business Server User Guide	**http://%sbsserver%/intranet/**
Small Business Server Administration Console	**http://%sbsserver%/myconsle/**

ISA Server Settings

The following ISA Server settings are implemented:

- The Firewall Client is configured to access the Internet through ISA Server.
- The ISA Server name and port are set for HTTP, FTP, Secure Sockets Layer, and Socks services.
- All protocols are set to use the ISA Server.
- Internet Explorer 5.0 is set to bypass ISA Server for local IP addresses.

Microsoft Outlook 2000

This section describes the configuration setup for the Outlook 2000 client.

Outlook First Run Wizard

The following registry keys are set to configure Outlook 2000 in the corporate mode, instead of the Internet mode, so that the user does not see the Outlook First Run Wizard:

HKLM, "SOFTWARE\Clients\Mail\Microsoft Outlook", "MSIComponentID", "{FF1D0740-D227-11D1-A4B0-006008AF820E}"

HKLM, "SOFTWARE\Microsoft\Office\9.0\Outlook\Setup", "MailSupport",0x00010003,1.

E-mail Profile

An e-mail profile is created for each Small Business Server user. The following services are added to the user profile:

- Outlook Client
- Microsoft Exchange 2000 Server
- Outlook Address Book

If the user has an existing profile, these services are appended to the profile. For further details on profile creation, refer to the section on Modprof later in this chapter.

Welcome Mail

A welcome e-mail is sent to all new Outlook 2000 users. So that the message appears properly, it is named Offer.msg and is copied into the following location on the server during client setup:

Program Files\MicrosoftOffice\Office

Outlook Client Profile Updates with Modprof Utility

All Outlook 97 and Outlook 98 clients have an existing e-mail profile. The Modprof utility automatically updates these existing client profiles to include the basic Exchange services a Small Business Server client needs. Modprof does this by appending the following services to existing Outlook profiles:

- Outlook Client
- Exchange Server
- Outlook Address Book

Modprof Scenarios

Modprof is used in the following scenarios:

- Scenario 1.

  An Outlook 98 Internet Mode (IMO) user is upgrading to Outlook 2000 corporate.

  Modprof is used to add Exchange Server to the configuration without eliminating the existing Internet configuration.

- Scenario 2.

  An Outlook 98 corporate user is connecting to MS Mail or cc: Mail.

  Modprof is used to add Exchange Server to the configuration while preserving existing Internet connectivity.

What the Utility Does

New Outlook client profiles are created by the Newprof utility, which uses the information specified in a Small Business Server .prf file to create the profile. For existing Outlook 97 and Outlook 98 client profiles, Modprof extends the format of this file to include the following new information in Outlook 2000 profiles:

- Identifies the profile to modify and includes an option to modify the default profile.

- Decides whether to abort, replace, or append the existing profile.

- Decides whether to overwrite or leave intact current settings for services that can only have a single instance in the profile, such as Exchange Server.

- Inserts a flag in all service definitions to indicate that each service can have only one instance in the profile.

Starting Modprof

The first run of Outlook 2000 starts Modprof. For this to occur properly, Small Business Server client setup writes the following registry key for each new user:

Key: HKCU\Software\Microsoft\Office\9.0\Outlook\Setup\Execute

Value: The path to Modprof, including command line parameters.

\\%sbsserver%\Clients\Setup\Modprof.exe

This registry key instructs Outlook 2000 to first run a custom executable file before doing a Mail Application Programming Interface (MAPI) logon. If there is no profile, Modprof is executed after Newprof runs. If there is an existing profile, Newprof does not run and Outlook starts Modprof.

> ☑ **Note** Since an Outlook first run condition may also occur when switching mail support modes or after new component installation, Modprof deletes the *execute* registry key after successfully modifying the profile to avoid running Modprof multiple times.

Compatibilities

Modprof functions the same on Windows Me, Windows 95, Windows 98, and Windows NT Workstation clients. Modprof only runs on Outlook 2000 and operates on profiles created by the following applications:

- Windows Messaging Subsystem

- Exchange versions 4.0, 5.0, and 5.5

- Outlook 97, Outlook 98, and Outlook 2000

Shared Modem Service

The Shared Modem Service can be installed on the client computer, enabling the client computer to use the shared modem pool on the Small Business Server 2000 computer.

Firewall Client

The Firewall Client can be installed on the client computer. This enables the client computer to seamlessly direct Internet-bound traffic through the ISA Server 2000 component on the Small Business Server 2000 computer.

Other Client Interactions

MS-DOS®, Windows 3.1, and Macintosh clients interact with Small Business Server 2000 just as they would with a normal Windows 2000 Server. However, Small Business Server does not provide client setup software or client applications for MS-DOS, Windows 3.1, and Macintosh client operating systems.

MS-DOS Clients

MS-DOS clients running one of the following components can use shared network resources on the respective servers:

- Microsoft LAN Manager for MS-DOS version 2.2. Enables computers running MS-DOS to interact with Windows NT Server and LAN Manager 2.x domain controllers.

- Microsoft Network Client for MS-DOS version 3.0. Enables computers running MS-DOS to interact with a Windows 2000 Server or Windows NT domain controllers and with computers running Windows 2000 Professional, Windows NT Workstation, and LAN Manager 2.x.

Since MS-DOS-based computers cannot store user accounts, they do not participate in domains the way Windows 2000-based computers do. Each MS-DOS computer usually has a default domain for browsing. An MS-DOS user with a domain account can be set up to browse any domain, not just the domain containing the user's account.

Windows 3.1 and OS/2 Clients Running LAN Manager

Windows 2000 Server interoperates with Microsoft LAN Manager 2.x systems. Windows 3.1, IBM OS/2, and MS-DOS computers running LAN Manager workstation software can connect to Windows 2000 Server.

Microsoft LAN Manager for OS/2 version 2.2 is a component of Windows 2000 Server that enables client computers running OS/2 version 1.3x to interact with Windows 2000 Server (and LAN Manager 2.x servers) and share network resources.

Macintosh Clients

Microsoft Windows 2000 Server Services for Macintosh is a component of Windows 2000 Server that enables Windows and Apple Macintosh clients to share files and printers. This means that a Windows 2000 Server computer can act as a server for both these types of clients and that Macintosh computers can share resources with any client supported by Windows 2000 Server.

Summary

This chapter addressed Small Business Server 2000 client computer issues, including:

- Configuring a support client computer to join a Small Business Server 2000 network.
- Defining the client computer setup process.
- Removing a client computer from the Small Business Server network.
- Client application optimizations.
- How a Small Business Server network interacts with non-supported clients such as MS-DOS and Macintosh.

CHAPTER 13

Remote Connectivity

Remote users can access Microsoft® Small Business Server 2000 securely across the Internet backbone by establishing a virtual private network (VPN) using Routing and Remote Access Service (RRAS) and Point-to-Point Tunneling Protocol (PPTP). The information in this chapter will help you install and configure VPN remote connectivity in Small Business Server 2000, including:

- Preliminary setup steps

- VPN configuration on Small Business Server

- Configuration of remote client connections to Small Business Server

Preliminary Setup Steps

Before installing and configuring VPN-based remote connectivity on Small Business Server 2000, verify that you have met the following requirements:

- Small Business Server 2000 has been successfully installed.

- One or more network adapters are installed.

    ☑ **Note** For VPN connectivity, two or more network adapters are required—one to connect to the Internet and one to connect to the Small Business Server network. Microsoft Internet Security and Acceleration (ISA) Server's best practices require the second network adapter to properly implement firewall features in Small Business Server 2000.

- TCP/IP is installed and bound to the internal network adapter. This is the default condition. One adapter must be connected to the Internet.

- The internal network adapter card on the Small Business Server computer is configured with a static IP address. This is the default condition. Additional network adapter cards located in the Small Business Server computer may have dynamic Internet Protocol (IP) addresses.

- RRAS is installed. This is the default condition.

Setting Up the Server

Configuring Small Business Server as a VPN server involves the following steps:

- Configuring the RRAS Server through ISA Server 2000 for VPN.

- Configuring encryption and authentication options.

- Configuring the user accounts to enable dial-in.

> ☑ **Note** Configuring Small Business Server 2000 for VPN and dial-up remote connectivity has been revised and simplified compared with Microsoft Small Business Server 4.5.

Configure RRAS Through ISA Server 2000 for VPN

RRAS is installed by default with Small Business Server 2000. It is configured through the ISA Server VPN Wizard.

> ☑ **Note** Do not configure RRAS for VPN in Small Business Server by using the Routing and Remote Access Server Setup Wizard, available from the Routing and Remote Access Microsoft Management Console. This will result in ISA firewall settings that are required for use by Small Business Server being improperly configured.

To configure RRAS

1. On your Small Business Server 2000 computer, click **Start**, point to **Programs**, point to **Microsoft Small Business Server**, and then click **Small Business Server Administrator Console**.

2. Select and expand the **Internet Security and Acceleration Server 2000** icon in the Console Tree, and then expand **Servers and Arrays**.

3. Expand the server icon, and then select **Network Configuration**. The **Configure Network Connection** page appears in the Details Pane.

4. Double-click the **Setup virtual private network (VPN) (Local)** shortcut to start the ISA Server VPN Wizard.

5. Click **Next** on the **Welcome to the ISA Virtual Private Network Setup Wizard** page.

   ☑ **Note**   If the **ISA VPN Wizard** dialog box appears, informing you that the Routing and Remote Access Services must be started before the VPN Wizard can continue, click **Yes**.

6. On the **ISA VPN Identification** page, type the name of the Small Business Server computer in the **Type the name of the local ISA VPN computer** field.

7. Type the name of the remote VPN computer, such as a client computer, in the **Type the name of the remote ISA VPN computer** field, and then click **Next**.

8. On the **ISA VPN Protocol** page, select **Use PPTP**, and then click **Next**.

9. Complete the **Two-way Communications** page, and then click **Next**.

10. On the **Remote VPN Network** page, click **Add** to provide an IP address range for the remote VPN network. Complete the **From** and **To** fields in the **ISA VPN Network** dialog box that appears. Click **OK** to close the **ISA VPN Wizard** dialog box.

11. Click **Next**, and then click **Finish**.

    ☑ **Note**   The PPTP and VPN ports are automatically configured as part of the ISA Server VPN Wizard, an improvement over previous versions of Small Business Server.

Configuring VPN Server Encryption and Authentication Options

This section provides information for configuring Small Business Server with encryption and authentication options.

To configure VPN-related encryption and authentication

1. On your Small Business Server 2000 computer, click **Start**, point to **Programs**, point to **Administrative Tools**, and then click **Routing and Remote Access**.

2. Right-click the server icon in the Console Tree of the **Routing and Remote Access** management console.

3. Click **Properties** in the shortcut menu.

4. In the **Properties** dialog box, click the **Security** tab.

5. Click **Authentication Methods**. The **Authentication Methods** dialog box appears, as shown in Figure 13.1.

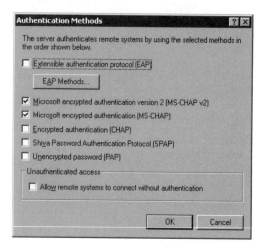

Figure 13.1 Authentication and encryption selections

6. After configuring the **Authentication Methods** dialog box, click **OK**.

7. Click **OK** to quit the **Properties** dialog box.

Configuring for Data Encryption on VPN Devices

Encryption of data is performed by the remote access protocol known as Point-to-Point Protocol (PPP). Encryption is enabled by configuring a remote access policy.

To enable data encryption from a remote access policy

1. On your Small Business Server 2000 computer, click **Start**, point to **Programs**, point to **Administrative Tools**, and then click **Routing and Remote Access**.

2. Expand the server node in the Console Tree of the **Routing and Remote Access** management console.

3. Click **Remote Access Policies**.

4. Right-click **Allow access if dial-in permission is enabled**. This is the default remote access policy when you configure RRAS.

5. Click **Properties** on the shortcut menu. The **Properties** dialog box appears.

6. Click **Edit Profile**.

7. On the **Edit Dial-in Profile** page, click the **Encryption** tab.

8. Select the data encryption level you want, as illustrated in Figure 13.2.

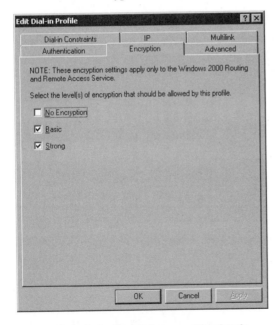

Figure 13.2 Selecting data encryption levels

You can select any or all levels of data encryption, including:

- **No encryption**. Data is not encrypted.

- **Basic**. Specifies that members of this group dial-in profile can use IPSec 56-bit or MPPE 40-bit data encryption.

- **Strong**. Specifies that members of this group dial-in profile can use IPSec 56-bit or MPPE 56-bit data encryption.

9. Click **OK**.

10. Click **OK** to quit the **Properties** dialog box.

Configure User Account for Remote Access

By default, Small Business Server denies dial-in access for users.

To enable dial-in access

1. Click **Start,** point to **Programs**, point to **Microsoft Small Business Server,** and then click **Small Business Server Administrator Console**.

2. In the Console Tree, click **Active Directory Users and Computers**, the **server** icon, and then **Users**. Select a user in the Details Pane.

3. On the taskpad, click **Change User Properties**. The **Properties** dialog box for the user appears.

4. Click the **Dial-in** tab.

5. Select **Allow Access**, as shown in Figure 13.3.

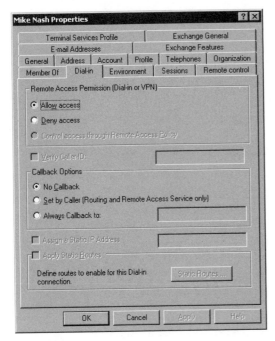

Figure 13.3 Allows dial-in access for this user

6. Click **OK**.

7. Click **OK** to quit the **Properties** dialog box.

> ✓ **Note** You can also access the property sheet for a user and enable remote access from the Microsoft Active Directory™ directory service Users and Computers management console.

Setting Up the Client

After Small Business Server is configured for VPN connectivity, a VPN client can connect to Small Business Server in the following three ways:

- Dialing into the Small Business Server server computer directly.

- Dialing into an Internet service provider (ISP) and then connecting to the Small Business Server server computer through a VPN.

- Using an existing Internet connection, such as broadband, and connecting to the Small Business Server server computer through a VPN.

Before the remote client can connect to Small Business Server, you must install and configure VPN capabilities on the client computer. The following sections explain VPN installation and configuration for Microsoft Windows® 2000 Professional, Windows NT® Workstation and Windows 95, Windows 98, and Windows Me client computers.

Installing and Configuring VPN on Windows 2000 Professional Remote Clients

Before installing and configuring VPN on Windows 2000 Professional clients, verify that the clients meet the following requirements:

- Windows 2000 Professional is installed on the remote client computer.

- TCP/IP is installed.

- An analog modem, DSL/ADSL router, cable modem, Integrated Services Digital Network (ISDN) device, or other modem device is installed and configured to enable the remote client for dial-out connection.

- If the Internet is used to connect to Small Business Server with PPTP protocol, a PPP account is established with an ISP.

To configure VPN capabilities on a remote Windows 2000 Professional client

1. Click **Start**, point to **Settings**, and then click **Network and Dial-up Connections**.

2. Double-click **Make a New Connection**.

3. The Network Connection Wizard appears. Click **Next**.

4. Select **Connect to a private network through the Internet**, and then click **Next**.

5. On the **Public Network** page, select **Automatically dial this initial connection** or **Do not dial this initial connection**. Click **Next**.

6. On the **Destination Address** page, provide the host name or IP address of the Small Business Server server computer. Click **Next**.

7. On the **Connection Availability** page, configure this connection for all users or just yourself. Click **Next**.

8. On the **Complete the Network Connection Wizard** page, type a name for the connection, and then click **Finish**.

9. The **Connect Virtual Private Connection** dialog box appears, enabling you to initiate a VPN session. Click **Connect** to start a VPN session, or click **Cancel** to close the dialog box.

> ☑ **Note** The **Properties** button on the **Connect Virtual Private Connection** dialog box enables you to further configure the connection, including data encryption, found on the **Security** tab. You can select PPTP-based VPN session settings from the **Networking** tab.

If you intend to dial up an ISP as your primary connection to the Internet, you need to create a dial-up connection to the Internet.

To create a dial-up connection to the Internet

1. Click **Start**, point to **Settings**, and then click **Network and Dial-up Connections**.

2. Double-click **Make a New Connection**.

3. The Network Connection Wizard appears. Click **Next**.

4. Select **Dial-up to the Internet**, and then click **Next**.

5. At the **Internet Connection Wizard Welcome** page, select your type of Internet account, and then click **Next**.

6. Follow the onscreen instructions to complete the Internet Connection Wizard for your dial-up Internet connection.

> ☑ **Note** After a dial-up Internet connection has been created, you can return to the property page for the VPN connection and select the Internet dial-up configuration (on the **General** tab, under **First connect**, click **Dial another connection first**).

Installing and Configuring VPN on Windows NT-Based Remote Clients

Before installing and configuring VPN on Windows NT-based remote clients, verify that the clients meet the following requirements:

- Windows NT Workstation 4.0 or Windows NT Server 4.0 is installed on the remote client computer.

- TCP/IP is installed.

- RAS with Dial-Up Networking is installed.

- An analog modem, ISDN device, or other modem device is installed and configured in RAS to enable the remote client for dial-out connection.

- If the Internet is used to connect to Small Business Server (PPTP-configured), a PPP account is established with an ISP.

    ✍ **Note**   In a Windows NT 4.0 environment, the Remote Access Service is referred to as RAS. In a Windows 2000 environment, the remote access service is referred to as Routing and Remote Access Service (RRAS).

Installing the VPN Client

As part of the VPN client installation, you must first install the PPTP protocol. Use the following steps to install PPTP on a Windows NT-based remote client computer.

To install a PPTP protocol on a Windows NT-based remote client computer

1. Click **Start**, point to **Settings**, and then click **Control Panel**.
2. Double-click **Network**.
3. Click the **Protocols** tab, and then click **Add** to display the **Select Network Protocol** dialog box.
4. Select **Point-To-Point Tunneling Protocol**, and then click **OK**.

5. Type the drive and directory location of your installation files in the **Windows NT Setup** dialog box, and then click **Continue**. The PPTP files are copied from the installation directory, and the **PPTP Configuration** dialog box appears.

6. Select the **Number of Virtual Private Networks** the client will support. You can select a maximum of 256. Typically, however, only one VPN is installed on a remote client.

7. Click **OK**, and then click **OK** again.

8. Click **Add** to continue the installation and add the VPN device installed with the PPTP.

Adding a VPN Device as a RAS Port on the Client

After installing PPTP, a VPN device must be added to Remote Access Service (RAS) on the PPTP client computer, per the following steps.

To configure a VPN device on the client

1. Click **Start**, point to **Settings**, and then click **Control Panel**.

2. Double-click **Network**.

3. Click the **Services** tab, and then click **Remote Access Service**.

4. Click **Properties** to display the **Remote Access Setup Properties** dialog box.

5. Click **Add**. The **Add RAS Device Properties** dialog box appears.

6. From the **RAS Capable Devices** drop-down list, select the VPN devices you want to use.

7. Click **OK**. If you installed PPTP with more than one VPN device, repeat steps 5, 6, and 7 until all the VPNs are added.

8. By default, the VPN device on a Windows NT Workstation computer is configured to dial out only. Select the VPN port, and then click **Configure**. Verify that the **Dial out only** option in the **Port Usage** dialog box is the only option selected. Click **OK** to return to the **Remote Access Setup Properties** dialog box.

9. Click **Network** to display the **Network Configuration** dialog box.

10. Verify that only **TCP/IP** is selected in **Dial out Protocols**. Click **OK**.

11. Click **Continue**.

12. Click **Close** to quit the **Network Configuration** dialog box, and then restart the computer.

Configuring Dial-Up Networking on the Client

When a VPN connection is configured for remote client access to the small business network, the VPN client must have two phonebook entries—one to connect to the ISP and one to connect to the Small Business Server (VPN server). The following procedures describe how to use dial-up networking to create both phonebook entries. Before performing the following steps, however, verify that the clients meet the following requirements:

- All network protocols used on the small business network, to which the remote connection is being made, are installed.

- RAS is configured to dial out, using those network protocols.

To create a new ISP entry, using the Phonebook Wizard

1. Click **Start**, point to **Programs**, then **Accessories**, and then click **Dial-Up Networking**. If this is the first phonebook entry created, the **Dial-Up Networking** dialog box appears. Click **OK**.

2. Click **New**. The New Phonebook Entry Wizard appears.

3. Type the name of the ISP in **Name the new phonebook entry,** and then click **Next**. An ISP name can be no longer than 20 characters and cannot contain spaces.

4. Click **I am calling the Internet**, and then click **Next**. This configures the phonebook entry to use TCP/IP and PPP as the dial-up networking protocols.

5. Select your modem device in **Select the modem or adapter this entry will use** in the **Modem or Adapter** dialog box, and then click **Next**.

6. In the **Phone Number** dialog box, type the ISP phone number in **Phone number**. Click **Use Telephony dialing properties** if you need to add an area code or other prefix. Click **Alternatives** if you have an alternative phone number for your ISP.

7. Click **Next**, and then click **Finish**.

8. Verify the phonebook entry in the following steps.

To verify or edit your ISP phonebook entry

1. In **Dial-Up Networking**, click **More**, and then click **Edit entry and modem properties** to verify the entry in the **Edit Phonebook Entry** dialog box.

2. Click the **Basic** tab, and then verify that the phone number is correct and the correct modem or ISDN device is selected. Make any necessary changes.

3. Click the **Server** tab, and then verify that the **Dial-up server type** displays "PPP: Windows NT, Windows 95 Plus, Internet."

4. In **Network protocols**, ensure that **TCP/IP** is selected.

5. Click **TCP/IP Settings** to display the **PPP TCP/IP Settings** dialog box. Ensure that the TCP/IP settings conform to the IP address and server name specified by the ISP. Click **OK** to close the dialog box.

6. By default, the options **Enable Software Compression** and **Enable PPP LCP extensions** are selected. These settings are compatible with most ISP services; check with the ISP, however, before changing the settings.

7. Click the **Script** tab, and then select **None**. The PPP protocol provided in RAS is designed to automate remote logon. If the ISP requires a manual logon, obtain the correct configuration.

8. Click the **Security** tab, and then select an encryption and authentication scheme supported by your ISP.

9. Click **OK**, and then click **Close** to complete the ISP phonebook entry.

Creating a Phonebook Entry to Dial a PPTP Server

A phonebook entry must also be created to connect to Small Business Server with VPN configured.

> ☑ **Note** You do not need to create a phonebook entry for your PPTP server if your computer is not PPTP-enabled and you are using a PPTP service provided by your ISP.

Before performing the following steps, verify that you have met the following requirements:

- TCP/IP and PPTP network protocols are installed on the small business network to which the remote connection is being made.

- RAS is configured to dial out, using the TCP/IP network protocol.

To create a phonebook entry to dial up a VPN server

1. Click **Start**, point to **Programs**, point to **Accessories**, and then click **Dial-Up Networking**. If this is the first phonebook entry, a **Dial-Up Networking** dialog box appears. Click **OK**.

2. Click **New**. The New Phonebook Entry Wizard appears.

3. Type the name of your PPTP server in **Name the new phonebook entry**, and then click **Next**. A PPTP server name can be no longer than 20 characters and cannot contain spaces.

4. Click **I am calling the Internet**, and then click **Next**. This configures the phonebook entry to use TCP/IP and PPP as the dial-up networking protocols.

5. Select **RASPPTPM(VPN1)** in the **Select the modem or adapter this entry will use** list in the **Modem or Adapter** dialog box, and then click **Next**.

6. Type the IP address of the adapter on the PPTP server that is connected to the Internet in the **Phone Number** dialog box.

   > **Note** If your VPN server has an Internet registered Domain Name Service (DNS) name, you could, alternatively, enter its DNS name in this field. However, if your VPN connection fails, revert back to using an IP address.

7. Click **Next**, and then click **Finish**.

8. Verify the phonebook entry in the following steps.

To verify or edit your phonebook entry for the VPN server

1. In **Dial-Up Networking**, click **More**, and then click **Edit entry and modem properties** to verify the entry in the **Edit Phonebook Entry** dialog box.

2. Click the **Basic** tab, and then check that the phone number is correct and the **RASPPTPM (VPN1)** device is selected. Make any necessary changes.

3. Click the **Server** tab and ensure that the **Dial-up server type** displays "PPP: Windows NT, Windows 95 Plus, Internet."

4. In **Network protocols**, ensure that the TCP/IP network protocol used on the small business network is selected. This protocol must already be installed and RAS must be configured to use this protocol to dial out.

5. Because TCP/IP is used on the small business network, click **TCP/IP Settings** to display the **PPP TCP/IP Settings** dialog box. Ensure that the TCP/IP settings conform to the settings required by the RAS configuration on the PPTP server. This includes the **Enable Software Compression** and **Enable PPP LCP extensions** settings. Click **Close**.

6. Click the **Script** tab, and then select **None**. The PPP protocol used in RAS is designed to automate remote logon. If the ISP requires a manual logon, consult them for the correct configuration.

7. Click the **Security** tab. Click **Accept only Microsoft encrypted authentication**. The PPP protocol encrypts the user name and password for remote logon. The user name and password used to log on for all current sessions can be used by selecting **Use current username and password**. The client is prompted by the PPTP server if this box is not selected. Both methods are encrypted and are therefore secure.

8. Close all open dialog boxes.

Installing and Configuring VPN on Windows Me-based Remote Clients

This section explains how to install and configure VPN capabilities on a Windows Me-based client computer.

To install VPN capabilities on a client running Windows Me

1. Click **Start**, point to **Settings**, click **Control Panel**, and then click **Add/Remove Programs**.

2. Click the **Windows Setup** tab.

3. Select **Communications**, and then click **Details**.

4. Select **Virtual Private Networking**.

5. Click **OK**.

6. Click **OK** to close **Add/Remove Programs**.

7. Click **Yes** to restart your Windows Me client.

Installing and Configuring VPN on Windows 95- and Windows 98-based Remote Clients

This section explains how to install and configure VPN capabilities on a Windows 95- or Windows 98-based client computer.

> ☑ **Note** VPN, which includes PPTP, is provided as a stand-alone upgrade to Windows 95 under the software title "Dial-Up Networking 1.2 Upgrade" (also known as DUN 1.2). No upgrade is required for Windows 98. You can find the upgrade at the following Web site: http://www.microsoft.com/ms.htm.

Before performing the steps in this section, verify that the client meets the following requirements:

- Windows 95 or Windows 98 is installed on the remote client computer.

- An analog modem, DSL/ADSL router, cable modem, ISDN device, or other modem device is installed and configured in Dial-Up Networking to enable a dial-out connection from the remote client computer.

- There is an established ISP PPP account, if the Internet is being used to connect to the PPTP server.

- All ISP and private network protocols are installed.

- The Dial-Up Networking upgrade is installed, including the most recent version of the executable file **Msdun.exe**. Refer to the following Web site for the latest version of Dial-Up Networking: http://www.microsoft.com/ms.htm.

Installation of the VPN Client

To install VPN capabilities on a Windows 95 or Windows 98-based remote client, complete the following procedures.

To install PPTP protocol on a client running Windows 95 (not required for Windows 98)

1. Insert the Windows 95 DUN upgrade disk into the disc drive, and then double-click **Msdun12.exe**.

2. Click **Yes** when you are asked if you want to install Microsoft Dial-Up Networking.

3. Setup displays a license agreement. After reading it, click **Yes** if you accept the terms.

4. Setup copies several files and asks you to restart the computer. Click **Yes**. Depending on your configuration, a logon may be required after computer restart.

5. Setup copies more files, including some files from your original Windows 95 installation source. If setup cannot locate your installation source, it will ask you for your original Windows 95 compact disc or setup disks.

   Note If a version conflict is identified, setup asks you if you want to keep your original file. Click Yes.

6. If you are running setup for the first time, a dialog box appears explaining that the DHCP client was unable to obtain an IP address. You will be asked if you want to see this message again later. Click **Yes**.

7. Setup restarts the computer. Depending on your configuration, another logon may be required after computer restart. Dial-Up Networking is now ready to be configured.

To install VPN capabilities on a client running Windows 98

1. Click **Start**, point to **Settings**, click **Control Panel**, and then click **Network**.

2. Click **Add**.

3. Select **Adapter**, and then click **Add**.

4. Select Microsoft as the manufacturer and Microsoft Virtual Private Networking Adapter as the network adapter.

5. Click **OK**.

6. Click **Add**.

7. Select **Adapter**, and then click **Add**.

8. Select **Microsoft** as the manufacturer and **Dial-Up Adapter** as the network adapter.

   Note This is the second dial-up adapter required for the VPN capability.

9. Click **OK**.

10. Click **OK**, and then restart your Windows 98 client computer.

Configuring Dial-Up Networking on the Windows Me, Windows 98, and Windows 95 VPN Client

A VPN configuration enables secure and encrypted communications to the small business network through a connection to the Internet. When setting up dial-up networking on a Windows 95 client, both the following connections must be configured:

- A connection to the Internet through an ISP.

- A tunnel connection to the VPN-configured server on the target network.

The exception is when using a dial-up modem link through the Public Switched Telephone Network (PSTN) to access Small Business Server with VPN configured. In this case, only the connection to the VPN server must be configured. The following steps describe how to configure dial-up networking to configure ISP and VPN connections for the remote Windows 98 or Windows 95 client.

To create a connection to the Internet through an ISP

1. Click **Start**, point to **Programs**, point to **Accessories**, and then click **Dial-Up Networking**. The **Dial-Up Networking** dialog box appears.

2. Click **Make New Connection**.

3. The **Make New Connection Wizard** appears. Click **Next**.

4. Type a name for the connection (for example, an ISP name) in the **Type a name for the computer you are dialing** box.

5. Select your modem device in **Select a modem**, and then click **Next**.

6. Type the ISP phone number in the **Telephone number** box.

7. Click **Next**, and then click **Finish**. A connection icon is created in the Dial-Up Networking folder.

8. Verify your connection by using the steps that follow.

To verify or edit the ISP connection

1. In **My Computer**, right-click the **ISP connection** icon in the Dial-Up Networking folder. Click **Properties** to verify that your ISP connection is correctly configured.

2. Click the **General** tab, verify that the phone number is correct, and that the correct modem or ISDN device is selected. Make any necessary changes.

3. Click the **Server Types** tab, and then verify that the **Type of Dial-Up Server** box displays "PPP: Windows 95, Windows NT, Internet."

4. In **Advanced options**, clear **Log on to the network**. This option is not necessary for ISP connections. However, clearing it will enable a quicker connection to the ISP.

   ☑ **Note**   Generally, it is not necessary to change the Enable software compression or Require encrypted password options.

5. Make sure that **TCP/IP** is selected in the **Allowed network protocols** box and that other network protocols are not selected. Canceling the selection of other network protocols will enable a quicker connection to the ISP.

6. Click **TCP/IP Settings** to display the **PPP TCP/IP Settings** dialog box. Make sure that TCP/IP settings conform to the settings required by your ISP.

   ☑ **Note**   Generally, do not change the values on the **Scripting** tab. If your ISP requires a manual logon, however, you can use a script to automate the process. If you want to use a script, consult your ISP for the correct configuration.

   The values on the **Multilink** tab usually do not need to be changed. Multilink enables you to use two devices (such as modems or ISDN devices) of the same type and speed for a single dial-up link. If you have two such devices and your ISP supports the multilink feature, consult your ISP for the correct configuration.

7. Click **OK**.

Creating a Connection to the VPN Server for Windows Me, Windows 98, and Windows 95 Clients

The connection to Small Business Server (VPN-configured) for remote Windows Me, Windows 98, and Windows 95 clients is created by using a VPN device. Perform the following steps to set up a VPN connection to Small Business Server.

To create a connection to dial up to a VPN server

1. Click **Start**, point to **Programs**, point to **Accessories**, and then click **Dial-Up Networking**. The **Dial-Up Networking** window appears.

2. Click **Make New Connection**. The Make New Connection Wizard appears.

3. Type a connection name (for example, the Small Business Server name), in the **Type a name for the computer you are dialing** box.

4. Select **Microsoft VPN Adapter** from the **Select a modem** box, and then click **Next**.

5. In the **Host name or IP address** box, type the name or IP address of Small Business Server (PPTP-configured).

6. Click **Next**, and then click **Finish**. A connection icon is created in the Dial-Up Networking folder.

7. Verify the VPN server connection by using the steps that follow.

To verify or change the connection to your VPN server

1. In **My Computer**, right-click the **VPN Server Connection** icon in the Dial-Up Networking folder.

2. Click **Properties** to verify that your PPTP server connection is correctly configured.

3. Click the **General** tab, and then verify that the host name or IP address is correct and that **Microsoft VPN Adapter** is selected. Make any necessary changes.

4. Click the **Server Types** tab and, in the **Advanced options** box, select **Log on to network** only if the target small business network requires workstation logons.

5. In **Allowed network protocols,** make sure **TCP/IP** is selected because it is the default protocol used on Small Business Server.

    ✓ **Note**   TCP/IP must already be installed on the remote client Windows 98 or Windows 95 workstation.

6. Click **TCP/IP Settings** to display the **TCP/IP Settings** dialog box. Make sure that TCP/IP settings conform to the settings required for a client on the small business network. The default settings are appropriate for most networks.

7. Click **OK** and quit all open windows.

Connecting to Small Business Server from a VPN by Dialing an ISP

A VPN-enabled client needs two phonebook entries to connect to Small Business Server with VPN configured, as described earlier. The following section explains how to make the connection. After the connection has been made, all traffic through the remote client modem is routed by the ISP over the Internet to Small Business Server, and then routed to the correct computer. This concept is explained in more detail in Chapter 5, "Planning for an Internet Presence."

To connect to a VPN server, using a VPN client to dial up an ISP

1. If the client computer is running Windows NT Workstation, click **Start**, point to **Accessories**, and then click **Dial-Up Networking**.

2. If the client is Windows 98 or Windows 95, right-click **My Computer** on the desktop, and then click **Dial-Up Networking**.

3. When the **Dial-Up Networking** dialog box appears, click **More**.

4. Select **User Preferences**, and then click the **Appearance** tab. Clear the **Close on dial** checkbox, and then click **OK**.

5. In the **Dial-Up Networking** dialog box, select the entry for your ISP phonebook from the drop-down **Phonebook entry to dial** list, and then click **Dial**.

6. After connecting to your ISP, select the entry for your VPN server from the **Phonebook entry to dial** drop-down list, and then click **Dial**.

Dialing up to an ISP PPTP Service to Connect to a PPTP Server

A PPP client can be used to make a connection to Small Business Server with VPN configured across the Internet if the ISP provides a PPTP service. This can be done by using Dial-Up Networking and a modem or other communication device to connect to the ISP server. A second dial-up call is not required because the ISP server configured as a PPTP client makes the connection to the Small Business Server for the PPP client.

Contact your ISP for information about whether they provide a PPTP service, and if so, how to connect to their server that provides the PPTP service.

Summary

This chapter discussed remote connectivity with Small Business Server 2000, including configuring:

- Small Business Server 2000 for VPN.

- Routing and Remote Access Service with the ISA Server VPN Wizard.

- VPN connectivity including encryption and user account settings.

- VPN capabilities on client computers.

CHAPTER 14

Windows 2000 Configurations

Microsoft® Windows® 2000 Server is the underlying operating system in Microsoft Small Business Server 2000. In previous Small Business Server releases, the underlying operating system was Microsoft Windows NT® Server 4.0.

Windows 2000 Server represents an improvement over Windows NT Server 4.0 in the following ways:

- **Stability**. Windows 2000 Server produces fewer STOP conditions and requires fewer restarts when performing network administration.

- **Features**. Windows 2000 Server has additional features, such as Microsoft Management Console (MMC).

- **Services**. Windows 2000 Server has additional services, such as Terminal Services.

- **Security**. Windows 2000 Server strengthens security, with Public Key Infrastructure (PKI) security solutions, such as Kerberos.

- **Management**. Windows 2000 Server Active Directory™ directory service and Group Policy offer greater management capabilities.

Active Directory

Active Directory is a directory services tool that provides the ability to manage (1) objects, such as users and computers, and (2) the entire information infrastructure, including other networks and operating systems. Active Directory, oriented toward large enterprises, has powerful searching capabilities that enable network administrators to quickly locate network resources. Active Directory has a much more robust security model than was previously available, based on PKI, a feature appreciated by large enterprises and small businesses alike.

Small businesses can benefit from Active Directory in several ways. First, many applications are now Active Directory aware. These applications modify the Active Directory schema—similar to a data dictionary—to use many Active Directory strengths. One of these strengths is the ability to have a single sign-on (SSO) in your company. For example, after a user is authenticated on the Small Business Server network, the same user can automatically be authenticated by an Active Directory–aware accounting application.

Another benefit of Active Directory for small businesses is that it includes organizational units, discussed in the following section. If the small business is using Microsoft Windows 2000 Professional client computers, it also can benefit from Group Policy objects, which allow for rich configuration of workstations.

☑ **Note** In-depth discussion of Active Directory concepts is beyond the scope of this resource guide. Refer to Windows 2000 Server Help by selecting **Help** on the **Start** menu in Small Business Server 2000. You can also refer to Part 3, "Active Directory Infrastructure," in the *Windows 2000 Server Resource Kit Deployment Planning Guide*.

Organizational Units

Organizational units, a key part of Active Directory, are containers placed inside a domain in which you can put objects such as users, computers, printers, and even other organizational units, because organizational units can be nested inside each other. Most technology consultants use organizational units that map the business organization directly. For example, members of the marketing department are placed in a "Marketing" organizational unit. The organizational units can also be mapped by geographic region; for example, there can be a "West" unit. You can even map by project teams and create an organizational unit called "Road Construction Project A-1," for example.

Small Business Server creates a default organizational unit during setup called **MyBusiness**. Three additional organizational units are created under **MyBusiness**, as follows:

- **Distribution Groups**. This unit contains distributions groups created by using the Distribution Group Wizard. To start this wizard, follow these steps:

    a. Click Start, point to Programs, and then click Microsoft Small Business Server.

    b. From the Small Business Server Administrator Console Favorites tab, click Small Business Server Tips, and then click Exchange Server 2000. The Tips – Exchange Server 2000 page appears.

    c. Click Add E-mail Group. The Add Distribution Group Wizard appears.

    d. Click Next.

    e. On the Group Identity page, in the Name field, type a name for the distribution group, and then click Next.

    f. On the Membership page, select users and groups that are members of the distribution group, and then click Next.

    g. On the Completing the Add Distribution Group Wizard page, click Finish.

- **Folders**. This unit contains shared folders that are published to Active Directory by the Add Shared Folder Wizard. To start this wizard, follow these steps:

  a. Click Start, point to Programs, and then click Microsoft Small Business Server.

  b. From the Small Business Server Personal Console, click Shared Folders.

  c. Click Add Folder to start the Add Shared Folder Wizard.

  d. Click Next.

  e. On the Folder Identity page, in the Folder Path field, specify a path for the folder that you want to share, and in the Shared folder name field, type a share name for the folder, and then click Next.

  f. On the Permissions page, select the users and groups that have permissions (Full, Read, Change) to the shared folder, and then click Next.

  g. On the Complete the Add Shared Folder Wizard page, click Finish.

- **Groups**. This unit contains security groups created by the Add Security Group Wizard. To start this wizard, follow these steps:

  a. Click Start, point to Programs, and then click Microsoft Small Business Server.

  b. From the Small Business Server Administrator Console Favorites tab, click Small Business Server Tips, and then click Active Directory. The Active Directory page appears.

  c. Click Add Security Group to start the Add Security Group Wizard.

  d. Click Next.

  e. On the Group Identity page, in the Name field, type a security group name, and then click Next.

  f. On the Membership page, select the users and groups that will be members of the security group, and then click Next.

  g. On the Completing the Add Security Group Wizard page, click Finish.

The **Groups** organizational unit also contains the default Small Business Server security groups, which are created during setup. These default security groups are:

- Microsoft BackOffice® Fax Operators

- BackOffice Folder Operators

- BackOffice Internet Users

- BackOffice Mail Operators

- BackOffice Remote Operators

- BackOffice Template Users

Benefits

There are many benefits of using organizational units in Active Directory, including the following:

- Conversion of Windows NT Server resource domains.

- Application of Group Policy objects to Windows 2000 client computers.

- Delegation of administrative control.

Windows NT Server 4.0 resource domains convert to organizational units under Windows 2000 Server. Organizational units hold and manage resources much like resource domains previously did. This is a key fact to consider if you want to collapse multiple domains in an existing small business network into a single domain for a Small Business Server 2000 implementation.

Organizational units also enable you to apply Group Policy, a configuration tool discussed in the next section.

Another popular feature of organizational units is the ability to delegate management control to the organizational unit level. You can create, in effect, sub-administrators with administrative powers limited to just one organizational unit container. This sub-administrator does not have administrative powers across the entire domain or network.

> **Note** To simplify the Small Business Server experience for administrators and users, the Small Business Server Administrator Console provides direct configuration and management of organizational units by using Active Directory Users and Computers, an important MMC-based administration management tool in the underlying Windows 2000 Server operating system. Active Directory Users and Computers is where you manage users and computers (on the **Start** menu, point to **Small Business Server Administrator Console**, and then click **Active Directory Users and Computers**). Organizational units are typically deployed at the enterprise level instead of multiple domains. Because Small Business Server allows only one domain, organizational units have been de-emphasized. In addition, the concept of organizational units being used by directory services was created with large enterprises, not small businesses, in mind. Whereas large enterprises are complex organizational structures— with perhaps hundreds of departments, branch offices, and/or several subsidiaries—the same characteristics are not typical in small businesses with 50 client computers or less; thus there is an overall de-emphasis of using organizational units in Small Business Server 2000. The technology consultant might, however, have sound technical and business reasons to implement organizational units in Small Business Server.

Creating Organizational Units

To create an organizational unit, perform the following steps.

To create an organizational unit

1. Log on to your Small Business Server 2000 computer as an administrator.

2. Click **Start**, point to **Programs**, point to **Microsoft Small Business Server**, and then click **Small Business Server Administrator**.

3. Select **Active Directory Users and Computers**.

4. In the Details Pane, right-click, point to **New**, and then click **Organizational Unit**.

5. Type a name for the organizational unit, and then click **OK**.

The organizational unit will appear beneath the server object in the Console Tree. You can place objects in the organizational unit by right-clicking on the organizational unit and then selecting an object to create from the **New** menu. For example, you can create a new user in the organizational unit. You can easily move objects to organizational units from other organizational units. The inability to easily move users was a fundamental problem with Windows NT Server 4.0, but organizational units in Active Directory, and thus Small Business Server 2000, resolve this difficulty.

> ☑ **Note** Active Directory allows a user to belong to only one organizational unit at a time. This is an Active Directory optimization, not a Small Business Server 2000 optimization. For this reason, organizational unit names typically reflect a department or location. For example, members of the marketing department would belong to the Marketing organizational unit. As mentioned earlier, Small Business Server 2000 creates an organization unit called **MyBusiness**, which contains distribution groups, folders, and security groups.

Groups

> ☑ **Note** It is important to distinguish between organizational units and Groups in Windows 2000 Server, and thus Small Business Server 2000. Organizational units are typically used for organizational, management, and configuration purposes. Groups are typically used for security-related and communication purposes. Whereas groups can be placed in organizational units, organizational units cannot be placed in groups.

Groups in Windows 2000 Server are largely unchanged from Windows NT Server 4.0. However, Windows 2000 Server does a better job of distinguishing the two types of groups: security and distribution. Security groups are used for applying share-level and NTFS file system permissions. Distribution groups are used for communication purposes, such as e-mail with Microsoft Exchange 2000 Server.

> ☑ **Note** A security group and a distribution group may have the same name—for example, Accounting—if the two groups are not located in the same container in Active Directory. Active Directory enables these two group types to have the same name as long as the Lightweight Directory Access Protocol (LDAP) distinguished name, which is based on the object's exact location, is different. That way, members of the Accounting security group can be granted sufficient permissions to run the accounting application. You can then send an e-mail message to the Accounting distribution group informing them, for example, that new permissions have been granted. Security groups can have an e-mail address for its membership to receive messages. This is significant because in many instances, the ability of a security group to receive messages eliminates the need for a distribution group to accomplish the same purpose.

> The membership of distribution groups is published to Active Directory and is viewable when you select users and groups to send e-mail to by using an e-mail client such as Microsoft Outlook® 2000. The membership of security groups is not visible when you send messages.

Unlike its predecessors, Small Business Server 2000 emphasizes the use of groups. This enables adherence to the traditional network administration best practice of placing users in groups and assigning permissions to groups.

Group Policy Objects

If your network has Windows 2000 Professional clients, you can use Group Policy objects. Group Policy objects enable you to configure the user and computer environments. For example, you could redirect My Documents to a network location, restrict what program groups are displayed on the **Start** menu, or not allow a user to install new hardware on a computer. In addition, Group Policy objects can be used to install software for roving users and to implement additional security features outside the traditional permissions model—for example, not allowing the user to use the floppy disk drive to store data.

Group Policy objects can be applied only at the site, domain, or organizational unit level. Site-level applications are more relevant to larger enterprise implementations. For Small Business Server 2000, Group Policy objects are typically applied at the organizational unit level by using the following steps.

To apply Group Policy objects at the organization unit level

1. Log on to your Small Business Server computer as an administrator.

2. Click **Start**, point to **Programs**, point to **Administrative Tools**, and then click **Active Directory Users and Computers**.

3. Right-click an organizational unit, and then click **Properties**.

4. Click the **Group Policy** tab.

5. Click **New**, type a name for the Group Policy object (for example, General Marketing Policy), and then press ENTER.

6. Click **Edit**. The **Group Policy** console appears.

7. Expand the **Computer Configuration** and **User Configuration** settings and modify the Group Policy object as you like. You can choose from many software, Windows 2000 Server, and administrative settings.

8. Close the **Group Policy** console.

9. Click **Close**. You have now implemented a Group Policy object for the organizational unit.

   ☑ **Note** For more information about Group Policy objects, refer to Chapter 23, "Defining Client Administration and Configuration Standards," in the *Windows 2000 Server Resource Kit Deployment Planning Guide*. You can also refer to Part 3, "System Configuration and Management," in the *Windows 2000 Professional Resource Kit*.

Windows 2000 Professional Clients

Using Windows 2000 Professional clients is a "best practice" implementation of Small Business Server 2000. Not only do you receive the benefits of better hardware detection, greater stability, and better multimedia support at the user desktop, but you also can fully implement Windows 2000 Server features. In addition, Windows 2000 Professional clients can run applications designed specifically for Windows 2000 by independent software vendors (ISVs).

Windows 2000 Professional requires a higher level of hardware than other Microsoft desktop operating systems, a fact the technology consultant will not want to overlook when planning a Small Business Server 2000 network. For more information, refer to the Windows 2000 Professional Web site at: http://www.microsoft.com/windows2000/.

Two benefits of using Windows 2000 Professional clients on a Small Business Server network are the ability to deploy applications and the ability to lock down workstations by using Group Policy objects.

Deploying Applications

A key feature of Group Policy is the ability to deploy applications by using the Assign and Publish tool. You can install applications on the Windows 2000 Professional client when the user logs on, but more importantly, you can centrally deploy application upgrades in a similar manner. This saves the technology consultant time when bug fixes, service packs, and new applications are released. The Group Policy Assign and Publish tool can also be configured to install an application on different computers when the user "roves" from computer to computer. This feature is especially beneficial when a user gets a new computer. The technology consultant can minimize the time needed for application installations.

> **Note** The Group Policy Assign and Publish tool is different from the application installation capability of the Small Business Server Set Up Computer Wizard. Group Policy Assign and Publish is a very sophisticated tool that requires a Microsoft Silent Installation (.msi) file for each application being installed. Group Policy Assign and Publish only works with Windows 2000 clients, which is a limitation. The Set Up Computer Wizard works well for installing Small Business Server client applications, such as Outlook 2000, and applications that allow unattended installations without user interaction. The Set Up Computer Wizard works with all Small Business Server–supported client platforms, including Microsoft Windows 95, Microsoft Windows 98, Microsoft Windows Me, and Windows 2000.

Locking Down Workstations

Group Policy objects enable the technology consultant to restrict what a user can do on a Windows 2000 Professional client. In secure environments, it is common to lock down a Windows 2000 Professional client computer so that only one business application can run. This lock-down strategy is also used in point-of-sale scenarios in retail environments. The ability to lock down Windows 2000 Professional clients increases the productivity of users, administrators, and technology consultants. Users are unable to run non-business applications, allowing them to stay focused on their jobs. Users also make fewer mistakes and configuration errors on Windows 2000 Professional client computers that have lock-down configurations. Administrators and technology consultants spend less time troubleshooting, repairing, and rebuilding Windows 2000 Professional clients that have lock-down configurations.

Terminal Services

Terminal Services is a multifaceted solution that comes with Windows 2000 Server and is installed in Small Business Server 2000. Previously, you had to purchase Windows NT Server 4.0 Terminal Server edition to receive the remote session capabilities now provided by Terminal Services. Terminal Services supports remote connections from client computers that run the Terminal Services client.

Remote Administration Mode

By default, Small Business Server 2000 installs Terminal Services in remote administration mode, not application mode. This configuration enables up to two Terminal sessions to run so that you can perform network administration on the Small Business Server computer. This approach is designed to replace the use of Microsoft NetMeeting® on the Small Business Server computer (which was the remote control network administration solution in previous editions of Small Business Server). Terminal Services should remain in remote administration mode on the Small Business Server 2000 computer to avoid placing undue strain on the computer's memory and processor resources.

Application Mode

Many technology consultants would like to provide their customers a Terminal Services solution to run business applications from remote locations. This is best accomplished by purchasing another copy of Windows 2000 Server with the appropriate number of licenses and installing it as a non-domain controller server on another powerful business-class server computer. That allows another server to be responsible for the heavy processing workload of Terminal sessions.

Using Terminal Services for Remote Administration

To use Terminal Services for remote administration, you can run the Terminal Services client setup program across the network by performing the following steps.

To use Terminal Services for remote administration

1. On a client computer, log on to the Small Business Server network.

2. On the desktop, double-click **Network Neighborhood** if you are using a computer running Windows 95 or Windows 98, or double-click **My Network Places** if you are using a computer running Windows Me or Windows 2000.

3. Browse to the Small Business Server computer. Double-click the computer icon to display the shared resources on the computer.

4. Open the **TSClient** shared folder.

5. Open the **Net** folder.

6. If you have a 32-bit client computer, open the **win32** folder. If you have a 16-bit client computer, such as Microsoft Windows 3.x, open the **win16** folder.

7. Run **Setup.exe**.

8. On the **Terminal Services Client Setup** page, click **Continue.**

9. On the **Name and Organization Information** page, type a name and organization, and then click **OK**. To confirm the name and organization, click **OK**.

10. On the **License Agreement** page, click **I Agree**.

11. Click the **setup** button.

12. Click **OK** on the completion dialog box that appears. You have now installed the Terminal Services client on a client computer.

13. You can also create the Terminal Services client disks and then install the Terminal Services client at the client workstation. Do so when using disks is more convenient than installing over a network connection.

To create a Terminal Services client disk and install Terminal Services at a client workstation

1. Log on to the Small Business Server computer as an administrator.

2. Click **Start**, point to **Programs**, point to **Administrative Tools**, and then click **Terminal Services Client Creator**.

3. Select the type of network client that you want to create (16-bit or 32-bit), select the destination floppy drive, and then click **OK**.

4. Insert the first and second floppy disks when asked, and then click **OK**.

5. When the **Network Client Administrator** dialog box appears, click **OK** to confirm that two floppy disks were created.

6. On the client computer, click **Start**, click **Run**, and then type *a:\setup* (where *a:* is the floppy disk drive letter).

7. On the **Terminal Services Client Setup** page, click **Continue**.

8. On the **Name and Organization Information** page, type a name and organization, and then click **OK**. To confirm the name and organization, click **OK**.

9. On the **License Agreement** page, click **I Agree**.

10. Click the **setup** button.

11. When asked, insert Terminal Services Client Setup Disk 2, and then click **OK**.

12. Click **OK** on the completion dialog box that appears. You have now installed the Terminal Services client on a client computer.

To start a Terminal session from the client computer with the Small Business Server 2000 computer

1. Click **Start**, point to **Programs**, point to **Terminal Services Client**, and then click **Terminal Services Client**.

2. In the **Available Servers** list, select the Small Business Server computer. Modify the Terminal session screen resolution area (for example, 800x600) if necessary, and then click **Connect**.

3. In the **Terminal Services** session window, in the **Log On to Windows** dialog box, type your user name and password. You have now successfully started a remote session with Terminal Services.

Terminal Services Manager

You manage Terminal Services with the Terminal Services Manager. To do so, click **Start**, and then click **Administrative Tools** on the Small Business Server 2000 computer. With Terminal Services Manager, you can view connected computers and open files. You can also terminate Terminal sessions that do not properly log off with Terminal Services Manager.

☑ **Note** For more information about Terminal Services, refer to Chapter 16, "Deploying Terminal Services," in the *Windows 2000 Server Resource Kit Deployment Planning Guide.*

Terminal Services WebConsole

A Web-based Terminal Services session can be started inside a Microsoft Internet Explorer Web browser by typing the following URL in the Address field of the Internet Explorer Web browser on a client computer on the Small Business Server network:

http://<server name>/myconsole

where <server name> is the name of the Small Business Server computer. At this point, the Terminal Services WebConsole starts, enabling you to initiate a Terminal Services session and log on to the Small Business Server network.

☑ **Note** Myconsole directory is a virtual directory in Microsoft Internet Information Services (IIS).

Scripting

With the inclusion of Windows Script Host (WSH), scripting in Windows 2000 Server is much improved over Windows NT Server 4.0. WSH enables administrators and users to automate actions, such as setting environmental variables for use by applications and making network connections and disconnections. WSH enables direct execution of Microsoft Visual Basic® Script, Java, and other scripts from the user interface or command line.

☑ **Note** For more information about scripting in Windows 2000 Server, refer to Chapter 7, "Introduction to Configuration and Management," in the *Windows 2000 Professional Resource Kit.*

Security

Windows 2000 Server offers many security improvements over Windows NT Server 4.0. Although many of these security improvements are most relevant to the large enterprise, small businesses running Small Business Server 2000 also benefit. The primary Windows 2000 Server security features are listed in Table 14.1.

Table 14.1   Windows 2000 Server Security Features

Feature	Description
Kerberos V5 trust	A PKI-based security solution that uses complex encryption algorithms.
Kerberos V5 network logon authentication	The logon security model in Windows 2000 Server.
Universal security groups	A type of group in Windows 2000 Server oriented toward larger enterprise deployments.
Group Policy fully integrated with Active Directory	Group Policy is full integrated and protected by Active Directory.
Delegation (administration, management functions)	The ability to delegate administrative responsibilities at the organizational unit level prevents users from having complete administrative permissions at the domain level.
PKI	A strong encryption security model.
Encrypting File System (EFS)	EFS enables local protection of sensitive data without a network-based security authority being present. For example, a laptop user could encrypt local data so that if the laptop is lost, the data cannot be compromised.
Internet Protocol Security (IPSec)	IPSec enables host-to-host IP-based secure tunnel configurations to prevent intrusion attempts.
Remote access network logon authentication based on public key technology and Smart Card logon.	Ensures secure remote network access.
Share-level Security	Share-level security based on user and group membership.
NTFS Security	NTFS security based on user and group membership.
Certificate Services	Windows 2000 Server can easily be configured as a certificate server.

☑ **Note**   Windows 2000 Server security is complex. For more information, refer to Chapter 11, "Planning Distributed Security," and Chapter 12, "Planning Your Public Key Infrastructure," in the *Windows 2000 Server Resource Kit Deployment Planning Guide.*

Summary

This chapter introduced Windows 2000 Server, the underlying network operating system in Small Business Server 2000. The following topics were discussed:

- Defining Active Directory
- Defining and creating organizational units
- Defining groups
- Defining Group Policy objects
- Windows 2000 Professional client computers on a Small Business Server network
- Terminal Services for remote administration
- Using scripting on a Small Business Server network

CHAPTER 15

Small Business Server Wizard Processes

Microsoft® Small Business Server uses wizards to streamline and automate administrative tasks. The wizards combine multiple administrative tasks into a few steps, within a single interface. They operate across the server applications of the Small Business Server platform to automatically configure them.

The processes of Small Business Server 2000 wizards are typically transparent to the technology consultant. The sections that follow present the background processes of the wizards, with a primary focus on the Add User Wizard. Some of the Microsoft Windows® 2000 Server wizards are also discussed. One of the major enhancements in Windows 2000 Server, the underlying operating system in Small Business Server 2000, is the extensive use of wizards compared to previous Microsoft business operating systems, such as Microsoft Windows NT® Server 4.0.

Add User Wizard Architecture

The Small Business Server 2000 Add User Wizard architecture is described in this section. Note that most other Small Business Server wizards are not as lengthy and complex as the Add User Wizard, by using both default (common) and unique information. Typically, other Small Business Server wizards do not offer default information, emphasizing unique information input instead.

The Add User Wizard architecture is discussed in this section; the detailed step-by-step use of the wizard is discussed in the Console Wizards section later in the chapter.

User Interface

Wizards rely on the user interface (UI) to display information in a step-by-step manner. The early screens of a wizard request unique information—for example, in the Add User Wizard, this includes First Name, Last Name, Logon name, and so on—and the later screens of a wizard request confirmation of common information. Common information consists of group memberships, remote access settings, and so on, which are common to all users or computer, depending on the type of wizard. In between the unique information that is initially requested) and the common information that is requested later, Small Business Server wizards often have a transition page. In the Add User Wizard, the transition page contains standard user templates. It is from these templates that common information is derived for future wizard pages. For example, common user information may be selected from a template presented on the User Properties page of the Add User Wizard. The Add User Wizard UI architecture is shown in Figure 15.1.

Figure 15.1 Add User Wizard architecture, displaying unique and identical information

Behavior

In Figure 15.2, the technology consultant starts the Add User Wizard from the Small Business Server Microsoft Management Console (MMC-based) console (the Add User Wizard is available from both the Small Business Server Administrator Console and Small Business Server Personal Console). After you click on the Add User task icon, multiple variables can be passed through Adduser.vbs (a Microsoft Visual Basic® script) command line to the Addusr.exe file. Three of the commonly used parameters are identified in Table 15.1. The Addusr.exe file is the Add User Wizard as it appears on the client computer's desktop.

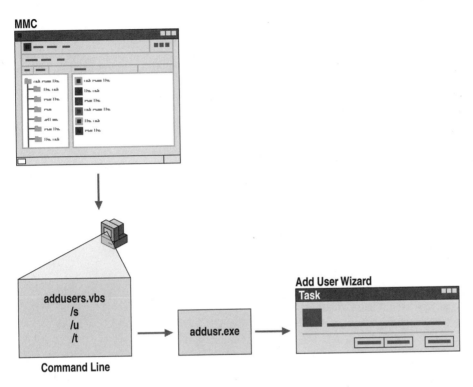

Figure 15.2 Add User Wizard processing architecture

Table 15.1 Adduser.vbs command-line variables

Variable	Description
/s	Simple Mode. This is the default condition for the Small Business Server Personal Console. The Small Business Server Administrator Console, however, does not use this command-line variable. The command line hides complex information and makes default selections in the background.
/u	Located in Microsoft Active Directory™ directory service where the user is created.
/t	Modifies the display of user templates. By default, the user templates contained in the Microsoft BackOffice® Templates Users group are displayed. You could modify this parameter to point to a different group containing user templates, which are effectively user accounts. Users of this new group you are pointing to would then be displayed and available as a user template selection in the Add User Wizard.

✍ **Note** Developers can customize setup processes of the Small Business Server wizard architecture. For information, refer to "Appendix C: Customization and Extensibility Options."

User Templates

User templates represent the transition between unique and common information. At mid-point in the Add User Wizard process, the technology consultant can select an existing user template, create a template, or proceed without a template—effectively providing unique information for the entire Add User Wizard process instead of leveraging the default templates.

Starting Additional Wizards

Small Business Server 2000 wizards often start other wizards through a process known as chaining. This is normal and by design. For example, the Add User Wizard starts the Set Up Computer Wizard so the technology consultant can create a computer for the newly added user.

Console Wizards

The following console wizards are used during Small Business Server administration:

- Add User Wizard
- Add Distribution Group Wizard
- Add Security Group Wizard
- Add Shared Folder Wizard
- Migrate User Wizard
- Set Up Computer Wizard
- Small Business Server Internet Connection Wizard

  ☑ **Note** Usability studies and experience have shown that the Add User Wizard is the most popular and frequently used wizard in Small Business Server. This is followed by the Set Up Computer Wizard.

The steps each console wizard follows to perform its task are described in the following sections.

Add User Wizard

The Add User Wizard simplifies the creation of a fully functional user account, which helps the technology consultant reduce the time and steps needed to:

- Add a fully functional Windows 2000 user account and password to Active Directory.
- Create an Exchange 2000 Server mailbox for the user.
- Assign the user to one or more distribution groups.
- Assign the user to one or more security groups.
- Grant the user access to network resources and applications (shared folders, shared printers, computers, fax printers, modems, and network connections).
- Deploy software on the user's computer.
- Train a power user, through the Small Business Server Personal Console, to perform the steps necessary to add a user to the network.

The Add User Wizard can be started from several locations in Small Business Server 2000, including:

- **BackOffice To Do List** page in the Small Business Server Administrator Console.
- **Active Directory** link on the **Small Business Server Tips** page in the Small Business Server Administrator Console.
- **Add User** link on the **Users** page in Small Business Server Personal Console.

The steps of the wizard process follow.

To create a user account using the Add User Wizard

1. Start the Add User Wizard from any of the locations just listed.
2. On the **Welcome to the Add User Wizard** page, click **Next**.
3. On the **User Account Information** page, type basic user information, including first and last name, telephone, office location, and logon name. Click **Next**.

4. On the **Password Generation** page, type password information and account conditions, and then click **Next**.

> ☑ **Note** You may disable an account on the **Password Generation** page by selecting the **Account is disabled** check box.

5. On the **Mailbox Information** page, select the **Create a mailbox** check box and confirm or change the default e-mail alias, Exchanger Server, and Exchange store information, and then click **Next**.

6. On the **User Properties** page, complete information, and then click **Next**. This page enables you to select a user template to implement generic settings for the user. You may view and modify the template details by selecting the **View the template to change properties for this user** check box. The templates that you select from include:

   - Small Business Administrator. Administrators have full access to the computer and domain.

   - Small Business Power User. Power users have all user rights. They can manage users, groups, printers, shared folders, and faxes. They also have Internet access and can log on to the Small Business Server 2000 server computer.

   - Small Business User. Users have access to all printers, shared folders, and fax devices, and they have Internet access.

   > ☑ **Note** Selecting a template results in permissions and settings being applied to the user. By default, you are not presented with the following specific pages for configuration. However, if the **View the template to change properties for this user** check box is selected as described in the preceding Step 6, these pages are displayed and can be modified.

   - Group Membership

   - E-Mail Distribution Groups

   - Address Information

   - Connection Access (for remote access and Terminal Services)

To avoid applying generic template-based permission settings to the user, select **Specify individual settings for this user**. When you select the **Use these settings to create a new template** check box, the new setting that you specify may also be used to create a custom template for future use. You may find custom templates particularly helpful in situations where you specify application-specific settings, such as granting certain permissions to specified users to run an accounting application.

> ☑ **Note**   You can also create a user template by taking an existing user account and making that account a member of the BackOffice Users Templates security group. The user account is then displayed as an available user template on the **User Properties** page.

7. On the **Run the Set Up Computer Wizard** page, choose whether to set up a computer now or later, and then click **Next**.

    If you decide to set up the computer now, the Set Up Computer Wizard is spawned and computer set up information is collected. The Set Up Computer Wizard is discussed later in this chapter. If you decide to set up the computer later, proceed to the next step.

8. Click **Finish** to complete the Add User Wizard.

Add Group Wizards

In Small Business Server 2000, there are two types of Add Group Wizards:

- Add Distribution Group Wizard

- Add Security Group Wizard

The goals for both wizards are to simplify the creation of groups for the technology consultant and power users, and to improve the efficiency of the native Windows 2000 Add Group Wizard.

Add Distribution Group Wizard

The technology consultant or power user may use the Add Distribution Group Wizard to create or modify Exchange 2000 Server distribution groups. The wizard may be started from either of the following locations:

- Small Business Server Administrator Console, **Favorites** tab, **Small Business Server Tips** page, **Exchange 2000 Server** link.

- Small Business Server Personal Console, **E-mail** page, **Add E-mail Group** link.

The steps of the wizard process follow.

To create a distribution group using the Add Distribution Group Wizard

1. Start the Add Distribution Group Wizard from any of the locations just listed.

2. On the **Welcome to the Add Distribution Group Wizard** page, click **Next**.

3. On the **Group Identity** page, complete the information shown in Figure 15.3, and click **Next**.

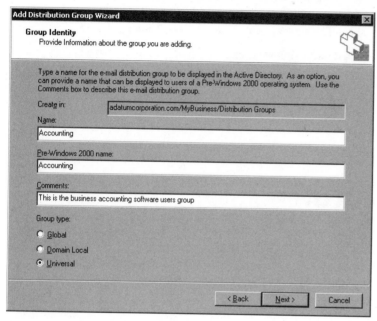

Figure 15.3   Defining and naming your distribution group

4. On the **Membership** page, add members to this distribution group. This may be any available user or group.

5. Click **Next**.

6. Click **Finish** to complete the wizard.

Add Security Group Wizard

The technology consultant or power user can use the Add Security Group Wizard to create or modify security groups. The wizard can be started from either of the following locations:

*   Small Business Server Administrator Console, **Favorites** tab, **Small Business Server Tips**, **Active Directory** page, **Add Security Group** link.

*   Small Business Server Personal Console, **Security Groups** page, **Add Group** link.

The steps of the wizard process follow.

To create a security group using the Add Security Group Wizard

1. Start the Add Distribution Group Wizard from any of the locations just listed.

2. On the Welcome to the Add Security Group Wizard page, click Next.

3. On the Group Identity page, type a group name and select a group type, and then click Next.

   Global. Can contain members only from the domain containing Global Groups and users (including contacts).

   Domain local. Can contain members from Global Groups, Universal Groups, and users (including contacts).

4. On the **Membership** page, add members to this distribution group. This may be any available user or group.

5. Click **Next**.

6. Click **Finish** to complete the wizard.

Add Shared Folder Wizard

The Add Shared Folder Wizard can be used to share an existing folder or to create a new folder, and then share it. The wizard can be started from either of the following locations:

- Small Business Server Administrator Console, **Favorites** tab, **Small Business Server Tips**, **Active Directory** page, **Add Share Folder** link.

- Small Business Server Personal Console, **Shared Folders** page, **Add Folder** link.

The steps of the wizard process follow.

To share a folder using the Add Shared Folder Wizard

1. Start the Add Shared Folder Wizard from the **Shared Folders** taskpad in the Small Business Server Personal Console.

2. On the **Welcome to the Add Shared Folder Wizard** page, click **Next**.

3. On the **Folder Identity** page, type a folder path, share name, and optional comments, and then click **Next**.

4. On the **Permissions** page, select from the list of available groups and users. Also, select the permissions for the groups and the users who can access the shared folder, and then click **Next**.

5. Click **Finish** to complete the wizard.

   Note Security on shared folders is enforced through the file system. Share permission is set to Everyone = Full access, so that everyone can see the share. Permissions are set on the file system itself (folders and files) so that if the share is removed, the permissions still exist.

Migrate User Wizard

The Migrate User Wizard is a three-page wizard used to migrate existing Windows 2000-based accounts into Small Business Server 2000. You have the ability to migrate user accounts, user e-mail mailboxes, and group settings (including adding the migrated user to existing groups). The Migrate User Wizard is started from the BackOffice **To Do List** in the Small Business Server Administrator Console.

> ☑ **Note** You can use the Moveuser.exe tool in the Windows 2000 Server Resource Kit to move users between Windows NT domains, in preparation for migration to a Windows 2000 Server-based network, such as Small Business Server 2000. For example, you might use this tool to move users from multiple Windows NT domains to a single domain, to adhere to the one-domain limitation in Small Business Server 2000.

Small Business Server Internet Connection Wizard

For a description of the background processes of the Internet Connection Wizard, refer to Chapter 11, "ISP Connectivity Tasks."

Windows 2000 Server Wizards

When logged on as an administrator, the technology consultant has full access to all Windows 2000 Server wizards. There are many enhanced wizards available with Windows 2000 Server. For example, one wizard, the Upgrade Device Driver Wizard, enables you to update your device drivers. This wizard is shown in Figure 15.4.

Figure 15.4   The Upgrade Device Driver Wizard is Windows 2000-based

Set Up Computer Wizard

The Set Up Computer Wizard creates and configures all necessary files and settings to process client logons and install client applications. The wizard starts the following server-based files:

- **SCW.exe.**The Set Up Computer Wizard.

- **SCWdll.dll.** All wizard components for the Set Up Computer Wizard are implemented through this dynamic link library.

The Set Up Computer Wizard initiates the client computer setup from the server. The SCW.exe file starts the Set Up Computer Wizard, which uses the Wizard Setup Engine   (WSE) developed for Small Business Server 2000.

Computer Account

The Set Up Computer Wizard creates a Windows 2000 computer account for the client if one does not already exist. Setup does not distinguish between Windows 2000 Professional, Windows Me, Windows 98, Windows 95, and Windows NT Workstation client computers, even though Windows Me, Windows 98, and Windows 95 clients do not require a computer account to access a Windows 2000 domain. All of the computer accounts created are Windows 2000 Professional or Server accounts.

Configuring Client Networking

The Set Up Computer Wizard creates client installation files and a Networking Setup Disk for use on the client computer.

Client installation files that are created, but not placed on the floppy disk, are as follows:

- **SBSClnt.exe**. This file replaces the Startcli.exe in previous versions of Small Business Server. This program, also known as Application Launcher (and App Launcher), performs the following tasks:

  a. Checks for applications that need to be installed.

  b. Enables the user to install the applications now or later (if applications are to be installed).

  c. Checks whether the computer receiving the installed applications is running as a Windows 2000 Terminal Services computer. If so, the computer is placed in Terminal Services application installation mode.

  d. Verifies and creates, as necessary, numerous registry entries for user information, user and company shortcut creation, Microsoft Internet Explorer 5.0 configuration settings, and Microsoft Outlook® 2000 configuration settings. These entries are found under HKEY_LOCAL_MACHINE\software\microsoft\small business.

  e. Confirms or denies the existence of Outlook.prf and Default.prf. These files are used in setting up Outlook for each user on the client computer.

- **SBSOSUpd.exe**. This program applies Windows NT 4.0 Service Pack 6, and the file ensures that the service pack is only applied once. The file also checks the operating system, as it only works with Windows NT-based clients—other client operating systems are ignored. A log file is created on the client computer at:

  %windir%\support\SBSOSUpdate.log

Using the Networking Setup Disk

The completed Networking Setup Disk, to be used on the client computer, contains the following five files:

- Setup.exe

- Netparam.ini

- IpDetect.exe

- Ipdx86.exe

- Ipd2000.exe

    Note   With Small Business Server 2000, you need to create only one Networking Setup Disk, as the same disk can be used on all network client computers. This is a change from Small Business Server 4.5, where each network client computer had its own client configuration floppy disk.

Setup.exe

On the client computer, run Setup.exe from the floppy disk, by using information from the Netparam.ini file. Setup.exe creates a setup log on the client computer, found at:

%windir%\support\SBSNetworkinggSetup.log

Setup.exe displays three pages for user input:

- **Computers page**. Displays a list of known computers, obtained from the Netparam.ini file. You can select a computer name or type a new computer name.

- **Users page**. Enables you to add users to the Windows 2000 local administrator's group, entitled Administrators. You can select multiple users from a list of known users, obtained from the Netparam.ini file. This page is not displayed in Windows Me, Windows 98, or Windows 95 client computers.

- **Admin credentials page**. Enables you to type a user name and password, with authority for the client computer to join the domain. This page is only displayed for Windows 2000 or Windows NT client computers.

Setup.exe updates the Netparam.ini file and then runs IpDetect.exe for Windows 95 and Windows 98 clients, Ipdx86.exe for Windows NT 4.0 clients, and Ipd2000.exe for Windows 2000 clients.

Netparam.ini

When Setup.exe starts, setup data is read from Netparam.ini on the floppy disk. This is a text file that contains configuration information. At the end of the Setup.exe process, the Netparam.ini file is updated with the selected computer name and user name. The name is then provided to the Admin credentials page.

IpDetect.exe

IpDetect.exe, Ipd2000.exe, and Ipdx86.exe provide similar functions for different client operating systems. IpDetect.exe reads the computer name and domain information from the Netparam.ini file. The client computer is renamed and the workgroup name is changed to the Small Business Server domain name. IpDetect.exe performs the following actions:

- Invokes the native network card selection screen of Windows 95 and Windows 98

- Installs TCP/IP networking protocol

- Installs client for Microsoft networking

- Installs file and print sharing

IpDetect.exe writes information to the following log on the client computer:

> %systemdrive%/IPDETECT.log

Ipdx86.exe

Ipdx86.exe reads the computer name from the Netparam.ini file and joins Windows NT client computers to the Small Business Server domain. Ipdx86.exe installs the following, as necessary:

- Network adapter card

- TCP/IP protocol

- Client for Microsoft networking

- File and print sharing

Ipdx86.exe does not create a log file. One update in Ipdx86.exe for Small Business Server 2000 is that the ADMINS key is read from Netparam.ini, and all its users are added to the Windows NT local administrators group, entitled Administrators.

> **Note** The client computer name account must already exist on the Small Business Server computer before Ipdx86.exe is used to join the domain. In addition, the client computer name cannot have been used before—there is no recycling of computer names. This can be problematic if a client computer is replaced with a new computer and the user wants to retain the same computer name.

Former Windows NT Workstation client computers might require an intermediate restart in order to fully configure their network, so Ipdx86.exe might create **RunOnce** entries to handle the continuation of setup.

Ipd2000.exe

The Ipd2000.exe file configures networking on a Windows 2000 computer by completing the following tasks:

- Installs a network card with Network Driver Interface Specification (NDIS) drivers (only one network card can be installed).

- Installs TCP/IP.

- Sets TCP/IP to access a DHCP server.

- Binds TCP/IP to the network interface card (NIC).

- Changes the computer name. Reads the computer name from Netparam.ini.

- Changes the domain name to the Small Business Server domain name, based on information read from the Netparam.ini file.

- Changes the workgroup name for Windows 95 and Windows 98 client computers.

- Sets Windows 2000 domain name.

- Installs client for Microsoft networking.

- Installs file and print sharing.

- Joins the domain (Windows 2000 clients and Windows NT Workstation only). Verifies that the computer name is unique and not already in use.

- Adds users to the local administrators group, entitled Administrators. Reads the ADMINS key from the Netparam.ini file.

Installing Applications on the Client

The Application Launcher, SBSClnt.exe, installs applications on the client computer. This file, discussed earlier in this chapter, checks to see if the client computer requires applications to be installed by reading the Apps.ini file in the client computer's Response folder. After reading the Apps.ini file, the Application Launcher does the following:

- If no response directory for the computer exists, or if the Apps.ini file is missing, Application Launcher quits.

- If the client computer does not need applications to be installed, Application Launcher quits.

- If the client computer requires applications to be installed, Application Launcher checks to see if the client computer is a Terminal Services server. If so, it changes the Terminal Server to application install mode. Application Launcher changes the Terminal Server back to normal mode before quitting.

- Next, a dialog box appears, asking you to click either **Start Now** or **Postpone**. If you are working across a slow link or do not want to install applications at this time, click **Postpone**. Each time users log on from that client computer, they will see this dialog box until they install the applications.

Summary

This chapter provided technical information for the technology consultant to better understand what Small Business Server 2000 wizards are and how they function. Typically wizards appear in a simple user interface, yet they run complex processes in the background. Topics discussed in this chapter include:

- Wizard architecture

- Console wizards

- Windows 2000 wizards

- Detailed architectural view of the Set Up Computer Wizard

CHAPTER 16

Terminal Services and Group Policy Administration

Small Business Server 2000 provides strong administration tools that let the technology consultant work on-site or off-site for the customer. These tools include Terminal Services, Microsoft® NetMeeting®, and Group Policy, the subjects of this chapter.

Remote Administration with Terminal Services

By running Terminal Services on a computer with Microsoft Small Business Server 2000 and an appropriately configured Terminal Services client installed, the technology consultant can manage the network either on-site or off-site, speeding customer response time.

Introducing Terminal Services

Terminal Services is installed and configured in remote administration mode as part of Small Business Server 2000 Setup. The underlying Windows 2000 Server operating system is modified to support a multi-session kernel. This enables multiple computing sessions to run simultaneously on the same computer. Each session runs as a virtual computer with its own memory space. Access to the processors is managed by Microsoft Windows® 2000 in a time-sliced, priority-based fashion.

Terminal Server also facilitates a remote control connection. Compare this to the traditional remote node connection facilitated by Routing and Remote Access Service (RRAS). In Terminal Services' remote control scenario, the technology consultant interacts with the "desktop" of the Small Business Server computer. All features and functions are available, but only screens depicting the desktop activity, keystrokes, and mouse movements are passed between the server and the remote client.

> ☑ **Note** Because Terminal Services transmits only screen images between the server and remote client, additional network traffic such as broadcast-based activity, packets sent to node address FFFFFFFF, is not forwarded. A traditional remote node connection that uses RRAS enables broadcast traffic to be sent to the remote client. The form of traffic filtering used by Terminal Services results in significantly higher remote communications performance than node-based RRAS connections under most connection scenarios.

Small Business Server 2000 supports Terminal Services in remote administration mode, not application mode. Remote administration mode is designed to minimize the impact on the operating system and the server computer by limiting the number of concurrent connections. Likewise, it is not recommended that Terminal Services run in application mode on Small Business Server 2000 because the demand on the server resources is considered too great.

Terminal Services Scenarios

The following are common Terminal Services scenarios in Small Business Server.

Remote Administration

Terminal Services is intended primarily to enable the Small Business Server 2000 technology consultant to connect to the customer's server from remote locations. For example, the technology consultant might maintain a business office separate from customer locations. He or she might also be traveling and could perform remote administration from a laptop computer.

☑ **Note** The recommended way to make a remote connection to Terminal Services occurs in two stages. First, a connection to the customer's local area network must be established. The two most common methods for connecting are dialing in to the Small Business Server computer running the RRAS by modem and connecting through a virtual private network (VPN) session (using RRAS) over the Internet. After a remote connection has been established, the Terminal Services client application on the remote computer is used to establish a Terminal Services session. Note that a VPN session for an Internet-based connection is not required but is recommended to increase security.

On-site Remote Desktop Administration

If the small business customer site is dispersed over several floors or significant distances, such as a manufacturing plant or a car dealership, the technology consultant can use a client computer to perform on-site remote administration.

Same Server Terminal Service Sessions

Before deploying new applications or desktop settings (such as Group Policy-based settings), it is often wise to perform tests. One such test is to install the Terminal Services client directly on the server computer and run a Terminal Services session for testing purposes.

☑ **Note** This may place a significant workload on the Small Business Server computer.

Application Mode

Some small businesses can benefit from having a second Windows 2000 Server computer for users to use for Terminal Services sessions. The computer could be used for such applications as an accounting program, a tax preparation program, or a business database. One benefit of running applications through a Terminal Services session is that the session can persist despite a lost connection. For example, if a tax preparer was working from home after hours to prepare tax returns, and the remote connection was lost during this session, the completed work would not be lost. When reconnected, the tax preparer would be returned to the previous Terminal Services session, with the work in progress displayed on the screen.

Another scenario includes thin clients, which are typically cheaper to deploy and maintain. A second server can also be used to enforce Terminal Services profiles and use Group Policy. One example of using a thin client in conjunction with Terminal Services profiles and Group Policy is retail point-of-sale. Here, a thin client acts as a cash register, and employees cannot misuse the computer system.

> ✔ **Note** The technology consultant should implement Terminal Services in application mode on a second, power server-class computer running as a non-domain controller Windows 2000 Server. Terminal Services session running on the Small Business Server 2000 computer is designed to run in remote administration mode, not application mode.

Web-based Remote Administration

Using a Microsoft ActiveX® control, a Terminal Services session can run on an Internet Explorer Web page. This lets the technology consultant gain access to the server from any desktop without needing to install the Terminal Services client.

It is also possible to expose the ActiveX control to the Internet, allowing the technology consultant to log on from any computer connected to the Internet and running the Internet Explorer browser. However, this is not considered a best practice because it potentially exposes the Small Business Server network to the Internet in unintended ways.

Configuring Terminal Services

Terminal Services is installed and deployed in remote administration mode by default in Small Business Server 2000. This is different from a standard Windows 2000 Server installation, in which Terminal Services is not installed by default.

Power users and administrators are granted access to Terminal Services and have permission to log on to the Terminal Services server. Users are not granted this permission by default.

Terminal Services is primarily configured and managed with two tools: Terminal Services Manager and Terminal Services Configuration.

Terminal Services Manager

Terminal Services Manager is a tool that enables you to monitor the logon status of remote users at a glance. It also enables you to observe which resources, such as open files, a remote user is using. Terminal Services Manager is shown in Figure 16.1.

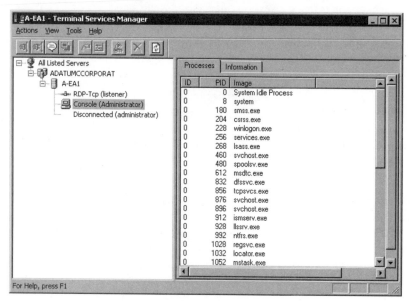

Figure 16.1 Terminal Services Manager

You can use Terminal Services Manager to send messages to or disconnect Terminal Services users. This is useful when the occasional Terminal Services session does not properly terminate. The Terminal Services Manager is accessed from the Administrative Tools program group, not from the Small Business Server consoles.

To start Terminal Services Manager

- Click **Start**, point to **Programs**, point to **Administrative Tools**, and then click **Terminal Services Manager**.

Terminal Services Configuration

This tool is less frequently used than Terminal Services Manager and is used primarily to configure the Remote Desktop Protocol (RDP) and server settings, such as specific Terminal Services computer-based Group Policy.

To use Terminal Services Configuration

1. Click **Start**, point to **Programs**, point to **Microsoft Small Business Server**, and then click **Small Business Server Administrator Console**.

2. In the Console Tree, click **Terminal Services Configuration**.

3. In the Details Pane, configure **Server Settings**.

Terminal Services Configuration can also be accessed from the Configure Access for Terminal Services link in the Small Business Administrator Console To Do List.

Terminal Services Configuration is shown in Figure 16.2.

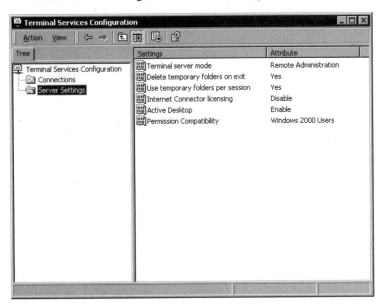

Figure 16.2 Terminal Services Configuration

Terminal Services uses RDP as its communication protocol. This is a stable protocol suite that is optimized for remote session connectivity. It is integrated with Windows 2000 Server down to the kernel level. RDP is configured on the **RDP-tcp Properties** dialog box, which is displayed when you right-click the **RDP-tcp protocol** in the **Connections** folder and then click **Properties**. The **RDP-tcp Properties** dialog box is shown in Figure 16.3.

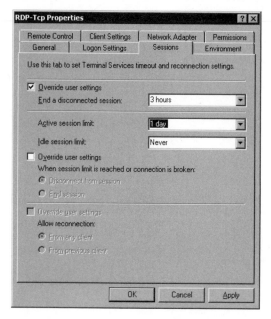

Figure 16.3 RDP protocol configurations include session settings

Client and Server Interaction with Terminal Services

The first step in Terminal Services client and server interaction is to create client disks. The client disks are used to set up the Terminal Services client-side application that enables a session between the client and server. Follow these two procedures to create the client disks.

To create Terminal Services client disks from a network share point

1. From a client computer, navigate using **My Network Places** (Windows 2000 or Windows Me) or **Network Neighborhood** (Windows 98 and Windows 95, Microsoft Windows NT®) to the Small Business Server computer.

2. Open the **TSClient** shared folder.

3. Open the **net** folder.

4. If your client computer is 32-bit, open the **win32** folder. If your computer is 16-bit, such as Windows 3.x, open the **win16** folder.

5. Run **Setup.exe.**

6. On the **Terminal Services Client Setup** page, click **Continue.**

7. On the **Name and Organization Information** page, type a name and organization, and then click **OK**. To confirm the name and organization, click **OK**.

8. On the **License Agreement** page, click **I Agree**.

9. Click the **setup** button.

10. Click **OK** in the dialog box that appears. You have now installed the Terminal Services client on a client computer.

To create Terminal Services client disks at the server computer

1. Click **Start**, point to **Administrative Tools**, and then click **Terminal Services Client Creator**.

2. In the **Create Installation Disk(s)** box, select the appropriate client environment (**16-bit Windows** or **32-bit Windows**), and then click **OK**.

   ☑ **Note**   The 16-bit option requires four floppy disks. The 32-bit option requires two floppy disks.

3. Label and insert the first floppy disk, and then click **OK**.

4. Insert additional floppy disks as instructed, and then click **OK**.

5. In the **Network Client Administrator** box, click **OK** to acknowledge the end of the client disk creation process.

You can use the floppy disks you have just formatted to install the Terminal Services client on a client computer.

To install Terminal Services on a client computer

1. Insert the first Terminal Services client setup disk into the floppy disk drive. From the command line, type *a:\setup*, where *a* denotes the floppy disk drive.

2. On the **Welcome** page, click **Continue**.

3. Type a user and organization name in the **Name and Organization Information** field.

4. Click **OK** to proceed, and then click **OK** to confirm the user and organization name.

5. In **License Agreement**, click **I Agree**.

6. In the **Terminal Services Client Setup** box, click the large setup button. Change the installation folder, if necessary.

7. Click **Yes** to confirm that all users will have the same initial Terminal Services client-side settings.

8. When asked, insert the remaining disks, and then click **OK**.

9. Click **OK** when notified that the Terminal Services client setup was successful.

With Terminal Services running on the server and the Terminal Services client software installed on the client computer, you are ready to initiate a Terminal Services session. You should have a network connection to the server computer running Terminal Services (this could occur through the local network or with a dial-up or Internet VPN connection through RRAS).

To start a Terminal Services session

1. At the client computer, click **Start**, point to **Terminal Services Client**, and then click **Terminal Services Client**.

2. In the **Server** field, select the Terminal Services server or type in the Internet Protocol (IP) address of a Terminal Services server. Modify the screen area (800X600 minimum recommended), and then click **Connect**.

3. Type your Windows 2000 user name and password when the **Log On to Windows** dialog box appears in the Terminal Services session window. Click **OK**.

You can also create a Terminal Services client connection setting that retains the server name, screen resolution, user name, and password. Each time an administrator or power user wants to connect to Terminal Services on the Small Business Server computer, the client connection is initiated, saving time and keystrokes.

To use Client Connection Manager

1. On the client computer that has the Terminal Services client installed, click **Start**, point to **Programs**, point to **Terminal Services Client**, and then click **Client Connection Manager**.

2. On the **File** menu, click **New Connection** to start the Client Connection Manager Wizard.

3. Click **Next**.

4. Type a connection name in the **Connection Name** field on the **Create a Connection** page.

5. Type a Terminal Services server name or IP address in the **Server name or IP address** field, and then click **Next**.

6. On the **Automatic Logon** page, type domain logon credentials.

7. Type the logon account name in the **User name** field, type a password for the logon account name in the **Password** field, type a logon domain name in the **Domain** field, and then click **Next**.

8. On the **Screen Options** page, select a screen resolution. The minimum screen size recommended for sufficient desktop space in the Terminal Services session is 800 X 600. Click **Next**.

9. On the **Connection Properties** page, click **Enable data compression** if you plan to work over a slow WAN link (such as a modem).

10. Click **Cache Bitmaps** if you want to save frequently used bitmaps to your local hard disk, and then click **Next**.

11. On the **Starting a Program** page, select **Start the following program** if you want to start a program or script at Terminal Services session logon. Click **Next**.

12. On the **Icon and Program Group** page, confirm or change the icon in the **Icon** field and program group in the **Program group** field, and then click **Next**.

13. Click **Finish**, and then start the connection from the Terminal Services Client program group.

You may now log onto and create a Terminal Services session. You will interact with the Small Business Server computer as if you were sitting at the actual console. For example, you might view the Microsoft Active Directory™ directory service Users and Computers console, as shown in Figure 16.4, to modify a user account.

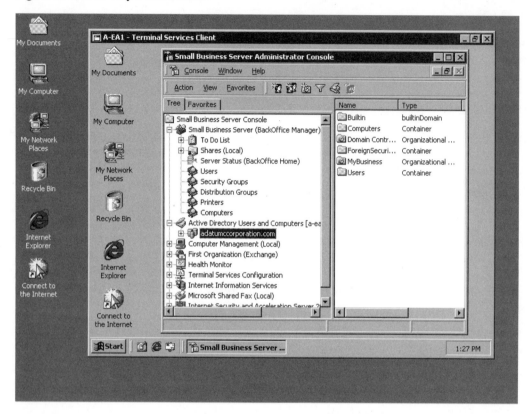

Figure 16.4   A Terminal Services session allows you access to the Small Business Server computer and its management tools

Remote Connection Considerations

You should keep in mind several remote connection issues when using Terminal Services for remote administration of the Small Business Server 2000 computer.

Screen Refresh Delays

Depending on the remote connection being used, you may experience screen refresh delays. For example, after selecting an option on the Small Business Server Administrator Console, you might experience a slight delay before the screen is refreshed. This can typically be traced to remote connection contention at the telecommunications level. This is normal.

Security

There are four security considerations when using Terminal Services:

- **Firewall port openings**. A remote access session over the Internet requires that port 3389 remain open on a firewall. This is a well-known configuration for RRAS and Terminal Services.

- **Autologon**. Terminal Services may be configured for automatic user logons. If poorly planned, this can expose a security risk in that any user can turn on a client computer and automatically log on to the Small Business Server 2000 network.

- **FTP**. It is recommended that you disable anonymous File Transfer Protocol (FTP) to prevent access to the file system. This only applies if you have installed FTP on your Small Business Server 2000 computer. Also note that FTP sends passwords as clear text. Thus, you should consider allowing anonymous access so users do not transmit logon credentials in an unsafe manner.

- **Remote Control.** This security risk applies more to scenarios in which Terminal Services is used in application mode. It is possible to configure a user account to allow remote control of a user's session without the user's explicit permission. For example, an executive's e-mail correspondence could be observed without the executive knowing it. This capability is configured in Active Directory Users and Computers on a per-account basis, as shown in Figure 16.5.

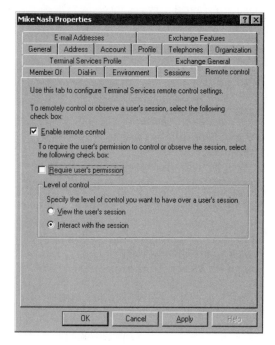

Figure 16.5 Configuring a user account for remote control

When the user account is configured to allow remote control, you can right-click an active Terminal Services session listed in Terminal Services Manager and then select Remote Control to view that active session.

WebConsole

You can run a Terminal Services session in a standard Internet Explorer browser to facilitate easy client connections. In this way, you can avoid installing the Terminal Services client application on each computer. To use WebConsole, start Internet Explorer and run the following Uniform Resource Locator (URL) command:

http://<server name>/myconsole

The WebConsole session is shown in Figure 16.6.

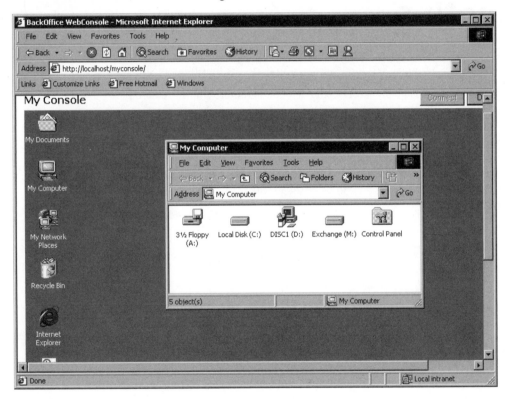

Figure 16.6 WebConsole session

Other Resources

For more information about remote administration using Terminal Services, refer to the *Windows 2000 Server Resource Kit Deployment Planning Guide*, Part 4, "Windows 2000 Upgrade and Installation."

Administration with NetMeeting

NetMeeting is included with Small Business Server 2000 even though its remote management role has largely been replaced by Terminal Services. NetMeeting performs four functions:

- **Remote Desktop Sharing**. This feature works similarly to the remote control feature in Terminal Services, but with NetMeeting, multiple users can participate in a single remote-control session. This capability is typically used for user training and collaboration. The remote-control capabilities of NetMeeting also extend to the user's desktop. For example, a user having printing difficulties could deploy NetMeeting to accept a call from the technology consultant. The technology consultant, by remote control, could fix the printing problem while the user observes the session to learn how to solve the problem.

- **Chat**. A real-time chat conference room is provided. This is useful when a conference-call-like chat session is desired.

- **Whiteboard**. This enables users to create simple drawings in real time in a paint application similar to Microsoft Paint.

- **Video**. Unicast video capabilities enable the technology consultant to interact with a customer, using a low-cost video camera, potentially improving communications between the technology consultant and customer.

    Note The video capabilities in NetMeeting are unicast, which means that a video session can occur only between two parties. Multicast video solutions, allowing multiple video participants in a conference-like format, can be deployed by acquiring Microsoft's Windows Media Services (WMS) solution.

NetMeeting is installed from the **File** menu in Internet Explorer. From **File**, point to **New**, and then click **Internet Call**.

You can download the NetMeeting Resource Kit from Microsoft's download Web site at: http://www.microsoft.com/downloads.

You can also visit Microsoft's NetMeeting Web site at: http://www.microsoft.com/windows/netmeeting/.

Group Policy

In a complete Windows 2000 scenario—that is, where all client computers on the Small Business Server 2000 network run Windows 2000 Professional—it is possible to take advantage of Group Policy. Group Policy is a way to invoke configuration settings in a manner similar to that used in previous editions of Small Business Server with System Policies and User Profiles.

> ☑ **Note** Group Policy replaces System Policies and User Profiles in Small Business Server 2000. Group Policy is often referred to as Group Policy Objects (GPO), and the terms can be used interchangeably.

Defining Group Policy

Group Policy interacts with Windows 2000 in three major ways:

- Desktop settings
- Software deployment
- Administrative settings

Desktop Settings

Desktop Group Policy settings can be applied to the computer or the user. Group Policy can be used for the following computer configurations:

- Event log settings, such as maximum log size for the application.
- Account policies, such as enforcing password history.
- Local policy configurations, such as auditing logon events.
- Computer-specific startup and shutdown scripts.
- System services, such as which services start at computer startup and which services are disabled.
- Registry entries. This is handy for implementing fixes and making additions or deletions to the Registry.
- Public Key policies, including encrypted data recovery agents.
- IP Security policies. This includes the three IPSec policies: Client (Respond Only), Secure Server (Require Security), and Server (Request Security).

Group Policy can be used for the following user configurations:

- User-based logon/logoff scripts.

- Folder redirection for application data, the desktop, My Documents, and the Start menu.

- Public Key security settings.

- Internet Explorer maintenance.

Software Deployment

Using Assign and Publish, a capability similar to the software installation capabilities of Microsoft Systems Management Server (SMS), the following software deployment capabilities are available in Group Policy for both the computer and the user.

- Installation of applications that have a Windows Installer package.

- Installation and configuration of software, using the Group Policy-based Software Installation feature.

- Upgrade, repair, and application of fixes to software, using the Group Policy-based Software Installation feature.

- Uninstallation and clean removal of software, using the Group Policy-based Software Installation feature.

- Management of installed software, including deployment and removal options and associated file extensions, using the Group Policy-based Software Installation feature.

Administrative Settings

Group Policy provides preconfigured templates that let the technology consultant efficiently deploy standard settings on Windows 2000 Professional clients and users on a Small Business Server 2000 network. These templates include:

- Windows Components (NetMeeting, Microsoft Internet Explorer, Task Scheduler, Windows Installer)

- System (Logon, Disk Quotas, Domain Name Service (DNS) Client, Group Policy, Windows File Protection)

- Network (Offline Files, Network and Dial-up Connections)

- Printers (for example, printer publishing permissions)

- Start Menu and Taskbar (for example, the ability to disable programs on the Settings Menu)

- Desktop (Active Desktop)

- Control Panel (Add/Remove Programs, Display, Printers, Regional Options)

Applying Group Policy

Group Policy may be applied to three locations:

- Sites, which typically map to the physical network or IP subnet.

- Domains, the primary administrative boundary in Windows 2000 Server.

- Organizational units, which typically reflect the functional organization's departments such as Manufacturing.

  ☑ **Note** In Small Business Server 2000, the technology consultant will most likely apply Group Policy at the organizational-unit level, given the one-domain limitation and limited number of sites.

Installing and Creating Group Policy

Group Policy is installed by using the Active Directory Users and Computers console.

To install and create Group Policy

1. Click **Start**, point to **Programs**, point to **Small Business Server Administrator Console**, and then click **Active Directory Users and Computers**.

2. Right-click the organizational unit to which you want to apply Group Policy. In Small Business Server 2000, that might be the built-in MyBusiness organizational unit.

3. Select **Properties**.

4. Click the **Group Policy** tab.

5. Click **New**. A Group Policy object link is created. Type a name for the link.

6. Select the newly named link, and then click **Edit**. The Group Policy console for the link appears, as shown in Figure 16.7.

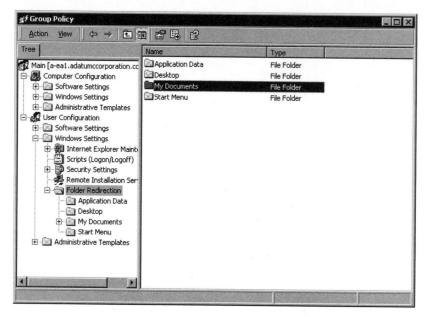

Figure 16.7   Group Policy console

7. Right-click an item that you want to configure, and then click **Properties**.

8. Configure the properties as necessary (see Figure 16.8).

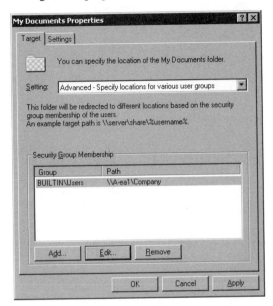

Figure 16.8 Implementing a Group Policy configuration

9. Close the **Group Policy** box.

10. Close the **Organizational Unit Properties** box.

Group Policy has now been applied to an organizational unit.

Group Policy Scenarios

Here are ten tasks the technology consultant might complete by implementing Group Policy.

Task 1.   Do not allow users to configure off-line folders.

Task 2.   Change the Internet Explorer browser title bar to "A Datum Corporation."

Task 3.   Set the Internet Explorer settings for Proxy Server to 131.107.68.11.

Task 4.   Run a logon script named SBS1.bat.

Task 5.   Disable Control Panel.

Task 6.   Direct desktop properties to different locations. Move the contents of this desktop to the new location.

Task 7.   Redirect the My Documents folder to a new location on the network.

Task 8.   Do not save desktop settings upon quitting.

Task 9.   Disable the "Run only allowed Windows applications" command.

Task 10.   Limit the application log size to 1,024 kilobytes.

The initial steps to complete each task

1. Log on to the Small Business Server 2000 computer as an administrator.

2. Click **Start**, point to **Programs**, point to **Microsoft Small Business Server, Small Business Server Administrator Console**.

3. Click **Active Directory Users and Computers**.

4. Right-click an organizational unit (for example, MyBusiness), and then click **Properties**.

5. Click the **Group Policy** tab.

6. If a Group Policy object has been created, highlight it in the **Group Policy Object Links** list, and then click **Edit** to start the Group Policy console.

You are now ready to complete each task.

Task 1. To prevent users from configuring off-line folders

1. In the Console Tree, expand **User Configuration**.

2. Click **Administrative Templates**.

3. Click **Network**.

4. Click **Offline Files**.

5. Double-click **Disable user configuration of Offline Files**.

6. Select **Enabled**.

7. Click **OK**.

Task 2. To change the Internet Explorer browser title bar to "A Datum Corporation"

1. In the Console Tree, expand **User Configuration**.

2. Click **Windows Settings**.

3. Click **Internet Explorer Maintenance**.

4. Click **Browser User Interface**.

5. Double-click **Browser Title**.

6. Select the **Customize Title Bars** check box, and then type the following text in the **Title Bar Text** box: *A Datum Corporation*.

7. Click **OK**.

Task 3. To set the Internet Explorer settings for Proxy Server to 131.107.68.11

1. In the Console Tree, expand **User Configuration**.

2. Expand **Windows Settings**.

3. In the **Internet Explorer Maintenance** folder, select **Connections**.

4. Double-click **Proxy Settings**.

5. Select **Enable Proxy Settings**.

6. Under **Address of Proxy**, type *131.107.68.11*. The **Use the same proxy server for all addresses** box should be selected so that the same proxy server is used for all protocols.

7. Click **OK**.

Task 4. To run a logon script named SBS1.bat

1. In the Console Tree, expand **User Configuration**.

2. Expand **Windows Settings**.

3. Click **Scripts (Logon/Logoff)**.

4. In the Details Pane, double-click **Logon**.

5. Click **Add**. The **Add a Script** box appears.

6. In the **Script Name** box, type *SBS1.bat*.

7. Click **OK**, then click **OK** again to close the **Logon Properties** box.

Task 5. To disable Control Panel

1. In the Console Tree, expand **User Configuration**.

2. Click **Administrative Templates**.

3. Click **Control Panel**.

4. Double-click **Disable Control Panel**.

5. Select **Enabled**.

6. Click **OK**.

Task 6. To direct desktop properties to different locations

1. In the Console Tree, expand **User Configuration**.

2. Expand **Windows Settings**.

3. Under **Folder Redirection**, right-click **Desktop**.

4. Click **Properties**.

5. Click the **Target** tab.

6. In the **Settings** box, select **Advanced – Specify locations for various user groups**.

7. Click **Add**. The **Specify Group and Location** box appears.

8. Click **Browse**.

9. Select **Guests**, and then click **OK**.

10. In the **Target Folder Location** box, type a network location as a Uniform Naming Convention (UNC) location.

11. Click the **Settings** tab and verify that the **Move the contents of the Desktop** box is selected.

12. Click **OK**.

Task 7. To redirect My Documents to a new network location

1. In the Console Tree, expand **User Configuration**.

2. Expand **Windows Settings**.

3. Select **Folder Redirection**.

4. Right-click **Application Data**, then click **Properties**.

5. Click the **Target** tab.

6. In the Setting drop-down list, select **Basic – Redirect everyone's folder to the same location**.

7. In the **Target Folder Location** box, type a network location as a Uniform Naming Convention (UNC) location.

8. Click **OK**.

Task 8. To prevent saving desktop settings upon quitting

1. In the Console Tree, expand **User Configuration**.

2. Click **Administrative Templates**.

3. Click **Desktop**.

4. Double-click **Don't save settings at exit**.

5. Select **Enabled**.

6. Click **OK**.

Task 9. To disable the "Run only allowed Windows applications" command

1. In the Console Tree, expand **User Configuration**.

2. Click **Administrative Templates**.

3. Click **System**.

4. Double-click **Run only allowed Windows applications**.

5. Select **Disabled**.

6. Click **OK**.

Task 10. To limit the application log size to 1,024 kilobytes

1. In the Console Tree, expand **Computer Configuration**.

2. Click **Windows Settings**.

3. Click **Security Settings**.

4. Click **Event Log**.

5. Click **Settings for Event Logs**.

6. Double-click **Maximum application log size**.

7. Select the **Define this policy setting** check box.

8. In the **Kilobytes** box, type *1024*.

9. Click **OK**.

> ☑ **Note**   These Group Policy tasks are examples only and should not necessarily be implemented on your Small Business Server network. You will need to create your own Group Policy configurations.

Summary

This chapter focused on two new Small Business Server 2000 features: Terminal Services and Group Policy. Terminal Services enables the technology consultant to manage customer sites more efficiently. Group Policy offers near-limitless configuration possibilities for the technology consultant in configuring the customer site.

This chapter addressed the following:

- Using Terminal Services in remote administration mode to manage the Small Business Server network.

- Using NetMeeting for user support and training.

- Applying Group Policy to assist in the management of Windows 2000 Professional clients.

Monitoring and Optimizing Small Business Server Components

Microsoft® Small Business Server 2000 and its integrated application suite is uniquely optimized for use in small business networks that support up to 50 client computers. This optimization makes it easy for the small business to share documents, faxes, printers, modems, and other company resources on one server platform, while also facilitating communication with employees, customers, and suppliers. Although the number of client computers supported by Small Business Server is limited to 50, there is no limit to the number of user accounts that can be created.

The stand-alone version of the Microsoft Windows® 2000 Server operating system and Microsoft server products were built to scale to the needs of larger organizations. As such, these products provide sophisticated and detailed mechanisms for optimization. Although Small Business Server 2000 was not designed for large organizations, it was designed with the same sophistication and performance of Microsoft Windows NT® and Microsoft server products.

Because Small Business Server was built specifically for small businesses, it is by default optimized for maximum performance in the small business environment. By design, Small Business Server provides a simple and efficient installation process and management system to lower the total cost of ownership. In addition, because technology consultants do not need to devote their time to optimizing, the Small Business network provides optimum performance immediately.

Maximizing Performance

The optimizations of Small Business Server can be best understood with respect to the installation process, which is divided into the following two parts:

- Operating system—Microsoft Windows 2000 Server installation and configuration.

- Applications—Microsoft Exchange 2000 Server, SQL Server™ 2000, Internet Security and Acceleration (ISA) Server 2000, Shared Fax Service, and Shared Modem Service.

The following sections discuss:

- How the optimizations of Small Business Server streamline the installation process.

- How server application capabilities are optimized for Small Business Server 2000.

- Small Business Server management optimization and additional optimization features.

Windows 2000 Server Default Installation Optimizations

The 50 client computer limit on the small business network does not limit the number of user accounts or mailboxes that can be created on Small Business Server, which is discussed further in Chapter 24, "Small Business Server Licensing and Upgrades." The limit of a set number of clients enables specific configurations and settings to save time, resources, and money. The resulting Small Business Server 2000 installation process produces the following optimizations:

- NTFS file system is required by Small Business Server but is not selected by default.

  When installing Windows 2000 Server as part of the Small Business Server Setup, the user must specify either the file allocation table (FAT) file system or NTFS. Small Business Server requires NTFS.

- The Small Business Server server computer is installed as the root of the forest.

- Windows 2000 Server is installed as a domain controller. It is unnecessary to understand complex domain security issues, such as transitive trusts, to set up Small Business Server.

  Small Business Server can be installed only as a domain controller, and so by default Windows 2000 Server is installed as a domain controller. In fact, the **Domain and Workgroup** page in the Windows 2000 Server Setup Wizard is not displayed. Additional Windows 2000 servers not running Small Business Server can be installed as additional domain controllers or as stand-alone servers. The additional Windows 2000 servers not running Small Business Server are often used as application servers to run specialized programs such as accounting or manufacturing applications. Other Small Business Servers cannot be added to the existing Small Business Server domain. The effect of the restrictions is that you may have only one Small Business Server computer on a network. All the issues involving domain structures and security between the domains and the server are excluded by designing Small Business Server to install in this fashion.

- Domain trusts are disabled.

- Client Access Licenses. Small Business Server limits the number of client computer connections based on the number of installed Client Access Licenses.

- Default shared folder configuration.

  So that shared folder configuration is streamlined and optimized, company and user files are created with appropriate permissions during setup. At the end of setup, Small Business Server sets access control lists (ACLs) on the appropriate folders. As a result, users who have logged onto the Windows 2000 domain can access only the company shared folder. The default ACLs in Small Business Server are:

  - Company Shared Folders. Everyone = Full Control

  - Users Shared Folders. Everyone = Full Control

Network Setup Optimizations

The network setup portion of Small Business Server 2000 setup has been optimized to provide small business customers with exactly what they need for an efficient, reliable, and secure network. The sections that follow discuss this in more detail.

Default Network Protocol

The TCP/IP protocol is installed by default in Windows 2000 Server for intranet and Internet connectivity.

> ☑ **Note** The network basic input/output system (NetBIOS) Enhanced User Interface (NetBEUI) and Internetwork Packet Exchange (IPX) protocols are included but not used by default.

Default IP Addressing

Small Business Server optimizes the server's Internet Protocol (IP) address as follows:

- The IP address of Small Business Server is set to 192.168.16.2.

  This address automatically provides security because it is non-routable—this prevents routers on the Internet from routing packets directly to Small Business Server. Inbound packets must first be routed through ISA Server, which uses network address translation (NAT) to convert its Internet service provider (ISP)-assigned IP address to the Small Business Server base IP address of 192.168.16.2.

- The subnet mask is set to Class C by default at 255.255.255.0.

- IP forwarding is turned off on the server to minimize the possibility of intrusive attacks on client computers because of exposure to the Internet.

  ☑ **Note** You may provide your own static IP address for your Small Business Server computer through the Server Network Configuration page in the Small Business Server Setup Wizard.

DHCP and WINS Configured Automatically

Another way that the networking environment is simplified is that the Dynamic Host Configuration Protocol (DHCP) is enabled by default, so that the technology consultant and small business customer do not need to be concerned with client IP address configuration issues. In addition, the Windows Internet Naming Service (WINS) is installed and started. The DHCP service assigns IP addresses to clients dynamically when they log on,so it is unnecessary to configure clients on an individual basis with static IP addresses.

☑ **Note** If you select a non-routable IP address for your server, you may make an alternative configuration during setup to have your client computers use static IP addresses.

DHCP is automatically configured, based on the non-routable IP addresses selected for the server network adapter. The IP subnet is a reserved, non-routable address set, so that all network workstations are inaccessible from the Internet. WINS is configured for name resolution.

Enabling DHCP in Small Business Server is an optimum configuration for dealing with the complexities of IP address allocation.

To configure client IP addresses manually on Windows Me, Windows 98, and Windows 95 clients

1. Click **Start** on the client computer, point to **Settings**, and then click **Control Panel**.

2. Double-click **Network**.

3. Select **TCP/IP network card**.

4. Click **Properties**, and then do the following:

   a. Click the **IP Address** tab, and then select **Specify an IP address**.

   b. Type the **IP address** and **Subnet Mask** of the client computer.

   c. If the computer is a virtual private networking (VPN) client, configure it to use the Small Business Server 2000 server computer as its WINS server. Click the **WINS Configuration** tab, select **Enable WINS Resolution**, type the internal IP address of the Small Business Server 2000 server (for example, 192.168.16.2) in the **WINS Server Search Order** field, and then click **Add**. Click **OK**.

   d. Click the **Gateway** tab, and then type the **Default Gateway** address, which should be the internal IP address of the Small Business Server 2000 server computer (for example, 192.168.16.2).

   e. Click **Add**, and then click **OK** to quit the **Network** dialog box.

   f. Click **Yes** to restart the client computer.

   g. Repeat these steps for all Windows Me, Windows 98, and Windows 95 client computers on the network.

To configure client IP addresses manually on Windows 2000 clients

1. Click **Start** on the client computer, point to **Settings**, and then click **Network and Dial-up Connections**.

2. Right-click **Local Area Connection**, and then click **Properties**.

3. Click **Internet Protocol (TCP/IP)**.

4. Click **Properties**, and then complete the following tasks:

   a. Click the **IP Address** tab, and then select **Specify an IP address**.

   b. Type the **IP Address, Subnet Mask,** and **Default Gateway** address. The default gateway address should be the internal IP address of the Small Business Server 2000 server computer (for example, 192.168.16.2).

   c. Click **OK**.

   d. Repeat these steps for all Windows 2000 clients on the network.

   Note Client IP addresses must match the ISA Server local address table (LAT) of Small Business Server, which in turn must be compatible with other services that use the base IP address for packet routing. Refer to the "ISA Local Address Table" section in Chapter 18, "Administering Small Business Server Components."

Client Networking Configuration

The Set Up Computer Wizard of Small Business Server 2000 automatically configures client computers to take advantage of Windows 2000 domain networking features, as well as DHCP (provided that the client computers' dynamically assigned addresses were selected during setup), WINS, and the ISA Server security configuration.

Server Application Installation Optimizations

After setup completes the installation of Windows 2000 Server, it begins to install the Small Business Server applications. One of the most significant features of Small Business Server setup is that everything can be installed at the same time. Microsoft Exchange Server 2000, SQL Server 2000, Microsoft Internet Information Services (IIS) 5.0, ISA Server, and all the services and components needed by a typical small business can be installed and configured in one process. The integration of server applications optimized for small businesses essentially makes Small Business Server 2000 a single product serving many business needs.

> ☑ **Note**   You can return to Small Business Server setup at a later time to install additional Small Business Server 2000 applications. To do so, click **Start**, point to **Settings**, and then click **Control Panel**. Double-click **Add/Remove Programs**, and then select **Microsoft Small Business Server 2000**.

The Small Business Server consoles are provided as a simple, centralized management tool to administer Small Business Server applications. The two Small Business Server consoles include the Administrator Console for administrators, and the Personal Console for power users. After the Small Business Server applications have been installed and configured, the **To Do List** is typically the first stop for technology consultants. From here, technology consultants can configure the To Do List items necessary to get the server up and ready-to-use.

> ☑ **Note**   For more information about increasing the performance of specific Small Business Server applications, refer to Chapter 18, "Administering Small Business Server Components."

Server Application Capabilities

Because the individual server applications (Exchange, SQL Server, ISA Server, IIS, and so on) of Small Business Server have been optimized and tested to work together on a single server platform, their capabilities are uniquely tuned for single Small Business Server installations. The sections that follow describe the capabilities of the server applications in this configuration.

Exchange 2000 Server

Small Business Server ships with Exchange 2000 Server Standard Edition, which includes Simple Mail Transfer Protocol (SMTP)-based Internet mail support by default, including:

- Network News Transfer Protocol (NNTP) Service, used for news group implementation.

- Microsoft Small Business Server Post Office Protocol version 3 (POP3) Connector, a POP3 gateway for Internet e-mail.

- Microsoft Outlook® Web Access, for access to e-mail and public folders, using a Web browser.

Exchange 2000 Server Installed as Its Own Organization

Significant efforts have gone into making Exchange 2000 Server perform at an optimum level in a single-server environment. As a result, only a single Exchange organization is needed.

Setup configures the organization name based on the company name. The service account is set to log on as the Local System account. In addition, a default global e-mail distribution list is created, which is useful for listing Small Business Server network users with Microsoft Exchange 2000 Server e-mail accounts.

SQL Server 2000

Small Business Server includes the standard edition of SQL Server 2000. Because some types of data, such as multimedia-related information (for example, video) consume significant space even in a small business environment, no limitations are imposed.

ISA Server

The ISA Server LAT is configured during installation to contain non-routable IP addresses. This ensures that all internal site addresses are stored in the LAT, so ISA Server does not initiate a dial-up connection to find them. Also, ISA Server permissions are set and enforced. By default, user Internet access is allowed by ISA Server. However, users can be denied access to the Internet by running the Change User Properties Wizard from the Small Business Server Administrator Console.

When packet filtering is turned on by using the Small Business Server Internet Connection Wizard, the majority of TCP/IP ports are disabled to prevent Internet exposure through these connections.

✓ **Note** Microsoft recommends that small businesses host their Web sites with their ISP, for security and performance reasons.

Internet Information Services 5.0

IIS 5.0 is tightly integrated with Windows 2000 Server. One of the services that Windows 2000 Server supports is File Transfer Protocol (FTP). Because most small businesses do not typically transfer large files by FTP, this service is generally not needed. By removing the FTP service from the IIS installation, memory is saved. However, Small Business Server is configured by default with *outbound* FTP services, to enable client access to Internet resources using this protocol. Also, basic authentication and Windows NT Challenge Response is set up and configured on IIS during the installation process, reinforcing IIS security. Internet security is as significant to small businesses as it is to medium- and large-sized organizations.

Other Server Application Optimizations

Additional Small Business Server 2000 optimizations include:

- Shared Modem Service support for up to four shared modem devices.

- Shared Fax Service support for up to four Class 1 fax modems.

  ☑ **Note** During the installation process, the service account for **Shared Fax Service** is set to the administrator account, along with the password specified in setup.

Fault Tolerance

Fault tolerance of Small Business Server is optimized to support the same options for software-level fault tolerance (RAID 1 and 5) as the standard version of Windows 2000 Server. Random array of independent disks (RAID) arrays enable the server to continue to operate with all production data intact in the event of a hard disk failure, and you can replace the hard disk when users log off the system. Hard disk redundancy for Small Business Server can be either of the following:

- RAID 1—Disk mirroring

- RAID 5—Stripe set with parity configuration

A RAID array requires small computer system interface (SCSI) hard disks, as well as two hard disks for RAID 1 and a minimum of three hard disks for RAID 5.

  ☑ **Note** For more information about fault tolerance, refer to Appendix A, "Networking and Storage Basics."

Value-Added Monitoring Tools

Small Business Server 2000 provides several robust monitoring tools to assist the technology consultant in proactively managing customer networks. These tools include:

- Health Monitor 2.1

- Server Status View and Server Status Report

- System Monitor

- Schedule Tasks

- Application programming interfaces (APIs) for independent software vendor (ISV) monitoring tools

The value-added monitoring tools in Small Business Server 2000 enable the technology consultant to engage in management behaviors ranging from the simple at-a-glance view provided by Task Manager, to complex quantitative analysis using Health Monitor 2.1 and System Monitor. Server Status View and Server Status Report are management oriented, as is the ability to schedule tasks with the Scheduled Tasks tool. The ability to use APIs is more likely to be of interest to developers.

Health Monitor 2.1

Health Monitor 2.1 is included and set up by default with Small Business Server 2000.

Defining Health Monitor

Health Monitor 2.1 enables you to monitor the health of computers running Small Business Server 2000. This tool draws from many data sources and includes an easy-to-read user interface. You can configure actions that are automatically performed when monitored threshold values are crossed. For example, having a low free available disk space reading might generate an alert that is sent to the technology consultant. Health Monitor 2.1 may be extended to include measurements of particular interest to the technology consultant.

Health Monitor 2.1 supports the following data sources:

- Windows Management Instrumentation (WMI) instances

- WMI event queries

- WMI data queries

- Performance Monitor counters

- Windows 2000 and Windows NT events

- Application services and processes

- Hypertext Transfer Protocol (HTTP) addresses

- Internet Control Message Protocol (ICMP) properties

- COM+ applications

The user interface for Health Monitor 2.1 is the Microsoft Management Console (MMC). You can perform the following tasks in the Health Monitor user interface:

- Logically group monitored items in the MMC tree.

- Do advanced sorting, enabling you to view monitored information from different views.

- Customize column headers.

- Reset data collection values to zero, and manually reset the state of any item back to normal.

Small Business Server 2000 lists critical server status alerts in the Server Status View when you start the Small Business Server Administrator Console and display the **Server Status (BackOffice Home)** page (the default view). This is illustrated in Figure 17.1. Note that the Health Monitor alerts in the center of the page.

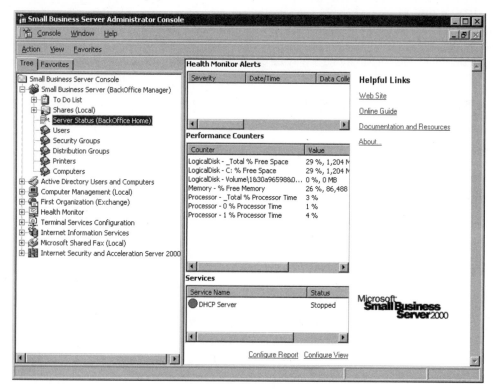

Figure 17.1   Viewing Health Monitor alerts in the Small Business Server Administrator Console

> ✍ **Note**   The view shown in Figure 17.1 is part of the Server Status View, which is discussed in the next section of this chapter.

The complete Health Monitor 2.1 application, shown in Figure 17.2, is available from Health Monitor in the Administrative Tools program group.

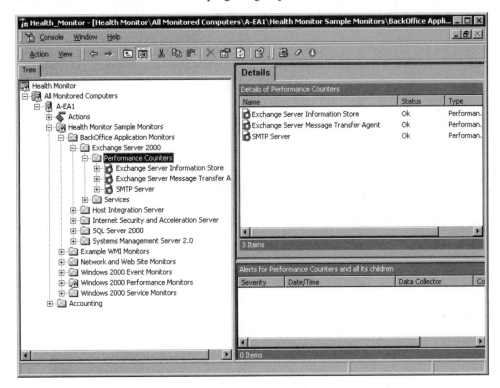

Figure 17.2 Health Monitor 2.1 as a stand-alone application

A sample set of monitored items and threshold values is provided with Small Business Server in the following file:

%systemroot%\WINNT\system32\wbem\HealthMonitor\stdrules.mof

A sample set of monitored items are as follows:

- BackOffice Application Monitors

- Example WMI Monitors

- Network and Web Site Monitors

- Windows 2000 Event Monitors

- Windows 2000 Performance Monitors

- Windows 2000 Server Monitors

    ☑ **Note** Health Monitor 2.1 is also available with Microsoft BackOffice Server 2000.

Configuring Health Monitor

Health Monitor 2.1 can be configured to respond to information it receives, such as alert conditions. Five actions are possible, as follows:

- Send an e-mail message as an alert to the technology consultant.

- Generate a Windows 2000 Event Log entry, with a detailed information (Event ID 2000) message in the Application Log.

- Log data statistics to a log file, where ASCII-text information describing the alert condition is written to c:\healthmon.log.

- Perform a command-line action.

- Execute a script.

The e-mail, command line, and script actions all require manual user configuration; the other four options are configured to run by default. The following example procedure shows how to manually configure e-mail properties on a global basis for use by all of Health Monitor 2.1.

To configure e-mail action in Health Monitor 2.1

1. Click **Start**, point to **Programs**, and then click **Administrative Tools**.

2. Double-click **Health Monitor**.

3. On the **Action** menu, right-click **E-mail <username>**, and then click **Properties**.

4. Click the **Details** tab, complete the fields as shown in Figure 17.3, and then click **OK**. The **SMTP server** name is the name of the Small Business Server 2000 server computer.

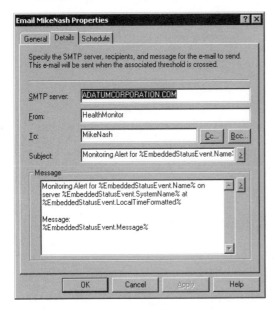

Figure 17.3 Configuring global e-mail properties in Health Monitor 2.1

> ✓ **Note**   You can specify additional e-mail recipients by using the **CC** and **BCC** buttons.

You can configure individual alerts to respond to an alert condition, as follows.

To configure individual alerts to perform an action in Health Monitor 2.1

1. Click **Start**, point to **Programs**, and then click **Administrative Tools**.

2. Double-click **Health Monitor**.

3. Right-click an alert condition (for example, **Is DiskPerf running?**), and then click **Properties**.

4. Click the **Actions** tab.

5. Click **New Action Association**.

6. Complete the **Execute Action Properties** dialog box, as shown in Figure 17.4, and then click **OK**.

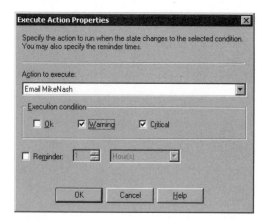

Figure 17.4   Configuring an action for an individual alert

The **Execution Condition** selection in Figure 17.4 enables you to define the status upon which to execute the action. **Throttle** is the length of time after which a new action will execute. Throttling prevents an action from taking place more than once within a given time period. **Reminder** is the length of time after which the action will execute again (as a reminder) if the problem has not been resolved.

🗹 **Note**   The technology consultant typically configures actions for alerts on an individual basis. However, it is possible to configure actions for a data group, such as operating system, from the **Properties** dialog box for the data group.

Extending Health Monitor

Health Monitor can be extended to meet the needs of the technology consultant and the customer. This is typically done to monitor third-party applications. For example, you might want to monitor an accounting system database file to make sure it's been reindexed. This type of task might be performed in the evening, when no one is using the system.

To configure a custom alert in Health Monitor 2.1

1.   Click **Start**, point to **Programs**, and then click **Administrative Tools**.

2.   Double-click **Health Monitor**.

3.   Right-click the server object in the Console Tree, click **New**, and then click **Data Group**.

4.   In the **Data Group Properties** dialog box, click the **General** tab, and then type the name of the data group (for example, Accounting) in **Name**.

5.   Click **OK**.

6.   Right-click the newly created data group, click **New**, click **Data Collector**, and then click one of the following selections. (In this example, shown in Figure 17.5, Performance Monitor is selected.)

   - Performance Monitor

   - Service Monitor

   - Process Monitor

   - Windows NT Event Log Monitor

   - Component Object Model (COM)+ Applications

   - HTTP Monitor

- TCP/IP Port Monitor

- Ping (Internet Control Message Protocol [ICMP]) Monitor

- WMI Interface

- WMI Event Query

- WMI Data Query

> ☑ **Note** If you install a third-party application that creates performance monitors, you need to reboot twice or reboot once and then type the following at the command line: **_net stop wmimgmt_**. The first reboot applies the performance counters and the second reboot exports the performance counters to Health Monitor. You do not need to use the **net start wmimgmt**, because Health Monitor 2.1 automatically restarts the wmimgmt service when it runs.

7. Select the object and counter you intend to monitor. In the example shown in Figure 17.5, the Memory object and Available MBytes counter will be monitored.

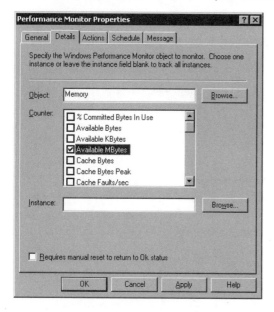

Figure 17.5 Selecting an object and counter for monitoring

8. Click the **Schedule** tab, and then select the days and times you want this property modified. In the example shown in Figure 17.6, the selection is for each weekday, from 8:00 A.M. to 5:00 P.M.

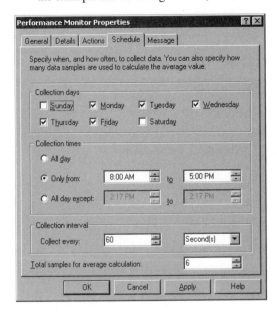

Figure 17.6 Setting a schedule for monitoring to occur

9. Click the **Actions** tab, and then click **New Action Association**.

10. In the **Execute Action Properties** dialog box, specify what type of action you want to occur (for example, send e-mail, generate Windows 2000 event, write to log file, and so on).

11. Click **OK** to quit the **Execute Action Properties** dialog box. Click **OK** to quit the **File Information Properties** dialog box.

It is possible for ISVs to have their applications interact with Health Monitor 2.1 by shipping a configuration file (in text file format). This is a capability that appeals to ISVs because they often integrate their applications with the health-monitoring capabilities of Health Monitor 2.1. When an ISV has its applications integrated with Health Monitor 2.1, technology consultants can monitor the performance of the ISV's application and can identify issues such as poor performance before larger problems, such as the application failing, occur. The configuration file provided by an ISV for its applications, known as a .mof file, can be compiled into the existing monitoring configuration either as part of the vendor's setup, or at a different time. The .mof file contains settings to configure Health Monitor 2.1.

> ☑ **Note** Health Monitor 2.1 is designed to provide on-going monitoring and a dynamic view of the Small Business Server computer's health. Server Status View and Server Status Report, discussed in the next section, provide a static or snapshot view of the Small Business Server computer's activity.

Server Status View

The Server Status View appears when you start the Small Business Server Administrator Console. As shown in Figure 17.7, the Server Status View includes:

- Health Monitor alerts

- Performance counters

- Services

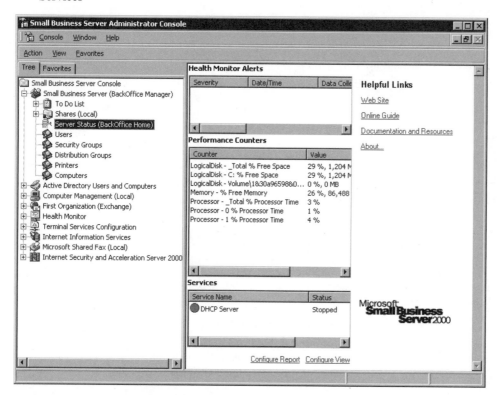

Figure 17.7 The Server Status View

It is possible to configure the Server Status View to display the most meaningful information to the technology consultant.

To configure the Server Status View

1. Open the Small Business Server Administrator Console.

2. Click **BackOffice Home** in the Console Tree if the Server Status View does not appear.

3. Click **Configure View**. The **Server Status View Configuration Properties** dialog box appears.

4. Select the performance counters and services you want to display, and then click **OK**. Your selections should look similar to the one shown in Figure 17.8.

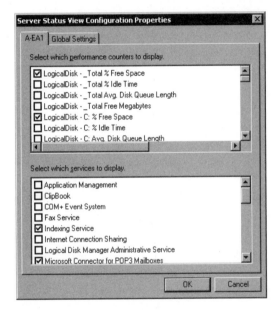

Figure 17.8 Modifying the Server Status View to display different performance counters and services

5. Click **OK**. The Server Status View is updated with the new configuration.

> ☑ **Note**   You may configure how often the Server Status View is updated from the **Server Status View Configuration Properties** dialog box, **Global Settings** tab. Specify the **Automatically refresh every** value with the number of minutes between refreshes.

Server Status Report

By configuring the Server Status Report, the technology consultant can receive valuable Small Business Server computer activity reports on a regular basis, through e-mail, fax, or both.

To configure the Server Status Report

1. Open the Small Business Server Administrator Console.

2. Click **BackOffice Home** in the Console Tree if the Server Status View does not appear.

3. Click **Configure Report**. The **Server Status View Report Properties** dialog box appears.

4. On the **Report Options** tab, select the data and log files that you want to include, as shown in Figure 17.9. To add new reports, click **Add**. You might, for example, need to add new tape backup and virus detection log reports.

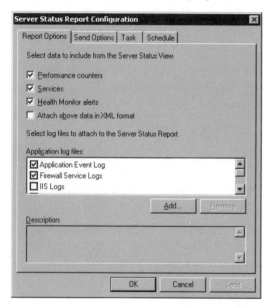

Figure 17.9   Configuring Server Status Report options by selecting the information to report

The following can be reported through Server Status Report:

- Performance counters
- Services
- Health Monitor alerts
- Application Event Log
- IIS Logs
- Security Event Log
- System Event Log
- Web Proxy Log
- Firewall Service Log
- Custom Logs

> ☑ **Note** You can attach the basic performance counters, services, and Health Monitor alerts data in extensible markup language (XML) format. This reporting format enables third-party tools (for example, databases) to import and parse report information so that you can view it more easily. The XML specifications are stored in the following folder:
> \%systemdrive%\Program Files\Microsoft BackOffice\Monitoring

5. Click the **Send Options** tab to configure e-mail and fax information. Type an e-mail address in the **blank field** designated for the e-mail address or enter a fax telephone number in the **Area code** and **Phone number** field for faxing. Remember that the delivery method you select (e-mail or fax) dictates where the technology consultant is to receive the report.

6. Click the **Schedule** tab to schedule the report.

7. Click the **Task** tab, type a **Run as: name** (such as Administrator), and type the **password**, specifying that this is an account with sufficient rights to run as a task. To specify the password, click **Set password**, and then complete the **Set Password** dialog box by typing a password into the **Password** and **Confirm password** fields.

8. Click **OK** to close the **Set Password** dialog box.

9. Click **OK** to close the **Server Status Report Configuration** dialog box.

> ☑ **Note** You can force Server Status Reports to send at any time by clicking the **Send Now** button on the **Server Status Report Configuration** page.

System Monitor

System Monitor was known as Performance Monitor in Windows NT Server 4.0. Small Business Server includes System Monitor as a tool that provides detailed analysis, using the following monitoring capabilities:

Charts. In real-time, you can chart system activity, ranging from admission control service (ACS) activity to Web service activity. Charts can be scaled to see different time scales on the X-axis and different value ranges on the Y-axis.

Reports. Reports show the same monitoring information as charts, but in a column and row format.

Logs. Logs enable you to capture and record data sets over extended periods of time.

Alerts. Alerts are triggered by an observed condition, such as an excessive processor utilization rate. Alerts trigger an action, make an entry in the Application Event Log, send a network message to a computer on the network, start a Performance Log of the activity, or execute a program (such as a batch or command file).

> ☑ **Note**   A common use of System Monitor is to track Small Business Server performance information over time, recording log data. The logs can then be charted for analysis.

To create an alert in System Monitor

1. Click **Start**, point to **Programs**, and then click **Administrative Tools**.

2. Double-click **Performance** to start System Monitor.

3. Right-click the **Alerts** icon in the Console Tree, and then click **New Alert Settings**.

4. Type the name for the new alert in the **Name** field, and then click **OK**. A property dialog box for the alert appears.

5. Click **Add** to add object:counters on which you want alerts generated. Next, configure the alert values (in the **Alert when the value is** drop-down list) and limits (in the **Limits** field) for the object:counters. You may want to consider monitoring the following three object:counters, illustrated in Figure 17.10:

- Select the **Processor: \%Processor Time** object:counter, and configure an alert to be generated when the value is over 80 percent.

- Select the **System\Processor Queue Length** object:counter, and configure an alert to be generated when the value is over two.

- Select the **Processor: \Interrupts/sec** object:counter, and configure an alert to be generated when the value is over 7,000 for 60 seconds.

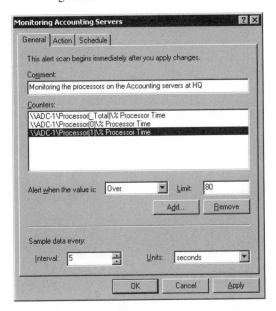

Figure 17.10 Configuring the general alert settings for System Monitor

6. Click the **Schedule** tab to specify when the alert should start and end.

7. Click the **Action** tab to specify what action the alert should generate (for example, send a network message to a computer).

   ✒ **Note** You can monitor real-timer server conditions by configuring an alert message to be sent to a computer other than the Small Business Server computer, such as a Windows 2000 Professional client.

After creating an alert condition, test the alert with an appropriate load on the computer. For example, to test a processor utilization rate of greater than 80 percent, consider playing the **Pinball** game found in the **Games** program group. (Click the **Start** menu, point to **Programs**, point to **Accessories**, point to **Games**, and then click **Pinball**.) Games such as Pinball are an easy way to increase the processing load placed on a computer. Check the Application Log in the Event Viewer of Computer Management to observe the alerts triggered because of the test. (Click the **Start** menu, point to **Programs**, and then click **Administrative Tools**.)

To modify an existing alert, right-click the alert in System Monitor, and then click **Properties**. From here, you can change alert thresholds as needed.

> ☑ **Note**   Experience has shown that alerts may need to be modified several times before the alert threshold conditions are satisfactory.

Scheduled Tasks

Scheduled Tasks is a tool that enables you to schedule processes to run in an attended manner. It replaces the use of the AT command at the command line.

To create a scheduled task

1. Click **Start**, point to **Programs**, and then click **Administrative Tools**.

2. Double-click **Scheduled Tasks**.

3. Click **Add Scheduled Task**. The Scheduled Tasks Wizard appears.

4. Click **Next**.

5. Select the program you want to run. Click **Next**.

    > ☑ **Note**   A popular use of Scheduled Tasks is to run a batch or command file to perform a specific function. For example, a third-party database program may require you to run a batch file to close all databases, completing a backup process. After the backup, you might run another batch file to reopen the databases.

6. Name the task, and then, in the **Perform this task** list, select the frequency with which the task should be performed. Click **Next**.

7. Specify a **Start time** and **Start date**, and then click **Next**.

8. Type a user name in the **Enter the User name** field, and then type a password in both the **Enter the password** and **Confirm password** fields for the account that will run the task. Click **Next**.

> ☑ **Note** The ability to use different user accounts to run different tasks is an important part of security in task scheduling. For example, many tasks require administrator-level permissions to run, but you might need to run a task on a computer on which you don't want the user logged on as an administrator. This is common for tasks scheduled to run on a Windows 2000 Professional computer. By using a separate logon account, however, to run a task, you effectively protect the computer.

9. Click **Finish** to complete the wizard.

To modify an existing task, right-click the task listed in Scheduled Tasks, and then click **Properties**. You can select multiple schedules to run on (for example, different times on different days) and specify whether a task will run when power to the computer is low or if the task will run from a backup battery.

APIs for ISV Monitoring Tools

Published APIs that enable third-party developers to provide integrated solutions enhances the management of Small Business Server 2000. For example, Microsoft Active Directory™ directory service has a published API entitled Active Directory Services Interface. This API enables developers to integrate Active Directory with third-party applications. An example of this would be a third-party software application, such as an accounting program, that uses Active Directory users for logon authentication. Numerous other APIs exist, and most are discussed in the Windows 2000 Software Development Kit (SDK). For more information, you can search the Microsoft Web site at http://www.microsoft.com, using the phrase "Windows 2000 SDK."

Summary

This chapter discusses the Small Business Server optimizations and tools available for you to use in monitoring and managing your Small Business Server 2000. These tools include:

- Health Monitor 2.1
- Server Status View
- Server Status Report
- System Monitor
- Scheduled Tasks

Specific Small Business Server optimizations, such as TCP/IP addressing, were also discussed.

Administering Small Business Server Components

This chapter provides concepts and procedures to help you administer the following Microsoft® Small Business Server 2000 applications and components:

- Shared Fax Service
- Shared Modem Service
- Microsoft Exchange 2000 Server
- Microsoft Internet Security and Acceleration (ISA) Server 2000
- Microsoft SQL Server™ 2000
- NTFS/FAT volume security
- Microsoft Outlook® Team Folders

Shared Fax Service

Shared Fax Service provides fax services to client computers on the small business network. After fax client software is installed, users can send and receive faxes with fax devices installed on the server. At least one high-quality Class 1 fax modem must be installed on the Small Business Server computer to use Shared Fax Service.

> ☑ **Note** Unlike previous versions of Small Business Server, a fax modem is no longer required to install Shared Fax Service. However, to use the Shared Fax Service, you need at least one fax modem installed on the server computer. It is preferable that one fax modem be dedicated to inbound fax traffic and another to outbound fax traffic.

Faxing Model

The Shared Fax Service uses a fax printer to send and receive faxes. During installation, the Shared Fax Service creates a default shared fax printer. Users then fax documents by printing them to the shared fax printer, just as if they were sending a document to a shared printer. The fax printer instructs the fax device to send the fax.

The three components of Shared Fax Service are:

- **Shared Fax Service**. The core server component.

- **Microsoft Shared Fax (Local)**. Used to configure, manage, and monitor the Shared Fax Service.

- **Microsoft Shared Fax Console**. The Microsoft Management Console (MMC) snap-in, used to send and receive faxes, monitor the fax queue, and archive sent and received faxes.

The Shared Fax Service is set up by default when Small Business Server is installed.

Managing Shared Fax Service

You can manage the Shared Fax Service by selecting **Microsoft Shared Fax (Local)** in the Console Tree of Small Business Server Administrator Console. The Shared Fax Service Manager appears, called **Tips—Microsoft Shared Fax**, as shown in Figure 18.1. It enables you to:

- Observe and modify the fax properties, including general properties, receipts, event reports, activity logging, outbox, inbox, sent items, and security settings.

- Start the Microsoft Shared Fax Console.

- Manage devices, providers, and incoming and outgoing routing objects.

- Manage cover pages.

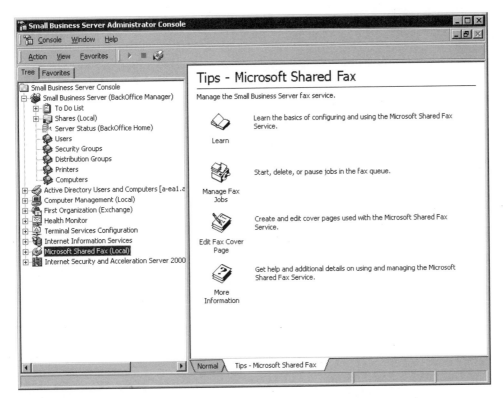

Figure 18.1 The Shared Fax Service Manager (right pane) in the Small Business Server Administrator Console allows extensive Shared Fax Service configurations

 Note You need to configure Shared Fax Service manually to receive faxes, a configuration that is disabled by default.

Adding a Fax Modem

When Small Business Server installs Shared Fax Service, it configures any fax modems installed during setup to send faxes. If your fax modem was not automatically installed, make sure your fax modem is a high-quality Class 1 fax modem. Shared Fax Server enables faxing activity automatically for those fax modems installed after setup.

Shared Fax Service can be configured to work with high-quality specialized fax cards. For more information, refer to the Microsoft Small Business Server Web site at: http://www.microsoft.com/smallbusinessserver/.

If you need to install additional modems after setup, you can do so by using the **Add/Remove Hardware** program group in Control Panel.

 Note Shared Fax Service does not support advanced Private Branch Exchange (PBX) routing features such as Direct Inward Dialing (DID).

User Access to the Fax Printer

You can control who uses a fax printer in the same way that access to any printer is controlled—by changing the security and sharing settings for the fax printer. To do this, perform the following steps.

To control user access to the fax printer

1. Click **Start**, click **Small Business Administrator Console**, and then right-click **Microsoft Shared Fax (Local)**.

2. Click **Properties**.

3. Click the **Security** tab (shown in Figure 18.2).

4. Click **Add** to add users and groups to the **Name** list.

5. Click **Remove** to remove users from the **Name** list.

6. In the **Name** list, highlight the user or group, and then in the **Permissions** list, modify the permissions listed as necessary. For example, to grant the Everyone group the permission to manage fax jobs, in the **Name** list, select **Everyone** and then in the **Permissions** list, click **Allow** for the **Manage fax jobs** permission.

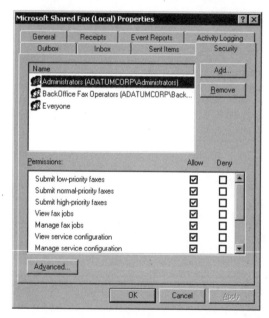

Figure 18.2   User access to the fax printer is configured on the Security tab

> ✍ **Note**   If you are upgrading from Small Business Server 4.5 to Small Business Server 2000, you must reset the user permissions for users who were denied fax access. In Small Business Server 2000, all users are allowed fax access.

Monitoring Fax Activity

Shared Fax Service provides reporting capabilities for outgoing and incoming faxes through the Microsoft Shared Fax Console, shown in Figure 18.3.

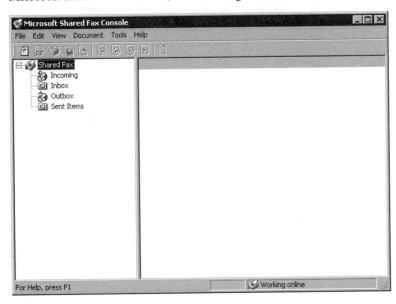

Figure 18.3 Microsoft Shared Fax Console

Start the Microsoft Shared Fax Console by selecting **Manage Fax Jobs** on the **Tips—Microsoft Shared Fax** page (see Figure 18.1).

Monitoring Outgoing Faxes

You can monitor outgoing faxes from the following Shared Fax Console folders:

- Outbox
- Sent Items

Outbox Folder

The Shared Fax Console Outbox folder is the queue for outgoing faxes, displaying information about outgoing faxes in the **Status** column. Faxes are in one of the following stages when shown in the Outbox folder:

- **Pending**. The fax is waiting in the outgoing queue for an available transmission group device, according to priorities in the group (in this case, a group of fax devices).
- **Sending**. Sub-stages in the sending stage include dialing, initializing, or transmitting the fax.

- **Paused**. The fax is pending because while it was in the queue, it was paused by either a user or the administrator.

- **Retrying**. Following receipt of a busy signal or of finding no free telephone line, the service redials the recipient fax number to attempt to send a fax to the recipient's fax device.

- **Retries exceeded**. The service has attempted to transmit the fax the maximum number of times allowed by the administrator.

Sent Items Folder

After an outgoing fax has been successfully transmitted, it moves to the Sent Items folder in the Shared Fax Console. This folder archives all successfully sent faxes and displays information about them.

Monitoring Incoming Faxes

You can monitor incoming fax queue status from the Inbox folder. The folder displays information about incoming faxes while they are being processed and after they have been processed.

Logging and Events

Shared Fax Service provides a log for all incoming and outgoing faxes. You can configure logging by using the **Activity Logging** tab in the **Microsoft Shared Fax (Local) Properties** dialog box. Set the location for the activity logs in the **Log database folder location** field.

You can also generate fax-related events in the in Event Viewer Activity Log by using the **Activity Logging** tab in the **Microsoft Shared Fax (Local) Properties** dialog box.

Shared Fax Service generates the following four types of events:

- General

- Incoming

- Outgoing

- Initialization or shutdown

You can view a description and the properties of generated events in the Event Viewer. View log entries by using the Event Viewer Application log (available from the **Start** menu, **Programs**, **Administrative Tools**, Computer Management snap-in, Event Viewer, Application log).

Fax Queue

The Fax Queue is the printer device used for sending and receiving faxes. You view it from the Printers folders, just like any other printer. Received faxes are placed in the Store Directory, a folder on the Small Business Server computer. Sent faxes are placed in the Archive Directory.

Received Faxes

The Store Directory is a folder entitled Received Faxes located on the Small Business Server computer. The built-in group Everyone has Read and Execute, List Folder Contents, and Read NTFS–based permissions. Received faxes are stored at the following location:

%systemroot%\Documents and Settings\All Users\Application Data\Microsoft\Shared Fax\Inbox

Archive Directory

The Archive Directory is a folder entitled Sent Faxes located on the Small Business Server computer. It can only be enabled on an NTFS file system partition. The built-in group Everyone has Read and Execute, List Folder Contents, and Read NTFS–based permissions. Sent faxes are stored at the following location:

%systemroot%\Documents and Settings\All Users\Application Data\Microsoft\Shared Fax\SentItems

Cover Pages

A cover page is the first page of a faxed document. It provides the recipient and sender with information, such as sender name, company, and fax number. Typically, a cover page is sent as an introduction to an accompanying document, but it can also be sent alone as a note.

The following two cover page template groups are available for fax printers in Small Business Server:

- Global
- Existing (Stored)
- Personal

Global Cover Pages

When Small Business Server installs Shared Fax Service, it sets up a fax printer and assigns four default cover pages—called global cover pages—that users can send with faxes. Shared Fax Service provides global cover page templates for simplicity, speed of use for first-time users, and controlled access to personal cover pages.

There are four global cover page templates:

- Confident
- FYI
- Generic
- Urgent

These templates are stored at the following location:

%systemroot%\Documents and Settings\All Users\Documents\My Faxes\Common Cover Pages\Personal Cover Pages

Users can choose personal cover pages by using the Send Fax Wizard if the administrator has enabled the option for them. Sometimes this option is not enabled. Denial of access to personal cover pages is a Small Business Server feature that the technology consultant can use to prevent employees from using inappropriate fax cover pages on a Small Business Server network. For example, some independent software vendors (ISVs) provide fax cover pages that contain cartoon characters uttering humorous phrases. Many businesses find these covers pages unacceptable and distasteful in a business climate. Access to all personal cover pages, even those created in other fax programs, depends on whether the administrator has enabled the option for each user individually.

Creating Cover Pages

Users can create and modify cover pages and store them on the server or local workstation. They can do this by selecting **Edit Fax Cover Page** on the **Tips—Microsoft Shared Fax** page, and then working in the Fax Cover Page Editor.

Receiving and Routing Incoming Faxes

When Small Business Server installs Shared Fax Service, all the fax modems on the computer are enabled to only *send* faxes. To *receive* a fax, complete the following steps.

To receive a fax

1. Click **Start**, point to **Small Business Server Administrator Console**, and then click **Microsoft Shared Fax (Local)**.

2. Expand the **Devices and Providers** folder.

3. Expand **Devices**.

4. Right-click the modem device, and then click **Receive**.

For each fax modem, you can specify the following routing options for received faxes. The options are accessed by using the **Fax Administration Tool**, and then clicking **Global methods** in the **Incoming Faxing** folder:

- **Print**. Automatically print faxes as they are received.

- **Store in a folder**. Save faxes in a shared folder anywhere on the network. You can view these faxes by using a Tagged Image File Format (TIFF) viewer. In a typical installation, all client computers have access to the share. To select the folder that will store the faxes, in the **Microsoft Shared Fax (Local) Properties** dialog box, on the **Inbox** tab, complete the **Archive folder** field. The box can be accessed from the Small Business Administrator Console by right-clicking on **Microsoft Shared Fax (Local)**, and then selecting **Properties**.

   ☑ **Note** If you archive sent and received faxes, delete them periodically from the saved location to conserve disk space.

- **Routing through e-mail**. You can send faxes to a Simple Mail Transfer Protocol (SMTP) e-mail address if Exchange Server is installed. Faxes are saved as an attachment to the e-mail message by using the TIFF file format. After received, you can view the fax with a TIFF viewer. You can configure fax routing in the **Microsoft Shared Fax (Local) Properties** box, on the **Receipts** tab. Select the **Use this configuration for the Microsoft Route through e-mail incoming routing method** check box and complete the **From e-mail address** and **Server address** fields.

After installation, fax modems can be disabled or enabled to receive faxes, and the routing of faxes can be changed. For example, all received faxes could be sent to an office manager's mailbox. The office manager could then open the faxes in the fax viewer and use the **Send** command to forward each fax to the addressee on the cover page.

Figure 18.4 illustrates the various ways a fax can be received and routed.

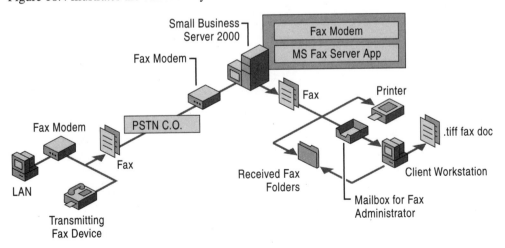

Figure 18.4 Receiving a fax with Small Business Server

Fax and E-mail Integration

Small Business Server 2000 integrates fax and e-mail services by routing messages between the Shared Fax Service and Exchange Server. With Small Business Server 2000, you can:

- Receive and view incoming fax messages in your Outlook 2000 Inbox.

- Send fax messages to a contact from Outlook 2000.

- Create distribution lists that contain both e-mail addresses and fax numbers.

- Send faxes to contacts by using the Microsoft Windows® **Send To** command.

Faxing Documents from the Small Business Server Network

On the Small Business Server 2000 network, there are several ways to fax documents, as described in the sections that follow. The discussion begins with creating a fax address in Exchange 2000 Server.

Creating a Fax Address

A fax address is required when faxing documents and messages by using Outlook 2000. Outlook 2000 automatically creates a fax address for each contact's fax number entered in the Outlook 2000 Contacts folder. To fax by using Outlook 2000, however, you must first create a fax recipient contact record in Exchange 2000 Server.

Use the following procedure to create a fax address record in Exchange 2000 Server.

To create a fax address in Exchange 2000 Server

1. Click **Start**, point to **Programs**, point to **Microsoft Small Business Server**, and then click **Small Business Server Administrator Console**.

2. In the Console Tree, select **Active Directory Users and Computers**.

3. Right-click the folder (for example, Users) or organizational unit (for example, MyBusiness) in which you want to create a fax address, click **New**, and then click **Contact** to start the New Object – Contact Wizard.

4. In the **First Name** and **Last Name** fields, type the fax recipient's first and last name. The **Full Name** field will automatically appear with the contents of the **First Name** and **Last Name** fields. Completing the **Initials** field is optional because not all fax recipients have a middle name. Click **Next**.

5. On the untitled page that appears, you can create an Exchange e-mail address for this fax recipient. To do so, click **Create an Exchange e-mail address**, and then click **Next**.

6. On the next untitled page that appears, click **Finish** to close the New Object – Contact Wizard.

7. In the Details Pane, right-click the contact you just created, and then click **Properties**.

8. The contact's property sheet appears. Click the **Telephones** tab.

9. In the **Fax** field, type the fax telephone number, and then click **OK**.

   Note Outlook 2000 supports dial-as-entered faxing capabilities. This allows you to enter a fax telephone number directly in the **To** field of an Outlook 2000 message. In the **To** field, type [**fax:** *xxxxxxx*] where *xxxxxxx* is the fax telephone number.

Faxing a Document with the Print Command

By using an application's **Print** command, you can fax any document by using the Send Fax Wizard (as described in the following procedure). You can also fax a document by choosing a fax address from the Outlook 2000 Address Book if an e-mail client is installed.

To send a fax by using the Print command, perform the following steps.

To fax a document by using the Print command

1. Open the document you want to fax.

    ☑ **Note**   You can also right-click the document, and then click **Print**.

2. On the **File** menu, click **Print** (or follow the procedure for printing documents in your application).

3. Select a fax printer, and then in the **Print** dialog box, click **OK**. The Send Fax Wizard appears.

4. On the **Welcome** page, click **Next**.

5. On the **Recipient Information** page, click **Address Book** (if an e-mail client is installed) or type a name in the **To** field and a fax number in the **Fax number** field. If you are sending a fax to another country, in the **Location** list, select a country dialing code (for example, 011).

6. Click **Next**.

7. To send a fax to more than one recipient, click **Add**, and then repeat Steps 5 and 6.

8. Click **Next**, and then follow the on-screen instructions to add a cover page and send the fax.

    ☑ **Note**   Do not use the **Fax Recipient** command on the **File** menu to send a fax with Shared Fax Service. This menu item is intended for use with the stand-alone version of Microsoft Fax and does not work in Small Business Server 2000 Shared Fax Service.

    ☑ **Note**   To enable a user to send faxes from Microsoft Access, change the spool settings of the client computer's fax printer to a Windows Enhanced Metafile (EMF).

Faxing a Message from Outlook 2000

A message can be sent from Outlook 2000 to fax and e-mail addresses separately or concurrently. Messages are composed and documents can be inserted as in any other message, either from Outlook 2000 or from your desktop by using the **Send-To** command.

Almost any type of file can be sent through Outlook 2000 as an e-mail message; however, the file must be rendered properly to be sent to a fax contact. To send a fax from Outlook 2000, follow the steps below.

To fax a message from Outlook 2000

1. Compose an e-mail message.

2. In the **To** or **Cc** fields, specify one or more fax addresses.

3. If you are sending messages to both fax and e-mail addresses, specify the e-mail addresses.

4. Click **Send** to send the message.

To fax a message from your desktop

1. Right-click a document, point to **Send To**, and then click **Mail Recipient**.

2. The **Outlook New Message** dialog box appears with the Global Address List and Personal and Shared Contact lists available. Specify your recipient, and then click **Send**. The document is routed to the fax server.

Faxing a Document from Office 2000 Applications

Faxes can also be sent from Office 2000 applications. This is typically accomplished by using the **Print** command, as described previously. For more information, refer to the *Microsoft Office 2000 Resource Kit* or Online Help for any Office 2000 application.

Shared Fax Service—Remote Administration

This section discusses the remote administration of the Shared Fax Service. The service has two components: remote administration setup and client setup.

- **Remote Administration Setup**. When installed on an additional Windows 2000-based computer (connected through a network to the server running Shared Fax Service), this configuration enables a technology consultant to remotely configure and monitor the system, set security permissions, define routing methods, send and receive faxes, and view, manage, and archive faxes in the server's queues.

To install the Shared Fax Service on another Windows 2000-based computer

a. On the remote computer, insert the Small Business Server 2000 Disc 2 into the disc drive, and then in the \FAX\Server folder, double-click **setup.exe**.

b. On the **Welcome** page, click **Next**.

c. On the **Customer Information** page, type a user name in **User Name** and an organization name in **Organization**, and then click **Next**.

d. On the **Setup Type** page, select **Complete**, and then click **Next**.

e. On the **Ready to Install the Program** page, click **Install**.

f. On the **Completing the Microsoft Shared Fax Setup Wizard** page, click **Finish**.

g. On the desktop of the computer on which **Shared Fax Service** was installed, right-click **My Computer**, and then click **Manage**.

h. In the **Computer Management** snap-in, right-click **Computer Management (Local)**, and then click **Connect to another computer**.

i. In the **Select Computer** dialog box, select the computer running Shared Fax Service to manage, and then click **OK**.

j. Expand the Services and Applications folder, and then select **Microsoft Shared Fax** to manage the Shared Fax Service on the remote computer.

- **Client Setup**. This configuration installs only the Shared Fax Console, including the necessary printer drivers and the Outlook extensions required to send faxes. After the console is installed, the user can send and receive faxes and can view and archive faxes in the server's incoming and outgoing fax queues.

Shared Modem Service

The Shared Modem Service enables Small Business Server users to use modems installed on the server and to connect to remote networks, bulletin board systems, and online services hosted by Internet service providers. When modems installed on the Small Business Server computer are shared, hardware costs are reduced because users do not need modems for their individual computers. Users can connect to and use the modem pool in the same way they use modems connected to the Component Object Model (COM) ports on their computers. When users need access to a remote network or online service, the modem sharing application is started. This application uses a COM port connected over the network to a modem pool on Small Business Server.

Shared Modem Service also enables you to pool together modems on the Small Business Server computer. When a modem from the modem pool becomes available, it dials the remote network or online service. If there is more than one modem in the modem pool, the server automatically uses the next available (idle) modem in the pool.

> ☑ **Note** Unlike previous versions of Small Business Server, a fax modem is no longer required to install Shared Modem Service. However, to use the Shared Modem Service, you need a business-class modem installed on the server computer.

Administering the Shared Modem Service

The technology consultant has the option of installing the Shared Modem Service as part of Small Business Server Setup. The following section explains how to administer and configure the Shared Modem Service.

To manage the Shared Modem Service

1. Click **Start**, point to **Settings**, and then click **Control Panel**.

2. Double-click **Shared Modem Service** to start the Shared Modem Service Admin application.

3. You can now perform the following tasks:

   - Add, remove, and configure modem pools.

   - Add or remove a modem from a pool.

   - View the status of a modem pool.

   - Troubleshoot modem pool problems.

Viewing and Configuring Modem Pools

To view the modem pool from the Small Business Server 2000 server computer, you must specify the modem pool name when connecting to it on the server. You can view modem pool names on the Shared Modem Service Admin **Configuration** tab.

After installing Small Business Server, you must configure the modem pool in Shared Modem Service if you plan to use this capability.

To manually configure modem pools on the server

1. Click **Start**, point to **Settings**, and then click **Control Panel**.

2. Double-click **Shared Modem Service** to start the Shared Modem Service Admin program.

3. Click the **Configuration** tab.

4. In the **Pool** pane, select the modem pool name.

5. Add or remove COM ports as follows:

   - To add a COM port to the modem pool: In the **Available for Pool** box, select the COM port, and then click the right arrow. The COM port appears in the **Assigned to Pool** box along with the other COM ports assigned to the pool.

   - To remove a COM port from the modem pool: In the **Assigned to Pool** box, select the COM port, and then click the left arrow. The COM port appears in the **Available for Pool** box.

6. Click **Apply**.

7. Click the **General** tab, click **Stop**, and then click **Start** to restart the service and apply the changes to Shared Modem Service.

You can also automatically configure the modem pool. If your server has no modem pools configured, you can use the Auto Configure option to configure a modem pool. Auto Configure scans your server for modem devices and groups them into modem pools according to the modem type. If a modem is not defined on a port, the serial port is added to the list of available ports.

You can manually start the application by performing the following steps.

To use the Auto Configure option

1. Click **Start**, point to **Settings**, and then click **Control Panel**.

2. Double-click **Modem Sharing**.

3. Click the **Configuration** tab, and then click **Auto Configure**.

4. Click **Apply**.

5. Click the **General** tab, click **Stop**, and then click **Start** to restart the service and apply the changes to Shared Modem Service.

Configuring Clients for Modem Pool Connection

Shared Modem Service supports client computers running Microsoft Windows 95, Microsoft Windows 98, Microsoft Windows Me, Microsoft Windows NT® 4.0 Workstation, and Windows 2000. The modem sharing client must be installed by the Set Up Computer Wizard, and a modem driver (the same as the one on the server) must be configured before connecting to the modem pool.

☑ **Note** Performing these client configuration procedures disconnects all users from the modem pool.

Connecting Windows 2000–Based Clients to the Modem Pool

During client setup, a modem sharing port is installed on the client computer. To use this shared port, you must first add the shared port, then install a modem, and then configure it to use the shared port. This configuration starts after you open the following file:

\\%servername%\ClientApps5\Modem Sharing Client\win2k\netsetupwin2k –a install –c client –i \\server\share\win2k\netsetupwin2k\netsrdr.inf

- Follow the on-screen instructions to complete the configuration. For more information about how this is accomplished, refer to Microsoft Knowledge Base Article Q224791 at: http://www.microsoft.com/technet/.

Connecting Windows NT 4.0 Workstation–Based Clients to the Modem Pool

During client setup, a modem sharing port is installed on the client computer. To use this shared port, you must first install a modem and then configure it to use the shared port by performing the following steps.

To install a modem

1. Click **Start**, point to **Settings**, and then click **Control Panel**.

2. Double-click **Modems**.

3. Follow the on-screen instructions to install a modem. Install the modem that matches the modem attached to the server computer.

To configure the modem sharing port

- Run the following command, and then follow the on-screen instructions:

  \\%servername%\ClientApps5\Modem Sharing Client\nt4\mpsetupnt4.cmd
  \\%servername%\ClientApps5\Modem Sharing Client\nt4\

Connecting Windows Me, Windows 98, and Windows 95–Based Clients to the Modem Pool

During client setup, a modem sharing port is installed on the client computer. To use this shared port, you must first install a modem and then configure it to use the shared port by performing the following steps.

To install a modem

1. Click **Start**, point to **Settings**, and then click **Control Panel**.

2. Double-click **Modems**.

3. Follow the on-screen instructions to install a modem. Install the modem that matches the modem attached to the server computer.

To connect Windows Me, Windows 98, and Windows 95–based computers to the modem pool

- Run the following command, and then complete the on-screen instructions:

  \\%servername%\ClientApps5\Modem Sharing Client\win95/setup.exe

After the client computer is connected to the modem pool, the remote serial port is used as if it were a local serial port. To run client applications that require a shared modem—for example, Routing and Remote Access Service (RRAS) or an Internet service provider (ISP)–hosted service—you must first install a modem on the newly connected remote port. For more details, refer to Small Business Server Online Help.

Status Monitoring

Follow these steps to view the status of a modem pool, including the number of active connections and the users that are connected.

To view the status of a modem pool

1. Click **Start**, point to **Settings**, and then click **Control Panel**.

2. Double-click **Shared Modem Service**.

3. Click the **Status** tab.

4. In the **Modem Pool** list, select the modem pool you want to view. The status of the modem pool, including connection information, appears.

5. Click **OK**.

Exchange 2000 Server

Exchange 2000 Server is a client/server messaging system that integrates e-mail, rules, group scheduling, electronic forms, groupware, and Internet connectivity. As an integrated application of Small Business Server 2000, the Exchange Server platform is scaled and optimized for the typical small business application. When Small Business Server 2000 is installed, Exchange Server is set up automatically to support the small business configuration.

When Small Business Server is up and running, Exchange is managed with console wizards to create the appropriate operating configurations for Exchange and other integrated applications. However, Exchange Server is also accessible as a stand-alone application on Small Business Server, which gives the technology consultant more manual control of certain Exchange features and interactions beyond the Small Business Server automatic configuration.

This section discusses several Exchange features and tools available to the technology consultant for fine-tuning the messaging system of the small business network.

System Manager Interface

All Exchange Server components can be accessed through System Manager. System Manager displays the small business organization hierarchically, making it easy to navigate and manage the elements at each level. System Manager is the tool displayed when you select **First Organization (Exchange)** in the Small Business Server Administrator Console.

> **Note** Most of the time, Exchange Server–related management occurs through the Active Directory Users and Computers snap-in. For example, this is where you would manage mailboxes, the subject of the next section.

Mailboxes

You can configure end-user mailboxes manually through Active Directory Users and Computers (available from the Small Business Server Administrator Console). By selecting the properties for an end user, you can see the additional Exchange Server–related tabs, as shown in Figure 18.5.

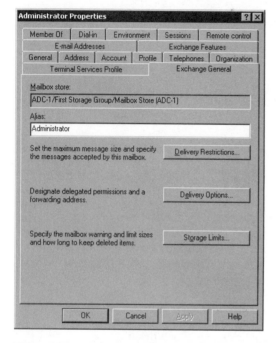

Figure 18.5   Exchange Server–related user properties

Mailboxes can be used as a repository for a wide range of data about each employee in the small business.

Distribution Groups

Distribution groups are groups of users combined into one list, allowing the users to be addressed as one user. A large mail system might include many distribution lists, often totaling more than the number of single mailboxes. Distribution groups are created with Small Business Server wizards, but can also be generated manually with Active Directory Users and Computers, available from the Small Business Server Administrator Console.

End-User Management of Distribution Groups

The Exchange permissions model can be used to delegate management of certain distribution lists to specified users, providing an element of decentralized control in a centralized administration model. The model also facilitates departmental distribution lists, allowing members to be added to a team-specific distribution list, controlled at the team level.

To create or add users to a distribution list

- From the Small Business Server Personal Console, click the **Add E-mail Group** taskpad.

    -Or-

- From the Small Business Server Administrator Console **Favorites** tab, click **Small Business Server Tips**, click **Exchange 2000 Server**, and then click **Add E-mail Group**.

Distribution List Options

Exchange Server automates distribution list management, making it cost effective for the small business to offer users a wide range of distribution list options.

Custom Recipients

Custom recipients are addresses of users on other mail systems that appear in the Exchange Server address book because they are used frequently by users in the small business network. The technology consultant can use Active Directory Users and Computers to create custom recipients.

Address Formats

Custom recipient addresses can appear in two ways:

- In a format that clearly depicts them as users of another mail system.

- In a format indistinguishable from Exchange Server user addresses.

The latter is particularly useful in a migration/coexistence scenario in which users will be migrated to Exchange Server gradually. For instance, representing IBM PROFS users in the Exchange Server format sets the stage for a seamless migration strategy.

When users are migrated to Exchange Server, their display names remain unchanged in the address book. Therefore, other users do not need to change the way they communicate with migrating colleagues.

Custom recipients appear in the address book in the same way as users of Exchange Server. They can be sent mail or included in distribution lists in the same way as regular Exchange Server users. You can create, manage, and delete custom recipients by using the same methods employed for mailboxes and distribution lists.

Address Lists

Address lists are virtual containers that enable the technology consultant to group recipient objects together logically, based on common directory attributes. By grouping recipients together in views, the technology consultant can sort recipient lists according to tasks or functions.

For example, the technology consultant needs to scroll to a particular recipient or use the Find feature to modify or obtain information in a directory with a large number of entries. Although there are tools to do this easily, having users grouped specifically by job functions allows the technology consultant to locate the entry in a manner more suitable to the small business context. Views do not provide filtering; they provide only groupings of users.

To create address lists by using System Manager

1. Click **Start**, point to **Programs**, point to **Microsoft Exchange**, and then click **System Manager**.

2. Click **Recipients**.

3. Right-click **All Address Lists**, point to **New**, and then click **Address List**.

The technology consultant can create a display name for the Address List and can control how the address view is grouped, based on filters assigned to the mailbox user (city, state, site, custom attributes, and so on).

Recipient Policies

Recipient Policies is an object found in the System Manager's Recipients container. It allows an organization to manage numerous Internet e-mail identities by Internet domain names. For example, a small business might use more than one Internet domain name because several small businesses in the same office space use the same Small Business Server network. By using Recipient Policies, the Exchange Server in Small Business Server can manage the distribution of e-mail to different Internet domain names. This happens when a customer has registered multiple domain names, a common occurrence in the business community. For example, a customer might have registered adatumcorporation.com and adatumcorporation.net. Recipient policies would then allow Exchange 2000 Server to manage and distribute Internet e-mail bound for recipients of either of the Internet domains.

> **Note**   Recipient Policies interact with the Small Business Server Post Office Protocol 3 (POP3) E-mail Connector by changing the Reply To address for a user to the POP3 e-mail address.

Public Folders

The public folder is another object on an Exchange Server that can be configured manually by using System Manager. Although the technology consultant can create public folders from either System Manager or the e-mail client, public folders are managed from System Manager in the same way as other end-user objects.

Exchange public folders can be created by using Outlook 2000. They can contain company-wide shared fax and e-mail contacts, which can then be configured as a shared contacts list (address book) for use in Outlook 2000. Individual users can add contacts to this public address book. In contrast, however, the Global Address List can only be configured by using the Exchange Administrator application, which is used to administer Exchange 2000 Server

To start Exchange 2000 Server

- Click **Start**, point to **Small Business Server Administrator**, and then click **First Organization (Exchange)**. The Exchange Administrator application appears in the Detail Pane. Note that **First Organization** is the default name. After you select it, however, its name refreshes to reflect your network basic input/output system (NetBIOS) domain name (for example, ADatumCorp).

To create a company-wide shared contacts list in Exchange Server by using Outlook 2000, perform the steps below.

To create a shared contacts list in Exchange Server by using Outlook 2000

1. In Outlook 2000, expand **Public Folders**.

2. Right-click **All Public Folders**, and then click **New Folder**.

3. In the **Name** field, type a name for the shared contacts list, and then in the **Folder contains** list, select **Contact Items**.

4. Click **OK**.

Off-Line Folder Synchronization

Exchange Server enables users to automatically perform two-way synchronization between a server folder and a copy of that folder on a local computer. Offline folder synchronization enables users to maintain up-to-date information without having to be continuously connected to the small business network.

For example, a user can create an off-line folder (a snapshot or replica) of a customer-tracking application to take along on a business trip. He or she can then update the folder based on customer interactions during the trip. By reconnecting to the server—either remotely through a modem or through the small business local network when the user returns to the office—the user can bidirectionally synchronize the off-line and server folders. Changes made on the local computer, including forms and views, are updated to the server, and changes to the server-based folders automatically show up on the user's computer.

Creating an off-line folder is different from simply copying a server folder to the hard disk because an off-line folder remembers its relationship with the server folder and uses that relationship to perform the bidirectional update. Only changes are copied—not the whole folder. This helps minimize network traffic and congestion.

An off-line folder is created in Outlook. First, users specify that they want an off-line folder (.ost), and then they set up offline synchronization in the folder properties. For more information, refer to Outlook Help.

Off-line folder synchronization provides an alternative to continuous network connection. Exchange Server supports off-line folder synchronization sessions from many different locations simultaneously. Built-in conflict resolution for public folders ensures that all changes are added. The owner of the folder is notified of any conflicts and is asked which version to keep.

Protecting Exchange Data

Exchange Server includes an enhanced version of the Windows 2000 Backup utility. This utility includes all the standard file and directory backup functions and includes the ability to back up and restore Exchange Server directories and information stores.

Backups are performed while Small Business Server is up and running, so downtime is not necessary to secure the data. The new Windows 2000 Backup utility recognizes Exchange Server and backs up the directory and/or information store as an object. It is not necessary to know which files make up the service; you must know only the components that are to be backed up.

Backups can be full, differential, incremental, or copy. Exchange Server backup capabilities are also included in the command-line mode of Windows 2000 Backup, which allows backup tasks to be batched and scheduled. For more information about using the Backup utility, refer to Chapter 26, "Disaster Recovery," or the Small Business Server Help.

Exchange Administration Tips

This section provides several tips for Exchange Server administration, including the automation of e-mail forwarding and Web access to Exchange.

Automating E-mail Forwarding

You can configure automatic e-mail forwarding by performing the steps below.

Configuring e-mail forwarding

1. Click **Start**, point to **Programs**, and then click **Small Business Server Administrator Console**.

2. Select **Active Directory Users and Computers**.

3. Select the **Users** folder.

4. Right-click on a user, and then click **Properties**.

5. Click the **Exchange General** tab.

6. Click **Delivery Options**.

7. Select **Forward to**, and then specify the forwarding e-mail address for the user.

8. Click **OK** to close the **Delivery Options** dialog box.

9. Click **OK** to close **Properties** for the user.

Web Access to Exchange

Exchange Server can be accessed over the Internet by using a Web browser. This feature, also known as Outlook Web Access (OWA), is automatically installed and configured when Small Business Server is set up. OWA is shown in Figure 18.6.

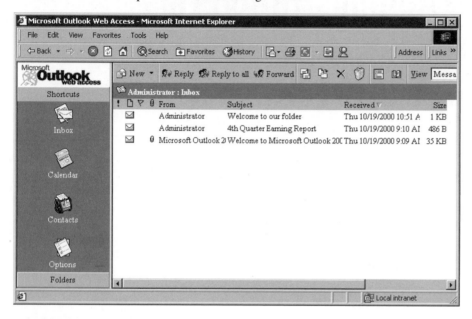

Figure 18.6 Outlook Web Access

Accessing Exchange from the Internet does not compromise security because ISA Server blocks all access to client computers on the small business network. When OWA establishes a connection to Exchange Server, the user can do the following:

- Send and receive e-mail.

- Use Calendar.

- Use Contacts.

- Review and publish to public folders.

- View the Global Address List.

When an e-mail message, public folder, Global Address List, or other Exchange resource is viewed with a browser, OWA converts it to HTML. In addition, inbound access to Exchange resources (through a browser) requires conversion from HTML to a MAPI-based call. OWA uses Exchange Active Server Pages (ASP) and Collaboration Data Objects (CDOs) for the conversion.

Monitoring the Performance of Exchange Server

Small Business Server 2000 includes tools for monitoring the performance of Exchange Server. Two such tools are System Monitor and Health Monitor, both of which are discussed in the sections that follow. The technology consultant can use the performance monitoring information to make decisions about improving the performance of Exchange Server.

System Monitor

Windows 2000 System Monitor is a tool that enables the technology consultant to collect and analyze performance data on the Exchange Server. This tool was used to preconfigure several key performance monitors supplied with Exchange Server, and it enables the technology consultant to maintain an accurate view of the overall health of Exchange Server in the small business network.

System Monitor (which can be accessed on the **Start** menu by pointing to **Programs**, clicking **Administrative Tools**, and then clicking **Performance**) provides quick system feedback and statistics to help the technology consultant detect and eliminate problems before they occur.

System Monitor can provide the technology consultant with statistics on more than 300 system characteristics for processor, process, memory, disk, and network objects. The counters in System Monitor can be used to view such things as access bottlenecks and errors, browse operations, reads/writes, and thread use on the Exchange directory, Exchange Information Store, and other Exchange services. By using the features of System Monitor, the technology consultant can easily determine the load and activity of users requesting addresses or updating directory information in the small business network.

Exchange Server Performance Monitoring

Figure 18.7 provides an overview of the processes involved in setting up accurate and meaningful performance monitors for Exchange Server.

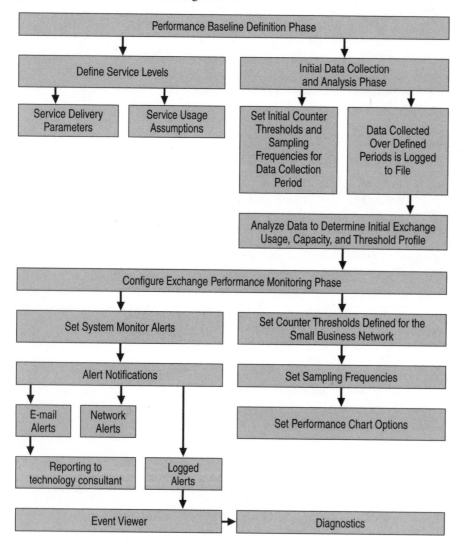

Figure 18.7   Exchange Server performance monitoring process

Health Monitor 2.1, accessed from the Small Business Server Administrator Console, has several performance counters for monitoring Exchange Server in real time. Sample Exchange Server performance counter data groups include Exchange Server Information Store, Exchange Server Message Transfer Agent, and SMTP Server. You can also create your own performance counter data groups for Exchange Server in Health Monitor.

Ways to Monitor Performance

The sections that follow describe ways in which you can use System Monitor to assess Exchange Server performance.

Data Collection and Analysis

Exchange 2000 Server is a complex application with multiple components that place varying performance demands on Small Business Server. For example, the Information Store must manage all communication with the various clients connecting to the server. To understand how this and other demands translate to actual system performance in the small business environment, it is useful to collect and analyze data.

Data collection involves running a number of performance monitor tests over defined periods and logging the results to a file for analysis. If the correct set of counters is used in the tests, you can easily assess the major performance characteristics of Exchange Server. It is recommended that you perform this process periodically to identify long-term trends in server performance.

> ☑ **Note** Only a small subset of the counters used in the data collection process is used in the key performance monitors that continuously track the health of Exchange Server.

When using the counters for data collection, you create performance monitor charts that write performance data to log files. The duration of the logging process depends on user capacity. In most cases, the data collection period is a minimum of one day and a maximum of one week. It is important to consider the counter sampling rate. The sampling frequency must be short enough to get a realistic average, but not so long that you run the risk of missing temporary spikes. In general, sampling ranges between 20 minutes and 120 minutes are suitable for data collection purposes.

Disk space requirements must also be considered because log file growth will vary proportionally with the sample frequency selected. For more information about log configuring, refer to "Configuring Log Files for Data Collection" later in this chapter.

In Small Business Server, Exchange 2000 Server and Windows 2000 Server are tightly integrated. As a result, several areas of both servers should be monitored. The critical subsystems are:

- System memory
- Disk input/output (I/O)
- System CPU
- Information Store (IS)

The first three in the preceding list deal with standard Windows 2000 Server counters used to detect degradation in performance. The fourth deals with counters that monitor user access to the IS.

Collecting and analyzing data is invaluable for developing a comprehensive understanding of Exchange Server performance characteristics. Such understanding is essential for defining realistic baselines for Exchange Server usage and capacity.

When a performance problem is detected, System Monitor can be used to identify the system component that may be the cause of the problem. However, the effectiveness of using System Monitor in this way is greatly dependent on the technology consultant's level of understanding.

Performance Baseline Definition

The predefined performance monitors included with Exchange Server are set up with counters, but not with counter thresholds, because counter threshold levels are uniquely dependent on the usage characteristics of the small business network. Before using the predefined Exchange performance monitors, you need to establish an Exchange usage, capacity, and performance counter threshold profile by collecting initial data on the system.

By using the information gathered in the data collection process, baseline performance thresholds can be defined. These thresholds are based on the load characteristics present during the data collection period. It will become obvious if these thresholds are incorrect—thresholds set too low will generate unnecessary alerts, and those set too high might result in undetected problems.

After thresholds have been defined, System Monitor can be configured to alert the appropriate support group when a particular threshold has been exceeded. Methods for configuring System Monitor are discussed in Chapter 17, "Monitoring and Optimizing Small Business Server Components."

Exchange Usage Characteristics

Over time, the usage characteristics of Exchange Server may change, impairing performance. Changes in usage levels can be detected early if they are measured on a regular basis.

For example, a common characteristic of e-mail systems is the gradual increase in the average message size. Continuous monitoring of message size can provide early warning of any trends. To detect changes in usage levels, you must first define basic service expectations so you can establish a substantial basis for comparison.

Defining Service Levels

Defining baseline service levels is the most effective way to measure future performance. Some service levels that you may want to define are as follows:

- Service delivery parameters, including:

  - System availability

  - Average message delivery time

  - Average time to read a message

  - Average time to send a message

- Service usage assumptions, including:

  - Maximum user mailbox size

  - Average message size

  - Average number of active users

  - Average number of messages sent per user per day

When these levels are defined and understood by both the service delivery and user groups, a clear framework in which to work can be established.

Conducting Performance Monitoring

The technology consultant should read the following resources to create appropriate system monitors in System Monitor and to engage in performance analysis:

- *Microsoft Exchange 2000 Server Resource Kit*

- *Microsoft Windows 2000 Professional Resource Kit*, Part 6, "Performance Monitoring"

- *Microsoft Windows 2000 Server Resource Kit, Operations Guide*, Part 2, "Performance Monitoring"

Configuring Log Files for Data Collection

By default, Exchange Server performs basic logging, which includes information events such as backup and restore success or failures, service initialization or shutdown, and background maintenance notifications. More importantly, it also logs events such as low disk space warnings or IS and directory services database errors. Exchange Server generally logs any event errors or warnings that may cause degradation or disruption of service.

To implement the initial data collection phase, you need to set up a System Monitor log file for the counters and an alert log.

During normal Exchange Server operation in the network, alerts should be reported to the Event Log to maintain a record of alerts in real time. Figure 18.8 provides an overview of the processes involved when setting up Exchange Server logs for both the initial data collection phase and thereafter.

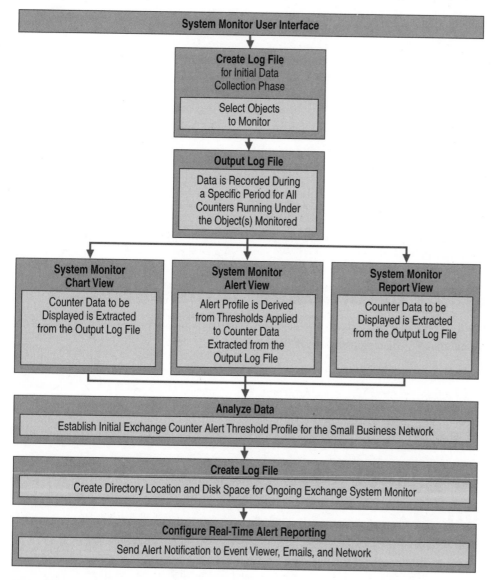

Figure 18.8 Exchange Server logging processes

Health Monitor 2.1 and Exchange Server Monitoring

Small Business Server's Health Monitor 2.1 provides built-in sample monitors for monitoring and alerting the technology consultant about Exchanger 2000 Server performance. The sample monitors can be accessed in Exchange 2000 Server by using the steps that follow.

Using Exchange Server sample monitors in Health Monitor

1. Click **Start**, point to **Programs**, and then click **Small Business Server Administrator Console**.

2. Select **Health Monitor**.

3. Expand **All Monitored Computers**.

4. Expand the server icon named after your Small Business Server 2000 server computer (for example, ADC1).

5. Expand **Health Monitor Sample Monitors**.

6. Expand **BackOffice Application Monitors**.

7. Expand the **Exchange 2000 Server 2000** folder, and then observe the predefined monitors in the **Performance Counters** and **Services** folders.

8. Right-click on any performance counter, and then click **Properties** to observe how the performance counter has been configured.

    ☑ **Note** Health Monitor is discussed in more detail in Chapter 17, "Monitoring and Optimizing Small Business Server Components."

Internet Security and Acceleration Server

ISA Server is an extensible firewall with high-performance content caching that provides secure and managed Internet access for small business client computers. As an integrated application of Small Business Server 2000, the ISA Server platform is optimized for the typical small business application. When Small Business Server 2000 is installed, ISA Server is set up automatically to support the small business configuration.

Protection features used by ISA Server that contribute to its ability to provide security on a single Small Business Server 2000 computer include:

- Dynamic port filtering; ports are opened only when needed.

- Domain filtering to restrict visited domains.

- Network Address Translation (NAT) to shield the internal network from external browsing.

After Small Business Server is up and running, the ISA Administration Tool, available from the Microsoft ISA Server program group, allows management of Internet access permissions on a per-user basis.

This section discusses several key ISA features that can be configured manually by the technology consultant to enhance small business Internet access management. This information is supplementary to the ISA online documentation. ISA Server system monitoring is also discussed.

User Access Control

A small business might be concerned that too much employee time is spent surfing the Internet, which detracts from productivity, and might want a way to control Internet access selectively. You can use ISA Server to limit employee Internet activity on the small business network or to deny access altogether.

With ISA Server, the technology consultant has control over Internet and intranet resources. Access privileges can be applied to the entire small business organization or only to individual users.

For example, the technology consultant may allow browser-based World Wide Web access for all employees, yet permit only certain managers to use the Internet for conferencing or other multimedia services. By configuring the access protocol for users, the technology consultant controls the type of resources users can access on the Internet.

Windows 2000 Active Directory and User Access Control

User names and domain information in the Windows 2000 Server Active Directory™ directory service is the basis for user access control, because ISA Server is tightly integrated with this directory service. As a result, the technology consultant does not have to maintain a separate database or directory of Internet users.

Note By default, Small Business Server 2000 allows the Small Business Server Users group access to the Internet. You can manually configure Internet access settings for users by creating and configuring an access policy. For more information, refer to the ISA online documentation and Chapter 21, "Firewall Security and Web Caching with ISA Server."

Security

To configure ISA security—including packet filtering, site and content rules, alerting, and logging—select **Internet Security and Acceleration Server 2000** in the Small Business Server Administrator Console. The technology consultant can configure these services manually to enhance or customize ISA in several ways.

Dynamic Packet Filtering

Packet filtering is a security feature of ISA Server. When packet filtering is enabled, all ports in the firewall are closed until opened by an access request. After the request, the ports are shut again unless a response is required, in which case the port stays open until the request is received. When a request opens a port, only certain types of packets are allowed to be interchanged at the external interface, depending on the protocols specified.

Dynamic packet filtering is configured by using the Small Business Server Internet Connection Wizard for most Small Business Server needs. You can manually configure dynamic packet filtering by using the ISA Administration Tool. To create an Internet protocol (IP) packet filter, perform the steps that follow.

To create an IP packet filter

1. Click **Start**, point to **Programs**, and then click **Microsoft Small Business Server Administrator Console**.

2. Expand **Internet Security and Acceleration Server 2000**.

3. Expand the **Servers and Arrays** folder, expand the array named after your Small Business Server, and then click **Access Policy**.

4. Right-click **IP Packet Filters**.

5. Click **New**, and then click **Filter**.

6. Follow the on-screen instructions to create the IP packet filter.

To enable packet filtering

1. Click **Start**, point to **Programs**, and then click **Microsoft Small Business Server Administrator Console**.

2. Expand **Internet Security and Acceleration Server 2000**.

3. Expand the **Servers and Arrays** folder, expand the array named after your Small Business Server, and then click **Access Policy**.

4. Right-click **IP Packets Filters**, and then click **Properties**.

5. Click the **General** tab, and then select the **Enable Packet** filtering check box.

6. Click **OK**.

Alerting

If intrusion detection is enabled, you can configure alerts to occur on rejected packets. These alerts are usually a sign that a network intruder is trying to breach the server. (Even though the ports are closed, they are still monitored.) To configure alerting, perform the steps that follow.

To enable intrusion detection and alerting

1. Click **Start**, point to **Programs**, and then click **Microsoft Small Business Server Administrator Console**.

2. Expand **Internet Security and Acceleration Server 2000**.

3. Expand the **Servers and Arrays** folder, expand the array named after your Small Business Server, and then click **Access Policy**.

4. Right-click **IP Packets Filters**, and then click **Properties**.

5. Click the **General** tab, and then select the **Enable Intrusion detection** check box.

6. Click the **Intrusion Detection** tab. Configure the options on the **Intrusion Detection** tab, as shown in Figure 18.9, and then click **OK**.

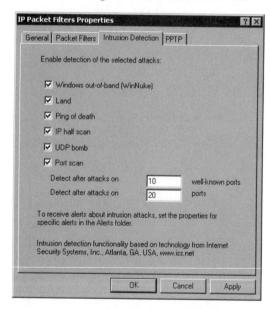

Figure 18.9 Configuring intrusion detection

7. Expand the **Monitoring Configuration** folder.

8. Click **Alerts**. In the Details Pane, observe the alerts that have been configured.

9. Double-click on an alert.

10. Click the **General** tab, and then click **Enable**.

11. Click **OK**.

Alerts are reported to the Event Viewer, which the technology consultant should monitor regularly, especially for attempted intrusion events. Alert notification can be sent by SMTP mail to a recipient. Click the **Action** tab in an alert's property dialog box to configure e-mail notification.

Site and Content Rules

Site and content rules in ISA Server allow the technology consultant to selectively deny or allow small business network access to specific Web sites, computers, or groups of computers. This rule-based filtering feature applies to sites on the Internet or on the small business intranet. The technology consultant has the ability to indicate a specific IP address, a range of IP addresses for a group of computers, or a domain name for any ISA service (Web, Winsock, or SOCKS). Defaults can be set to grant access with exceptions or to deny access with exceptions. The following steps describe how to create a site and content rule.

To create a site filter

1. Click **Start**, point to **Programs**, point to **Microsoft Small Business Server**, and then click **Microsoft Small Business Server Administrator Console**.

2. Expand **Internet Security and Acceleration Server 2000**.

3. Expand the **Servers and Arrays** folder, expand the array named after your Small Business Server, and then click **Access Policy**.

4. Expand the **Site and Content Rules** folder.

5. In the Details Pane, click **Create site and content rule**, and then follow the on-screen instructions to create the site filter.

Value-Added Site Filtering Services

With new Web sites going live every day, it can be an ongoing challenge for a technology consultant to know the address of every Internet site that has material that should be filtered for users. This has initiated the development of value-added services that complement the core site-filtering features of ISA Server.

Third-Party Filtering Services

Third-party solution developers that use the extensibility of ISA Server can offer subscription services that plug in to ISA Server site filtering. With these services, a technology consultant does not need to know the Web address for every undesirable Web site to be able to deny user access to those sites. Instead, the technology consultant can use a check box to select the *categories* of Web content to be filtered. The third-party companies offering filtering services maintain continuously updated lists of those sites by category as a value-added service.

Logging

ISA log files are text files that display ISA Server traffic activity. The technology consultant can configure several ISA log file parameters useful to the small business by performing the following steps.

To configure ISA Server logging

1. Click **Start**, point to **Programs**, point to **Microsoft Small Business Server**, and then click **Microsoft Small Business Server Administrator Console**.

2. Expand **Internet Security and Acceleration Server 2000**.

3. Expand the **Servers and Arrays** folder, expand the array named after your Small Business Server, and then click **Monitoring Configuration**.

4. In the Details Pane, double-click a component (log type). The properties for the log type appear.

5. Click the **Log** tab, and then select whether to log to a file or a database. The **File** option logs to a text file. The **Database** option logs to a database table.

6. Click **OK**.

    ☑ **Note**   By default, logs are compressed to save space on the local hard disk.

Reporting

ISA Server provides reports that the technology consultant can review to monitor firewall and Web browsing activity. The following reports are included with ISA Server:

*   Summary

*   Web Usage

*   Application Usage

*   Traffic and Utilization

*   Security

To view ISA Server Reports

1. Click **Start**, point to **Programs**, point to **Microsoft Small Business Server**, and then click **Microsoft Small Business Server Administrator Console**.

2. Expand **Internet Security and Acceleration Server 2000**.

3. Expand the **Servers and Arrays** folder, expand the array named after your Small Business Server, and then click **Monitoring**.

4. Expand **Reports**, and then select the report of your choice.

ISA Local Address Table

The Local Address Table (LAT) maintains a record of the IP address range that spans the internal network address space. This tells ISA Server whether client-requested IP addresses are to be found on the intranet or Internet so appropriate routing can occur. When a client computer in the small business network makes a URL request from the Internet, the LAT tells ISA Server to route that request outside the local address space and to the Internet. When the resource is retrieved, ISA Server consults the LAT, which then tells it where to route the request to the requesting network client.

The IP address range for the Small Business Server computer (the static IP address assigned to the internal network card) in the ISA LAT is also configured by default during Small Business Server Setup. The only time the LAT may need to be reconfigured is if the base IP address of Small Business Server is changed. If this is required, the IP address range in the LAT must be changed for compatibility with the new base IP address of the server. This is also necessary because the LAT enables ISA Server to distinguish between internal non-routable network IP addresses and external Internet-routable IP addresses. This is a security feature that prevents direct client connection with Internet hosts (having external IP addresses). Before the LAT is modified, the Dynamic Host Configuration Protocol (DHCP) Server scope must be changed to accommodate the new IP address range. The appropriate changes to the LAT can then be added automatically by performing the following steps.

To modify the LAT

1. Click **Start**, point to **Programs**, point to **Microsoft Small Business Server**, and then click **Microsoft Small Business Server Administrator Console**.

2. Expand **Internet Security and Acceleration Server 2000**.

3. Expand the **Servers and Arrays** folder, expand the array named after your Small Business Server, and then click **Network Configuration**.

4. Right-click **Local Address Table (LAT)**, and then click **Construct LAT**.

5. In the **Construct LAT** dialog box, configure the LAT, and then click **OK**.

   ✓ **Note** You can add and delete IP address ranges manually.

Viewing Active Internet Sessions

The technology consultant can monitor ISA Server active sessions by performing the steps that follow.

To view active Internet sessions

1. Click **Start**, point to **Programs**, point to **Microsoft Small Business Server**, and then click **Microsoft Small Business Server Administrator Console**.

2. Expand **Internet Security and Acceleration Server 2000**.

3. Expand the **Servers and Arrays** folder, expand the array named after your Small Business Server, and then click **Monitoring**.

4. Click the **Sessions** folder.

Caching

Caching is enabled by default during Small Business Server Setup. Caching helps to minimize the number of Internet accesses on frequently visited sites. However, it is not recommended that small businesses with dial-up Internet connections use active caching because this results in nonstop dial-ups at regular intervals to the Internet to update the cached sites.

To configure caching

1. Click **Start**, point to **Programs**, point to **Microsoft Small Business Server**, and then click **Microsoft Small Business Server Administrator Console**.

2. Expand **Internet Security and Acceleration Server 2000**.

3. Expand the **Servers and Arrays** folder, expand the array named after your Small Business Server, and then click **Cache Configuration**.

4. In the Details Pane, click **Configure cache policy**, and then follow the on-screen instructions to configure the cache.

   ☑ **Note** The size of the cache can be limited to conserve disk space.

Using FTP

By default, File Transfer Protocol (FTP) for inbound requests from the Internet is not installed by Small Business Server 2000 Setup, although an optional installation procedure is provided in the *Small Business Server 2000 Planning and Installation* guide. Only FTP Read service is enabled on Small Business Server 2000 for outbound requests.

To use the FTP protocol for inbound requests, the FTP service must be installed and the FTP default site properties must be configured by performing the steps that follow.

To install FTP

1. Click **Start**, point to **Settings**, and then click **Control Panel**.

2. Double-click **Add/Remove Programs**.

3. In the **Currently installed programs** list, select **Microsoft Small Business Server 2000**.

4. Click **Change/Remove**.

5. Click **Next** until the **Component Selection** page appears.

6. Expand the **Windows 2000 Optional Components** folder.

7. Expand the **Internet Information Services** folder.

8. Configure **Action to Maintenance**.

9. Configure **Action to Install** for the FTP Service.

10. Click **Next** until the **Completion page** appears.

11. Click **Finish**.

To configure FTP

1. From the Small Business Server Administrator Console, expand the **Internet Information Services** folder.

2. Right-click the server object, click **New**, and then click **FTP Site**.

3. Follow the on-screen instructions to configure the FTP.

   ☑ **Note** Technology consultants should be aware that using the FTP protocol with a full-time Internet connection to accommodate inbound requests poses a security risk to the small business network. This is not an issue for typical Small Business Server installations in which the ISP hosts the Web site. Also note that you will need to run the Small Business Server Internet Connection Wizard and select the FTP check box on the Configure Firewall Settings page to open Port 21 for FTP traffic.

Configuring System Monitor Alerts for ISA Server

ISA Server is heavily instrumented for performance counters. Several of these can be set up for ISA services to monitor Internet-related activities on the server and provide performance data and alerts that are meaningful to the small business application. To learn more about configuring System Monitor for ISA Server services, refer to the *Microsoft Internet Security and Acceleration Server Resource Kit*.

Firewall Client

The Firewall Client can be installed on the client computers from the Set Up Computer Wizard, which is integrated with the Add User Wizard when users are added. Alternatively, the Firewall Client can be installed by selecting **Define Client Applications** from the Small Business Server Administrator Console To Do List. The Firewall client directs Internet-bound traffic from the client computer through ISA Server on the Small Business Server network. By doing this, you can restrict what Internet activity is allowed and also protect client computers from potential outside intruders. The Firewall Client can be configured on the client computer by opening the **Firewall Client** icon in Control Panel.

SQL Server 2000

SQL Server 2000 is a component of Small Business Server 2000. It contains a very powerful and scalable database designed to facilitate solutions, ranging from mobile laptops running Windows 95/98/Me to small user group applications to terabyte symmetric multiprocessor clustering environments. As the small business expands, SQL Server 2000 easily supports growth in transactions, data handling, and users while maintaining essential security and reliability necessary for mission-critical business systems.

Migrating Access to SQL Server 2000

Access 2000, included with Microsoft Office 2000, is a relational database application for desktops that works best for individuals and workgroups who manage data in the scale of megabytes. The small business might be using Microsoft Access as a client database, or might want to create an Access 2000 prototype database by using the Microsoft Data Engine (MSDE), before migrating to SQL 2000.

Access enables multi-user access to the same database by using the file-server architecture (rather than client/server architecture). However, if the small business encounters one of the following situations by using either Access 2000 or an earlier version, upgrading to SQL Server 2000 is recommended:

- The database expands to more than 2 gigabytes (GB).

- The database must support a mission-critical application.

- The application's usage grows beyond the individual or small group it was intended to support.

- The data must be accessed through the Internet.

- The application requires a more comprehensive security infrastructure.

SQL Server 2000 resolves these problems for the small business owner. It provides scalability, advanced database management, replication, advanced and easy-to-manage security features, and Web page–building wizards to support the small business application. When migrating data to SQL Server 2000, the small business can continue to use Access as the development environment, or the database application can be redeveloped by using Microsoft Visual Studio®. For more information about Access to SQL Server migrations, refer to Chapter 25, "Migrating Data to SQL Server 2000."

Small Business Database Scenarios

One of the following scenarios might apply to database planning in the small business network. Follow the directives specified for the respective scenario to prepare for implementation of the small business database.

- A new database application will be created by using SQL Server 2000.

  For information about setting up a database, refer to the SQL Server Web site for SQL Server 2000 online documentation and various white papers at: http://www.microsoft.com/sql/

- Access 2000 will serve as the new database.

  If you are planning to use Access 2000 as your new database in the small business network and future expansion is anticipated, MSDE should be used instead of Microsoft Jet 4.0. This will better accommodate migration to SQL 2000 when the small business has expanded to the point at which it can take advantage of the advanced features of SQL Server. For more information about setting up a database, refer to Access 2000 online documentation.

When you are ready to migrate to SQL Server 2000, the Access 2000 Upsizing Wizard (available in Office 2000) can be used to move Access tables and queries into SQL Server 2000. For Access 2000 migration procedures, refer to Chapter 25, "Migrating Data to SQL Server 2000."

> ☑ **Note** Another common small business database scenario is to install third-party business applications on SQL Server 2000. This is common with many popular business accounting packages. For installation instructions, contact the vendors of these specific software applications.

SQL Server 2000 Administration

Whether you have developed a new database application for SQL Server 2000 or you have migrated Access to SQL 2000, all the administrative techniques necessary for a small business implementation are found in the SQL online documentation provided with Small Business Server 2000.

The online SQL documentation describes key counter statistics recorded by predefined performance monitors for SQL 2000. The performance monitors, which gather the data, are discussed along with how to set them up for alert notification when critical operating threshold points are exceeded. This allows the technology consultant to oversee the health and status of the server and to be notified of problematic trends in server usage.

Outlook 2000

Outlook 2000 is a messaging and collaboration client for Small Business Server 2000 users. It supports Internet and Exchange Server e-mail standards, combining them with integrated calendar, contact, and task-management features. The Exchange Server and Outlook 2000 combination is an ideal platform for creating collaborative applications by using your existing messaging infrastructure.

Team Interaction

Collaborative applications facilitate team interaction, enabling individuals and teams to do such things as share information, coordinate projects, and conduct online meetings across the network. To help individuals and teams in the Small Business Server network interact, the following information is discussed in this section:

- Configuring Outlook 2000 with public folders for information sharing

- Publishing to a public folder

- Creating discussion groups

- Testing a discussion group

- Allowing anonymous access to public folders

- Setting up group task and contact lists

Configuring Outlook 2000 with Public Folders

Public folders are configured for accessibility to small work groups or the entire small business network. They can contain any type of information, including e-mail messages and documents. They are well suited to be accessed by discussion groups in the organization or made public on the Internet. Public folders reside on the Exchange Server. However, they can be synchronized to the local hard drive for offline access. To create a public folder, perform the following steps.

To create a public folder in Outlook 2000

1. Click **Start**, point to **Programs**, and then click **Microsoft Outlook**.

2. On the **View** menu, click **Folder List**. The **Folder List** appears.

3. Double-click **Public Folders**.

4. Right-click **All Public Folders**, and then click **New Folder**. The **Create New Folder** dialog box appears.

5. In the **Name** field, type a new folder name.

6. In the **Folder contains** drop-down list, select the type of folder you want.

7. Click **OK**.

8. When asked to add this folder to the Outlook 2000 bar, click **Yes**.

9. In the Outlook 2000 Folder List, right-click the newly created folder, and then click **Properties**. The **Folder Properties** dialog box appears.

10. On the **Administration** tab, click **Personal Address Book** to add the folder to your personal address book, which is usually your Outlook 2000 Contact folder.

11. Click **OK**.

Publishing to a Public Folder

To publish to a public folder, you can either drag it to the public folder in the Outlook 2000 bar or send an e-mail to the folder, as described in the following steps.

To publish to a public folder by dragging and dropping

1. In Outlook 2000, click **Inbox**.

2. Select a message, and then drag it onto the Outlook 2000 bar public folder that you created in the previous procedure.

3. In the Outlook 2000 bar or Folder List, click the public folder, and then verify that the message appears there.

    ☑ **Note**   You can drag any type of item to the public folder, including Word documents.

To publish to a public folder by sending an e-mail

1. On the Outlook 2000 **Actions** menu, click **New Mail Message**. The **Untitled - Message** dialog box appears.

2. Compose a message, and then in the **Subject** box, type a subject for the message.

3. Click **To**. The **Select Names** dialog box appears.

4. In the **Show names from the** drop-down list, select **Public Folders**.

5. Select the public folder to which you are publishing, and then click **To**.

6. Click **OK**.

7. In the **Message** dialog box, click **Send**.

8. In the Outlook 2000 bar or Folder List, select the public folder, and then verify that the message appears there.

Creating a Discussion Group

Discussion groups enable users to collaborate and share information. They can also be used to host list servers and knowledge bases for use by coworkers, business partners, and customers. Discussion groups are accessed by using any Internet newsreader, a Web browser, or Outlook 2000.

☑ **Note**   The Network News Transfer Protocol (NNTP) connector must be configured on Exchange Server to allow anonymous client access for reading and posting Internet news articles in public folders. For information about configuring the NNTP properties, refer to the Exchange Server Help.

To create a discussion group, perform the following steps.

To create a discussion group in Outlook 2000

1. Click **Start**, point to **Programs**, and then click **Microsoft Outlook**.

2. On the **View** menu, click **Folder List**.

3. On the **File** menu, point to **Folder**, and then click **New Folder**. The **Create New Folder** dialog box appears.

4. In the **Name** field, type a name for your discussion group.

5. In the **Folder contains** drop-down list, select **Mail Items**.

6. Click **OK**.

7. When asked to add this folder to the Outlook bar, click **Yes**.

Testing the Discussion Group

You can test the discussion group you just created by posting messages to the discussion group folder by performing the following steps.

To test the discussion group

1. On the Outlook 2000 **View** menu, click **Folder List**.

2. From the **Folder List**, double-click **Public Folders**, click **All Public Folders**, and then select the discussion group folder created in the previous procedure.

3. Click **New** above the Outlook 2000 bar. The **Untitled - Discussion** dialog box appears.

4. Create several messages with different subject fields. To do so, on the **Actions** menu, click **New Post in this Folder** when you want to open more **Untitled - Discussion** dialog boxes.

5. In each open **Discussion** dialog box, click **Post**, and then observe that postings are automatically filtered by message topic.

6. On the Outlook 2000 **View** menu, point to **Current View**, and then select **By Conversation Topic** to group the postings according to conversation topic.

Allowing Anonymous Access to Public Folders

To be able to open a discussion group to customers of the small business and other users on the Internet, you must allow anonymous access to the public folder. With anonymous access, users do not need a Windows 2000 account on Small Business Server to participate in discussions. To allow anonymous user access to Exchange Server public folders, perform the following steps.

To configure anonymous user access to public folders

1. On the Outlook 2000 **View** menu, click **Folder List**.

2. From the **Folder List**, double-click **Public Folders**, click **All Public Folders**, and then right-click the discussion group folder. The **Folder Properties** dialog box appears.

3. On the **Permissions** tab, select **Anonymous**.

4. In the **Roles** drop-down list, select **Author**.

5. Click **Apply**, and then click **OK**.

Before anonymous users can access a public folder, the Hypertext Transfer Protocol (HTTP) public properties of Exchange Server must be configured with a shortcut to the public folder. To do so, perform the following steps.

To configure public folder shortcuts on the Exchange Server

1. Click **Start**, point to **Programs**, point to **Microsoft Exchange**, and then click **System Manager**.

2. Expand the site object, expand **Servers**, expand the server object, expand **Protocols**, expand **HTTP**, and then expand **Exchange Virtual Server**.

3. Right-click the public folder, and then click **Properties**.

4. Click the **Access** tab.

5. Click **Authentication**.

6. In the **Authentication Methods** dialog box, select **Anonymous access**.

7. Click **OK**, and then quit all open dialog boxes.

To verify anonymous user access to the discussion group folder

1. On the **Start** menu, point to **Programs**, and then click **Internet Explorer** to start the Microsoft Internet Explorer 5.x Web browser.

2. In the **Address** field, type *http://CompanyServerName/Exchange* to display the **Outlook Web Access** page.

3. Click **click here** to display the Outlook All Public Folders view.

4. Click the public discussion group folder you created with anonymous access.

5. In the **Compose New** drop-down list, select **Posting to this Folder** to post a message to the discussion group folder.

6. Click **Compose New**. The **New Post - Microsoft Internet Explorer** dialog box appears.

7. In the dialog box, type all appropriate information, and then on the **File** menu, click **Post**.

8. Verify that the posted message appears in the **Outlook discussion group** folder.

Setting Up Group Task Lists and Contact Databases

Public folders can be used to host other shared information such as task and contact lists, thus creating easy ways for users or groups to manage projects or contact databases. Perform the following steps to set up a group task list and a contact database.

To configure Outlook 2000 for a group task list

1. Click **Start**, point to **Programs**, and then click **Microsoft Outlook**.

2. On the **View** menu, click **Folder List**. The Outlook **Folder List** appears.

3. From the **Folder List**, double-click **Public Folders**, and then click **All Public Folders**.

4. On the **File** menu, point to **New**, and then click **Folder**. The **Create New Folder** dialog box appears.

5. In the **Name** field, type **Group Tasks**

6. In the **Folder Contains** drop-down list, select **Task Items**.

7. Click **OK**.

8. When asked to add this folder to the Outlook 2000 bar, click **Yes**.

To create a group task in Outlook 2000

1. On the Outlook 2000 bar, click **Group Tasks**. The **Outlook 2000 Group Tasks** list appears.

2. On the **File** menu, point to **New**, and then click **Task**. The **Untitled - Task** dialog box appears.

3. In the **Untitled - Task** dialog box, type all appropriate information, and then in the **Subject** box, type a task name.

4. Click **Save and Close**.

5. Verify that the task appears in the **Outlook 2000 Group Tasks** folder.

To configure Outlook 2000 for a group contact database

1. Click **Start**, point to **Programs**, and then click **Microsoft Outlook**.

2. On the **View** menu, click **Folder List**. The Outlook 2000 **Folder List** appears.

3. From the **Folder List**, double-click **Public Folders**, and then click **All Public Folders**.

4. On the **File** menu, point to **New**, and then click **Folder**. The **Create New Folder** dialog box appears.

5. In the **Name** field, type **Group Contacts**

6. In the **Folder Contains** drop-down list, select **Contact Items**.

7. Click **OK**.

8. When asked to add this folder to the Outlook 2000 bar, click **Yes**.

To create a group contact in Outlook 2000

1. On the Outlook 2000 bar, click **Group Contact** to display the Outlook 2000 Group Contacts list.

2. On the **File** menu, point to **New**, and then click **Contact**. The **Untitled - Contact** dialog box appears.

3. In the **Untitled - Contact** dialog box, type all appropriate information, including a contact name.

4. Click **Save and Close**.

5. In the **Group Contact** list, verify that the new contact appears.

    ✎ **Note** If you want to define permissions for the **Group Contact** list, right-click the **Group Contact** folder, click **Properties**, and then click the **Permissions** tab.

Outlook 2000 Team Folders

Outlook 2000 team folders make it easy for any user to create and manage a team collaboration application by using Outlook 2000 and Exchange Server public folders. A team folder combines the ease of use of a Web-style user interface with the powerful collaboration features of Outlook and Exchange Server.

After running a simple setup program to install the Team Folders Wizard in Outlook 2000, the user opens the Outlook **File** menu, clicks **New**, and then clicks **Team Folder**. The wizard guides the user through the steps of building the Team Folder application, including creating an Exchange Server public folder, publishing Web files, and even sending out an announcement to team members. Users can choose from six standard templates or custom templates that they create.

Depending on the type of application installed, the Team Folders application can contain one or all of the following modules:

- Threaded discussion

- Document repository

- Team calendar

- Team task list

- Contacts list

Because the Outlook 2000 Team Folders application was designed with end users in mind, the user who creates the team folder can also administer it by using a simple, wizard-like Web page. The user/administrator can add and remove team members, assign access permissions, and manage messages displayed by the team folder home page. Because it is easy for users to manage their own applications, the network administrator is relieved of having to manage the collaboration applications used by workgroups and teams throughout the organization.

Downloading the Outlook 2000 Team Folder Kit

You can download the Outlook 2000 Team Folder Kit from the Microsoft Web site at: http://www.microsoft.com/outlook/.

The Outlook 2000 Team Folders Kit consists of four components:

- An invitation form and a utility for installing the form in the Organizational Forms Library.

- Microsoft ActiveX® controls and utility files to allow the controls to be accessed from an organization's intranet.

- Team Folders Wizard setup.

- Supporting documentation.

Invitation Form

After a user creates a team folder by using one of the Outlook 2000 team folders templates, the user can send a message to team members that tells them about the team folder and provides a button they can click to add a shortcut to the team folder on their Outlook Bar. To prevent users from receiving a warning about macros in the invitation message, the form this message is based on must be published in the Microsoft Exchange Server Organizational Forms Library. The Team Folders Kit includes a personal folders file (Invite.pst) that contains the form and a utility (Vbinvite.exe) that an Exchange Server administrator can run to publish the form automatically.

ActiveX Controls

The folder home pages of the team folders templates use two ActiveX controls: the Microsoft Outlook View Control and the Microsoft Outlook Permissions Control. By default, the folder home pages download these controls from the Microsoft Web site (http://www.microsoft.com/). However, organizations in which users do not have access to the Internet can configure the folder home pages to download the controls from a server on the organization's LAN. The Team Folders Kit includes .cab files containing the controls and utility files (Codebase.bat and Codebase.ini) that are used to specify the location of the source files.

Team Folders Wizard Setup

Before a team folder can be created, the user must install the Team Folders Wizard and the team folders templates. Team Folders Wizard Setup is a self-contained executable file (Oltfwiz.exe) that a user can run from a network share or receive as an e-mail attachment.

Supporting Documentation

In addition to this guide, the Team Folders Kit contains programmer's reference files for the View Control (Ovctl.chm) and the Permissions Control (Oltfacl.chm), which is located in the Docs folder. There is also a Readme file in the installation folder, which contains information that developed too late to be included in this guide.

Installing the Team Folders Wizard

After the Team Folders Kit has been downloaded and installed on your computer, you start the Install Team Folders Wizard from the Outlook 2000 Team Folders Kit. From here, you can create a team folder by using Outlook 2000.

> ✒ **Note** You need an Internet connection before you can fully deploy Outlook 2000 team folders so that client computer Active X controls can be downloaded and installed. Also, be sure to create a public folder by using Outlook 2000 that will hold the Outlook 2000 team folder you create. You cannot create a folder in the Favorites public folder.

You must have Owner permissions to this public folder to be able to install the Team Folders application. You also must create a folder on the server that is shared as a Web folder where you have Full Control permission.

Building Outlook 2000 Team Folders

After the Install Team Folders Wizard is complete, you use Outlook 2000 to create a team folder as follows.

To create a team folder by using Outlook 2000

1. Click **Start**, point to **Programs**, and then click **Microsoft Outlook**.

2. On the **File** menu, point to **New**, and then click **Team Folder**. The Outlook Team Folders Wizard appears.

3. Click **Next**.

4. Select the type of team folder you want to create, and then click **Next**.

5. Type a name for the team folder, and then click **Next**.

6. Click **Choose Folder**, and then select a public folder in which that the team folder will be located, as shown in Figure 18.10.

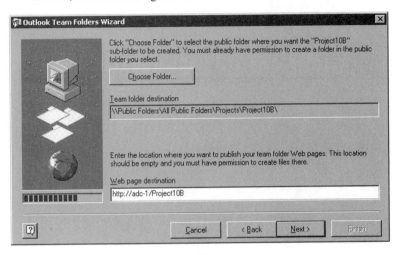

Figure 18.10 Selecting the public folder to host

7. In the **Web page destination** box, replace **<YourServerName>** with the NetBIOS name of your server.

8. Click **Next**.

9. Select members for the team, set permission levels (see Figure 18.11), and then click **Next**.

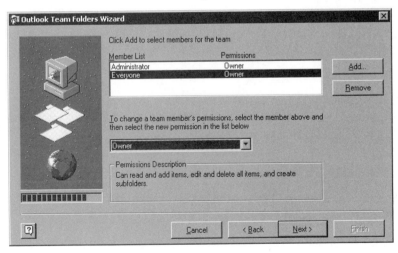

Figure 18.11 Selecting team folder members

10. Review the summary information, and then click **Finish**, as shown in Figure 18.12.

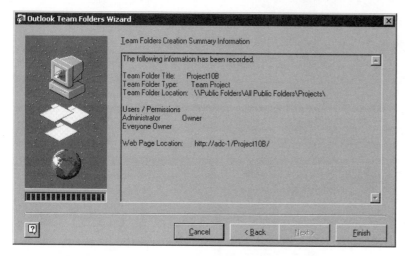

Figure 18.12 Reviewing summary information for team folders

11. Click **OK** when the **Ready to administer Team Folder** dialog box appears.

12. Click **Yes** when the **Security Warning** dialog box appears, warning you that the Microsoft Outlook View Control (consisting of the olTFACL.ocx and oltfacl.inf files) will be installed over the Internet. This is shown in Figure 18.13.

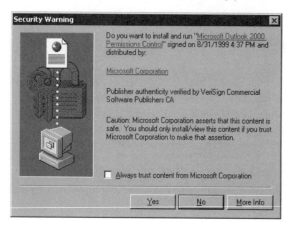

Figure 18.13 Internet security warning about downloading the ActiveX controls

After the installation is complete, you are ready to administer and use team folders, as shown in Figure 18.14.

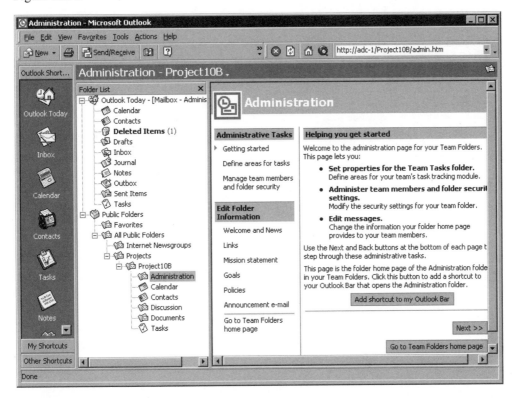

Figure 18.14 Team folders are ready for administration and use

Extending Team Folders

You can extend team folder usage beyond that available in the Team Folders Kit. For more information about extending team folders, refer to the Microsoft Outlook 2000 Team Folders Online Help.

Summary

This chapter discussed several key Small Business Server 2000 components from an administration perspective, including SQL Server, Exchange Server, ISA Server, and Outlook.

E-mail and Internet Connectivity Alternatives

Overview

When setting up an Internet connection for Microsoft® Small Business Server 2000, you can use either an existing Internet service provider (ISP) account or set up a new account. This chapter shows you how to configure e-mail and Internet access for new and existing ISP accounts, with an emphasis on modem usage.

E-mail and Web Browsing Support

Any ISP with e-mail and Web-browsing support can support Small Business Server. Users in the small business network can connect to the Internet, either to browse the Web or to connect to mail services through a Web-based account. The sections that follow describe two ways that Web-browsing support can be configured to work with the Small Business Server to provide Web access for users on the small business network.

Single ISP Account Configured with ISA Server

A single ISP configuration can be established by using the Internet Security and Acceleration (ISA) Server 2000, an application of Small Business Server 2000. ISA Server is configured so that when a client computer starts its Web browser, a connection to the ISP account is initiated. All clients on the network can share access to the Internet through this single connection, as illustrated in Figure 19.1.

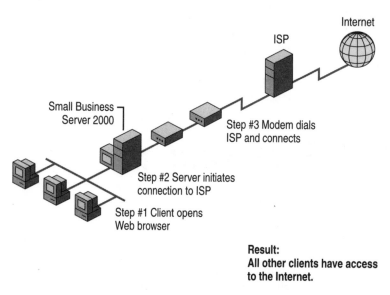

Figure 19.1 Single ISP account configured by using ISA Server

To configure a single ISP account, use the Small Business Server Internet Connection Wizard, and perform the following steps.

To configure Small Business Server to use ISA Server through a modem for Web browsing support

1. From the Small Business Server Administrator Console To Do List, click the **Small Business Server Internet Connection Wizard**.

2. Click **Next**.

3. On the **Configure Hardware** page, click **Modem**, and then click **Next**.

4. On the **Set up Modem Connection to ISP** page, select or type the dial-up connection information for your ISP. Complete the required fields, as illustrated in Figure 19.2. You need to type an ISP account name and password.

5. If your ISP has assigned you a static IP, select the **I have a static IP address from my ISP with this connection** check box, and then type an IP address.

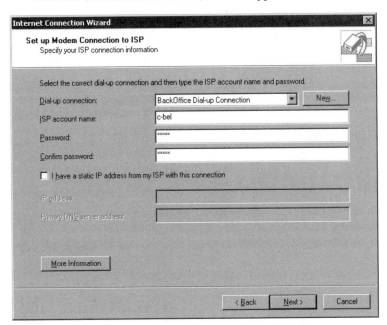

Figure 19.2 Completing required fields for an ISP connection

6. Click **Next**.

7. Complete the **Configure Internet Mail Settings** page, and then click **Next**. You configure Exchange Server e-mail settings on this page for either SMTP or Post Office Protocol (POP3) e-mail. Note that you can select **Do not change my Exchange Server settings** and **Do not change my POP3 settings** if you do not want to configure e-mail at this time.

8. Complete the **Configure Firewall Settings** page, and then click **Next**. If you have previously configured the ISA Server firewall settings, click **Do not change firewall settings**.

To manually configure Internet Explorer to use ISA Server when initiating an Internet connection, perform the following steps.

To manually configure Internet Explorer to use ISA Server for an Internet connection

1. Click **Start**, point to **Programs**, and then click **Internet Explorer**.

2. On the **Tools** menu, click **Internet Options**.

3. On the **Connections** tab, click **LAN Settings**.

4. In the **Local Area Network (LAN) Settings** dialog box, click **Use a proxy server**, and then click **Bypass proxy server for local addresses**.

5. In **Address**, type *http://servername*, where *servername* is the name of the Small Business Server server computer.

6. In **Port**, type *8080*.

7. Click **Advanced**.

8. In the **Proxy Settings** dialog box, click **Use the same proxy server for all protocols**.

9. Make sure the server name and port number specified in steps 5 and 6 appear in the **HTTP** protocol.

10. Click **OK**, and then close all remaining dialog boxes.

Multiple ISP Accounts Configured with Microsoft Shared Modem Service

A multiple ISP configuration can be established by using the Shared Modem Service, a Small Business Server component that enables users to share modems. A client computer uses the Shared Modem Service to connect, using a modem attached to the server computer. This type of modem sharing eliminates the need for an individual modem for each client computer. The resulting connection between the client computer and ISP, however, cannot be shared with other client computers on the network, as illustrated in Figure 19.3.

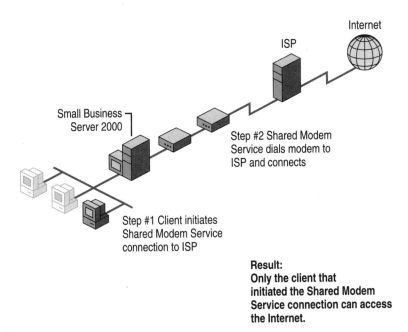

Figure 19.3 Multiple ISP accounts configured by using Microsoft Shared Modem Service

To enable Web-browsing support on a client by using Shared Modem Service, perform the following steps.

☑ **Note**   The Shared Modem Service application must be installed before you can follow this procedure. This client computer application is installed as part of the Set Up Computer Wizard.

To configure a dial-up connection for client Web-browsing support for Microsoft Windows® 2000

1.   Click **Start**, point to **Settings**, and then click **Network and Dial-up Connections**.

2.   Double-click **Make New Connection**.

3.   On the **Welcome to the Network Connection Wizard** page, click **Next**.

4.   On the **Network Connection Type** page, select **Dial-up to the Internet**, and then click **Next**.

5.   On the **Welcome to the Internet Connection Wizard** page, select the appropriate Internet account configuration. Choices include creating a new Internet account, using an existing Internet account, manually configuring your Internet account, or connecting manually through a LAN. Complete the pages that follow based on your ISP configuration selection, account, and password information. You also need to select a modem for dialing out. Be sure to select the modem associated with, through modem sharing, the Small Business Server 2000 computer—typically, an upper-level Component Object Model (COM) port on the client computer, such as COM3 or COM4.

6.   Click **Finish**.

To configure a dial-up networking entry for client Web-browsing support for Windows Me, Windows 98 or Windows 95

1. Click **Start**, point to **Programs**, point to **Accessories**, point to **Communications**, and then click **Dial-Up Networking**.

2. Double-click the **Make a New Connection** icon. The Make New Connection Wizard appears.

3. Name the connection in the **Type a name for the computer you are dialing** field, and then select a device (modem). Be sure to select the modem associated with, through modem sharing, the Small Business Server 2000 computer—typically, an upper-level COM port on the client computer, such as COM3 or COM4. Click **Next**.

4. Provide the area code and telephone number of the ISP. Click **Next**.

5. Click **Finish**.

Internal E-mail Configured with Exchange Server

Microsoft Exchange 2000 Server is selected by default during the Small Business Server installation and is automatically set up and configured for internal e-mail. Internal e-mail is, by definition, e-mail sent to Microsoft Exchange 2000 Server-based e-mail accounts on the internal Small Business Server network. Also, if the Microsoft Outlook® 2000 client is installed by using the Set Up Computer Wizard, the client computer is automatically set up to use the Microsoft Exchange 2000 Server for internal e-mail.

POP3 Support

With an Internet connection, Small Business Serer 2000 supports internal e-mail and external POP3-based e-mail. The three scenarios discussed in this section that involve Outlook 2000 and Microsoft Exchange 2000 Server are supported, including:

*   The first scenario—a single POP3 account that enables a single POP3 account to receive Internet e-mail.

*   The second scenario—a situation where multiple POP3 accounts receive Internet e-mail.

*   The third scenario—detailing how the Microsoft Connector for POP3 mailboxes for Exchange Server is implemented.

Single POP3 Account

A single POP3 account configuration can be established by using Outlook to receive corporate Internet mail. This single account dials out to the ISP to receive and send *all* Internet e-mail for the small business.

If the single POP 3 account is used in combination with the Exchange Server, the account owner can manually forward Internet e-mail received to other clients on the network. Forwarding is accomplished by using the internal mail features of Exchange Server, as illustrated in Figure 19.4.

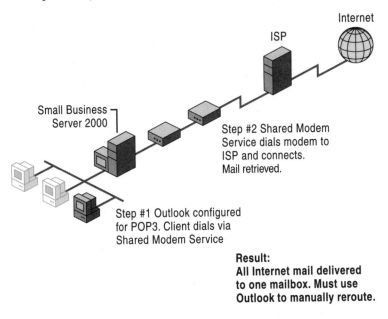

Figure 19.4 Single POP3 account, using Microsoft Outlook

> ☑ **Note** Using a single POP3 e-mail account for a small business is not recommended. It is recommended that every user have an individual Internet e-mail account, which can be either a POP3 account or an Exchange 2000 Server-based e-mail account, supporting Internet e-mail.

Multiple POP3 Accounts

A multiple POP3 configuration of individual accounts is established on client computers when Outlook is configured to receive mail from individual POP3 accounts. Each client computer can dial out to the designated ISP to receive Internet e-mail. This could occur when an individual has e-mail accounts for work, family, hobby, and volunteer work. Each of the individual's activities may require a separate Internet e-mail identity; thus the need for multiple POP3 accounts.

> ☑ **Note** Although having multiple POP3 accounts individually connect to the POP3 e-mail server at the ISP is possible, it is not recommended. Consider instead using the POP3 e-mail gateway discussed next.

Using Exchange Server for Internal and POP3 E-mail

For this configuration, users have normal access to Exchange Server and Outlook for their internal e-mail, POP3 e-mail, and scheduling. To establish the configuration, you need to specify the Microsoft Connector for POP3 mailboxes for Exchange Server to accept Internet e-mail from a POP3 server, and redirect it to the appropriate internal e-mail account.

To configure Exchange Server to receive and redirect POP3 e-mail

1. From the Small Business Server Administrator Console To Do List, click **Internet Connection Wizard** to start the Small Business Server Internet Connection Wizard.

2. Click **Next**.

3. On the **Configure Hardware** page, do one of the following:

    *   Select the type of hardware to configure, and then click **Next**. Complete the hardware pages that follow, which vary, depending on the hardware you selected (modem, router, full-time broadband, and so on).

    *   If you don't need to configure hardware or your hardware has previously been configured, select **Do not change my networking configuration**.

    *   Click **Next**.

4. On the **Configure Internet Mail Settings** page, select **Use POP3 for Internet mail**, and then click **Next**.

5. Complete the **Review POP3 Mailboxes** page as follows:

   - Click **Add**, and then complete the **Create POP3 Account dialog box** for each user by typing basic POP3 account information—including mail server, login name, and password.

   - Select an Exchange user account, and then click **OK**.

   - In the **Review POP3 Mailboxes** page, shown in Figure 19.5, click **Next**. On this page, you can map POP3 e-mail accounts to existing Microsoft Exchange 2000 Server accounts.

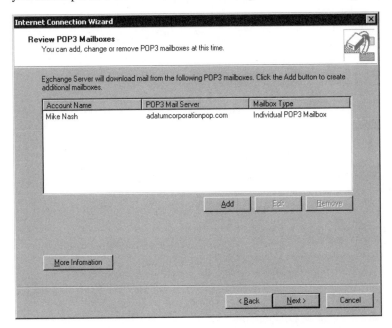

Figure 19.5   Mapping POP3 e-mail accounts to Exchange 2000 Server e-mail accounts

6. Complete the **Mail Delivery Frequency** page, and then click **Next**.

7. Complete the **Configure Firewall Settings** page, and then click **Next**.

8. Click **Finish**.

   📝 **Note**   The POP3 e-mail gateway included with Small Business Server for Exchange Server 2000 is designed to work with POP3 e-mail from national, regional, and local ISPs. The POP3 e-mail gateway does not, however, work with proprietary POP3 e-mail providers— America Online (AOL) and Microsoft Hotmail®, for example. ISPs that use secure password authentication (SPA), such as Microsoft Network (MSN®) are also not supported.

SMTP and Web Hosting Support

Although POP3 support does offer Internet e-mail access and a single inbox for users, in some cases manual mail forwarding is required and the number of e-mail addresses and distribution lists you can have is limited. If POP3 is inadequate for the needs of the small business, Simple Mail Transfer Protocol (SMTP) is the next level of e-mail support to acquire. Experience has shown that many small businesses start with POP3 e-mail services and quickly migrate to SMTP-based e-mail service. This occurs for performance and Internet identity purposes. Many small businesses want to have an Internet domain closely related to the business name for marketing purposes.

SMTP Support

SMTP enables the use of Exchange 2000 Server for both internal and Internet e-mail, providing full control over the e-mail accounts you create and use. This improves manageability, and having a single log on to retrieve all Internet e-mail improves security and eliminates the need for multiple POP3 accounts. For information about using the Small Business Server Internet Connection Wizard to configure Exchange Server for dial-up and to receive e-mail messages from an ISP, refer to Chapter 11, "ISP Connectivity Tasks."

Web Hosting Support

Although Web-browsing support enables users to browse the Web, a small business can only host its own Web site with Web-hosting support from an ISP. With Web-hosting support, the ISP hosts the small business Web site on their server—they can post any changes to small business Web pages there. When an ISP hosts the Web site, a full-time Internet connection is not needed. Having an ISP host a small business Web site is recommended for several reasons, including performance and availability. For more information, refer to Chapter 11, "ISP Connectivity Tasks."

Summary

This chapter provided a discussion on e-mail and Internet connectivity alternatives in Small Business Server 2000. Topics included:

- Web browsing support
- Use of single and multiple ISP accounts
- POP3 support
- SMTP support
- Web browsing support and recommendations

CHAPTER 20

Cross-Platform Interoperability

Overview

Many networks were installed to provide basic file and printer sharing. As business requirements have expanded, however, so have the demands on computing infrastructures. These same networks must now support a growing number of new capabilities and services, such as electronic commerce, remote communications, Web publishing, e-mail, and database applications in a client/server processing model.

To provide these services to small and large businesses, many information technology professionals are using Microsoft® Windows® 2000 Server-based computing environments. Windows 2000 Server serves as a unifying foundation that does the following:

- Combines and enhances the capabilities of diverse server operating systems.

- Enables organizations to extend a consistent set of system services, applications, and user interfaces across a network. System services are typically core operating system functions running at either the executive- or user-mode in the Windows 2000 Server operating system architecture. Applications run in user mode and, more often than not, require a user logon to run.

The core server technology of Small Business Server 2000 is Windows 2000 Server, which is designed to work with the many client network operating systems. This protects the network investments of the small business and provides the necessary flexibility for a small business to keep up with evolving business computing demands.

This chapter describes the requirements for interoperability between Small Business Server 2000 and other operating system environments.

Interoperability Layers

When assessing interoperability issues, think of your organization's computing infrastructure in terms of four layers: network, data, applications, and management. Depending on the platforms combined, one or more of these areas must be addressed:

- **Network layer.** Consists of low-level communication protocols, such as Internet Packet Exchange (IPX) and TCP/IP, which are used to transport data. Also includes such functionality as terminal emulation or print services.

- **Data layer.** Provides access to both structured (primarily database) and unstructured (primarily file systems) data sources. In addition, includes access to other critical information, such as e-mail.

- **Application layer.** Addresses the way an organization's application infrastructure can allow applications running on different operating systems to work together. For example, this layer defines how two applications can participate in transactions, or how an application can be delivered to multiple client platforms.

- **Management layer.** Focuses on cross-platform user, system, and network management.

Operating System Environments Supported by Windows 2000 Server

Windows 2000 Server supports all the standards required to interoperate with the following operating systems:

- NetWare 2.x/3.x/4.x/5.x

- UNIX

- Macintosh System 6.0.7 or higher

- Windows 2000 Professional

- Windows NT® Workstation

- Windows Me

- Windows 95 and Windows 98

- Windows 3.x

- MS-DOS®

- OS/2

Windows 2000 Server also supports the following network protocols:

- TCP/IP

- Internet Packet Exchange/Sequenced Packet Exchange (IPX/SPX)

- Network Basic Enhanced User Interface (NetBEUI)

- AppleTalk

- Data Link Control (DLC)

- Hypertext Transfer Protocol (HTTP)

- Systems Network Architecture (SNA)

- Point-to-Point Protocol (PPP)

- Point-to-Point Tunneling Protocol (PPTP)

NetWare Interoperability

Small Business Server 2000 integrates easily with the infrastructures of NetWare 2.x, 3.x, 4.x, and 5.x (in bindery emulation mode). This helps to lower operating costs, increase resource use, and enables a platform for innovative client/server solutions. To ease the integration, Microsoft developed a set of utilities that enables Windows 2000 Server to fully integrate with most NetWare networks. These technologies address NetWare interoperability at the network, data, and management layers. The following utilities are part of the Windows 2000 Server application in Small Business Server 2000:

- Gateway Service for NetWare (GSNW)

- Client Services for NetWare (CSNW)

- NWLink (an IPX/SPX-compatible protocol)

Also, File and Print Services for NetWare (FPNW) can be purchased to further enhance Windows 2000 Server and NetWare interoperability.

Gateway Service for NetWare

GSNW is a Microsoft utility that enables a Windows 2000 Server-based computer to act as a gateway to resources on a NetWare LAN, as illustrated in Figure 20.1.

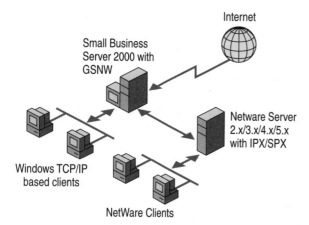

Figure 20.1 Gateway Service for NetWare configuration

GSNW offers the following features:

- Protocol availability.

  Enables the small business to use any protocol on client desktops without losing NetWare LAN connectivity. For example, Windows 2000 Professional-based clients can access NetWare resources by using TCP/IP without requiring a NetWare client redirector on an IPX/SPX protocol stack. The efficiency of GSNW reduces the administrative load for each client, improving network performance.

  GSNW also enables the technology consultant to deploy TCP/IP as the strategic protocol without incurring the additional costs of replacing older technologies.

- Remote access to NetWare file and print servers.

  Small Business Server can be deployed as a communications server to enable remote user access to the NetWare LAN. This feature of GSNW enables NetWare, MS-DOS, or Windows operating system-based clients to use the Windows 2000 Server Routing and Remote Access Service (RRAS) to maintain a reliable and secure connection when connecting to the LAN.

- Novell Directory Services (NDS) support.

  This feature enables users to do the following:

  - Navigate NDS trees.

  - Authenticate with an NDS-aware server.

  - Print from NDS.

  - Get NetWare 4.x and 5.x logon script support.

Client Services for NetWare

CSNW enables Windows 2000 Professional-based clients to gain access to files and print resources on a NetWare 4.x or 5.x server with a single logon and password. CSNW supports Novell's NDS authentication to multiple NDS trees and provides full support for NDS property pages, passwords, and processing of NetWare login scripts.

NWLink

NWLink is an IPX/SPX-compatible protocol that provides NetWare clients with access to Windows 2000 Server-based applications. With this protocol, NetWare clients can gain access to applications such as Microsoft SQL Server™ 2000 or Microsoft Exchange 2000 Server without changing any client-side software. NWLink also establishes a means of communication for the tools that interoperate with NetWare.

Microsoft's implementation of IPX/SPX and Novell NetBIOS-compatible protocols can coexist with other protocols on the same network adapter card. This means you can have several networks running independently on the same network hardware connection. NWLink also supports Windows Sockets, Novell NetBIOS, and Named Pipes protocols.

File and Print Services for NetWare

The FPNW component, an add-on purchased separately, enables Small Business Server to act like a NetWare Server to all NetWare clients currently on the network. It supports NetWare 2.x, 3.x, 4.x, and 5.x (in bindery emulation mode) clients without any changes to their configurations and enables Small Business Server to appear in each client's Windows Explorer list of NetWare-compatible servers. FPNW enables the Windows 2000 Server application of Small Business Server to emulate a NetWare file and print server while providing file and print resources that use the same dialog boxes as a NetWare Server.

With FPNW installed on Small Business Server 2000, a NetWare client can do the following:

- Map to a shared volume and directory on Small Business Server.

- Connect to a Small Business Server printer.

- Log on to Small Business Server and execute login scripts.

- Use Small Business Server applications and services.

More Information

For additional information about NetWare integration with Small Business Server 2000, refer to Appendix B, "Migrating from a NetWare Environment."

UNIX Interoperability

Small Business Server 2000 integrates easily with an existing UNIX infrastructure. This helps lower operating costs, increases resource utilization, and assures a smooth migration from legacy UNIX environments. To facilitate the integration of UNIX environments with the Windows 2000 Server application, Microsoft offers Services for UNIX. The components of this package include technologies for resource sharing, remote administration, password synchronization, and common scripting across platforms. Support for these technologies is described in the following sections with respect to the network, data, application, and management layers.

Network Layer Interoperability

For basic integration with UNIX systems, Small Business Server 2000 includes support for industry-standard protocols used by UNIX, such as TCP/IP, and Domain Name Service (DNS). These and other common protocols found on UNIX systems are all included in the underlying Windows 2000 Server operating system. The sections that follow describe the interoperability characteristics of Windows 2000 Server and UNIX at the network layer.

TCP/IP

Windows 2000 Server includes TCP/IP, the primary transport protocol for the Internet, intranets, and homogeneous or heterogeneous networks. With TCP/IP built into its operating system, Windows 2000 Server can exchange data with both UNIX hosts and the Internet.

File Transfer and Hypertext Transfer Protocols

With File Transfer Protocol (FTP) and HTTP services, users can copy files across heterogeneous networks and then manipulate them locally as text files or Microsoft Word documents.

Domain Name Service

The DNS is a set of protocols and services on a TCP/IP network that enables network users to employ hierarchical user-friendly names to find other computers rather than using Internet Protocol (IP) addresses. Windows 2000 Server has a built-in, standards-based DNS service. This enables the technology consultant to easily migrate an existing DNS to the Windows 2000 Server DNS, or coexist with a non-Microsoft DNS.

Dynamic Host Configuration and Boot Protocols

Dynamic Host Configuration Protocol (DHCP) configures a host during boot up on a TCP/IP network and can change IP settings while the host is attached. This allows storage of IP addresses in a central database, along with associated configuration information, including the subnet mask, gateway IP address, and the DNS server IP address. Because DHCP for Windows 2000 Server is based on industry standards, requests from any type of client platform using these standards are supported. The Microsoft DHCP server also offers Boot Protocol (BOOTP) support, used for booting diskless workstations.

Network File System

The Network File System (NFS) is included in the Services for UNIX, an add-on that is purchased separately, as a standard for sharing files and printers in the UNIX environment. The NFS client and server software allows Windows 2000 Server users to access files on UNIX, and UNIX users to access files on Windows 2000 Server.

> ✔ **Note** Services for UNIX does not provide print services. Windows 2000 Server, however, includes native line printer remote (LPR) and line printer daemon (LPD) UNIX print services. This printing support can be installed through Print Services for UNIX (from the Control Panel, double-click the **Add/Remove Programs** icon, click **Add/Remove Windows Components**, and then select **Other Network File and Printer Services**).

Data Layer Interoperability

At the data layer, Windows 2000 Server includes support for data source interoperability with UNIX systems, as described in the sections that follow.

Oracle Database Access

Microsoft Visual Studio® Enterprise Edition offers comprehensive support for Oracle 7.3 and later databases running on UNIX platforms. Using Visual Studio, developers can visually build or edit data-driven Web pages quickly from multiple data sources. In addition, developers can use Visual Studio to build and edit stored procedures, database diagrams, triggers, and scripts.

Database Connectivity Tools

Open Database Connectivity (ODBC) is a software interface that separates data access from the data sources, to make it easier to gain access to a database on a network. The ODBC database access interface enables programmers to gain access to data from a diverse set of sources, using a standard series of functions and commands. This means that application developers using ODBC can create applications that connect to databases running on UNIX or Windows 2000 Server, and their application code will run exactly the same way on either platform. With ODBC, developers avoid having to code to each specific data source's requirements—efficiency that significantly increases productivity.

Object Linking and Embedding Database (OLE DB) takes ODBC a step further. While ODBC is designed around accessing relational data sources using Structured Query Language (SQL), OLE DB is focused on providing access to *any* data, anywhere.

Application Layer Interoperability

At the application layer, Windows 2000 Server supports interoperability with UNIX systems, as described in the sections that follow.

Telnet

Users can access character-based UNIX applications through Windows 2000 Server support for remote logon. By running terminal emulation software (Telnet) built into Windows 2000 Professional, Windows Me, Windows 95, Windows 98, and Windows NT client operating systems, users can log on to a UNIX timesharing server. After entering an authorized user name and password, users can access applications residing on the remote UNIX system as if they were logged on locally.

Microsoft Internet Explorer for UNIX

Microsoft Internet Explorer for UNIX enables Web applications and Internet or intranet access to be delivered to UNIX desktops, using the familiar Internet Explorer interface. Also, client/server applications can be designed to operate within the browser, across multiple platforms. This application may be obtained free from:
http://www.microsoft.com/downloads

Transaction Internet Protocol

Transaction Internet Protocol (TIP) is a standard two-phase commit protocol that enables a UNIX transaction manager to coordinate distributed transactions. It can be used with any application protocol, but is especially important for the Internet HTTP protocol. For examples of TIP, review the TIP request for proposal (RFP) found at
http://ietf.org

Microsoft Transaction Server 2.0 and Oracle 7.3 Support

Microsoft Transaction Server (MTS) 2.0 is a component-based transaction processing system included with Small Business Server. It combines the features of a transaction processing monitor and an object request broker. MTS defines a programming model, provides a run-time environment, and is also a graphical administration tool.

Microsoft has enhanced the Microsoft Oracle ODBC driver to work with MTS 2.0. In addition, Oracle 8i supports the XA interface. As a result, Small Business Server users can access an Oracle database in a coexisting UNIX operating environment and the database can participate in MTS-based transactions.

For example, users can update a Microsoft SQL Server database in Small Business Server and an Oracle database on a UNIX system under a single atomic transaction. If the transaction commits, both databases are updated. If the transaction quits, all work performed on each database is rolled back to a pre-transaction state.

MTS interoperates with any Oracle platform accessible from Windows 2000, Windows NT, Windows Me, or Windows 95 and Windows 98. Microsoft Distributed Transaction Coordinator (DTC) does not need to be running on UNIX and other non-Windows 2000 platforms in order for an MTS component to update an Oracle database.

MTS also works with Oracle version 8 databases. However, users must access the Oracle 8 database server by using the Oracle 7.3 client. Also, the Microsoft Oracle ODBC driver supplied with MTS 2.0 must be used with the Oracle database, because it is the only Oracle OBDC driver that works with MTS.

Distributed Component Object Model and UNIX

The Component Object Model (COM) is a Microsoft specification for developing distributed transaction-based applications and defining the manner by which objects interact through an exposed interface. Distributed Component Object Model (DCOM) extends the COM model and provides applications with a way to interact remotely over a network.

Microsoft is working with partners to port DCOM onto UNIX and other platforms. This enables the DCOM application programming interface (API) of Windows 2000 Server to appear on UNIX servers. DCOM on a UNIX server enables consistent application behavior in a heterogeneous environment of Windows 2000 and UNIX clients. By employing DCOM on UNIX, users can do the following:

- Port DCOM server applications from Windows 2000 Server-based operating environments to UNIX operating environments.

- Create wrappers for existing UNIX applications, providing DCOM access to the applications by clients running Windows.

- Develop new distributed UNIX applications that take advantage of the DCOM distribution mechanism. These applications can make the most of the DCOM reuse, version independence, and language independence capabilities.

Management Layer Interoperability

At the management layer, Windows 2000 Server supports interoperability with UNIX systems, as described in the sections that follow.

Simple Network Management Protocol

Simple Network Management Protocol (SNMP) service is included in Windows 2000 Server and Windows 2000 Professional. This means that SNMP management software, such as Hewlett-Packard OpenView and IBM NetView, can be used to manage Windows systems. Using these products, the technology consultant can manage UNIX clients from the Windows 2000 Server operating system in Small Business Server 2000.

Administrative Tools

Services for UNIX offers the following three features to simplify the administration of combined Windows 2000 Server and UNIX networks:

- Password synchronization between Windows 2000 Server and UNIX servers. This reduces user confusion and the technology consultant's workload.

- Telnet administration of both UNIX and the Windows 2000 Server operating system, including access to network administration from a single client workstation.

- Korn Shell (a UNIX command line interface) and common UNIX commands, thus enabling UNIX shell scripts to run on Windows 2000 Server. This means that UNIX administrators can use familiar UNIX commands on Windows 2000 Server.

More Information

For additional information about Windows 2000 Server and UNIX interoperability, refer to:

- Services for UNIX at: http://www.microsoft.com.

- Chapter 11, "Services for Unix," in the *Internetworking Guide* of the *Windows 2000 Server Resource Kit.*

Macintosh Interoperability

Services for Macintosh is an integrated component of Windows 2000 Server that enables Windows and Macintosh clients to collaborate and share information across the small business network. Macintosh users can connect to a Windows 2000 Server in the same way that they connect to an AppleShare Server. The service supports an unlimited number of simultaneous Apple Filing Protocol (AFP) connections to a Windows 2000 Server, and the Macintosh sessions are integrated with Windows 2000 sessions. Windows 2000 Server is transparent to the Macintosh user—its presence is revealed only by the quick responsiveness of the network.

Graphics Performance

In the past, Macintosh clients used UNIX servers to facilitate the heavy performance requirements of moving large graphics files across a network. With optimization for high bandwidth networks, such as Fast Ethernet and its full-featured functionality, Windows 2000 Server can handle the most demanding needs of Macintosh users. Windows 2000 Server is also ideal for the publishing marketplace, because most of the major server applications are already using it.

File Sharing

Services for Macintosh enables Macintosh users to access and share files on a Windows 2000 Server-based network. The service includes a full AFP 2.0 file server. All Macintosh file system attributes, such as resource data forks, are supported. As a file server, all filenames, icons, and access permissions are intelligently managed. For example, a Word for Windows file appears on the Macintosh computer with the correct Word for Windows icons. These applications can also be run from the file server as Macintosh applications. When files are deleted, no orphaned resource forks remain to be cleaned up.

Macintosh-accessible volumes can be created in My Computer. Services for Macintosh automatically create a Public Files volume at installation time. At the same time, Windows 2000 file and directory permissions are translated into corresponding Macintosh permissions.

Printer Sharing

Services for Macintosh enables Macintosh users to gain access to and share printers on a Windows 2000 Server-based network. With Services for Macintosh, Macintosh users can gain access to the print server through the Chooser dialog box, and can print PostScript jobs to either PostScript or non-PostScript printers, using the Windows 2000 Server print services.

Administration

Services for Macintosh can be administered from Control Panel. It can also be started transparently, provided that the technology consultant has configured the server to use the service.

Connecting Macintosh Computers to the Internet

Windows 2000 Server application, included with Small Business Server, has all the features necessary to connect Macintosh clients to the Internet or corporate intranet. With built-in DHCP, Small Business Server has full compatibility with Macintosh clients running Open Transport 1.1, allowing them to use dynamically assigned IP addresses. For example, a Macintosh PowerBook can be moved anywhere in the network with no disruption to network services.

Security

With Internet Security and Acceleration (ISA) Server 2000, which is included with Small Business Server, Macintosh clients have fast and secure access to the Internet. Also, Services for Macintosh fully supports and complies with Windows 2000 security. It presents the AFP security model to Macintosh users and enables them to gain access to files on volumes that reside on compact discs or other read-only media. The AFP server also supports both clear text and encrypted passwords at logon time.

> **Note** The technology consultant has the option of configuring the server to not accept clear text passwords.

Interoperability Benefits of Services for Macintosh

The following table summarizes the interoperability benefits that Services for Macintosh, included in Small Business Server, has for Macintosh users.

Table 20.1 Services for Macintosh Interoperability Benefits

Feature	Benefit
Seamless connectivity for Macintosh users	Macintosh users can access the Windows 2000 Server as easily as an AppleShare Server, using the familiar **Chooser** dialog box.
High performance file and print services	Macintosh users can make the most of Windows 2000 Server performance, with its ability to move large graphics files faster than any other network operating system.
Full-featured AppleTalk routing	With its built-in Multi-Protocol Router, a Windows 2000 Server can replace a dedicated AppleTalk router.
Universal printing	Macintosh users can print PostScript jobs to either PostScript or non-PostScript printers, using the Windows 2000 print server. Server-side spooling means a faster return to the client application and increased user productivity.
	The Windows 2000 print subsystem handles AppleTalk de-spooling errors and uses the Windows 2000 Server built-in printer support. A PostScript-compatible engine enables Macintosh users to print to any Windows 2000 printer as if they are printing to a LaserWriter.

Table 20.1   Services for Macintosh Interoperability Benefits *(continued)*

Feature	Benefit
AppleTalk/PostScript printing for Windows users	Windows users can send print jobs to PostScript printers on an AppleTalk network, which provides them with access to more network resources.
	A user interface in Services for Macintosh allows for publishing a print queue on AppleTalk and for choosing an AppleTalk printer as a destination device.
User identification and directory permissions	Users can log on to Small Business Server from either a Windows PC or a Macintosh computer, using the same user identification. Windows 2000 Server directory permissions for Macintosh users can be set in exactly the same way as an AppleShare Server, eliminating the need for Macintosh users to learn a new security model.
High volume capacity	Macintosh users use a Windows 2000 Server NTFS volume.
Flexible server hardware options	Windows 2000 Server supports more hardware options than any other network operating system. Thus, Macintosh users can choose the server hardware platform that best suits their needs, including PowerPC platforms.

More Information

For additional information about setting up, configuring, and using Services for Macintosh, refer to Chapter 13, "Services for Macintosh" of the *Internetworking Guide* of the *Windows 2000 Server Resource Kit*.

Summary

A strength of Small Business Server 2000 is its support for different environments. To accomplish business tasks, small businesses, like larger businesses, need the ability to run multi-vendor networks and ISV applications. This is supported in Small Business Server 2000 in the following ways:

- Support for Novell NetWare
- Support for UNIX
- Support for Macintosh

Firewall Security and Web Caching with ISA Server

Microsoft® Internet Security and Acceleration (ISA) Server 2000 is an extensible firewall and content cache server that delivers a compelling combination of security and performance. ISA Server integrates high-performance content caching with firewall features for a complete small business solution. It provides an easy and secure way to bring Internet access to every desktop in the small business organization, while rendering an integrated network access management solution.

This chapter begins with an overview of ISA Server, including descriptions of ISA Server features and services offered with Microsoft Small Business Server 2000. System architecture is also discussed. The chapter concludes with a description of specific ISA Server firewall security features.

Overview of ISA Server

This section provides an overview of Microsoft ISA Server, including:

- Firewall and security overview
- Publishing overview
- Cache overview

Firewall and Security Overview

ISA Server can be deployed as a firewall that acts as the secure gateway to the Internet for internal clients. ISA Server protects all communication between internal computers and the Internet. In a simple firewall scenario, the ISA Server computer has two network adapter cards—one connected to the local network and one connected to the Internet. This scenario is illustrated in Figure 21.1.

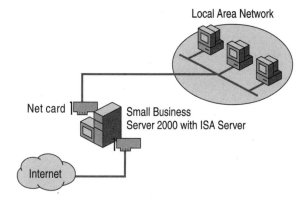

Figure 21.1   The two network adapter cards create a simple firewall between the public and private network

You can use ISA Server to configure the firewall, configure policies, and create rules to implement your business guidelines. By setting security access policies, you prevent unauthorized access and inappropriate content from entering the network. You can also restrict what traffic is allowed for each user and group, application, destination, content type, and schedule.

ISA Server includes the following firewall and security features:

- Outgoing access policy
- Intrusion detection
- Wizards
- Application filters
- Authentication

Outgoing Access Policy

You can use ISA Server to configure site and content rules and protocol rules (both described later in the chapter), which control how your internal users gain access to the Internet. Site and Content Rules specify which sites and content can be accessed. Protocol Rules indicate whether a particular protocol is accessible for inbound and outbound communication.

Intrusion Detection

Integrated intrusion detection mechanisms can alert you when a specific attack is launched against your network. For example, you can configure the ISA Server to alert you if a port-scanning attempt is detected.

Wizards

The ISA Server Security Wizard enables you to set the appropriate level of system security, depending on how ISA Server functions in your network. The ISA Server VPN Wizard (discussed later in the chapter) enables you to set ports to accept or filter out network traffic from the Internet.

Application Filters

ISA Server controls application-specific traffic by using data-aware filters. ISA Server uses the filters to determine whether packets should be accepted, rejected, redirected, or modified.

Authentication

ISA Server supports the following user authentication methods: Integrated Microsoft Windows® authentication, Client certificates, Digest, and Basic.

Publishing Overview

ISA Server enables you to publish services to the Internet without compromising the security of your internal network. You can use ISA Server to publish internal servers, making them available to Internet users, without putting your network at risk. You can configure Web publishing and server publishing rules that determine which requests should be sent to a server on your local network, providing an increased layer of security for your internal servers.

> ☑ **Note** Although you can use Small Business Server to publish some Web resources—such as intranet content for employees or extranet content for business partners—note that Small Business Server 2000 is not designed for true Web hosting. Instead, you should use an Internet service provider (ISP) to host Web pages that will be accessed by the general public.

For example, you can place your Microsoft Exchange 2000 Server behind the ISA Server and then create server publishing rules that allow the e-mail server to be published to the Internet. Incoming e-mail messages routed to the Exchange Server are then intercepted by the ISA Server computer, which gives the appearance of an e-mail server to clients. ISA Server filters the traffic and forwards it on to Exchange Server. In this scenario, your Exchange Server is never exposed directly to external users and is in a secure environment, maintaining access only to other internal network services. Figure 21.2 illustrates how you can use ISA Server in a similar way to securely publish Web servers.

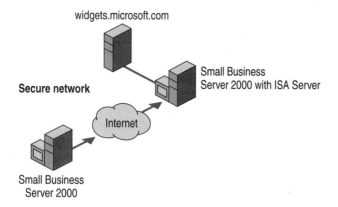

Figure 21.2 Publishing Web content securely to the Internet

When a user on the Internet requests an object from a Web server, the request is actually sent to an Internet Protocol (IP) address on the ISA Server. Web publishing rules configured on the ISA Server forward the request as applicable to the internal Web server. The publishing servers require no special configuration, because the servers benefit from ISA Server's extensible network address translation (NAT) architecture.

Cache Overview

ISA Server implements a cache of frequently requested objects to improve network performance. You can configure the cache to ensure that it contains the most frequently used data accessed by your organization or by Internet users.

ISA Server can be used to allow communication between your local network and the Internet. Communication may be internal users accessing servers on the Internet—in this instance, ISA Server would implement forward caching. Communication may also be external users accessing internal publishing servers—in this instance, ISA Server would implement reverse caching. Both scenarios benefit from ISA Server's ability to cache information, making it more quickly available to users.

ISA Server offers the following types of caching:

- Distributed
- Hierarchical
- Scheduled
- Forward
- Reverse

Distributed Caching

When you set up an array of ISA Server computers, you benefit from distributed content caching. ISA Server uses the Cache Array Routing Protocol (CARP) to enable multiple ISA Server computers to be arrayed as a single logical cache.

Hierarchical Caching

ISA Server further extends distributed caching by allowing you to set up a hierarchy of caches, chaining together arrays of ISA Server computers, so that users can access objects from the cache geographically closest to them.

Scheduled Caching

Configure the scheduled cache content download service when you want the ISA Server to retrieve commonly requested content from the Internet to its cache.

Forward Caching

ISA Server can also be deployed as a forward caching server, providing internal users with access to the Internet. ISA Server maintains a centralized cache of frequently requested Internet objects any Web browser client can access. Objects served from the disk cache require significantly less processing time than objects served from the Internet, improving client browser performance, decreasing user response time, and reducing bandwidth consumption on your Internet connection.

Figure 21.3 illustrates how users benefit when ISA Server caches objects.

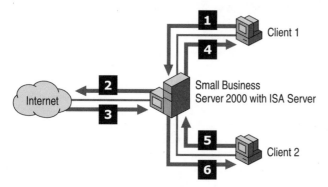

Figure 21.3 How ISA Server responds when a user requests an object

1. The first user (Client 1) requests a Web object.

2. ISA Server checks to find out whether the object is in the cache. Because the object is not in the ISA Server cache, ISA Server requests the object from the server on the Internet.

3. The server on the Internet returns the object to the ISA Server.

4. The ISA Server retains a copy of the object in its cache, and returns the object to Client 1.

5. The second user (Client 2) requests the same object.

6. The ISA Server returns the object from its cache, rather than obtaining it from the Internet.

Figure 21.3 focuses on a forward caching scenario (internal clients accessing the Internet). The process is identical for reverse caching, when Internet users access a corporate Web server.

Reverse Caching

ISA Server can cache content of publishing Web servers, thus improving their overall performance and accessibility. All ISA Server caching features are applicable for the content on published servers; however, reverse caching is typically beyond the scope of Small Business Server 2000 networks, and is mentioned here only for reference purposes.

Architecture Overview

ISA Server works at various communication layers to protect the Small Business Server 2000 network. At the packet layer, ISA Server implements packet filtering. When packet filtering is enabled, ISA Server statically controls data on the external interface, evaluating inbound traffic before it has the chance to reach any resource. If the data is allowed to pass the packet-filtering layer, it is passed to the Firewall and Web Proxy services, where ISA Server rules are processed to determine whether the request should be serviced.

As illustrated in Figure 21.4, ISA Server protects three types of clients: firewall clients, secure network address translation (SecureNAT) clients, and Web proxy clients.

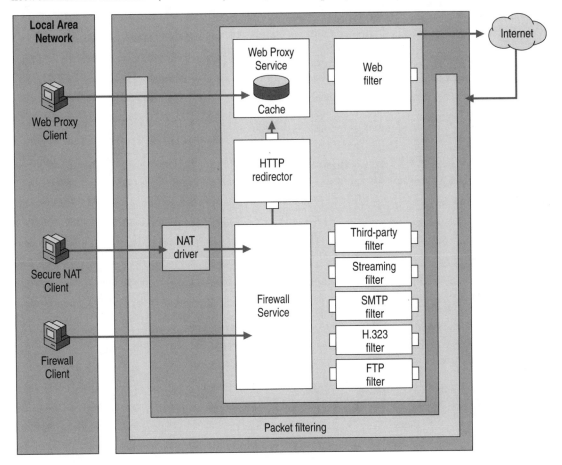

Figure 21.4 ISA architecture details from a client perspective

Firewall Client

In Small Business Server 2000, the Firewall Client, which was developed by the ISA Server team at Microsoft, is installed as part of client workstation setup. The Firewall Client participates in Internet-related network traffic in the following way. Requests from firewall clients are directed to the Firewall service on the ISA Server computer to determine whether access is allowed. Subsequently, they may be filtered by application filters and other add-ins. If the firewall client requests a Hypertext Transfer Protocol (HTTP) object, the HTTP redirector redirects the request to the Web Proxy service. The Web Proxy service may also cache the requested object, or serve the object from the ISA Server cache.

SecureNAT

SecureNAT clients are computers that do not have Firewall Client installed. Requests from SecureNAT clients are directed first to the NAT driver, which substitutes a valid Internet global IP address for the internal IP address of the SecureNAT client. The client request is then directed to the Firewall service to determine whether access is allowed. Finally, the request may be filtered by application filters and other extensions. If the SecureNAT client requests an HTTP object, the HTTP redirector redirects the request to the Web Proxy service. The Web Proxy service may also cache the requested object, or deliver the object from the ISA Server cache.

Web Proxy Clients

Web Proxy clients are any CERN-compatible Web application, such as a business application using the Web for data updates. Requests from Web Proxy clients are directed to the Web Proxy service on the ISA Server computer to determine whether access is allowed. The Web Proxy service may also cache the requested object, or serve the object from the ISA Server cache.

> ☑ **Note** Both Firewall Client computers and SecureNAT client computers might also be Web Proxy clients. By default, this is the case with client workstations on a Small Business Server 2000 network. If the Web application on the computer is configured explicitly to use the ISA Server, all Web requests (HTTP, File Transfer Protocol [FTP], and Hypertext Transport Protocol Secure [HTTPS]) are sent directly to the Web Proxy service. All other requests are handled first by the Firewall service.

Configuring ISA Server

This section highlights key ISA Server configuration areas. Topics discussed include policy elements, access policy, packet filtering, and the ISA Server VPN Wizard.

Policy Elements

Some rule properties can be set to values beyond the scope of the rule itself. The group of these properties is called policy elements, which are discussed in greater detail in the ISA Server Help. Policy elements include:

- Bandwidth priorities
- Client address sets
- Content groups
- Destination sets
- Dial-up entries
- Protocol definitions
- Schedule

Access Policy

You can use ISA Server to configure an access policy, which consists of Site and Content Rules, Protocol Rules, and IP packet filters. In Small Business Server 2000, you create an access policy for a stand-alone server. Access policy rules apply to all types of clients: firewall clients, SecureNAT clients, and Web Proxy clients.

Site and Content Rules

You can grant or deny access to the Internet by creating Site and Content Rules. Site and Content Rules determine if and when content on specific destination sets can be accessed by users or client address sets.

When a client requests an object, ISA Server checks the Site and Content Rules. If a Site and Content Rule specifically denies the request, access is denied. The request will be fulfilled only if a Site and Content Rule specifically allows the client access to the content and if the client is allowed to communicate by using the specific protocol. To allow access to the Internet, perform the following steps.

To allow access to the Internet

1. Create a site and content rule specifying which clients are allowed access to specific destination sets. Typically, a technology consultant creates rules in a Small Business Server environment.

2. Create a protocol rule indicating which protocols can be used to access the specific destinations. Typically, a technology consultant creates rules in a Small Business Server environment. For additional information, refer to the "Protocols" section later in the chapter.

Processing Order

Although Site and Content Rules are not in a specific order, rules that deny access are processed before rules that allow access. For example, if you create two rules, one of which allows access to all clients and one of which denies access to all users in the Sales department, the Sales department cannot gain access to the Internet.

Action

Site and Content Rules can either allow or deny access to specific sites. If access is denied, then for HTTP objects, the request can be redirected to a different URL—typically a page on an internal server—explaining why access is denied.

When you specify the destination to which to redirect the request, you can specify a different location by typing **http://** and then the URL of the location to which to redirect the request. When access is denied, ISA Server sends the URL specified here to the Web browser client. The client Web browser then tries to access the object from the destination to which ISA Server redirected.

For example, suppose a Site and Content Rule denies access to http://example.microsoft.com/, redirecting the request for this site to http://widgets.microsoft.com/accessdenied.htm. When a client requests an object on http://example.microsoft.com/, ISA Server denies the request, and returns http://widgets.microsoft.com/accessdenied.htm to the client. The client then requests http://widgets.microsoft.com/accessdenied.htm.

> ☑ **Note** If you choose to redirect the request, the URL you specify must be accessible to the selected clients or users. Either the URL must be on an internal computer or there must be a rule that explicitly allows access to the URL.

Protocol Rules

Protocol rules determine which protocols the client computers can use to access the Internet. You can define protocol rules that allow or deny the use of one or more protocol definitions.

Protocols

You can configure protocol rules to apply to all IP traffic, to a specific set of protocols definitions, or to all IP traffic. If ISA Server is installed in cache mode, protocol rules can be applied only to HTTP, HTTP-S, and FTP protocols. ISA Server includes a list of preconfigured, well-known protocol definitions, including the Internet protocols that are most widely used. You can also add or modify additional protocols.

When a client requests an object using a specific protocol, ISA Server checks the protocol rules. If a protocol rule specifically denies use of the protocol, the request is denied. The request will be processed only if a protocol rule specifically allows the client to communicate using the specific protocol, and if a site and content rule specifically allows access to the requested object. You must perform the following tasks to allow access:

1. Create a protocol rule indicating which protocols can be used to access the specific destinations.

2. Create a site and content rule specifying which clients are allowed access to specific destination sets.

Some application filters create and install new protocol definitions. When the application filter is disabled, all its protocol definitions are also disabled. Traffic that uses the protocol definition is blocked. For example, if you disable the streaming media filter, all traffic that uses the Windows Media® and Real Networks protocol definitions is blocked.

Other applications filter traffic of existing protocol definitions, either user-defined or those configured by ISA Server. When application filters are disabled, the protocol definitions they filter are not disabled. For example, even if you disable the Simple Mail Transfer Protocol (SMTP) filter, SMTP protocol definitions might still be allowed to pass (unfiltered).

Protocol Rules for SecureNAT Clients

Protocol Rules apply to firewall clients and to SecureNAT clients. If the protocol is defined by an application filter, the protocol rule applies to both firewall and SecureNAT clients. If the protocol rule applies to a protocol with only a primary connection—for example, HTTP—the rule applies to both firewall and SecureNAT clients.

If a protocol has secondary connections, and is not defined by an application filter, the protocol rule applies only to the primary connection. For example, if an application uses a protocol with a secondary connection, the application will work only on the firewall client. For SecureNAT clients, if you configure a protocol rule to apply to all IP traffic, the rule will only apply to all defined protocols.

Processing Order

Although protocol rules are not in a specific order, rules that deny protocols are processed before rules that allow access. For example, if you create two rules—one rule that allows use of all protocols and one rule that denies use of the SMTP protocol—the SMTP protocol will not be allowed.

Packet Filtering

The packet-filtering feature of ISA Server enables you to control the flow of IP packets to and from ISA Server. When you enable packet filtering, all packets on the external interface are dropped unless they are explicitly allowed—either statically by IP packet filters or dynamically by access policy or publishing rules.

☑ **Note** Even if you do not enable packet filtering, communication between your local network and the Internet is allowed only when you explicitly configure rules that permit access.

Since it is preferable to open ports dynamically in most instances, it is recommended that you create one of these two types of rules:

- Access policy rules to allow internal clients access to the Internet

- Publishing rules to allow external clients access to internal servers

This is because IP packet filters open the ports statically, whereas the access policy and publishing rules open the ports dynamically—as a request arrives. For example, suppose you want to grant all internal users HTTP access. You should not create an IP packet filter that opens port 8080. Rather, create the necessary site and content rule and protocol rule that allow this access.

In some scenarios, you must use IP packet filters. Configure IP packet filters if you:

- Publish servers that are located on a screened subnet (DMZ).

- Run applications or other services on the ISA Server computer that need to listen to the Internet.

- Want to allow access to protocols that are not User Datagram Protocol (UDP) or Transmission Control Protocol (TCP) based (IP protocols).

- Can configure IP packet filters to filter IP packet traffic (only if you install ISA Server in firewall mode or integrated mode).

Virtual Private Networks

ISA Server helps you set up and secure a VPN, which is an extension of a private network that encompasses links across shared or public networks, similar to the Internet. A VPN enables you to send data between two computers across a shared or public intranet in a manner that emulates the properties of a point-to-point private link.

VPN connections allow users who work at home or on the road a remote access connection to an organization server using the infrastructure provided by a public internetwork (such as the Internet). From the user's perspective, the VPN is a point-to-point connection between the computer, the VPN client, and an organization server (the VPN server). The exact infrastructure of the shared or public network is irrelevant because it appears logically as if the data is sent over a dedicated private link.

VPN connections also allow organizations to have routed connections with offices that are geographically separate or with other organizations over a public internetwork (such as the Internet), while maintaining secure communications. A routed VPN connection across the Internet logically operates as a dedicated WAN link. Figure 21.5 shows a VPN.

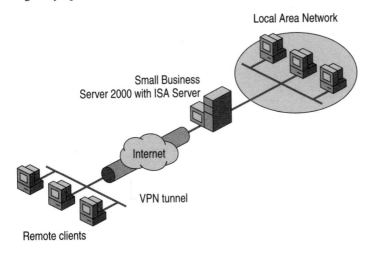

Figure 21.5 VPN overview

The ISA Server computer configured to be a VPN computer connects to its ISP. The remote client computer connects to its ISP. When a computer on the local area network communicates with a remote computer, data is encapsulated and sent through the VPN tunnel. A tunneling protocol (PPTP or L2TP) is used to manage tunnels and encapsulate private data. To be a VPN connection, data that is tunneled must also be encrypted.

The ISA Server VPN Wizard, shown in Figure 21.6, runs on ISA Server on the local area network. The ISA Server VPN Wizard is the preferred way to configure a VPN in Small Business Server, as it will not negatively impact other port settings created by other Small Business Server wizards.

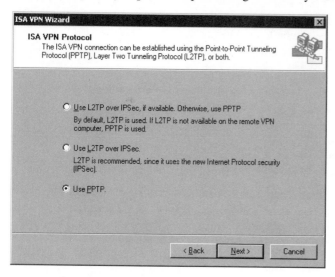

Figure 21.6 ISA Server VPN Wizard

Summary

This chapter described the firewall and caching capabilities of ISA Server. Specific topics discussed included:

- Access policy
- Detecting intruders
- Publishing
- Caching
- Client types, including firewall clients
- Virtual private networks

Computer Security and Windows 2000 Server

Because sensitive data—anything from financial data, to personnel files, to employee correspondence—is stored on computers, there is a need to protect these company resources. Small businesses also need to protect themselves against accidental or deliberate changes to the way the computer is set up. At the same time, the technology consultant should take into account the need of small business network users to do their work without barriers to the resources they need.

Microsoft® Windows® 2000 Server provides a range of security levels to address the needs of the small business. In this chapter, the various security levels are described. Because these levels vary according to the needs of each business, the technology consultant may want to create a unique combination of the characteristics of security levels presented in this chapter.

Overview of Security Needs

In small businesses, the level of security can vary depending on the specific requirements of the network. For example, maximum security may not be needed at all times, because it restricts access to resources and also takes additional work for the technology consultant to maintain.

The first step in establishing security is to make an accurate assessment of network needs. Next, the technology consultant can select and implement the appropriate measures. It is also important to make sure that users know how to maintain security and why security is important. The last step is to monitor the small business network and make adjustments as needed.

Physical Security Considerations

This section describes standard and high-level physical security considerations and recommendations for the small business organization.

Basic Security

For standard security, the Microsoft Small Business Server computer should be protected, as any valuable equipment would be. Generally, this involves keeping the computer away from unauthorized users in a locked building. In some instances, you may want to use a cable and lock to secure the computer to its location. If the computer has a physical lock, lock it and store the key in a safe place for added security.

Advanced Security

Standard security precautions are sufficient for most installations. However, additional precautions are suggested for computers that contain sensitive data, or those with a high risk of data theft or accidental (or unauthorized) disruption of the system. At a minimum, the physical security considerations described for standard security configurations should be followed. In addition, the physical link provided by your computer network should be examined. In some cases, it is wise to use controls built into certain hardware platforms that restrict who can start the Small Business Server computer.

Networks and Security

When a computer is placed in a network, an access route to the server is created. Make sure this route is secured. For standard-level security, user validation and file protection are sufficient. However, for high-level security, the network itself should be secure, and in some cases, the server must be completely isolated.

The risks to the server from the network include other network users and unauthorized network taps. If the network is entirely contained in a secure building, the risk of unauthorized taps is minimized or eliminated. If the cabling must pass through unsecured areas, optical fiber links rather than twisted pair wiring are recommended to foil any attempts at wiretapping data transmissions.

If Small Business Server is connected to the Internet, be aware of the security issues involved in providing access to and from the Internet. For additional information on using network topology to provide security, refer to Chapter 21, "Firewall Security and Web Caching with ISA Server" in this guide, and Chapter 17, "Determining Windows 2000 Network Security Strategies," in the *Deployment Planning Guide* in *Window 2000 Server Resource Kit.*

Controlling Access to the Computer

The Small Business Server computer is not completely secure if people other than authorized users can physically access it. For maximum security on a computer that is not physically secure (locked away), follow all or some of the following security measures:

- Disable floppy-disk-based startup. If the computer does not require a floppy disk drive, remove it.

- Keep the central processing unit (CPU) in a case that cannot be opened without a key. Store the key away from the computer.

- Ensure that the hard disk is formatted with an NTFS file system (NTFS).

- If the computer does not require network access, remove the network card.

Controlling Access to the Power Switch

Keep unauthorized users away from the power and reset switches on the computer, particularly if your computer rights policy denies them the right to shut down the computer. The most secure computers (other than those in locked and guarded rooms) expose only the computer's keyboard, monitor, mouse, and printer to users. The CPU and removable media drives can be locked away where only authorized personnel have access to them.

On many hardware platforms, the system can be protected by using a power-on password. A power-on password prevents unauthorized personnel from starting an operating system other than Windows 2000, which would compromise system security. Power-on passwords are a function of the computer hardware, not the operating system software. The procedure for setting up a power-on password, therefore, depends on the type of computer. Consult the computer vendor's documentation for additional information.

Standard Software Security Considerations

A secure system requires effort from both the technology consultant administering the system and network users. The technology consultant must maintain certain software settings, and users must cultivate habits such as logging off at the end of the day and memorizing their passwords rather than writing them down.

User Accounts

With standard security, a user should be required to provide a user account (user name) and password before using the computer. User accounts can be managed from the Microsoft Active Directory™ directory service Users and Computers snap-in.

1. Click **Start,** point to **Programs,** point to **Microsoft Small Business Server,** and then click **Small Business Server Administrator Console.**

2. In the Console Tree, click **Active Directory Users and Computers.**

3. Expand the server name of your server.

4. Click **Users.**

5. In the Details Pane, right-click a user, and then click **Properties.** The property sheet for the user account appears.

You may also use the Add User Wizard from the To Do List in the Small Business Server Administrator Console.

☑ **Note**   Changes to the Windows 2000 computer user rights policy take effect the next time the user logs on.

Administrative Accounts and User Accounts

You should use separate accounts for administrative activity and general user activity. Individuals who do administrative work on the computer should have two user accounts—one for administrative tasks and one for general activity. To avoid accidental changes to protected resources, use the user account with the fewest privileges (as long as that user can perform the tasks at hand). For example, viruses can do much more damage if activated from an account with administrator privileges.

☑ **Note**   It is also possible to run separate processes on a Windows 2000 computer under different user names. For example, while logged on as an administrator at the Small Business Server computer, you could start a Microsoft Internet Explorer Web browser that creates an Internet session using a different logon name. You might run the Web browser session as a low-level user account that does not allow downloaded files to be written to the local hard disk. This is accomplished by using the **RUNAS** command at a command prompt. The full syntax of the **RUNAS** command is:

RUNAS [/profile] [/env] [/netonly] /user:<UserName> program

/profile = if the user's profile needs to be loaded

/env = to use the current environment instead of the user's

/netonly = use if the credentials specified are for remote access only

/user = <UserName> should be in the form DOMAIN\USER or USER@DOMAIN

program = command line with complete path for .EXE program

Enter the user's password when asked.

The Guest Account

Limited access can be permitted for visitors through the default Guest account. If the computer is for public use, the Guest account can be used for public logons. You should prohibit the Guest account from writing or deleting any files, directories, or registry keys, with the possible exception of a directory in which information can be left.

In a standard security configuration, a computer that allows Guest access can also be used by regular users for those files they do not want accessible to the general public. These users can log on with their own user names to access files in directories in which they have set the appropriate permissions. They should be especially careful to log off or lock the workstation before they leave.

☑ **Note** The Guest account should be denied permission to log on locally at the server computer.

Logging On

All users should *always* press CTRL+ALT+DEL before logging on. Intrusive applications designed to collect account passwords can appear as a logon screen, waiting for user input. By pressing CTRL+ALT+DEL users will see the secure logon screen provided by Windows 2000, and any intrusive programs will be disabled.

Supported Client Authentication

Authentication, sometimes referred to as identification, allows initial access to an operating system, such as Windows 2000. The first step in authentication is to present credentials, followed by system validation of those credentials. After those credentials are validated, the user can access resources controlled by the system.

For Windows 2000 clients, the primary logon authentication is provided by Kerberos. Kerberos authentication is the primary security protocol for access within or across Windows 2000 domains. It provides for mutual authentication of clients and servers and supports delegation and authorization. If implemented, Internet Protocol Security (IPSec) supports network-level authentication, data encryption to secure intranets, extranets, and secure Internet Web sites.

Microsoft Windows NT®, Windows 95, Windows 98, and Windows Me clients are authenticated through Integrated Windows Authentication (formerly known as Windows NT Challenge Response). A user supplies a logon user name and password that is compared to the same user name and password stored in Active Directory. If these credentials match, the user is authenticated and a security token is attached to all processes (applications) that the user runs. All processes must have a token associated with them that identifies the user and the Windows 2000 security groups to which the user belongs. The token contains the user's security identifier (SID) and the SIDs of all the security groups to which the user belongs.

Non-Supported Client Authentication

The sections that follow describe how Microsoft MS-DOS®, Microsoft Windows 3.1, and Macintosh clients authenticate to a Windows 2000 Server.

MS-DOS Client Authentication

For an MS-DOS client to connect to a network, network software such as LAN Manager or Microsoft Networks must be installed and configured. Refer to the network software user documentation for installation instructions.

When the network software is installed, the Autoexec file is modified. The network software then starts automatically when the MS-DOS client is started. For the MS-DOS client to log onto Windows 2000 Server, the user account and appropriate permissions for the user must be created from the Small Business Server consoles, or in Active Directory from the Active Directory Users and Computers console. After the user account and permissions are created and the network is started, the MS-DOS user types the **Net Use** command (at the prompt) and then types the server name and share to which to connect. In the following example, the user is connecting to the payroll share on a payroll department server identified as *CAWPS30DPT01*:

Net Use * \\CAWPS30DPT01\Payroll

The user then presses ENTER. An available drive letter is assigned and a connection to the server is established.

Windows 3.1 Client Authentication

For a Windows 3.1 user to connect to a Windows 2000 Server-based network, network software such as LAN Manager or Microsoft Networking Client must be installed and configured. Refer to the network software user documentation for installation instructions.

When the network software is installed, the Config.sys and Windows\system.ini files are updated. This causes the network software to start up automatically when the Windows 3.1 client computer is started.

> **Note**   If LAN Manager is used, the LAN Manager Logon window is displayed every time the Windows 3.1 client computer starts up.

Before a Windows 3.1 user can log onto Windows 2000 Server, the user account and appropriate permissions for the user must be created from the Small Business Server consoles or in Active Directory from the Active Directory Users and Computers console. After the user account and permissions are set up, the Windows 3.1 user can log on and be authenticated on the Windows 2000 Server network. To gain access to file and print services, the Windows 3.1 user must supply the network path to connect to the required Windows 2000 Server resources.

Macintosh Client Authentication

Services for Macintosh is a completely integrated component of Windows 2000 Server, making it possible for Macintosh users to share files and printers in the Windows 2000 Server domain. Macintosh users need only the operating system software on their computers. However, the optional Microsoft Authentication module, an extension to AppleShare, may be set up to provide additional security for Macintosh client logon to the Windows 2000 Server.

Microsoft Authentication encrypts (scrambles) passwords so that they cannot be monitored when sent over the network. Microsoft Authentication also stores the passwords on the Windows 2000 Server. The technology consultant can set up the Macintosh Authentication file, or the Macintosh client computer can do so across the network. With Macintosh Authentication, the Macintosh client computer can also specify the domain when the user logs on or changes passwords.

Because Apple software, up to version 7.1, only has standard authentication modules, it is recommended that you install the Microsoft Authentication Module if increased security is necessary for Macintosh clients in the Windows 2000 Server domain.

More Information

For additional information on Macintosh client authentication, refer to Chapter 13, "Services for Macintosh," in the *Internetworking Guide*, part of *Windows 2000 Server Resource Kit*.

Logging Off or Locking the Workstation

Users should always log off or lock their workstations when away from them for any length of time. Logging off allows other users to log on (if they know the password to an account), whereas locking the workstation does not. The workstation can be set to lock automatically when it has not been used for a set period of time, using any 32-bit screen saver with a Password Protected option. For information about setting up screen savers, refer to Windows 2000 Server Help.

Passwords

Anyone who knows a user name and the associated password can log on as that user. Users should keep their passwords secret. The following list provides a few additional tips:

- Change passwords frequently, and avoid reusing them.

- Avoid using easily guessed words. A phrase or a combination of letters and numbers works well.

- Don't write a password down. Use one that is easy for you to remember.

For more information, refer to "Creating Strong Passwords" in Windows 2000 Server Help. To do so, click **Start**, and then click **Help**.

DNS Security

The Domain Name Service (DNS) system used in Small Business Server has a security setting for secure dynamic zone-file updates. This enables zone transfers between known DNS servers.

To set secure dynamic updates

1. Click **Start**, point to **Programs**, point to **Administrative Tools**, and then click **DNS**.

2. In the Console Tree, right-click on the zone file, and then click **Properties**.

3. Select **Only secure updates** from the **Allow dynamic updates** drop-down list.

4. Click **OK**.

Enforcing Strong User Passwords

The technology consultant should highly recommend that the customer implement strong passwords. Passwords must contain characters from at least three of the four classes described in the following table:

Table 22.1   Password characters for passfilt.dll

Description	Examples
English uppercase letters	A, B, C, ... Z
English lowercase letters	a, b, c, ... z
Western arabic numerals	1, 2, 3, ... 9
Non-alphanumeric (special characters)	Punctuation symbols

Passwords cannot contain the user name or any part of the full user name.

Protecting the Registry from Network Access

All the initialization and configuration information used by Windows 2000 Server is stored in the registry. The registry can be altered from the Registry Editor, which supports remote access to the Windows 2000 registry. To restrict network access to the registry, use the Registry Editor 32-bit version (Regedt32) to set permissions for the winreg Registry key:

HKEY_LOCAL_MACHINE\SYSTEM\CurrentcontrolSet\Control\SecurePipeServers\ winreg

The Permissions for winreg dialog box is shown in Figure 22.1.

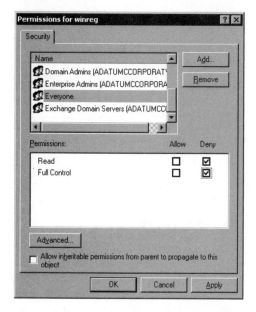

Figure 22.1 Denying everyone Read and Full Control access to the registry

In an all-Windows 2000 network with Windows 2000 Professional clients, you can restrict access
to the registry by using Group Policy (from the Group Policy Wizard, Windows Settings for the
Computer Configuration folder, Security Settings, Registry folder).

> **Caution** The Registry Editor should be used only by individuals who thoroughly
> understand the tool, the registry itself, and the effects of changes to various keys. Mistakes
> made in the Registry Editor could render all or part of the system unusable.

Secure File Sharing

The native Windows 2000 Server file sharing service is provided through the Server Messaging
Blocks (SMB)-based server and redirector services. Even though only administrators can create
shares, the default security placed on the share allows everyone full-control access. These
permissions control access to files on down-level file systems, such as the file allocation table
(FAT), which do not have built-in security mechanisms. Shares on NTFS enforce the security on
the underlying directory to which the shares map. It is recommended that proper security be
established with NTFS and not with the file-sharing service. Windows 2000 includes several
enhancements to the SMB-based file-sharing protocol, as follows:

- Support for mutual authentication as a countermeasure to person-in-the-middle attacks and
  other forms of network traffic interception.

- Support for message authentication, to prevent active message attacks.

These enhancements are provided by incorporating message signing into SMB packets, verified at both the server and client ends. There are registry key settings to enable SMB signatures on each side. To ensure that the SMB-based server responds to clients with message signing only, the following two registry key values should be configured on Small Business Server 2000:

- **Hive**: HKEY_LOCAL_MACHINE\SYSTEM

- **Key**: System\CurrentControlSet\Services\LanManServer\Parameters

- **Name**: RequireSecuritySignature

- **Type**: REG_DWORD

- **Value**: 1

  ☑ **Note**   A second key in the registry, shown in the following list, is already set to *1*. This enables the key you configured in the preceding list to function correctly. In Small Business Server 4.5, this key was set to *0* by default.

- **Hive**: HKEY_LOCAL_MACHINE\SYSTEM

- **Key**: System\CurrentControlSet\Services\LanManServer\Parameters

- **Name**: EnableSecuritySignature

- **Type**: REG_DWORD

- **Value**: 1

These values ensure that the Small Business Server communicates with only those clients that are aware of message signing. This means that, for installations with multiple versions of client software, the older versions will fail to connect to servers with this configured key value. It is extremely important that *both* keys be set to 1. Setting RequireSecuritySignature to 1 while EnableSecuritySignature is set to 0 prevents all access to server SMB shares. This should not be a problem, since EnableSecuritySignature is set to 1 by default.

Similarly, security-conscious Windows 2000 users can also decide to communicate with servers that only support message signing. The following registry key should be configured on the Windows 2000 client computer. Setting this key value implies that the user will not be able to connect to a server that does not have message signing support.

- **Hive**: HKEY_LOCAL_MACHINE\SYSTEM

- **Key**: System\CurrentControlSet\Services\Rdr\Parameters

- **Name**: RequireSecuritySignature

- **Type**: REG_DWORD

- **Value**: 1

For more information about SMB message signing enhancements, refer to Microsoft Knowledge Base Article Q161372.

Controlling Access to Removable Media

By default, Windows 2000 Server allows any application to access files on floppy disks and compact or digital video discs. For a highly secure multi-user environment, the technology consultant should allow only the person logged on to access these removable media devices. This ensures that only interactive users can write sensitive information to the drives, with confidence that no other user or application can see or modify the data.

You can manage the process from the Group Policy snap-in, in either of the following ways:

- Click **Start**, point to **Programs**, point to **Administrative Tools**, and then click **Active Directory Users and Computer**. Right-click the domain object or an organizational unit object, and then click **Properties**. Click the **Group Policy** tab, and then select **New** (to create a new Group Policy Object you will need to name) or **Edit** (to edit an existing Group Policy Object). Under the **Computer Configuration**, **Local Policies**, **Security Options**, **Allowed to eject removable NTFS media** option, select **Security Settings**.

- Click **Start**, point to **Programs**, point to **Administrative Tools**, and then click **Active Directory Users and Computer**. Right-click the domain object or an organizational unit object, and then click **Properties**. Click the **Group Policy** tab and then select **New** (to create a new Group Policy Object you will need to name) or **Edit** (to edit an existing Group Policy Object). Under the **User Configuration**, **Windows Components**, **Windows Explorer**, **Prevent access to drives from My Computer** option, select **Administrative Templates**.

Protecting Files and Directories

Small Business Server 2000 is installed on an NTFS partition. NTFS provides more inherent security features than the FAT system. With NTFS, the technology consultant can assign a variety of protections to files and directories, specifying which groups or individual accounts can access the resources. By using the inherited permissions feature and by assigning permissions to groups rather than to individual accounts, you can simplify the chore of maintaining appropriate protections.

For example, a user might copy a sensitive document to a directory that is accessible by people who should not be allowed to read the document, thinking that the protections assigned to the document in its old location still apply. This is not the case, as copying changes the permissions. Instead, set new permissions on the document as soon as it is copied. Conversely, if a file created in a protected directory is being placed in a shared directory so that other users can read it, copy the file, rather than moving it, to the new directory. If the file is moved, change the protections on the file so other users can read it.

When permissions are changed on a file or directory, the new permissions apply any time the file or directory is subsequently opened. Users who already have the file or directory open when you change the permissions are still allowed access according to the permissions that were in effect when they opened the file or directory.

Backups

Regular backups protect small business network data from hardware failures and mistakes, as well as from viruses and other harmful mischief. You can use the Windows 2000 Backup program found in the System Tools program group to make backups and to restore data. Obviously, files must be read to be backed up and they must be written to be restored. Backup privileges should be limited to administrators and backup operators. The latter are people to whom you are comfortable giving read and write access on all files.

> ☑ **Note** The Backup Utility included with Windows 2000 Server allows you to back up the registry and Active Directory by selecting the System State backup option, in addition to backing up files and directories.

For more information about backups, refer to Chapter 4, "Planning a Small Business Server Network," and Chapter 26, "Disaster Recovery."

Auditing

Auditing can inform you of actions that pose a potential security risk and identify user accounts from which audited actions were taken. Note that auditing only identifies which user accounts were used for the audited events. If passwords are adequately protected, this in turn indicates which user attempted the audited events. However, if a password has been stolen or if actions were taken while a user was logged on but away from the computer, someone other than the person to whom the user account is assigned could have initiated the action.

When establishing an audit policy, the cost (in disk space and CPU cycles) of the various auditing options should be weighed against the advantages. At a minimum, failed logon attempts, attempts to access sensitive data, and changes to security settings, should be audited. The following table describes some common security threats and the type of auditing that can help track them.

Table 22.2 Security Threats and Auditing

Threat	Action
Hacker-type break-in, using random passwords	Enable failure auditing for logon and logoff events.
Break-in, using stolen password	Enable success auditing for logon and logoff events. The log entries do not distinguish between real users and phony ones. Look for unusual activity on user accounts, such as logons at odd hours or on days when you would not expect any activity.
Misuse of administrative privileges by authorized users	Enable success auditing for user rights, user and group management, security policy changes, restart, shutdown, and system events. Because of the high volume of events that would be recorded, Windows 2000 does not typically audit the use of the backup files and directories and the restore files and directories rights.
Virus outbreak	Enable both success and failure write access auditing for program files such as files with .exe and .dll extensions. Enable both success and failure process tracking auditing. Run suspected programs, and examine their security logs to assess unexpected modification attempts on program files, or creation of unexpected processes. These auditing settings generate a large number of event records during routine system use. Use them only when you are actively monitoring the system log.
Improper access to confidential files	Enable success and failure auditing for file- and object-access events, and then use Windows Explorer to enable success and failure auditing of read and write access for suspected users or groups of sensitive files.
Improper access to printers	Enable success and failure auditing for file- and object-access events, and then use Print Manager to enable success and failure auditing of print access for suspected users or groups of printers.

Advanced Security

This section addresses advanced security topics, including Kerberos, Point-to-Point Tunneling Protocol, Layer Two Tunneling Protocol, and Internet Protocol Security.

Kerberos

The default protocol for network authentication in Windows 2000 is the Kerberos version 5 authentication protocol. An emerging authentication standard, the Kerberos protocol provides a foundation for interoperability. It also enhances the security of enterprise-wide network authentication. Key components of the protocol's implementation in Windows 2000 include the integration of initial authentication with the Winlogon single sign-on architecture, the use of Active Directory (the directory service included in Windows 2000) as the domain's security account database, and the implementation of the Kerberos client as a Windows 2000 security provider through the Security Support Provider Interface (SSPI).

Point-to-Point Tunneling Protocol

Microsoft virtual private network (VPN) technology, based on the Point-to-Point Tunneling Protocol (PPTP), was created to address secure, low-cost remote access to corporate LANs through public networks like the Internet. PPTP is a new networking technology that supports multiprotocol VPNs. Using PPTP, remote users of the small business network can employ Windows 2000 Professional, Windows Me, Windows 95, Windows 98, and Windows NT Workstation 4.0 operating systems or other PPP-enabled client systems to dial a local ISP and connect securely to the small business network through the Internet. VPN technology provides small business network users an economical and easy-to-implement solution for creating secure and encrypted communication across the Internet.

PPTP can also be used with dense and integrated communications solutions to support the V.34 standard and integrated service digital network (ISDN) dial-up. Small businesses can also use a PPTP-enabled VPN over IP backbones to outsource dial-up access to their corporate networks in a manner that is cost-effective, hassle-free, protocol-independent, and secure, and requires no changes to existing network addressing.

Layer Two Tunneling Protocol

Layer Two Tunneling Protocol (L2TP) is a combination of PPTP and Layer Two Forwarding (L2F), a technology proposed by Cisco Systems, Inc. Rather than having two incompatible tunneling protocols competing in the marketplace and causing customer confusion, the Internet Engineering task Force (IETF) mandated that the two technologies be combined into a single tunneling protocol that represents the best features of PPTP and L2F. L2TP is documented in RFC 2661.

L2TP encapsulates PPP frames to be sent over IP, X.25, Frame Relay, or asynchronous transfer mode (ATM) networks. Currently, only L2TP over IP networks is defined. When sent over an IP internetwork, L2TP frames are encapsulated as User Datagram Protocol (UDP) messages. L2TP can be used as a tunneling protocol over the Internet or over private intranets.

L2TP uses UDP messages over IP internetworks for both tunnel maintenance and tunneled data. The payloads of encapsulated PPP frames can be encrypted or compressed, or both. Windows 2000 L2TP clients do not, however, negotiate the use of Microsoft Point-to-Point Encryption (MPPE) for L2TP connections. IPSec Encapsulating Security Payload (ESP) provides encryption for L2TP connections.

It is possible to create L2TP connections in Windows 2000 that are not encrypted by IPSec. This is not a VPN connection, however, as the private data being encapsulated by L2TP is not encrypted. Non-encrypted L2TP connections can be used temporarily to troubleshoot an L2TP over an IPSec connection by eliminating the IPSec authentication and negotiation process.

L2TP assumes the availability of an IP internetwork between a L2TP client (a VPN client using the L2TP tunneling protocol and IPSec) and a L2TP server (a VPN server using the L2TP tunneling protocol and IPSec). The L2TP client might already be attached to an IP internetwork that can reach the L2TP server, or the L2TP client might have to dial into a network access server (NAS) to establish IP connectivity, as in the case of dial-up Internet users.

Authentication that occurs during the creation of L2TP tunnels must use the same authentication mechanisms as PPTP connections, such as EAP, MS-CHAP, CHAP, SPAP, and Password Authentication Protocol (PAP).

For Internet-based L2TP servers, the L2TP server is an L2TP-enabled dial-up server with one interface on the external network (the Internet), and a second interface on the target private network.

Internet Protocol Security

The IETF developed IPSec as the security protocol for IP. In fact, IPSec was designed for the next generation of IP, which is IP version 6. However, IPSec can be used with the current implementation of IP, which is IP version 4.

> ▨ **Note**   One of the issues with TCP/IP is that it was not designed with security in mind. For example, TCP/IP does not accommodate authentication or privacy.

IP Security and Authentication

It is easy for an unauthorized user to spoof IP packets—that is, to make packets appear to have come from another destination. This is achieved by writing applications that build complete, but invalid, IP packets and then sending them to a target computer. The packets are invalid in that the source IP address is incorrect, does not exist, or is unreachable because of router settings. The target computer attempts to set up a connection with the unreachable source but fails, and in so doing (although the target waits for a while to accommodate latencies in the network), the target must allocate memory for the connection anyway. If the system receives a large number of invalid packets, the target eventually runs out of memory and probably stops responding. This is a denial-of-service attack.

IPSec can provide strong authentication of packet data to help alleviate many common spoofing attacks.

IP Security and Privacy

No data is encrypted at the TCP or IP layers; it is up to higher-level protocols such as SSL and TLS to perform this work. Because the data is unencrypted, it is very easy to gather important information like user names and passwords by "sniffing" the network. IPSec can encrypt data in order to help prevent data sniffing.

For more information about IPSec, refer to "Internet Protocol Security (IPSec)" in the *TCP/IP Core Networking Guide,* a part of *Microsoft Windows 2000 Server Resource Kit.*

Additional Resources

For more security-related information and best practices, refer to the Microsoft security Web site at: http://www.microsoft.com/security/.

☑ **Note** Best practices on the Microsoft Security Web site include discussions on the following:

- For the latest security implementation, the need to test and install operating system and application service packs.

- Having an outside consulting firm perform an annual security audit.

Summary

This chapter defines Windows 2000 security—specifically, how Windows 2000 security interacts with Small Business Server 2000, including physical, network, software-based, logon/logoff, and file access security.

CHAPTER 23

Internet Information Server 5.0 Security Model

Microsoft® Internet Information Services (IIS) 5.0 is tightly integrated with the Microsoft Windows® 2000 Server operating system to provide a powerful Web server for the small business. This integration enables the small business to take advantage of Internet and intranet use, while still maintaining the highest levels of security for applications and information. This chapter describes the security model used by IIS 5.0.

IIS Integrated Security Model

The robust security architecture of Windows 2000 Server is used consistently across all system components, including IIS, with authentication tied to controlled access of all system resources. IIS integrates with the Windows 2000 Server security model and the operating system services, such as the file system and directory service. Because IIS uses the Windows 2000 Server user database, the technology consultant does not have to create separate user accounts on the Web server. IIS automatically uses the same common file, print, and group permissions set in the Small Business Server 2000 console. Small business network users need to log on to the network only once to use both Small Business Server and IIS.

IIS does not install a separate security implementation on top of the network operating system, as some Web servers do. When there are separate security systems in place, there is additional overhead and potential security exposure because there is no integration or synchronization. Rather, IIS integrates into Windows 2000 Server, which is inherently secure by design. Files and system objects can only be accessed with the proper permissions. User and group accounts are managed by a globally unique identification. When accounts are deleted, all access permissions and group memberships are also deleted. So even if a new account is created and a previous user name is used, none of the permissions are inherited.

Central Management

Permission to control access to files and directories can be set graphically because IIS uses the same Windows 2000 Server access control lists (ACLs) as all other Windows services. This includes such services as file sharing and Microsoft SQL Server™ 2000 permissions. Permissions for IIS are not separate from other file services, so the same files can be securely accessed over other protocols, including file transfer protocol (FTP), Common Internet File System/Server Messaging Block (CIFS/SMB), or Network File Systems (NFS), without duplicating administration.

> ☑ **Note**   IIS is integrated with Microsoft Active Directory™ directory service. It uses the object permissions maintained in Active Directory.

With IIS, the technology consultant does not have to maintain multiple user databases. All the services for IIS can easily be managed from a single graphical tool. The integration of IIS with Windows 2000 Server ensures that the technology consultant can give new network users access to valuable network resources, such as HTML pages, as well as shared files, printers, and corporate databases, with a few mouse clicks.

IIS produces standard Web server access logs to analyze usage. Integration with Windows 2000 Server means that IIS can also take advantage of system auditing for more secure monitoring of resource use. For example, failed attempts to access a secure file can be recorded in the Windows 2000 Event Log and audited with the same tools used for managing the server.

Comprehensive Security Solution

IIS tightly integrates with Microsoft Internet Security and Acceleration (ISA) Server, Certificate Server, Site Server Express, and other applications to provide a comprehensive security platform with a rich spectrum of built-in functionality. This enables the small business to deploy a fully featured Web server that is secure for both public and intranet Web sites. IIS supports integration with existing solutions and a new generation of Web applications.

New IIS 5.0 Security Features

This section briefly describes the new security features in IIS 5.0, outlining the changes from both IIS 4.0 and Microsoft Windows NT® Server 4.0:

- **Digest Authentication**. Adds security and reliability to user authentication across proxy servers and firewalls. IIS 5.0 still offers previous means of authentication: Anonymous, Hypertext Transfer Protocol (HTTP) Basic, Windows NT Challenge/Response, and NTLM authentication (now known as integrated Windows authentication).

- **Server-Gated Cryptography**. Allows financial institutions with export versions of IIS to use strong 128-bit encryption. Server-Gated Cryptography (SGC) is an extension of Secure Sockets Layer (SSL). Although SGC is built into IIS 5.0, a special SGC certificate from a certificate authority (CA) is required to use it.

- **New Security Wizards**. These wizards simplify server administration tasks, as follows:

  - **Web Server Certificate Wizard**. Simplifies certificate administration tasks in IIS 5.0; for example, creating certificate requests and managing the certificate life cycle.

  - **Permissions Wizard**. Simplifies editing and configuring Web site access, such as assigning access policies to virtual directories and files. The Permissions Wizard can also reflect these Web access policies to NTFS file system permissions.

  - **CTL Wizard**. Configures certificate trust lists (CTLs). A CTL is a list of trusted certification authorities for a particular directory. CTLs are especially useful for Internet service providers (ISPs) that have several Web sites on their server and that need a different list of approved certification authorities for each site.

- **Kerberos version 5 Authentication**. Passes authentication credentials among networked computers that are running Microsoft Windows. IIS 5.0 is fully integrated with the Kerberos version 5 authentication model implemented in Windows 2000 Server.

- **Certificate Storage**. Stores, backs up, and configures server certificates through a single point of entry. IIS certificate storage is now integrated with Microsoft CryptoAPI (CAPI) storage, which is provided with Windows 2000.

- **Fortezza**. Supports Fortezza, the U.S. government security standard. This standard satisfies the Defense Messaging System security architecture, by supplying a cryptographic mechanism that features message confidentiality, integrity, authentication, and access control to messages, components, and systems.

Importance of Web Server Security

The Internet has created the opportunity for businesses of all sizes to have better access to information and improved business processes and models. However, the open nature of the Web and its role as an information gateway underscores the need to use a Web server with a solid security foundation. It is also essential that the Web server be tightly integrated with the operating system on which the network and applications run. This security is vital for such considerations as:

- Application and database security

- Electronic commerce

- Business relationships and extranets

- Communicating with customers

Application and Database Security

Web browsers are being used increasingly to provide access to information and applications in databases and other existing business systems. For example, many businesses allow employees to manage their personal information and benefits plans through Web browsers that link back to human resources systems. These business systems must be protected so that users are allowed to access only applications for which they are authorized. In addition, they must be protected so that employees can change only their personal information.

To do this, systems must be in place to identify and validate users, and determine whether they have permission to view the information or to perform the requested task. This last step often requires integration with existing information systems. Also, the exchange between client and server must take place over a secure channel to ensure private information transfer. Windows 2000 Server and IIS 5.0 provide integrated services to enable the small business to securely connect to the Web with databases and business applications.

Electronic Commerce

Electronic commerce requires a greater degree of security than is currently deployed on many corporate networks. The lack of acceptable protection, verification, and payment methods has prevented electronic commerce from fulfilling its potential. The Internet can be a safe place for business if used with care. The integrated security technologies and services of IIS 5.0 and Microsoft Site Server Express 2.0 provide an infrastructure for building safe and secure applications, when used in conjunction with Windows 2000 Server.

Business Relationships and Extranets

Small business partnerships can benefit from the efficiency of electronic information transfer and communication. Many small businesses like to make selective information available to third parties while still maintaining complete security. For example, a small business may allow resellers limited access to its internal customer information database to streamline the generation of sales leads. But when the small business opens its network to contractors, suppliers, and other business partners, security is of paramount concern.

When a company allows outsiders to gain access to information or applications, the server must be able to identify and authenticate users. Access control is also needed so that the technology consultant can limit the areas that a user can visit. In addition, users must have the ability to transfer information privately, so that confidential information cannot be intercepted over the network. By using public key cryptography, Challenge Access Protocol, and other advanced security features, IIS 5.0 provides the security required for opening parts of a corporate intranet to the outside world.

This secure zone between a corporate intranet and the public Internet is sometimes referred to as an extranet.

Communicating with Customers

A small business that provides services across the Internet currently has to manage multiple user names and passwords. Personal digital certificates can help streamline the process of customer service by providing a secure, efficient way to identify customers. Digital certificates can store data customized to the buying patterns and other important characteristics of each customer.

For example, customers could be issued certificates based on services to which they subscribe. In the case of an online sports information service, one person might subscribe to football information only, while another subscribes to golf, and a third to all sports information offered. Customers can be issued personal digital certificates that are mapped to a Windows 2000 Server security group with access to certain portions of the site. With Site Server Express, a Web site can also easily track usage and related information to personalize and enhance the user's experience.

Framework for Using Security

Microsoft designed IIS 5.0 and Windows 2000 Server to provide the technology consultant with a powerful framework for deploying Web servers. Above all, IIS and Windows 2000 Server provide the technology consultant with a single integrated security model. This gives it a number of advantages, including the ability to:

- Take full advantage of the strong, secure underpinnings of the U.S. Government C2 and ITSEC FC2-rated Windows 2000 Server security.

- Eliminate possibilities for security weaknesses by not having to add redundant security layers. This sets IIS 5.0 apart from other Web servers or operating systems with multiple security layers, which increase their complexity and the subsequent possibility for security problems.

- Take advantage of existing Window 2000 Server knowledge, making it easy to learn and configure.

- Provide better performance by eliminating unnecessary performance-related overhead of additional security and access control layers.

This framework allows the technology consultant to determine everything from what type of end user authentication will be used on the Web server, to how the Web server itself will be physically locked down.

Access Control

One of the most important areas of focus for IIS 5.0 is providing powerful access control functionality for Web access to files and applications on Small Business Server. IIS 5.0 was designed to make it easy to use a wide range of mechanisms for access control to critical business data, depending on the needs of the small business. These include:

- Support for integrated Windows authentication (formerly known as New Technology LAN Manager (NTLM) authentication).

- IP address grant/deny restrictions.

- An ability to implement restrictions on virtual servers and directories.

- Support for the Windows 2000 File System (NTFS).

- Impersonation of users when running applications.

- Client and server digital certificates.

- Advanced security filters.

User Authentication and Authorization

IIS 5.0 security is integrated with Active Directory, which means that only a user with a valid Windows 2000 user account can access all resources. This enables the technology consultant to use the full power of Active Directory, including account management, the ability to audit and log all activity, setting time-of-day restrictions, expiring passwords, and forcing secure password policies.

Anonymous Access

When IIS 5.0 is set up, it creates an anonymous account for unauthenticated Web connections. When file security is not required, the request is processed by the server in the security context of the anonymous user account. The anonymous user account can only access files and applications for which permission has been granted.

User Name and Password

Access to files and applications can be restricted to specific users or groups. This requires obtaining and verifying the user name. IIS 5.0 can be configured to require basic HTTP authentication. Users are prompted for a name and password, which are then compared to accounts in the Windows 2000 Server directory. The name and password in basic authentication are passed as clear text over the network and can potentially be intercepted by a network packet sniffer.

Secure Windows Integration

Integrated Windows authentication, formerly known as both NT LAN Manager (or NTLM) and Windows NT Challenge/Response authentication, is more secure than basic authentication. This authentication scheme works especially well in an intranet environment in which users have Windows domain accounts.

In integrated Windows authentication, the browser attempts to use the current user's credentials from a domain logon. If those credentials are rejected, integrated Windows authentication asks the user for a user name and password. When integrated Windows authentication is used, the user's password is not passed from the client to the server. If a user has logged on as a domain user on a local computer, the user won't have to be authenticated again when accessing a network computer in that domain.

The user is not asked for a user name and password for each HTTP request. This only occurs when the cached credentials do not have sufficient permissions to access a specific page or file.

☑ **Note** Many third-party firewalls block the ports necessary for Windows Integrated Security. Check the documentation of your third-party firewall to enable Windows Integrated Security.

Digital Certificates

IIS 5.0 supports the use of X.509 certificates for access control. A certificate verifies a user's identity in much the same way as a driver's license or corporate identification card does. Certificates are issued by a trusted certificate authority, either within an organization or from a public company. When issuing a certificate, the degree of rigor for which IIS 5.0 checks the user's identity or credentials depends on the level of security required for the information or application being accessed. Users enter a password when signing their certificate. This password is required every time the certificate is activated for use. The possession of a certificate alone does not constitute proof of ownership. The password is the key to verifying access, because only the owner of the certificate should know this information.

Certificate-based client authentication requires a protocol able to handle certificates at both the client and server ends, in addition to the appropriate requests and replies. A server certificate is presented to a client so that the client may authenticate the identity of the server. When the SSL protocol is running, a server is required to have a server certificate. As an option, the server can ask for the client's certificate. The server certificate contains the Web site name, and the browser verifies that the Web site is the name that was entered.

☑ **Note** IIS can map client certificates to user accounts within Active Directory. Incoming client certificates are passed to the Active Directory mapper (DS Mapper), and Active Directory verifies incoming client certificates with client certificates stored in Active Directory.

Active Directory Holds Information

IIS holds user information related to IIS. However, configuring Web services can be time-consuming because of the number of parameters that you must set. The IIS Admin Objects (IISAO) feature can help reduce this work by allowing you to write scripts to automate the process.

The IISAOs are an Active Directory Services Interface (ADSI) implementation for accessing and setting IIS 5.0 settings. They are Component Object Model (COM) Automation-based, and can be used with any language that supports Automation, such as Microsoft Visual Basic® Scripting Edition (VBScript) or Microsoft JScript®, Visual Basic, Java, or C++. Table 24.1 provides some useful IISAO security-related settings.

Table 23.1 Security Settings with IISAO

IISAO property/object	Comment
AccessFlags	Sets access permissions such as Read, Write, and Script.
AccessSSLFlags	Sets SSL properties, requires 128-bit SSL, and requires client authentication certificate.
AnonymousPasswordSync	Allows IIS to synchronize the anonymous password with the Active Directory user database if necessary.
AnonymousUserName, AnonymousUserPass	Allows IIS to set the user name and password for Uniform Naming Convention (UNC) shares.
AuthFlags	Specifies the authentication scheme to be used.
IIsCertMapper	Manages mapping of client certificates to Windows user accounts.
LogonMethod	Specifies the log on method for Basic and Anonymous authentication.
PasswordCacheTTL	Specifies the amount of time in seconds that an expired password will be held in memory cache.
UNCAuthenticationPassThrough	Enables user authentication pass-through for Uniform Naming Convention (UNC) virtual root access. This applies to authentication schemes that support delegation.

Digest Authentication

Digest authentication helps resolve many of the weaknesses of Basic authentication. Most notably, in Digest authentication the password is not in clear text. In addition, Digest authentication can work through proxy servers, unlike integrated Windows authentication.

At the time of this writing, Digest authentication is only a draft standard. The version of digest authentication used in IIS 5.0 follows RFC2069, with some extensions from the IETF draft specification, which can be found at:
http://www.ietf.org/

Because Digest authentication is a challenge/response mechanism like integrated Windows authentication, passwords are not sent unencrypted, as in Basic authentication.

> ☑ **Note** One limitation is that the password has to be stored in "reversible encryption" in Active Directory.

Access Control, Using Custom Authentication Filters

IIS 5.0 provides a set of open application programming interfaces (APIs) that developers can use to create filters that authenticate users based on custom rules. This gives the technology consultant the flexibility to control access by using any authentication scheme or external directories.

Access Controls

After users are authenticated, IIS 5.0 checks to see if they have permission to access the requested file or application. Thus, IIS 5.0 takes advantage of the NTFS file system and Access Control Lists (ACLs). Refer to the "NTFS File System Permissions" later in this section for details.

Internet Protocol Addresses

On the Internet, each server and client (or proxy for a group of clients) has a specific Internet address called the Internet Protocol (IP) address. IIS 5.0 can be configured to grant or deny access to specified IP addresses. This provides the technology consultant with the ability to exclude users by denying access from a particular IP address, or to prevent entire networks from accessing the server. Conversely, the technology consultant can choose to allow only specific IP addresses to have service access.

NTFS File System Permissions

NTFS was designed to provide the security features required for high-end Web servers in both intranet and Internet scenarios. The NTFS file system supports discretionary access control and ownership privileges important to the integrity of critical small business data. NTFS allows the technology consultant to assign permission to individual files—not just to folders and directories. By using NTFS for the content made available by IIS 5.0, the technology consultant can help ensure that only authorized individuals have access to individual files on the Web server.

After the user's IP address restrictions are satisfied, the user name or password is validated, and the service's virtual directory permissions are completed, IIS 5.0 attempts to access the specified resource (based on the URL) by using the security context of the authenticated user. This allows Windows 2000 Server to enforce resource access control based on NTFS permissions, providing the technology consultant with detailed control over confidential resources and data.

Windows 2000 identifies each user by using a globally unique security identification (SID), known as a Global User ID in Active Directory—not by user name. The SID is mapped in the background to the user's account name, so that file permissions and group accounts are managed by using a friendly name, but are applied with the SID. When an account is deleted, all ACLs and group assignments for the account are also removed. SIDs and synchronization ensure that an account created later with the same user name cannot inherit permission to the old account.

Impersonation

IIS 5.0 accesses all files and runs all applications in the security context of the user requesting the file, restricting what can be accessed. This is either the anonymous user account specified in the server administration or an authenticated user account. This means that a Common Gateway Interface (CGI) application or component in a user directory cannot access data or services restricted to other users or the server administrator. Moreover, application developers have much more flexibility in developing applications than they would if all codes were required to run in the security context of the server itself. Impersonation allows Web-based applications to be used securely for applications or administrator-like functions to limit both who accesses the application and what they are allowed to do.

Permissions on IIS

IIS 5.0 enables the technology consultant to set read-only or execute-only permissions on virtual directories. For every request, IIS 5.0 examines the URL and type of request to ensure that the permissions set on the virtual directory or virtual root are honored. This ensures that users cannot read files with execute-only permission or execute files with read-only permissions.

Auditing Access

Auditing security events is one of the few ways to determine whether users are trying to gain access to secure content on your Web server. IIS 5.0 supports two forms of logging. The first is the standard Web server access log that records all file and object requests and errors. The second uses Windows 2000 Server capability to enable the technology consultant to log and audit all possible attempts to breach security through the Windows 2000 Server Event Viewer. For example, on a secure intranet Web server, a technology consultant is able to log the following:

- All access to server files

- Invalid logon attempts

- All logons

The audit log can be used in addition to the Web server access log for increased security monitoring. It is recommended that customers guard the audit logs generated by IIS, because some hackers try to cover failed attempts to gain access to your Web server's secure information. Restriction of access to the logs and periodic backup of all files is also recommended.

Confidentiality and Data Integrity

When there is a connection on the Internet between a Web browser and a Web server, the secure channel technology of IIS 5.0 provides privacy, integrity, and authentication in point-to-point communications for small business network users. SSL 2.0 and 3.0 for secure channel communication are included with Small Business Server 2000 as a base feature of IIS 5.0.

Developers of Internet applications running on Windows 2000 Server for the small business can provide SSL application support through the WinInet functions or through Windows Sockets (Winsock) 2.0, which is a communications mechanism. The Transport Layer Security Protocol (TLS), now under consideration by IETF, will provide a single standard, encompassing both SSL and Private Communications Technology (PCT).

Confidentiality

Confidentiality prevents the content of a communication from being reached by unauthorized parties. In the case of a small business sales transaction, for example, it is important to guarantee that only the intended party has access to the information being transferred. Privacy mechanisms, such as an SSL-encrypted channel, are used to ensure that sales and other sensitive transactions are secure over the Internet or other carriers.

Data Integrity

Integrity assures that vital data has not been modified and is critical for conducting small business commerce over the Internet. Without assured integrity, items such as purchase orders, contracts, specifications, and stock purchase orders could be modified with devastating effects. This is why IIS 5.0 supports digital signatures and message authentication codes. Digital signatures provide fingerprints of a document to determine if data has been changed from the original signed document.

Digital Signatures

Digital signatures are used in e-mail and file transfers to verify identity and encrypt messages. They are also used by Web servers and browsers to provide mutual authentication, confidentiality of the pages transferred, and integrity of the information. Signing data does not alter it, but simply generates a string that is attached to the data.

Public-key encryption algorithms, such as the RSA public-key cipher, are used to create digital signatures. A public-key algorithm uses two mathematically mated keys—the *public key* and the *private key*—which together are known as a key pair. A public key is available to anyone, whereas the private key is available only to its owner. Public-key algorithms are designed so that if one key is used for encryption, the other key is necessary for decryption. The private key is virtually impossible to derive from the public key. IIS 5.0 certificate technology uses 1024-bit public key cryptography, which is extremely secure protection.

> **Note** Data integrity and digital signatures are provided by SSL. There is no other mechanism in IIS 5.0 other than SSL that provides this functionality.

Secure Sockets Layer

IIS 5.0 supports SSL 3.0. SSL provides a security handshake that initiates a Transmission Control Protocol/Internet Protocol (TCP/IP) connection, such as when communication between a Web browser and a Web server is initiated in the small business network. A browser and server with mutual authentication must be in agreement about the use of SSL security with TCP/IP connections. SSL provides privacy, integrity, and authentication in a private point-to-point communications channel. SSL also provides for selectable encryption and decryption of both request and response data being passed across network connections. An example is credit card information in a shopping-payment scenario.

Spontaneous communication on a worldwide basis is possible because SSL uses world standard cryptography from RSA, which is shipped in every Microsoft operating system and copy of Microsoft Internet Explorer. Microsoft has proposed extensions to Winsock 2.0 in order to accommodate SSL and TLS. The goal is to make implementing an SSL-enabled application as easy as possible, while still providing an adequate amount of flexibility. An application that uses these Winsock 2.0 extensions should be just as secure as one that implements the protocol internally.

SSL always provides authentication of the server. If an SSL session is established, the server always provides a digital certificate to the client. Digital certificates are similar to an electronic license or a notarized document, because they allow both parties to confirm that they are talking with the server name that is being claimed. The browser checks the server name against the certificate and alerts the user if they are different.

Security Functionality for Developers

IIS 5.0 was designed to provide independent software vendor (ISV) developers with a powerful platform for designing Web-based applications for the small business. In addition to the Internet Server API (ISAPI) and Active Server Pages (ASP) for scripting the Web server, IIS makes the following secure technologies available to developers:

- Issuing Digital Certificates with Microsoft Certificate Server
- Using CryptoAPI for cryptography
- Using SSL certificates with Active Server Pages

Issuing Digital Certificates with Microsoft Certificate Server 2.0

Certificate Server 2.0 enables the small business to easily manage the issuance, renewal, and revocation of certificates without having to rely on external certificate authorities. With Certificate Server 2.0, the small business organization also has full control over the policies associated with the issuance, management, and revocation of certificates, as well as the format and contents of the certificates themselves. In addition, Certificate Server 2.0 logs all transactions,which enables the technology consultant to track, audit, and manage certificate requests. The default policy automatically grants certificates to a trusted set of users, based on a preset Windows 2000 Server group of administrators and accounts. It can authenticate users based on their Windows 2000 Server logon and enables the technology consultant to approve or deny a certificate request directly.

The technology consultant can issue certificates in standard formats (X-509 versions 1 and 3) and add extensions to certificates as needed. Certificate Server 2.0 does the following:

- Accepts standard PKCS #10 certificate requests

- Issues X-509 version 1 and version 3 certificates in PKCS #7 format

- Issues SSL client and server certificates

- Issues S/MIME certificates

- Issues SET-compliant certificates

- Supports open interfaces that enable writing of modules to support custom formats.

Certificate Server 2.0 functions with Microsoft and non-Microsoft clients, browsers, and Web servers. The technology consultant can choose to distribute and request certificates in many ways, including transport mechanisms that can be customized to small business needs. Certificate Server 2.0 can post certificates back to the user in e-mail, to a light directory access protocol (LDAP)-based directory service, or to any other custom mechanism.

Cryptography Application Program Interface

Cryptography Application Programming Interface (CryptoAPI), which is part of Windows 2000 Server and Internet Explorer 5.0, was designed to abstract the details of cryptography away from developers. It includes the Cryptographic Service Provider (CSP) interface, which makes accessing cryptography easier by enabling developers to change the strength and type of their cryptography without modifying application code.

CryptoAPI frees applications from having to perform their own encryption. It provides extensible, exportable, system-level access to common cryptographic functions such as encryption, hashing, and digital signatures. Any application written with CryptoAPI can use certificates that support the standard X.509 standard. This enables any standards-compliant application or system to access the server from any platform, including those on UNIX and Macintosh platforms.

CryptoAPI provides a set of high-level APIs that make it easier for the developer to sign, seal, encrypt, and decrypt data. ISV developers will easily be able to integrate identity and authentication into their applications, thereby securing private communications and data transfers over intranets and the Internet. Examples of certificate services are: functions for generating requests to create certificates, functions for storing and retrieving certificates, and functions for parsing certificates.

Programmatically Interacting with Client Certificates

The scripting power of ASP provides a programmatic way of interacting with client certificates. The certificate and its key fields can be exposed for scripting, thus allowing direct mapping, for example, into server-side databases. This provides the ability to map client certificates to Windows 2000 Server user accounts. In addition to specific client certificates being mapped on a many-to-one basis (multiple certificates mapping to the same Windows 2000 Server user account), wildcard mapping is also included. For even greater security, ASP allows Web masters to examine the content of a client-provided certificate.

Additional Resources

For additional information about IIS and security, refer to Chapter 9, "Security," in the *Internet Information Services 5.0 Resource Guide,* part of *Microsoft Windows 2000 Server Resource Kit.*

Summary

This chapter introduced the IIS 5.0 security model, including IIS-specific security features and Windows 2000 Server security features. The way in which IIS security integrates with Windows 2000 Server was also discussed.

Small Business Server Licensing and Upgrades

This chapter covers the following topics:

- Licensing requirements to expand the user base of Microsoft® Small Business Server 2000 up to 50 users and beyond.

- Client Access Licenses (CALs).

- Installation of Client Add Packs.

- Upgrading to Microsoft BackOffice® Server 2000 to accommodate small business growth.

Licensing

Because many small businesses have more users than computers, the Microsoft Small Business Server 2000 licensing model provides maximum flexibility and value. There is no limit to the number of user accounts that can be created on Small Business Server 2000. However, the maximum number of client computers that can be connected (physically attached) to a Small Business Server 2000 network is 50. For example, you can have 70 user accounts on the Small Business Server network that share 35 client computers.

> ✍ **Note** Licensing for Terminal Services on a Windows 2000 Server computer in application mode is handled separately. For more information, refer to: http://www.microsoft.com/Windows2000/guide/server/pricing/tsfaq.asp.

A CAL is required for each client computer that accesses Small Business Server 2000, including clients running Microsoft Windows® 3.x, Windows for Workgroups, Windows 95, Windows 98, Windows Me, Windows NT® Workstation, and Windows 2000 Professional.

> ✍ **Note** Printer server cards installed in network printers do not accumulate as outstanding occurrences against the CAL count.

Client Access Licenses

Client Access Licenses (CALs) (or Client Add Packs) are available in increments of 5 or 20 clients. They allow for expansion of the small business network up to a maximum of 50 clients. Client Add Packs are unique to Small Business Server and cannot be used with any other Microsoft server products—for example, a stand-alone Microsoft Windows NT Server computer.

A CAL is needed by a client to access any service such as file, print, Exchange 2000 Server e-mail, or the Microsoft SQL Server™ 2000 database. Users cannot apply CALs for any other BackOffice products to Small Business Server 2000.

The Small Business Server 2000 CAL also authorizes you to access and use the services and functionality of a Microsoft Windows 2000 Server that is in the same domain as the Small Business Server. This CAL does not grant you any rights of a Terminal Services CAL.

Adding Client Access Licenses

CALs are added by using the Client Add Pack Setup application, up to the allowed maximum of 50. An attempt to install more than 50 clients results in an installation error.

You can add licenses from the Small Business Server **About** page or the **To Do List** page, as follows.

To add client access licenses

1. Log on to the Small Business Server computer as an administrator. Only users with administrator privileges can add CALs.

2. Insert the **Small Business Server Client Add Pack** floppy disk.

3. Click **Start**, and then click **Run**.

4. Type *a***:\setup.exe**, and then click **OK** (where *a* is the letter of your floppy disk drive).

5. Read the license agreement, and then click **I Agree**.

    Follow the on-screen instructions.

    ☑ **Note** If you need to reinstall Small Business Server software at any time, use the last Client Add Pack disc to reinstall the CALs, as this disc maintains the total number of CALs for the server. It is important to mark the discs with the appropriate installation order.

Upgrading the Server Computer

If you are upgrading your server computer and reinstalling Small Business Server software along with the CALs, you will be asked for a password. A System ID number appears in a message, which asks you to call Microsoft Technical Support for a new password. The new password is required to unlock the floppy disk and to add the full number of licenses.

Windows 2000 License Manager Disabled

Adding or changing client licenses can only be done from the Small Business Server 2000 Administrator Console. The Windows 2000 Server license manager is disabled in Small Business Server 2000. If you attempt to start the license manager from the Control Panel, a message appears, which instructs you to use the Small Business Server Administrator Console.

Upgrading Small Business Server 2000

Small Business Server runs on a single server computer, supporting a maximum of 50 connected client computers. When a business expands beyond the 50 computers, or when integrated applications are used extensively, it is recommended that you upgrade to BackOffice Server 2000. This upgrade provides greater scalability and a broader base of BackOffice components, while retaining the usability of Small Business Server data. When expanding to BackOffice Server, you must buy BackOffice Server 2000 and the appropriate number of CALs. For more information about upgrading to BackOffice Server, refer to the following Web site: http://www.microsoft.com/backofficeserver/.

Summary

This chapter addressed important licensing and upgrade issues, including:

- Licensing issues
- Client Access Licenses
- Upgrading Small Business Server

Migrating Data to SQL Server 2000

As the needs of a small business grow and the demand for a high-performance database increases, it may be necessary to migrate from the file-server environment of the Microsoft® Access Jet engine to the client/server environment of Microsoft SQL Server™ 2000. The Access 2000 Upsizing Wizard included with Microsoft Office 2000 moves Access tables and queries into SQL Server 2000. If the small business has used an earlier version of Access, applications can be migrated to SQL Server 2000 by upgrading to Access 2000 and then using the Upsizing Wizard.

If the technology consultant prefers not to use Access 2000 and the Upsizing Wizard to migrate, the material presented in this chapter still serves as a general guide for moving an Access application to SQL Server 2000. Moving an Access application requires moving the data into SQL Server 2000 and then migrating the Access queries into the database or into SQL files for execution at a later time. The last step is migrating and optimizing the applications.

What's New in SQL Server 2000

SQL Server 2000 has several new features, which primarily focus on electronic commerce and Web-related activities, including:

- **XML support**. SQL Server 2000 delivers fully integrated, standards-based Extensible Markup Language (XML) support that is flexible, high performance, and easy–touse for Web developers and database programmers. Unlike competitive databases, SQL Server 2000 offers powerful tools for manipulating XML inside the database, and it enables developers to retrieve XML-based data from the database without writing code.

- **Microsoft BizTalk™ Server 2000 support**. SQL Server 2000 and BizTalk Server 2000 support an integrated XML infrastructure that allows documents to be managed and routed from database applications through BizTalk Server 2000.

- **SQL Server Analysis Services**. SQL Server 2000 Analysis Services includes unique, new features for analyzing Web click-stream data, performing closed-loop analysis, and sharing analysis results across the Web through firewalls. This capability also facilitates data mining of company data repositories.

- **English Query**. Simplifying access to strategic data resources, SQL Server 2000 English Query allows end users of all skill levels to pose questions in English to the database through the Web. English Query translates a user's question into a database query and returns the desired results from the relational store or Analysis Services.

SQL Server 2000 Tools Used in Migration

Several tools in SQL Server 2000 assist in the migration of Access data and applications. These tools are described in the sections that follow.

SQL Server Enterprise Manager

SQL Server Enterprise Manager allows for enterprise-wide configuration and management of SQL Server 2000 and SQL Server objects. SQL Server Enterprise Manager provides a powerful scheduling engine, administrative alert capabilities, and a built-in replication management interface. You can also use SQL Server Enterprise Manager to complete the following tasks:

- Manage logins and user permissions

- Create scripts

- Manage backup of SQL Server objects

- Back up databases and transaction logs

- Manage tables, views, stored procedures, triggers, indexes, rules, defaults, and user-defined data types

- Create full-text indexes, database diagrams, and database maintenance plans

- Import and export data

- Transform data

- Perform various Web administration tasks

SQL Server Enterprise Manager is included in the SQL Server 2000 application installed with Microsoft Small Business Server 2000. It can be accessed from the SQL Server program group, available from the **Start** menu. In migration procedures, Data Transformation Services (DTS) is started from the SQL Server 2000 Enterprise Manager interface.

Data Transformation Services

DTS allows you to import and export data between multiple heterogeneous sources that use an object linking and embedding database (OLE DB)-based architecture, such as Microsoft Excel spreadsheets. It also allows for transferring databases and database objects (for example, indexes and stored procedures) between multiple computers running SQL Server 2000. You can use DTS to transform data so that it can be used more easily to build data warehouses and data marts from an online transaction processing (OLTP) system.

The DTS Import Wizard and DTS Export Wizard allow you to interactively create DTS packages that use OLE DB and open database connectivity (ODBC) to import, export, validate, and transform heterogeneous data. Saving a DTS package to a Microsoft Visual Basic® file allows a package created by the DTS wizards to be incorporated into Visual Basic programs or to be used as prototypes by Visual Basic developers who need to reference the components of the DTS object model.

The wizards enable you to copy schema and data between relational databases, while DTS supports keys and constraints. You can use the import and export wizards to move primary and foreign keys and constraints.

The SQL Server 2000 DTS Designer and the DTS object model allow custom tasks, which means you can create packages that perform tasks or set variables based on properties of the run-time environment.

SQL Server Query Analyzer

SQL Server 2000 Query Analyzer is a graphical query tool that allows you to visually analyze the plan of a query, run multiple queries simultaneously, view data, and obtain index recommendations. SQL Server Query Analyzer provides the Showplan option, which is used to report data retrieval methods chosen by the SQL Server 2000 Query Optimizer.

SQL Server Profiler

SQL Server 2000 Profiler captures a continuous record of server activity in real time. SQL Server 2000 Profiler enables you to monitor events produced through SQL Server 2000, filter events based on user-specified criteria, and direct the trace output to the screen, a file, or a table. Using SQL Server 2000 Profiler, you can replay previously captured traces.

The Profiler Tool also helps application developers identify transactions that might be deteriorating the performance of an application. This can be useful when migrating an application from a file-based architecture to a client/server architecture, since the last step involves optimizing the application for its new client/server environment.

SQL Migration

Technology consultants working with previous versions of Small Business Server must know how to migrate data between the various SQL Server versions. This section discusses data migrations from SQL Server 6.5 to SQL Server 7.0, and SQL Server 7.0 to SQL Server 2000.

SQL Server 6.5 to SQL Server 7.0

Migrating from SQL Server 6.5 to SQL Server 7.0 occurs in the context of Small Business Server 4.5. Small Business Server 4.0 (and 4.0a) provided SQL Server 6.5.Small Business Server 4.5 provided SQL Server 7.0.

The Small Business Server 4.5 Version Upgrade setup application installs SQL Server 7.0 into a new folder but does not migrate your existing SQL Server 6.5 database to SQL Server 7.0. Many third-party software applications might have a dependency on SQL Server 6.5, so consult the appropriate software vendor to ensure their software is compatible with SQL Server 7.0.

If you want to migrate your own SQL Server 6.5 database to SQL Server 7.0, run the SQL Server Upgrade Wizard in Small Business Server 4.5, which walks you through the process of migrating an existing SQL Server 6.5 database to the new SQL Server 7.0 format. This wizard is accessible from the Small Business Server 4.5 To Do List.

The SQL Server upgrade is built on some fundamental assumptions. The Upgrade Wizard is designed to upgrade all the databases in a single pass. The purpose of the SQL Server Upgrade Wizard is to upgrade a single instance of SQL Server 6.5 to a single instance of SQL Server 7.0 in one pass. You can run multiple upgrades (for example, one database at a time) as long as they use the same SQL Server 6.5 installation. This is not recommended, however, as cross-database dependencies cannot be resolved if you upgrade only one database at a time.

SQL Server 7.0 to SQL Server 2000

To migrate data from SQL Server 7.0 to SQL Server 2000, start the SQL Server Upgrade Wizard from the SQL Server Switch program group. This upgrade occurs in the context of Small Business Server 2000. The SQL Server Upgrade Wizard in Small Business Server 2000 is designed to transfer your server configuration and databases from a single SQL Server 6.5 installation to the SQL Server 2000 installation on the server computer. The wizard upgrades any or all of your databases, transferring all catalog data, objects, and user data. It also transfers replication settings, SQL Server Executive settings, and most of the SQL Server 6.5 configuration options.

> ☑ **Note** To run the SQL Server Upgrade Wizard in Small Business Server 2000, you must have an instance of SQL Server 2000 already installed on your computer. SQL Server 2000 is not installed in Small Business Server 2000 by default. For more information, refer to the Small Business Server Online Help.

The SQL Server Upgrade Wizard in Small Business Server 2000 does not remove the SQL Server 6.5 installation from your server computer. You must manually uninstall SQL Server 6.5.

Migration Phase

This section covers the migration procedures involved in using the SQL Server 2000 tools described earlier in this chapter.

Access Database Backup

Before migrating tables and queries to SQL Server 2000, it is strongly advised that you run trial passes on a backup of the Access database, because the database format is converted by the Upsizing Wizard. To obtain the best possible SQL Server database, you will likely need to run the wizard through a few trial passes before performing your migration. You can experiment on the backup copy of the Access database until the best configuration is obtained, at which time the actual migration should be performed on the production database.

Moving Tables and Data

Access data can be transferred to SQL Server 2000 by using the DTS Import/Export Wizard, as follows.

To transfer Access data to SQL Server 2000

1. On the SQL Server Enterprise Manager, select a database in the Databases folder, and then select the **Tools** menu, point to **Data Transformation Services**, and click **Import Data**.

2. In the **Choose a Data Source** dialog box, select **Microsoft Access as the Source**.

3. Type the file name of your .mdb database, or browse for the file.

4. In the **Choose a Destination** dialog box, select **Microsoft OLE DB Provider for SQL Server**, select the database server, and then click the required authentication mode.

5. In the **Specify Table Copy or Query** dialog box, click **Copy tables**.

6. In the **Select Source Tables** dialog box, click **Select All**.

7. Click **OK** to complete the wizard.

Migrating Access Queries

Existing Access queries must be moved into SQL Server 2000 in one of the formats described in the sections that follow.

Transact-SQL Scripts

Transact-SQL statements are usually called from database programs, but you can use SQL Server 2000 Query Analyzer to run them against the database directly. SQL Server 2000 Query Analyzer helps developers test Transact-SQL statements against development databases and run Transact-SQL statements that perform queries, data manipulation (INSERT, UPDATE, DELETE), or data definition (CREATE TABLE).

Stored Procedures

Most Transact-SQL statements that originate from Access queries (SELECT, INSERT, UPDATE, and DELETE) can be moved into stored procedures. Stored procedures written in Transact-SQL can be used to encapsulate and standardize your data access, and are actually stored within the database. Stored procedures can run with or without parameters and are called from database programs or manually from the Query Analyzer. Table 25.1 describes Access queries.

Table 25.1 Access Queries

Access query type	SQL Server migration options and comments
SELECT	A SELECT statement can be stored in a Transact-SQL file, a stored procedure, or a view. Creating stored procedures is the best way to separate the database application development from the physical implementation of the database design. Stored procedures are created in one place and are called from the application. Calls to stored procedures do not "break" if the underlying database changes and the stored procedure is carefully modified to reflect the changes.
CROSSTAB	Crosstabs are used for summary reports. An Access CROSSTAB can be implemented as a Transact-SQL SELECT statement in a SQL script, a stored procedure, or a view. The data join is re-executed each time a query is issued, ensuring that the latest data is always used. Depending on the application, it might be appropriate to store data from the crosstab as a temporary table (see MAKE TABLE). The temporary table requires fewer resources but offers only a snapshot of the data at the time the temporary table is created.
MAKE TABLE	An Access MAKE TABLE can be implemented as a Transact-SQL CREATE TABLE statement in a Transact-SQL script or stored procedure. The syntax follows: SELECT [ALL I DISTINCT] [{TOP integer I TOP integer PERCENT} [WITH TIES]] *<select_list>* [INTO *new_table*] [FROM {*<table_source>*} [,...n]] [WHERE *<search_condition>*] [GROUP BY [ALL] group_by_expression [,...n]] [WITH { CUBE I ROLLUP }] CREATE TABLE mytable (low int, high int)
UPDATE	An UPDATE statement can be stored in a Transact-SQL script. However, the recommended way to implement an UPDATE statement is to create a stored procedure.
APPEND	An APPEND statement can be stored in a Transact-SQL script. However, the recommended way of implementing an APPEND statement is to create a stored procedure.
DELETE	A DELETE statement can be stored in a Transact-SQL script. However, the recommended way of implementing a DELETE statement is to create a stored procedure.

Views

Views are used as virtual tables that expose specific rows and columns from one or more tables. They enable users to create queries without directly implementing the complex joins that underlie the query. Views do not support the use of parameters. Views that join more than one table cannot be modified by using INSERT, UPDATE, or DELETE statements. Views are called from Transact-SQL statements and can also be used in *.scripts that run in SQL Server Query Analyzer. SQL Server views and the SQL-92 standard do not support ORDER BY clauses in views.

For more information about Transact-SQL, stored procedures, or views, refer to the SQL Server Web site at: http://www.microsoft.com/sql.

Migrating Access Queries into Stored Procedures and Views

Each Access query must be placed into this set of statements.

```
CREATE PROCEDURE <NAME_HERE> AS

< SELECT, UPDATE, DELETE, INSERT, CREATE TABLE statement from Microsoft
Access >

GO

CREATE VIEW <NAME_HERE> AS

<Place (SELECT only, with no parameters) Microsoft Access Query>

GO
```

For each Access query, perform the following steps.

To migrate Access queries into stored procedures and views

1. Start Access, and then start the SQL Server 2000 Query Analyzer.

2. In the **Database** window of Access, click the **Queries** tab, and then click **Design**.

3. On the **View** menu, click **SQL**.

4. Paste the entire query into the SQL Server Query Analyzer.

5. Either test the syntax and save the Transact-SQL statement for later use, or run the statement in the database. Transact-SQL can also be saved to a script, as described in the following section.

Migrating Access Queries into Transact-SQL Scripts

Most Access queries should be translated into stored procedures and views. Nevertheless, some statements that are run infrequently by an application developer can be stored as a Transact-SQL script, which is a text file that ends with the file extension .sql. These files can be run from within SQL Server Query Analyzer.

If you plan to transfer some of the small business Access queries into .sql files, consider separating the Transact-SQL statements into several scripts, depending on how they are used. For example, those Transact-SQL statements that must be run with the same frequency can be grouped together into a script. Another script might contain all Transact-SQL statements that are run only under certain conditions. Also, Transact-SQL statements that must be run in a specific order should be grouped together in a discreet script.

To move a statement from Access to a Transact-SQL file

1. Copy the statement into the SQL Server Query Analyzer.

2. Click the **Parse Query** icon on the toolbar to parse the statement.

3. Run the statement by using the **Execute Statement** button on the toolbar.

If there are MAKE TABLE Access queries, two options are available for SQL Server. Either of the following can be created:

- **A view**. A view creates the effect of having a dynamic, virtual temporary table that provides the latest information. This is input/output (I/O) intensive since it requires the rejoining of the data tables each time a query is issued.

- **A temporary table**. A temporary table creates a snapshot of data for a connected user's session. You can create local and global temporary tables. Local temporary tables are visible only in the current session, and global temporary tables are visible to all sessions.

  Prefix local temporary table names with single number sign (#table_name), and prefix global temporary table names with double number sign (##table_name). Queries run quickly against temporary tables as they typically use only one table rather than dynamically joining together several tables to obtain a result set. For more information about temporary tables, refer to the SQL Server Web site at: http://www.microsoft.com/sql.

  The DTS in SQL Server 2000 enables you to standardize, automate, and schedule the creation of temporary tables by creating packages. For example, when you migrate the Access 2.0 Northwind sample database, the Crosstab created for reporting quarterly data becomes either a view, or a data transformation creating a temporary table on a regular basis.

Other Migration Considerations

The following section describes other issues to consider when migrating the Access database to SQL Server 2000.

Using Parameters

SQL Server 2000 stored procedures that have parameters need a different syntax from Access queries, as described in Table 25.2. In the section following the table, an example is given of the syntax changes of an Access 2.0 query versus the equivalent SQL Server 2000 stored procedure syntax.

Table 25.2   Differences Between SQL Server 2000 and Access Syntax

Access	SQL Server
ORDER BY in queries	ORDER BY in views not supported
DISTINCTROW	DISTINCT
String concatenation with "&"	String concatenation with "+"
Supported clauses/operators	Supported clauses/operators
SELECT	SELECT
SELECT TOP N	SELECT TOP N
INTO	INTO
FROM	FROM
WHERE	WHERE
GROUP BY	GROUP BY
HAVING	HAVING
UNION (ALL)	UNION (ALL)
ORDER BY	ORDER BY

Table 25.2 Differences Between SQL Server 2000 and Access Syntax *(continued)*

Access	SQL Server
WITH OWNER ACCESS	COMPUTE FOR BROWSE OPTION
Not Supported: COMPUTE, FOR BROWSE, OPTION	Not Supported: WITH OWNERACCESS
Aggregate functions	Aggregate functions
AVG	AVG([ALL | DISTINCT] expression)
COUNT(column)	COUNT([ALL | DISTINCT] expression)
COUNT(*)	COUNT(*)
	GROUPING (column_name)
MAX	MAX(expression)
MIN	MIN(expression)
STDEV, STDEVP	STDEV, STDEVP
SUM	SUM([ALL | DISTINCT] expression)
VAR, VARP	VAR, VARP
FIRST, LAST	Not supported: FIRST, LAST
TRANSFORM (SELECT statement)	WITH ROLLUP, WITH CUBE on SELECT statements
PIVOT	Not applicable
MAKE TABLE, ALTER TABLE	CREATE TABLE, ALTER TABLE
Other supported clauses:	Other supported clauses:
CONSTRAINT	CONSTRAINT
ADD COLUMN	ADD COLUMN
DROP COLUMN	DROP COLUMN
DROP INDEX	Not applicable
Also, stand-alone statement: DROP INDEX	Stand-alone statement: DROP INDEX

Access and SQL Server Syntax

The following is a syntax example of an Access 2.0 query and the equivalent for a SQL Server 2000 stored procedure.

Access Query Name: Employee Sales By Country, in NWIND.mdb:

```
PARAMETERS [Beginning Date] DateTime, [Ending Date] DateTime;

SELECT Orders.[Order ID], [Last Name] & ", " & [First Name] AS
Salesperson, Employees.Country, Orders.[Shipped Date], [Order
Subtotals].Subtotal AS [Sale Amount]

FROM Employees INNER JOIN (Orders INNER JOIN [Order Subtotals] ON
Orders.[Order ID] = [Order Subtotals].[Order ID]) ON Employees.[Employee
ID] = Orders.[Employee ID]

WHERE (((Orders.[Shipped Date]) Between [Beginning Date] And [Ending
Date]))

ORDER BY [Last Name] & ", " & [First Name], Employees.Country,
Orders.[Shipped Date];
```

SQL Server stored procedure syntax:

```
CREATE PROCEDURE EMP_SALES_BY_COUNTRY

@BeginningDate datetime,

@EndingDate datetime

AS

SELECT Orders.[Order ID], [Last Name] + ", " + [First Name] AS
Salesperson, Employees.Country,

Orders.[Shipped Date], [Order Subtotals].Subtotal AS [Sale Amount]

FROM Employees INNER JOIN (Orders INNER JOIN [Order Subtotals] ON
Orders.[Order ID] = [Order Subtotals].[Order ID]) ON Employees.[Employee
ID] = Orders.[Employee ID]

WHERE (((Orders.[Shipped Date]) Between @BeginningDate And @EndingDate))

ORDER BY [Last Name] + ", " + [First Name], Employees.Country,
Orders.[Shipped Date]

GO
```

Nested Queries

Some Access queries are created on top of other queries in a nested fashion. Nested queries in Access become nested views in SQL Server. The ORDER BY clauses cannot be part of a view definition but are appended to the SELECT statement that queries the VIEW. If you have nested Access queries, create several views and then create stored procedures that perform both a SELECT operation on the view and append an ORDER BY clause to the SELECT statement.

For example, the following Access query:

```
SELECT *
FROM STUDENTS
WHERE COUNTRY = "USA"
ORDER BY LAST_NAME
```

becomes the SQL Server view and a stored procedure:

```
CREATE VIEW US_STUDENTS AS
SELECT * FROM STUDENTS
WHERE COUNTRY = "USA"
CREATE PROCEDURE US_STUDENTS_ORDER AS
SELECT * FROM US_STUDENTS_ORDER BY LAST NAME
```

Verifying SQL Server 2000–Compliant Syntax

You can use the Parse command on the Query menu in the SQL Server 2000 Query Analyzer to verify whether a view or stored procedure functions in SQL Server 2000. For example, an Access query might properly use the word "DISTINCTROW." However, SQL Server 2000 uses the Transact-SQL command DISTINCT to perform the same operation. The Parse command enables the technology consultant to isolate and modify syntax problems in Access queries.

Connecting the Applications

Many Access applications predating Office 2000 were written by using Microsoft Visual Basic for Applications, or the Visual Basic for Applications Access user interface. Applications that use Visual Basic for Applications as the development environment can run against SQL Server 2000, using the Jet ODBC driver. Applications that use the forms and reports found in the Access user interface can access SQL Server 2000 by using linked tables.

If the small business application is to use linked tables, make sure that all Access tables get moved to SQL Server 2000 to increase performance. Creating queries against a mix of Access (Jet) and SQL Server using linked tables can be very resource intensive.

Optimizing the Application

You can optimize the Access application for the client/server environment by:

- Monitoring Transact-SQL statements being sent to the server
- Implementing efficient indexes

Monitoring Transact-SQL Statements

SQL Server Profiler is a useful tool for monitoring how Transact-SQL statements are sent to the database. If you run an unmodified Access application on SQL Server 2000, you might send less-than-optimum Transact-SQL statements to the database by using Data Access Objects (DAO) with the Jet/ODBC driver. For example, a DELETE statement that uses the Jet/ODBC driver to delete 1,000 rows makes 1,000 calls to the database. This negatively impacts the performance of a production database. In this example, SQL Server Profiler displays 1,000 DELETE statements, allowing you to modify the application to use Microsoft ActiveX® Data Objects (ADO) with the Microsoft OLE DB Provider for SQL Server 2000, and thereby improve the application's efficiency.

Implementing Efficient Indexes

After determining that the Transact-SQL statements being sent to the database are efficient, you can fine-tune those statements by using indexes effectively. The Index Tuning Wizard enables you to locate index bottlenecks, and it also provides recommendations to help you resolve the issues. Although your Transact-SQL statements are not modified, their performance improves with the correct use of indexes.

> ☑ **Note** For additional information about optimizing the Access application for client/server performance, refer to Knowledge Base article Q128808 in the support section on the Microsoft Web site at: http://support.microsoft.com.

Additional Resources

For more information about SQL Server 2000, refer to the Microsoft SQL Server 2000 Web site at: http://www.microsoft.com/sql.

You may also want to acquire the *Microsoft SQL Server 2000 Resource Kit* through Microsoft Press at: http://mspress.microsoft.com.

Summary

This chapter addressed the three types of SQL Server 2000 data migrations within Small Business Server 2000. Discussions included migrating Access databases to SQL Server 2000, migrating SQL Server 6.5 data to a SQL Server 7.0 database, and migrating SQL Server 7.0 data to a SQL Server 2000 database.

Disaster Recovery

Protecting company data on Microsoft® Small Business Server 2000 is a critical consideration, as the small business may only have a fault-tolerant disk configuration providing limited protection from hardware failure. Furthermore, Small Business Server is not able to protect crucial company data from fire or other natural disasters. Two crucial methods of protecting company data include making backups and having a disaster plan. Disaster recovery planning for Small Business Server includes reducing the potential for problems to occur and developing the necessary plans and procedures to handle failure recovery.

Windows 2000 Server Backup Utility

The Microsoft Windows® 2000 Server component of Small Business Server has a comprehensive backup utility that permits the technology consultant to back up critical company data to tape media. You can schedule the time of your backup with the scheduling capability found in Windows 2000 Backup utility. It allows for backup of data on the server itself and for workstations in the small business network, including security information, file and share permissions, and registry data. For data security, only a user from the administrator or backup operator group should back up data to tape. Individual files and directories or the entire server can be restored by using the Windows 2000 Backup utility.

To use the Windows 2000 Backup utility in Small Business Server, you need access to some form of backup device. This can include a hard disk, removable disk, floppy disk, or a tape backup device. The Windows 2000 Backup utility does not support backups to CD-R, CD-RW or DVD-R devices because Remote Storage Management does not have the ability to recognize these devices as backup pool media.

If you are using a tape backup device, it must be connected to a compatible small computer system interface (SCSI) controller card or other controller card such as IDE, which uses the Atapi tape drivers in Windows 2000 Server as described in Knowledge Base article Q254153. The SCSI controller card must be properly installed and functional. Windows 2000 Server automates the installation of a controller card because Device Manager detects new hardware at system startup and automatically installs the appropriate drivers.

Note The Windows 2000 Backup utility does not back up open files. This is an important fact to know if you are running important business applications such as accounting systems on your server computer. You may need to shut down these applications to ensure a proper backup.

Selecting a Backup Scheme

You are encouraged to select a tape backup rotation scheme that ensures that your data is protected should a tape malfunction or become lost. A popular tape rotation scheme is the grandparent-parent-child, as follows:

- The tape used for backup on the last Friday of each month is called the grandparent tape. This tape is stored off-site.

- The tape used for backup every Friday, except the last Friday of the month, is the called the parent. This tape is also stored off-site.

- The tapes used for backup on Monday, Tuesday, Wednesday, and Thursday are called children. Often, all children tapes are stored on-site except for the tape from the previous day.

You can select from the following backup options:

- **Normal**. Backs up all selected files and marks the files as backed up.

- **Copy**. Backs up all selected files but does not mark the files as backed up.

- **Differential**. Backs up selected files only if they have not been previously backed up, or have been changed since the last backup, but does not mark the files as backed up.

- **Incremental**. Backs up selected files only if they have not been previously backed up, or have been changed since the last backup, and marks the files as backed up.

- **Daily**. Backs up only files that have been changed today and marks them as backed up.

Because small businesses typically do not have technology professionals on staff, a Normal backup, performed daily and according to the suggested grandparent-parent-child backup scheme, is recommended as part of the small business backup and disaster recovery plan.

System State Data Backup

Windows 2000 Backup utility can also back up System State data, including:

- Registry (found in both Windows 2000 Professional and Server)

- COM+, an extension of Component Object Model, Class Registration database, found in both Windows 2000 Professional and Server

- Boot files, found in both Windows 2000 Professional and Server

- Certificate Services database, Windows 2000 Server only

- Microsoft Active Directory™ directory service, Windows 2000 Server only

- SYSVOL directory, on Windows 2000 Server only; this is a shared directory that stores the server copy of the domain's public files, which are replicated among all domain controllers in the domain

- Cluster service information, found in Windows 2000 Advanced Server; this software component controls all aspects of server cluster operations and manages the cluster database

Possible backup locations for System State data include floppy disks, a hard disk, removable media, recordable compact discs, and tapes.

    ☑ **Note**   You can also make a Registry backup by exporting the Registry through the Registry Editor, Regedit.exe or Regedt32.exe.

Emergency Repair Disk

The Windows 2000 Backup utility allows you to create an Emergency Repair Disk (ERD). The ERD stores critical system information. You can use the ERD to repair and restart Windows 2000 if it is damaged. This option does not back up your files or applications, and it is not considered a replacement for regularly backing up your system.

Using Windows 2000 Backup Utility

To perform a backup using the Windows 2000 Backup utility

1. Click **Start**, point to **Programs**, point to **Accessories**, and then click **System Tools**.

2. In the System Tools program group, click **Backup**.

3. In the **Backup** dialog box, click **Backup Wizard**, and then click **Next**.

4. On the **What to Back Up** page, click **Back up everything on my computer**, and then click **Next**.

   > ✒ **Note** Be sure to back up the \%systemdrive%\WINNT folder, for example, C:\WINNT, so the Metabase.bin file in the \WINNT\system32\inetsrv folder is properly backed up. The Metabase.bin file contains critical configuration settings for Windows 2000.

   > Also, if you back up drive M, which is automatically created in Small Business Server to hold the Microsoft Exchange 2000 Server installable file system (IFS), you receive a message that the IFS could not be backed up. This is caused by an open file condition and should be ignored. To properly back up Microsoft Exchange 2000 Server, select the two Microsoft Exchange backup options: Microsoft Exchange and Microsoft Exchange Server.

5. On the **Where to Store the Backup** page, specify your backup media type in the **Backup media type** field. Type the name of the media in the **Backup media or file name** field, and then click **Next**.

6. On the **Completing the Backup Wizard** page, click **Advanced**.

7. On the **Type of Backup** page, specify the type of backup operation to perform. Although the default selection is Normal, another common type of backup is Incremental. Both are discussed earlier in this chapter. Click **Next**.

8. On the **How To Backup** page, select the **Verify data after backup** box, and then click **Next**.

9. On the **Media Options** page, specify whether to append to or replace backup media that already contains backup data, and then click **Next**.

10. On the **Backup Label** page, type a backup label in the **Backup label** field and media label in the **Media label** field. Notice that the backup and media label fields are automatically completed for you with the current date and time. Click **Next**.

11. On the **When to Back Up** page, specify whether the backup is to run now or later from a scheduled entry. If you schedule the backup for a later time, type a logon name and password. This is essentially the same as the RUNAS command, which allows the scheduled backup task to log on using a different logon name from the currently logged on user. If no user is logged on to the Small Business Server 2000 computer, this logon name and password allow the schedule backup task to run. Click **Next**.

12. On the **Completing the Backup Wizard** page, click **Finish** to complete the wizard.

To restore data from a backup using the Windows 2000 Backup utility

1. Click **Start**, point to **Programs**, point to **Accessories**, and then click **System Tools**.

2. In the **System Tools** program group, click **Backup**.

3. In the **Backup** dialog box, click **Restore Wizard**, and then click **Next**.

4. On the **What to Restore** page, select the backup file to restore from the **What to restore** list, and then click **Next**.

    ☑ **Note** If you elect to restore System State, you receive a warning informing you that system state data cannot be restored while Active Directory is running. You must restart the Small Business Server 2000 server computer and select the advanced start-up option **Directory Services Restore Mode** before restarting the computer. Also be aware of how Active Directory is restored, discussed later in the "Active Directory Restoration" section.

5. On the **Completing the Restore Wizard** page, click **Advanced**.

6. On the **Where to Restore** page, select a restore location. Selections include original location, alternative location, or single folder. Click **Next**.

    ☑ **Note** It is common to restore to an alternative location so that you do not risk overwriting good data with aged backup data. For example, if you are restoring an accounting database, you might restore it first to a temporary directory and then copy the database to the original location. This serves as a check-and-balance method to ensure proper restores.

7. On the **How to Restore** page, specify how to resolve file restore issues when a file with the same name exists overwrite it, do not restore, or restore based on aging. Click **Next**.

8. On the **Advanced Restore Options** page, select from the list of restore options, as follows, and then click **Next**.

   • Restore security

   • Restore Removable Storage database

   • Restore junction points, not the folders and file data they reference

9. Click **Finish** to complete the wizard.

   ☑ **Note** For more information about disaster planning, refer to the "Improving Your Disaster Recovery Capabilities" section in Chapter 19, "Determining Windows 2000 Storage Management Strategies" of the *Windows 2000 Server Deployment Planning Guide* in the *Windows 2000 Server Resource Kit*.

Active Directory Restoration

Distributed services such as the Active Directory directory service are contained in a collection known as the System State data. When you back up the System State data on a domain controller, you are backing up all Active Directory data that exists on that server, along with other system components, such as the SYSVOL directory and the registry. To restore these distributed services to that server, you must restore the System State data. However, if you have more than one domain controller in your organization, and your Active Directory is replicated to any of these other servers, you must perform what is called an authoritative restore in order to ensure that your restored data gets replicated to all of your servers.

During a normal restore operation, Backup operates in nonauthoritative restore mode. That is, any data that you restore, including Active Directory objects, have their original update sequence number. The Active Directory replication system uses this number to detect and propagate Active Directory changes among the servers in your organization. Because of this, any data that is restored nonauthoritatively appears to the Active Directory replication system as though it is old, which means the data will never get replicated to your other servers. Instead, the Active Directory replication system updates the restored data with newer data from your other servers. Authoritative restore solves this problem.

To authoritatively restore Active Directory data, you must run the Ntdsutil utility after you have restored the System State data but before you restart the server. The Ntdsutil utility lets you mark Active Directory objects for authoritative restore. When an object is marked for authoritative restore, its update sequence number is changed so that it is higher than any other update sequence number in the Active Directory replication system. This ensures that any replicated or distributed data that you restore is properly replicated or distributed throughout your organization.

For example, if you inadvertently delete or modify objects stored in the Active Directory directory service, and those objects are replicated or distributed to other servers, you need to authoritatively restore those objects so that they are replicated or distributed to the other servers. If you do not authoritatively restore the objects, they never get replicated or distributed to your other servers because they appear to be older than the objects currently on your other servers. Using the Ntdsutil utility to mark objects for authoritative restore ensures that the data you want to restore gets replicated or distributed throughout your organization. On the other hand, if your system disk has failed or the Active Directory database is corrupted, you can simply restore the data nonauthoritatively without using the Ntdsutil utility.

The Ntdsutil command-line utility can be run from the command prompt. Help for the Ntdsutil utility can also be found at the command prompt by typing **ntdsutil /?**

How to Test

All technology consultants should periodically test the fitness of a customer's data backups in either a monthly test restore or a fire drill.

Monthly Test Restore

Most technology consultants visit their Small Business Server customers periodically, often once per month. During that visit, the technology consultant should randomly select a recent backup tape and restore several files, such as word processing and spreadsheet files, to a temporary directory on the Small Business Server 2000 server computer. These restored test files should then be opened, changed, and saved. This is one of the best tests to ensure the customer that valid backups are taking place.

> ☑ **Note** If the customer is using a sophisticated business application such as accounting software, it is recommended that the technology consultant coordinate a test restore with the accounting software consultant. Complex business applications often need additional steps performed to restore data beyond a simple tape restore process.

Fire Drill

Small business owners, often without full knowledge of the business staff, have a technology consultant arrive unannounced at the site and create a simulated disaster. This is often contracted for once per year. It enables the customer to assess the fitness of its data backups and the ability to recover from a disaster. As part of this exercise, the technology consultant often invites an employee from the customer site, retains a recent backup tape, and visits another site, known as a hot site. The hot site may even be the technology consultant's office. At this site, a full restore is performed to another computer.

Fire drill exercises typically reveal weaknesses in the information system disaster recovery plan in a methodically and controlled environment, before a real disaster occurs.

Backup Calendar

The backup program in Small Business Server has a calendar utility that can be used to schedule backup jobs. The calendar is shown in Figure 26.1, a marked improvement over the use of the AT scheduling command in previous releases of Small Business Server.

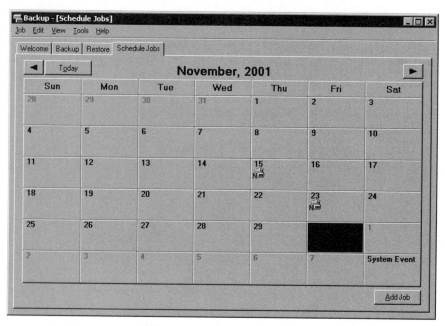

Figure 26.1 The Backup utility Schedule Jobs tab displays a calendar, with a backup job shown

Windows 2000 Clients

Using the synchronize capability, Windows 2000 users may effectively back up data, such as data files, to the Small Business Server 2000 computer. Synchronize is available from the Windows 2000 Professional Accessories program group. Here, you can configure those items that you want synchronized with the Small Business Server 2000 computer, including Web content, data files, e-mail messages, and calendar information.

Third-Party Applications

Several major independent software vendors have released Small Business Server tape backup programs. These programs are often used in environments that either need to back up more than one server, back up Microsoft Exchange Server e-mail at the mailbox level, and/or back up Microsoft SQL Server™. Check with a software reseller for availability of these Small Business Server backup applications.

Exchange 2000 Server Backup

The Windows 2000 Backup utility can back up the Exchange 2000 Server information store and directory services. Because Exchange 2000 Server is backed up at the post office-level when the Microsoft Exchange options are selected in Windows 2000 Backup, however, it is not possible to restore an individual mailbox or individual piece of e-mail using the Windows 2000 Backup utility. Some third-party tape backup applications have the ability to restore at the individual mailbox level. For more information about this or about Exchange 2000 Server disaster planning, refer to the *Microsoft Exchange 2000 Server Resource Kit.*

SQL Server 2000 Backup

The Windows 2000 Backup utility cannot back up SQL Server databases that are online. However, there is a solution to this. You can first create a backup of the SQL Server databases, using Enterprise Manager in SQL Server. Next, you can use the Windows 2000 Backup utility to make a backup of the databases that you just backed up with the SQL Server Enterprise Manager. This sequence of events can occur on predetermined schedules to automate the coordination of this backup process. The schedule for the SQL Server database backups would occur in SQL Server 2000 Enterprise Manager. The scheduling capability in the Windows 2000 Backup utility is shown earlier in Figure 26.1.

> ☑ **Note** For more robust, enterprise-level SQL Server backups, it is recommended that you purchase a third-party Windows 2000 Server tape backup application that has a SQL Server backup agent. More robust backup capabilities include saving SQL Server 2000-related account settings as an example. Note that some business applications that use SQL Server, such as accounting programs, use the internal backup capabilities found in SQL Server to back up critical data to a hard disk, usually several times per day. This form of backup is typically specified by the ISV that created the business application and should not be confused with a bona fide tape backup approach. For more information about SQL Server disaster planning, refer to SQL Server 2000 Books Online, available on the SQL Server Web site at: http://www.microsoft.com/sql/.

Summary

This chapter discussed Small Business Server disaster recovery issues and covered backing up critical data and system information. Discussion included how to restore System State data, in particular the Active Directory database, strategies for testing the fitness of backups, issues surrounding third-party backup applications, and Exchange 2000 Server and SQL Server 2000.

Networking and Storage Basics

Many technology consultants are new to the world of Microsoft® Small Business Server 2000—and even new to networking in general. In this appendix, a networking primer, you can learn the fundamentals of networking and the basics of storage management.

Defining a Network

A network is a business solution based on technology that enables the sharing of resources in a reliable and secure manner. These shared resources include information, printers, and communications, such as e-mail and an Internet connection. Small Business Server 2000 satisfies this basic definition of networking.

Server

At the center of the network is a computer known as a server. A server is usually a powerful machine that can accept and process many commands from multiple users and store data safely. Server-class computers are typically more expensive than workstations. This additional cost comes from hardware components that offer better performance and greater system availability.

Client

Clients are the computers that connect and log on to the server across the network. Client computers are typically workstation-class machines that are capable of performing local operations and participating in the network.

Other Hardware

A network is not just server computers and client workstations. Other components play a critical role in completing the definition of a network, including:

- Wiring
- Hubs
- Segments
- Routers
- Printers
- Power supply management, including uninterruptible power supplies
- Modems

Hubs gather and manage the wiring (or media) that connects all the client computers to the server and the network. Networks can be broken down into segments to accommodate geographic restrictions, such as different buildings on a campus. These networks often connect by means of routers that boost performance and improve manageability. Other hardware devices typically connected to networks include printers, uninterruptible power supplies (UPS) for power management, and modems for telecommunications.

Network Operating System

As you most likely know, an operating system provides basic functions such as accessing hardware devices and reading data from and writing data to storage media. Network operating systems extend this basic understanding of an operating system to include logon authentication services for security, management of shared devices such as printers, and reliable management of storage. Network operating systems typically have a more powerful command set than a desktop operating system, allowing the server to perform more functions and run more complex applications.

Network operating systems, working in conjunction with the network client software installed on the client computer, typically assume responsibility for executing computer commands directed to the network. The network client software, known in the past as a redirector, passes network-related activity to the server for processing by the network operating system. Similarly, local commands are directed to the local workstation for processing.

While this discussion oversimplifies the complete range of services provided by the network operating system Microsoft Windows® 2000 Server, it does form the foundation for a better understanding of Small Business Server 2000.

Connectivity

Critical components that enable connectivity and allow networks to function are protocols. Protocols facilitate connectivity by allowing the transfer of information on the network. Protocols can be thought of as an agreement between parties who want to communicate or collaborate. By selecting the same protocol, every node on the network agrees to communicate according to a certain set of rules.

Another component of connectivity is how networks connect to the Internet. By agreeing to use the same protocol—which in the case of the Internet is TCP/IP—your network can connect to the Internet. One reason this works is that the Internet is really nothing more than a network of networks, all connected by a common protocol.

Many small businesses decide to implement networks for connectivity reasons, such as high-speed Internet connections and e-mail capabilities. The technology consultant should not overlook the role of connectivity in helping a small business make the decision to network.

Files, Printers, and Applications

Major reasons that small businesses implement networks are to manage files (data and information), manage printers, and run applications. Files are discussed in "Storage," a later section of this appendix.

Printers are one of the main reasons that local area networks grew rapidly in the 1980s and early 1990s, a time when printers were relatively expensive. By sharing a laser printer, a small business could often justify the entire cost of developing the network in reduced printing costs.

Today, an important reason for developing networks is to run applications, specifically business applications. By allowing workers to share a common business database, for example, firms can dramatically improve both their productivity and competitiveness. Productivity improves because redundant operations are performed much faster and with less staff. Competitiveness improves because companies can mine their databases to find new customer relationships, sales cycles, unmet product demand, and so on.

Storage

One of the most important jobs of the network is to provide storage for data and information. This storage should be high-performance to avoid long read and write delays for the user. More important, the storage should be reliable so that the user has confidence that the data is recoverable in the worst-case data loss scenario.

Implementing an appropriate storage solution in Small Business Server 2000 starts with planning for a fault-tolerant disk configuration.

Planning a Fault-Tolerant Disk Configuration

A technology called Redundant Array of Independent Disks (RAID) may be used to minimize loss of data if hard disk access problems occur on Small Business Server. RAID is a fault-tolerant disk configuration in which part of the physical disk-storage capacity of a server contains a redundant data set. The redundant information enables the automatic regeneration of the data if either of the following occurs:

- A disk or its access path fails.

- A sector on the disk cannot be read.

Standard fault-tolerant disk systems are categorized in six levels, known as RAID levels 0 through 5. Each level offers various combinations of performance, reliability, and cost. RAID combines multiple disks with lower individual reliability ratings to reduce the total cost of storage. The redundancy feature offsets the lower reliability of each disk in a RAID array. Windows 2000 Server supports the following:

- Disk striping (RAID level 0)

- Disk mirroring (RAID level 1)

- Disk striping with parity (RAID level 5)

For more information about RAID arrays compatible with Windows 2000 Server, refer to the Windows 2000 Hardware Compatibility List located on the Internet at:
http://www.microsoft.com/windows2000/

To create a fault-tolerant disk configuration for Small Business Server 2000, use RAID level 1 disk mirroring or duplexing, or RAID level 5 disk striping with parity, as described in the sections that follow. The Computer Management management console, available from the Small Business Server Administrator Console located on the Start menu, configures mirrored or duplexed disk sets, disk striping with parity, and also reconstructs the volume if a failure occurs.

> **Note** For the highest performance, consider hardware-based RAID solutions instead of the RAID implementation provided natively with Windows 2000 Server. Hardware-based RAID solutions take advantage of the processor found on RAID controller cards, relieving Windows 2000 Server of the burden of managing the RAID process.

Disk Mirroring

Disk mirroring creates and maintains an identical redundant disk for duplication of data on a selected primary disk. Disk mirroring uses two partitions on different drives connected to the same disk controller, as shown in Figure A.1. All data on the primary disk partition is mirrored automatically onto the secondary (redundant) disk partition—sometimes referred to as a shadow partition. If the primary disk fails, no data is lost since the secondary partition can be used.

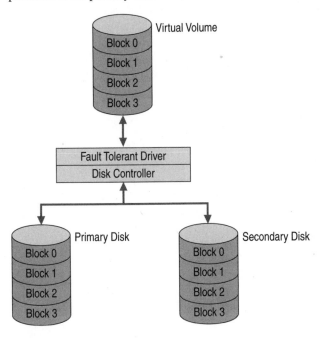

Figure A.1 Disk mirror configuration

I/O Requests in a Disk Mirroring Configuration

In a disk mirroring configuration, all data is written to both partitions, resulting in only 50 percent disk space utilization. From the perspective of the user, only a single read or write occurs to satisfy data requests, although FtDisk, the Windows 2000 Server fault-tolerant disk driver, creates separate input/output (I/O) requests for each disk in the mirrored set. If a read failure occurs on one disk, FtDisk reads the data from the other disk in the mirrored set. If a write failure occurs on one disk, FtDisk uses the remaining disk in the mirrored set to access data. Since dual-write operations can degrade system performance, many mirrored set implementations use duplexing, where each disk in the mirrored set has its own disk controller. Refer to the section "Disk Duplexing" later in this appendix.

Mirrored Partition Size

The secondary mirrored partition is not limited to the size, number of tracks, or the number of cylinders on the primary partition. This eliminates the requirement to replace the primary drive with an identical model, should it fail. In practice, however, mirrored partitions are usually created with identical disks, the same size as the primary partition. Note that the unpartitioned area you use for the shadow partition must not be *smaller* than the primary partition. If it is *larger*, the unused space can be configured as another partition if there are fewer than four existing partitions on the disk.

Advantages of Mirrored Disk Sets

Some of the advantages of using mirrored disk sets include:

- **Disk read operations on a mirrored set are more efficient than on a single partition**. FtDisk, the fault-tolerant disk driver, has the ability to load-balance read operations across the physical disks. With current small computer system interface (SCSI) technology, two disk read operations can occur simultaneously. In some cases, a disk read can be done in half the time it takes on a single partition.

- **Recovery from a disk failure is rapid**. Mirrored sets offer the fastest data recovery because the shadow partition contains all the data and rebuilding is not required for data restoration. If you configure your boot partition on a mirrored set, Windows 2000 Server reinstallation is not required to restart the computer in the event of disk failure.

- **Disk failure does not impact performance**. A disk mirroring configuration does not impact performance when a member of a mirrored set fails, as stripe sets do.

- **Disk mirroring has better overall read and write performance than stripe sets with parity**.

Disadvantages of Mirrored Disk Sets

Some disadvantages of mirrored disk sets include:

- **Disk write operations are less efficient**. Because data must be written to both disks, performance is slightly affected. However, because disk writes are done asynchronously, the impact is offset. In most situations, a user application is not affected by the extra disk update.

- **Space utilization inefficiencies**. Mirrored disk sets are the least efficient in terms of space utilization. Since data is entirely duplicated, the disk space requirement for mirroring is higher than a stripe set with parity.

- **Incomplete duplication of sectors**. Creating a mirrored set of a boot or system partition does not implement a sector-by-sector duplication of the primary disk. FtDisk does not copy either the Master Boot Record on track 0 or the Partition Boot Sector, which is the first sector of the partition. Some systems may save information in other parts of track 0 and this will not be duplicated either. Data corruption in these areas can make it much more difficult to recover from primary disk failure. If both disks are affected, it can be extremely difficult or impossible to recover the data.

- **More expensive than a disk striping configuration with large storage volumes**. Initially, with two small hard disks, mirroring is less expensive than disk striping with parity because you do not need to purchase a RAID controller card. However, the utilization rate of storage space in a mirroring scenario is 50 percent, which makes the cost per megabyte higher than disk striping with parity with large storage volumes when the cost of the RAID controller card is not significant.

Disk Duplexing

Disk duplexing is a mirrored pair with an additional adapter on the secondary disk drive. Duplexing provides fault tolerance for both disk and controller failure, and increases performance. Like mirroring, duplexing is performed at the partition level; therefore Windows 2000 Server sees no difference between the duplexed disks, with the exception of partition locations. A duplexed mirror set has very high data reliability because the entire I/O subsystem is duplicated, as shown in Figure A.2.

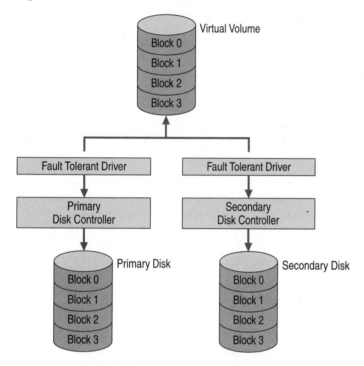

Figure A.2   Duplexed disk mirror configuration

Disk Stripe Sets

Stripe sets are composed of strips of equal size on each disk in a volume, with 2 to 32 disks in the configuration. For Windows 2000 Server, strip size is 64 kilobytes (KB). When data is written to a stripe set, it is written across the strips of the volume—as in the gray area across disks 1 through 4 in the following example. Table A.1 shows the order in which data is written to a stripe set and how a stripe set is similar to a table.

Table A.1 Stripe Set Configuration

	Disk 1	Disk 2	Disk 3	Disk 4
Stripe 1	1	2	3	4
Stripe 2	5	6	7	8
Stripe 3	9	10	11	12
Stripe 4	13	14	15	16
Stripe 5	17	18	19	20

If a 325 KB file was written to the configuration shown in Table A.1, it would occupy the following areas:

- 64 KB in strip 1.
- 64 KB in strip 2.
- 64 KB in strip 3.
- 64 KB in strip 4.
- 64 KB in strip 5.
- 5 KB in strip 6.

Disk Stripe Set with Parity

A stripe set with parity adds parity information to a stripe set configuration. A stripe set with parity dedicates the equivalent of a strip of disk space for the parity information and distributes this across all the disks in the group. The data and parity information is arranged on the volume so that they are always on different disks, as shown in Table A.2.

Table A.2 Stripe Set with Parity Configuration

	Disk 1	Disk 2	Disk 3	Disk 4	Disk 5
Stripe 1	Parity 1	1	2	3	4
Stripe 2	5	Parity 2	6	7	8
Stripe 3	9	10	Parity 3	11	12
Stripe 4	13	14	15	Parity 4	16
Stripe 5	17	18	19	20	Parity 5

The first strip on disk 1 is the parity strip for the four data strips included in stripe 1. The second strip on disk 2 is the parity strip for the four data strips included in stripe 2, and so on. The parity strip is the exclusive OR (XOR) of all the data values for the data strips in the stripe. If no disks in the stripe set with parity have failed, the new parity for a write can be calculated without having to read the corresponding strips from the other data disks. Thus, only two disks are involved in a write operation, the target data disk and the disk containing the parity strip. Figure A.3 illustrates the steps in writing data to a stripe set with parity.

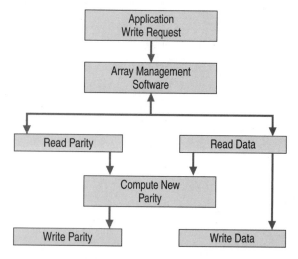

Figure A.3 Data write to a stripe set with parity

Disks and Partition Space in a Stripe Set with Parity

When implementing a stripe set with parity, you need at least three disks, but you can have no more than 32 disks in the set. The physical disks do not need to be identical, but they must have equal size blocks of unpartitioned space available. They can also be on the same or different controllers. After the initial configuration, you cannot add disks to a stripe set with parity to increase the size of the volume.

Disk Failure in a Stripe Set with Parity

If one of the disks in a stripe set with parity fails, no data is lost. When a read operation requires data from the failed disk, the system reads all the remaining good data strips in the stripe as well as the parity strip. Each data strip is subtracted (with XOR) from the parity strip, and the result is the missing data strip.

When the system needs to write data to a failed disk, it reads the other data strips and the parity strip and then backs them out of the parity strip, thus leaving the missing data strip. Calculations to modify the parity strip can now be made. Since the data strip has failed, it is not written to—only the parity strip is written to.

Read operations are unaffected if the failed disk contains a parity strip. The parity strip is not needed for a read operation, but only when there is a failure in a data strip. When the failed disk contains a parity strip, the system does not compute or write the parity strip when there is a change in a data strip.

Advantages of Stripe Sets with Parity

Some of the advantages of using a stripe set with parity include:

- **Read operations**. Disk read operations can occur simultaneously. All disks in the array can be in use at the same time.

- **Fault tolerance**. Provides a high degree of fault-tolerance at a lower cost than a mirrored set.

- **Utilization**. Utilization increases as the number of disks in the array increases.

- **Database applications**. Works well in large database applications where reads occur more often than writes. With the built-in load balancing of a stripe set with parity, database applications that do random reads are also well suited to this configuration.

- **Storage space**. A stripe set is several times more efficient with storage than a mirror set when large numbers of disks are used. The space required for storing the parity information is equivalent to 1/number of disks, therefore a 10-disk array uses 1/10 of its capacity for parity information.

Disadvantages of Stripe Sets with Parity

Some of the disadvantages of using a stripe set with parity include:

- **Partition limitations**. Neither the boot nor the system partition can be on a stripe set with parity.

- **Write operation speed**. Write operations are substantially slower than for a single disk because the software has to read the old data strip and the old parity strip, and then compute the new parity strip before writing it.

    ☑ **Note**   Applications that require high-speed data collection from a process are not well suited for use with a stripe set with parity. This type of application requires continuous high-speed disk writes, and does not work well with the asymmetrical I/O balance inherent to stripe sets with parity.

- **Read operation speed**. If a disk that is part of a stripe set with parity fails, read operations for data strips on that disk are substantially slower than for a single disk—the software has to read all of the other disks in the set to calculate the data.

- **Memory requirement**. A stripe set with parity requires more system memory than a mirrored set. This does not apply if you deploy a hardware-based RAID solution.

- **Data transfers**. Applications that require large sequential data transfers are not well suited for a stripe set with parity. This type of data transfer can prevent effective I/O load balancing.

Guidelines for Choosing Mirrored Sets and Stripe Sets with Parity

When choosing mirrored sets or stripe sets with parity, address the following issues:

- Software and hardware constraints

- Cost

- Reliability

Each vendor that you contact should have design guidelines for its system, whether you need a RAID array or want to use the fault-tolerant features of Windows 2000 Server.

Hardware Compatibility

Some configurations might not work as well as expected with a fault-tolerant disk system. To avoid problems, verify that your disk hardware is on the Windows 2000 Hardware Compatibility List, located on the Internet at: http://www.microsoft.com/windows2000/.

If any equipment you are using does not appear on the list, it may not work well.

Advantages of Using Identical Disks

Although using identical disks is not a requirement, if you use identical hardware for your fault-tolerant disk configuration, you have the following advantages:

- **Disk performance is the same**. Faster disks do not have to wait for slower disks.

- **Capacity is the same**. If you want to configure the entire disk for a mirrored set or stripe set with parity, identical disks have identical capacity.

- **Compatibility is better**. Fewer compatibility problems with the configuration occur.

Backup Hardware

When purchasing disks, acquire an extra disk for backup so that it is available when needed. In the event of a hardware failure, an identical backup disk guarantees compatibility without system performance degradation. You only need to install the new disk to become operational again. If you are using SCSI disks, you need to configure the SCSI ID as well.

If you are not using a duplexed disk controller scheme, obtain a backup disk controller identical to your existing one. A system can continue to operate when a disk fails, but not when a controller fails. There is no way to avoid system downtime if a controller fails, but you can minimize it by having a pre-configured disk controller available. If a non-identical disk controller is used as a replacement, you must install a new driver, which makes the configuration more complex.

> ☑ **Note** If you have configured your system partition on a mirrored set, use the same model controller for a backup. In addition, be sure to use the same translation for both the original and shadow partitions.

Other Resources

Two books that provide additional networking fundamentals and information are available from Microsoft Press:

Microsoft Corporation. *Networking Essentials Plus*, *Third Edition*. Redmond, WA: Microsoft Press. 2000. ISBN 0-7356-0912-8.

Tulloch, Mitch. *Microsoft® Encyclopedia of Networking*. Redmond, WA: Microsoft Press. 2000. ISBN 0-7356-0573-4.

Summary

For you to obtain the greatest value from Small Business Server and this guide, it is essential that you have a fundamental knowledge of computer networks. The intent of this appendix is to provide you with baseline knowledge, including how to:

- Define network components.

- Define a network operating system.

- Assess the types of storage.

- Address backup issues.

Migrating from a NetWare Environment

This appendix discusses deployment of Microsoft® Small Business Server 2000 into an existing Novell NetWare environment. The discussion continues with integration and procedures for migrating NetWare resources to Small Business Server 2000. Planning and testing criteria are also discussed.

The migration process is completed in the following five phases:

- Planning and overview
- Testing
- Integration
- Migration
- Project review

    ☑ **Note** In this appendix, some references are made to Microsoft Windows® 2000 Server. Anything applicable to Windows 2000 Server in this context is also applicable to Small Business Server 2000.

Integration and Migration Planning

Because Small Business Server 2000 contains the Windows 2000 Server operating system, all the built-in NetWare migration and integration features of Windows 2000 Server are included in Small Business Server 2000. This also means that the Windows 2000 Server add-on tools, which may be purchased separately to enhance integration and migration in a NetWare environment, will also work with Small Business Server 2000. NetWare tools discussed in this chapter include:

- Client Services and Gateway Service included with Small Business Server 2000.
- File and Print Services for NetWare, which may be purchased separately.

    ☑ **Note** While these tools will help at many stages of deployment, they do not substitute for a rigorous deployment plan.

Deployment Plan

Attention to planning increases the prospect of successful deployment and assures that functionality is achieved within the scheduled time. If you are considering skipping all planning, please consider the time that might be wasted without a clearly defined approach and support information. Even the most rudimentary planning will help avert serious, costly, and time-consuming problems during deployment.

General Agenda

The first step is to define your objectives. A clear, concise project objective will give the project focus. Describe the current small business network environment, any additional resources needed to deploy Small Business Server, and the necessary resources to migrate from NetWare to Small Business Server. The deployment plan should define the following:

- Proposed changes to the network
- Plans for preliminary testing (proof of technology and pilot)
- Details for deployment

Details of the Plan

While the details of the plan may differ from one small business network to another, the outline remains fairly consistent. It considers the following elements:

- Current network architecture
- Existing schedules or planned installation events
- Integration plans outside the scope of the project
- Network growth
- Business goals or objectives of the organization
- Business expectations of LAN service levels

Pre-Installation Checklist

A detailed step-by-step check and sign-off list should be used to control the process and order of the installation. A checklist ensures that steps are not missed. The following is a typical checklist of items to be addressed during the planning stages of a NetWare to Windows 2000 Server deployment:

- Ensure that all equipment and software have been ordered and are available.

- Run **Security** and **Modules** on the NetWare server to receive correct configuration information.

- Review the **Groups** and **Members** on the NetWare server.

- Review the **Security Equivalents** on the NetWare server.

- Determine whether some or all groups are to be migrated.

- Decide whether clients will be migrated at the same time as the server conversion, before or after server migration, or whether they will be left as is.

- Determine whether any applications will be migrated.

- Establish performance testing guidelines.

- Ensure that you have sufficient database and file capacity on the Small Business Server computer.

Integration Overview

Successful deployment (or "rollout") depends on successful planning and execution. The deployment of Small Business Server 2000 in a NetWare environment may consist of a NetWare and Small Business Server coexistence, a NetWare to Small Business Server migration, or a combination of the two.

Because you are deploying Small Business Server 2000—a tightly integrated suite of server applications for Windows NT—you must successfully test installation and basic use of this software before trying to integrate it with the Novell NetWare environment. The scope of these tests and the instructions for executing them are included later in this appendix.

Implementation of Rollout

To ensure successful implementation of Small Business Server 2000 into a NetWare environment, the rollout should be separated into two phases. Although it is possible to abbreviate the phases, the technology consultant should plan on executing both of them. These two phases are *test* and *integration*.

Test Phase

In the optimum situation, the deployment will progress exactly as anticipated with no unforeseen technological snags. However, in the real world, unexpected obstacles invariably arise. For this reason, you should spend some time trying out Small Business Server and experimenting with its functionality before trying to integrate it into the network environment of the small business. Even a short test phase can uncover and resolve problems that would prove costly when occurring in real time. The test phase is discussed in more detail later in this appendix.

Integration Phase

Once the initial testing of the new technology is complete, the next step is the integration of Small Business Server 2000 into the production network environment. The same approach may be followed as in the test phase, as follows:

- Small Business Server is installed and applications are tested, including any third-party applications.

- Services for NetWare are installed and configured, and connectivity between Small Business Server and the NetWare operating system is verified.

- After Small-Business-Server-to-NetWare communication is established with test clients, the actual users of the small business network begin using the Small Business Server 2000.

The test and integration phases should ensure the basic functionality of the networking environment and the Small Business Server operating system.

> ✔ **Note** Although it may be necessary to perform other tasks, such as implementing a database with Microsoft SQL Server™ 2000, this is beyond the scope of this appendix.

Failures During the Integration Phase

If something goes wrong during the integration phase that did not occur or was not anticipated during the testing phase, the technology consultant should document the precise configuration details, attempt to re-create the scenario, and then troubleshoot the situation with Small Business Server 2000 off the production network.

A failure during the integration phase may be an indication that the test phase was not performed thoroughly enough; that a configuration issue specific to the production network caused problems; or that something was not installed or configured in the same way as during the test phase. This is why a record of what was done during the test phase is highly encouraged.

The Test Phase

Before setting up the testing environment, you should determine the tests' impact on your equipment needs. The primary focus of the test phase is to verify that Microsoft Small Business Server 2000 installs and functions correctly on the hardware that you have allocated for this project. However, the testing process should encompass at least some of the typical functionality that you intend to implement on the network.

 Note The test phase should be performed in an environment separate from the production network—any computers involved should be set up on an isolated hub. During this phase, test and document everything, noting any unexpected behaviors.

Preparation Tasks

The sections that follow cover preparation for the test phase, including:

- Determining the physical location of the testing environment.
- Verifying hardware components.
- Determining the tests to be conducted.
- Securing the software needed.
- Preparing hardware.
- Documenting procedures.

Physical Location

The computers used in the testing process should not be connected to the small business network. The technology consultant should arrange for office space dedicated to testing and make sure that there are enough power outlets for all the hardware being used in the test phase.

Verify Hardware Components

Before setting up Small Business Server, consult the Windows 2000 Hardware Compatibility List to verify that all hardware components you intend to use (network cards, modems, and so forth) appear on the list. The list may be found at the following Web site: http://www.microsoft.com/windows2000/.

If a hardware component does not appear on the list, contact the hardware manufacturer to see if you can get a Windows 2000 Server-compatible driver.

✓ **Note** The Hardware Compatibility List in most cases provides links for downloads of device drivers.

In addition to the compatibility issues, make sure that the computer on which Small Business Server 2000 is to be installed has enough capacity. Confirm that the hardware meets or exceeds the specifications in Table B.1.

Table B.1 Small Business Server Hardware Requirements

Specification	Hardware
Processor	Intel Pentium 300 megahertz (MHz) or higher or compatible processor.
Memory	128 megabytes (MB) of random access memory (RAM).
Hard Disk	4 gigabytes (GB) of free space.
Video	Video Graphics Adapter (VGA) or higher resolution monitor is required. A VGA adapter with at least 800x600 resolution is recommended for both the monitor and adapter.
CD-ROM drive	Double speed or higher is recommended.
Network card	Network adapters supported by Windows 2000 Server.

Hardware for Client Connectivity Tests

For test purposes, make sure that you have the correct components for at least one client computer. The client computer should run the same operating system as the majority of the user desktop computers. If the client environment is mixed, set up one of each client type to be used on the network. It may be appropriate to set up one or more new client computers to prevent any disturbance to employees at work in the small business organization. If setting up new machines is necessary, refer to the procedures listed in the operating system's manual for verifying compatible hardware components.

Windows 2000 Professional and Windows Me, Windows 98, and Windows 95 Client Setup

Using the Set Up Computer Wizard in the Small Business Server 2000 console, you will be able to set up an existing Microsoft Windows 2000 Professional, Windows 98, or Windows 95 installation for use with Small Business Server 2000, without having to perform some of the typical manual setup tasks. The Set Up Computer Wizard automates the reconfiguration of an existing Windows Me, Windows 98, and Windows 95 installation, establishes network connectivity, and sets up applications such as Microsoft Outlook® and Microsoft Internet Explorer.

Network Hub

An additional piece of hardware that should be considered is the network hub—a component that allows computers to be networked together. It is possible to connect a small number of computers together simply by using cables. However, there will be fewer concerns and testing complications if a hub is used. In order for you to test client/server network connectivity with Small Business Server 2000, at least a four- or five-port hub should be available. A port is a singular connection from a computer's network adapter card to the hub.

The only detail about the hub that requires attention is the transceiver type. You should identify whether the jacks on the hub are 10Base-T (also known as Twisted Pair or RJ-45) or 10Base-2 (also known as thinnet, BNC, or coaxial). Be sure that the network adapter cards for all the testing machines are of the same transceiver type (connection type) and that the hub used for testing matches that type.

In practice, a prudent test environment will match that of the business network environment as closely as possible—the test hub connection type should be matched to what is actually used in the small business network. If the network uses a cabling scheme only, then it is most likely using thinnet cable. You may attempt to simulate this network setup if you wish, but be advised that it will be easier to use a hub configuration. 10Base-T tends to be a more popular connection type than 10Base-2 because it is the easiest to use. You will also need appropriate networking cable to match the network adapter and hub. Both the cable and hub can be purchased from a vendor of network hardware.

Determining Which Tests to Conduct

The goal of the test phase is to test the new server functionality without involving the NetWare components. Although it might be reassuring to test NetWare interoperability with a mock Small Business Server, the time required to do this may not make it a viable option. For this reason, during the integration phase, you should try to establish the required level of NetWare interoperability before deploying Small Business Server 2000 to users in the small business organization.

If you do have the time and resources to experiment with Novell functionality in a test environment, proceed to the integration section of this appendix and follow the procedures. However, be aware that you will need to create the interoperability environment again during the actual integration phase. In either case, the following installation, configuration, and application/functionality tests should be performed:

- **Installation of Small Business Server**. This is the essential part of the testing phase. If problems arise, consult the documentation provided with the software and double-check all hardware components against the hardware compatibility lists.

- **Peripheral devices**. If you plan to use a printer or modem in the small business network, the deployment should be tested at this time.

- **Adding and connecting users**. Through the Small Business Server Administrator Console, you can add users to the system. Next, you can test the ability to log onto the server from a client computer and gain access to shared files. Some shared folders are set up automatically during installation.

- **Small Business Server applications**. The test phase should also include a trial run for the Small Business Server 2000 applications that will be used most often in the small business organization, such as Microsoft Outlook.

- **Independent software vendor (ISV) applications**. The test phase should include running any third-party software that you intend to use on Small Business Server 2000, from both the server and client computers.

Secure the Installation Software

Before proceeding with the test phase, make sure the following items are available:

- Small Business Server 2000 compact discs 1 to 4, or the digital video disc (DVD).

- Small Business Server 2000 floppy disks 1, 2, 3 and 4. These can be created from Disc 1, if necessary, with the Makeboot program. These disks are needed if you do not plan to boot and install directly from the Disc 1.

- Two blank floppy disks for the Emergency Repair Disk and client setup disk.

- The Services for NetWare compact disc, which must be purchased separately.

- A network adapter configuration disk (if provided by the network card manufacturer). This disk may be needed to save modifications to settings on hardware memory, such as the transceiver type, before proceeding with the installation procedure.

- Drivers for hardware devices.

- Any required workstation operating system software.

- Any ISV software.

Network Hardware Setup

Before beginning the test phase, some final hardware preparation tasks are required, as described in the sections that follow.

Connect Computers to Hub

After the location for the testing environment has been secured and all necessary materials are obtained, the connection from the computer to the hub must be set up. On the back of the computer are the interfaces for the adapter cards. The network adapter card interface will either be a large telephone jack or a round, protruding connector, depending on whether you have twisted pair cabling (10 Base-T) or thinnet coaxial cabling (10Base-2).

If you have a twisted pair, insert one end of the cable into the jack and the other into the hub. You should hear a click when each end is inserted properly. If you are using thinnet, verify that both ends have a round or conical terminator attached and insert the cable connector into each device. Make sure all test computers are connected to the hub in this way. If you do not plan to use a hub, make sure that the thinnet cable used has the correct terminator on both ends of the wire and that all connecting pieces are inserted into all computers.

Configure Network Adapter Transceiver Type

The transceiver type for the network adapter in use is either a twisted pair or coaxial. Before you begin any software installation, power up all computers and boot from the network adapter configuration disk to verify that the setting on the network adapter matches the cabling scheme in use.

Documentation

During the test phase (and when preparing the testing environment), have a pen and paper ready to document the variables and settings chosen during the procedures. A legible record of what was done during this phase can be invaluable if something goes wrong and you need to figure out what happened.

Installation of Small Business Server 2000

For Small Business Server 2000 installation procedures, refer to Chapter 9, "Installing Small Business Server in Existing Environments," of this resource guide or refer to the *Small Business Server 2000 Planning and Installation* guide. The installation is led by the Small Business Server Installation Wizard and requires a minimum of effort on the part of the installer. Small Business Server 2000 will be optimized for the particular small business environment and, for the most part, the default information will be sufficient for a complete installation. This should help the installer understand what is happening on the computer and what information must be provided to complete the actual installation.

Client Setup

After Small Business Server is installed, you must set up a new user account using the Add User Wizard (to access the wizard, click **Add Users** on the To Do List that appears at the end of setup), and then configure the client computer with the Set Up Computer Wizard (which automatically starts from the Add User Wizard).

The purpose of the Add User Wizard and the chained Set Up Computer Wizard process is to complete the following steps:

- Add a user account to the Microsoft Active Directory™ directory service in Small Business Server 2000.

- Create a home folder.

- Create a logon script.

- Configure the server for the client.

- Configure client networking.

- Install and configure Small Business Server client applications (such as Microsoft Outlook).

  ☑ **Note** During the Set Up Computer Wizard, you will be asked to create a networking setup disk, which enables you to configure the client computer for use on the Small Business Server network. To ensure that all the user and computer data is on the disk, create it the last time you run through the Set Up Computer Wizard. This single disk can then be used to configure an existing Windows 2000 Professional, Windows Me, Windows 98, Windows 95, or Windows NT computer for use with Small Business Server.

Client Software Installation

If the client setup disk has difficulty installing applications on the client computer, verify that the network adapter on the client computer is properly connected to the hub or other computers, and that the transceiver type is correctly set. The correctness of these physical network connections and settings is very important, because the client software is installed over the network.

Client Computer Functionality Testing

After the client setup disk has successfully installed the client applications, a series of tests can run on the client computer. Testing begins with connecting to a share and then moves on to network printing and running client/server applications, such as Outlook 2000, for interaction with Small Business Server 2000.

Third-Party Application Testing

After Small Business Server 2000 and client-side components have been found to work as expected, the functionality of any third-party applications should be tested. If these applications are designed to run on Windows 2000 Server, there should be no problem running them on Small Business Server 2000. You should still verify that the software will install and run as expected, however. If the software is designed to run in the client/server model, test basic tasks on a typical client computer.

> **Note** Define Client Applications allows you to customize the Set Up Computer Wizard to install third-party client applications.

The Integration Phase

This next phase involves installing and configuring the various required services for NetWare. Procedures for setting up all the NetWare services are documented here, but you may not need to run all services. It depends on which functions are to be transferred to Small Business Server 2000.

For example, the small business may want to continue using an existing NetWare print server to service its client machines. In this case, the print functionality provided by File and Print Services for NetWare (FPNW) is not needed. A summary of what each service does is provided before detailed installation instructions. This should help you in making decisions about which services to run on Small Business Server.

You should isolate Small Business Server 2000 from users while it is being set up to interoperate with the NetWare server.

Integration of Small Business Server 2000 into the NetWare Network

You should begin the integration of Small Business Server and NetWare by following the same procedures to test functionality of the software. Set up and test a client computer, just as in the test phase, to ensure there are no communication problems in the small business network-testing environment.

In the integration phase, physical network connectivity is important, just as it is in the test phase. Make sure the network adapter cards are properly configured by using the manufacturer-supplied configuration utility. Check that physical links between computers and hubs are in place and that status indicators on the hub or network cards are signaling good connections.

Before installing Small Business Server 2000, verify that no Dynamic Host Configuration Protocol (DHCP) servers are present on the small business network. DHCP is a method of assigning Internet Protocol (IP) addresses to computers automatically in a TCP/IP network. Because Small Business Server 2000 uses DHCP by default, another DHCP server on the same network will cause interference. The presence of a DHCP server in the small business network is unlikely, especially because NetWare uses Internetwork Packet Exchange/Sequenced Packet Exchange (IPX/SPX), but it should be checked.

Installation of the NWLink Protocol

The first component to be installed to provide NetWare interoperability is the NWLink protocol. NWLink is a network protocol for Small Business Server 2000 that is compatible with IPX/SPX. It is the default protocol supported by NetWare. Although NWLink by itself does not provide a high degree of connectivity to NetWare servers, it is the core component that allows a Small Business Server-based computer to communicate with a NetWare client or server. The NWLink protocol must be installed to provide a means of communicating with the tools that interoperate with NetWare.

To install the NWLink protocol:

1. Click **Start**, **Settings**, **Network and Dial-up Connections**.

2. Right-click **Local Area Connection** and select **Properties**.

3. Click **Install**.

4. Select **Protocol** and click **Add**.

5. Select **NWLink IPX/SPX/NetBIOS Compatible Transport Protocol** and click **OK**. You may be asked to provide Small Business Server Disc 1.

6. Click **Close**.

> ☑ **Note** Instructions for installing and configuring the NWLink protocol are provided in Chapter 9, "Installing Small Business Server in Existing Environments."

Installation of Gateway Service for NetWare

Gateway Service for NetWare (GSNW) allows Small Business Server to function as a NetWare client. Once GSNW is installed, any NetWare servers configured for the same frame type as Small Business Server appear in a list under the heading "NetWare or Compatible Network."

Another feature of GSNW is the Windows 2000 Server to NetWare gateway. This provides Microsoft Network clients with access to NetWare resources and allows users to access what appears to be a standard Microsoft server resource, although they are actually connected to the NetWare resource through a gateway service.

GSNW may be found on the Small Business Server Compact Disc 1. It is installed using **Local Area Connection** Properties on the **Network and Dial-Up Connections** page. To access this page, click **Start**, point to **Settings**, and then click **Network and Dial-Up Connections**.

> ☑ **Note** Instructions for installing and configuring GSNW are provided in Chapter 9, "Installing Small Business Server in Existing Environments."

Uses of GSNW with Small Business Server 2000

One of the practical uses of GSNW in the small business network is the ability to provide Small Business Server 2000 and any connected client computers with access to file and print resources on a NetWare server.

For example, by using GSNW, Small Business Server can connect to a NetWare file server directory and share it as if the directory were on Small Business Server. The Small Business Server-based network clients can then access the directory on the NetWare server by connecting to the share created on Small Business Server.

> ☑ **Note** GSNW is not intended to function as a full-service router for NetWare services. It is designed only for occasional access to the NetWare servers, or to serve as a migration path. Network performance will degrade if it is used for unlimited server access, because all clients are receiving services through one NetWare connection.

Installing File and Print Services for NetWare

File and Print Services for NetWare (FPNW) is a separate, add-on product for Small Business Server 2000. The FPNW component allows the Small Business Server computer to act as a NetWare server to all NetWare clients currently on the small business network. Small Business Server will appear in the client's Windows Explorer list of NetWare and NetWare-compatible servers. A NetWare client can do the following tasks with FPNW installed:

- Map to a shared volume and directory on an FPNW-enabled Small Business Server just as if it were a NetWare server.

- Connect to a printer on Small Business Server 2000.

- Log on to the Small Business Server 2000 and have configured system and personal login scripts execute.

- Use Small Business Server 2000 applications services.

FPNW is a valuable component of Small Business Server integration, because it can provide a high degree of interoperability with the existing small business NetWare LAN, without the need to change the configuration of existing network computers.

After successfully completing the last step of the FPNW installation procedure, you have achieved Small Business Server 2000 coexistence in the NetWare environment. At this point, migration can be accomplished easily to replace the functionality of the NetWare servers and decommission them, if the deployment calls for it.

> ☑ **Note** Make sure that you document all the actions taken up to this point. Also document any problems encountered, along with the resolution.

NetWare Migration Phase

In most cases, migrating off the NetWare platform is preferable to coexistence with Small Business Server 2000. The migration from the NetWare server to Small Business Server 2000 is completed in the following four phases:

- Creating users and group accounts on Small Business Server 2000, using the Small Business Server Console.

- Migrating all data from the NetWare server directories to the Small Business Server as a copy-and-paste command with Windows Explorer.

- Configuring clients on the new network.

- Testing network connectivity. Several tests should be run before users in the small business organization can start to use the new network.

Creating User Accounts

By creating new user accounts, rather than migrating the NetWare accounts to Small Business Server 2000, the small business can take advantage of full-featured Small Business Server 2000 accounts. Also, creating new group accounts is an opportunity to reorganize company data in a more intuitive manner.

Before migrating data, new user accounts must be created on Small Business Server 2000 from the Users page icon on the Small Business Server Administrator Console. As described earlier, the Set Up Computer Wizard runs as part of this process to configure the client computer.

Migrating the Data

You should copy all user NetWare-based home directory files to the new user home folders and all company-shared data on the NetWare Server to the Company Shared Data folder on Small Business Server. With the Small Business Server Shared Folder Wizard, you can reorganize company data in any directory structure and permissions configuration desired.

Testing Basic Connectivity

Several tests should be conducted before users start accessing the new network setup. Depending on the NetWare services you select for configuration, you may run some or all of the following tests.

> ☑ **Note** These tests are required for a Small Business Server replacement of the NetWare preferred server. In an environment where the Small Business Server will coexist with current NetWare servers, these tests may not be necessary.

Tests for basic connectivity

- Log in from a NetWare client to Small Business Server with no login script.

- Log in from a NetWare client to Small Business Server with a system login script.

- Connect (map) to a shared volume on the Small Business Server (the SYS volume is created during the FPNW installation).

- Copy a large file (5 megabytes [MB]) from the client to the mapped drive on the Small Business Server computer.

- Copy a large file (5 MB) from the mapped drive on the Small Business Server computer to the client computer.

- Test file-level security. Check a user's permissions settings.

Documenting Migration Results

It is recommended that you summarize the success or failure of the various components used in your migration, including each NetWare service or tool used in the process. Note problems and their respective resolutions.

Project Review Phase

Compile all the information into a concise format for a formal project review with the small business owner. A project review will not only serve as a project summary for the small business, but will also provide a solid base for any further company network upgrades. Include the following in the project review document:

- Executive summary

- Project objective

- Schedule analysis

Executive Summary

The executive summary should not be longer than one page and should cover at least the following topics:

- Project objective

- High-level summary of changes performed

- Project schedule versus summary of actual results

- Project budget versus summary of actual results

Project Objective

This section should describe in detail the specific problems that the upgrade was intended to resolve and the plan used to address the problems. A quick summary of the plan will clearly identify your strategies to solve the problems. Where appropriate, include actual network diagrams used in analyzing the network.

As part of the plan, include how the objective fits into the overall small business' computing strategy, in one-, three-, and five-year network objectives. You may address factors such as scalability and upgrade paths as the small business grows beyond the 50-user limit.

Clearly specify issues excluded from the scope of the project, as they will likely be identified and discussed during the project review process. If the items are clearly documented, it saves time and also demonstrates that you and your team are aware of the issues, and that you decided not to include them in the project.

Schedule Analysis

A significant part of the review process is an analysis of scheduling, including any unexpected events that caused a schedule slip. This information is critical to future project planning schedules. One tool that you should consider is Microsoft Project 2000. You can use a Microsoft Project 2000 colored chart to compare the schedule with the actual results. This chart will highlight the areas of the project that are ahead of schedule and those that went beyond the target date. This provides the small business owner with a comprehensive overview of project scheduling.

Summary

This appendix provides information on migrating from NetWare environments to Small Business Server 2000, including:

- Integration and migration planning.

- The importance of testing.

- Specific steps for integrating Small Business Server 2000 and NetWare.

- Specific NetWare migrations phases.

- Conducting the project review phase.

Customization and Extensibility Options

This appendix focuses on the rationale, design, architecture, customization and use of the Small Business Server consoles. Two consoles are included in Small Business Server 2000: the Small Business Personal Console and the Small Business Server Administrator Console. These consoles provide user-friendly, consistent features—the trademark of Small Business Server since its inception. The two consoles are based on the Microsoft® Management Console (MMC).

- **Small Business Server Personal Console**. This console, shown in Figure C.1, displays basic commands for use by power users at the customer site. The power user may perform such tasks as configuring users and computers. These tasks are performed on an as-needed and regular basis.

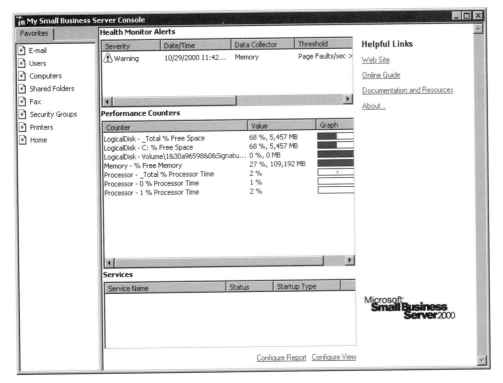

Figure C.1   Fewer options are available in the Small Business Server Personal Console

- **Small Business Server Administrator Console**. This advanced console, shown in Figure C.2, is for use by the technology consultant. All Small Business Server-specific administrative functions such as the Microsoft BackOffice® To Do List are presented and can run from this console. The design goal was to provide one place for the technology consultant to perform any and all Small Business Server 2000 tasks. Each Small Business Server application is represented by an item in the Console Tree. Selecting an item will allow you to manage the corresponding application. For example, selecting the Exchange 2000 Server organization item displays numerous Exchange 2000 Server-related objects, as illustrated in Figure C.2.

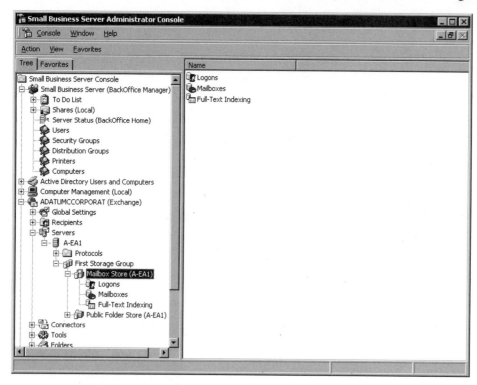

Figure C.2   All applications in Small Business Server 2000 can be managed from the Small Business Server Administrator Console

Defining the Microsoft Management Console

MMC is an independent software vendor (ISV)-extensible, common presentation user interface for management applications. MMC is included with Small Business Server 2000 and also the Microsoft Windows® 2000 operating system.

This section discusses the main graphical user interface (GUI) elements of MMC. The majority of these are standard Windows 2000-based software GUI elements, tailored for use with MMC.

> ☑ **Note** Snap-ins, a major functional component of MMC, are discussed in a later section of this appendix.

Menus

The MMC has a main menu, an Action band, and a toolbar. The main menus are Console, Window, and Help; these menus provide commands that affect the entire console. A newly created, empty console is shown in Figure C.3.

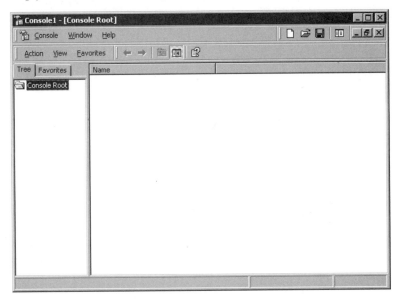

Figure C.3 Console interface elements

Action Band

A band is a rectangular area that contains menus and icons. The Action band contains the following menus:

- **Action**. Includes the same contents as a context menu in Windows (a context menu is accessed by right-clicking an object or container).

- **View**. Controls how information is displayed in the Details Pane.

- **Favorites**. This tab is displayed when you open a new console in Author mode, or when an item has already been added to the Favorites list in a console. The Favorites list can include shortcuts to tools, items in the console, or tasks. When you use MMC in Author mode, you have full access to all MMC functionality. You can add or remove snap-ins, create new windows, create taskpad views and tasks, add items to the Favorites list, and view all parts of the Console Tree.

Toolbars

The MMC contains two standard Windows toolbars:

- **Console toolbar**. Contains the main menu and author mode band (when used in Author mode).

- **Snap-in toolbar**. Includes the Action band, common commands bands, and one or more snap-in specific bands.

Property Sheets

A property sheet is a window that users can use to view and edit the properties of an item. A property sheet contains one or more overlapping property pages, which are child windows that contain controls for setting a group of related properties. Each page has a tab that the user can click to bring the page to the foreground of the property sheet.

For example, the **Computer Management Properties** page contains the controls for setting properties such as a textual description of the computer, setting environment variables, performance options, and startup and recovery options.

Dialog Boxes

MMC uses dialog boxes, which are secondary windows used mainly to obtain information from the user to complete a given task. Dialog boxes are usually modal, which means the dialog box must be closed before the user can access another window. However, MMC is primarily modeless, which allows users to move between open windows.

MMC Namespace

The MMC namespace represents the hierarchy of objects and containers that are displayed in the console window. The window consists of two panes; the left pane contains the Console Tree, and the right pane contains the Details Pane. The left pane also includes the **Favorites** tab, explained below.

The Console Tree contains a hierarchy of containers, most of which are represented by folder icons. Some containers are displayed as unique icons that graphically represent the type of items they contain.

The Details Pane displays the item selected in the Console Tree according to a selected view type.

Console Tree Pane

The Console Tree uses a standard Windows-based tree control to represent a set of containers and objects as an indented outline, based on their hierarchical relationship.

Containers

In this guide, the term *container* refers to an item in the Console Tree that displays child containers beneath it in the expanded tree and, when selected, its details in the Details Pane.

Objects

Object refers to an item in the Console Tree that does not have child items displayed beneath it in the Console Tree. An object displays information in the Details Pane when it is selected in the Console Tree.

Console Root

The console root is a container that holds the snap-in root nodes.

Snap-in Root Node

The snap-in root node is the uppermost node in the snap-in; it is labeled according to the product or task that it manages. Only one snap-in root node exists for each stand-alone snap-in. MMC supports stand-alone and extension snap-ins. A stand-alone snap-in provides management functionality without requiring support from another snap-in, whereas an extension snap-ins requires a parent snap-in above it in the Console Tree. Extension snap-ins extend the functionality provided by other snap-ins.

Favorites List

When you create a console in Author mode, the left pane of the new console includes the **Favorites** tab. This tab is also displayed if an item has been added to the Favorites list in a console.

You can use the Favorites list to:

- Create shortcuts to tools or items in the Console Tree.

- Simplify navigation for novice users. For example, you can include shortcuts only to the tasks users need to perform, providing a simplified view of a console.

- Organize taskpad views. For example, if a console has multiple taskpad views that are distributed in several places in the Console Tree, you can add these views to the Favorites list, allowing users to access all the views from a single location.

Details Pane

The Details Pane displays the view of the selected item in the Console Tree. The Details Pane can display information in a variety of formats: a list view, a taskpad view, as Microsoft ActiveX® controls (.ocx files), or as an HTML page.

List View

The list view displays a collection of items, each consisting of an icon and a label, and provides several ways to display and organize the items. For example, additional information about each item can be displayed in columns to the right of the icon and label. The following view type modes are supported:

- Large icons

- Small icons

- List

- Detail

- Filtered

Column Customization

MMC supports column configuration, which allows users to customize the configuration of columns in a details list view. The changes the user makes to the column configuration are saved, or persisted, by the console. Not all of the snap-ins support column customization.

By making changes to the column configuration, you can:

- Customize the display of columns and rows. For instance, you can rearrange or hide columns. Or you can click the column heading to reorder rows alphabetically or chronologically.

- Filter columns, based on particular attributes. This applies to some snap-ins only. If you enable this feature, a row of drop-down list boxes that contain options for filtering is displayed beneath the column headings.

Taskpad View

A taskpad view is a DHTML page that presents shortcuts to commands available for a selected item in the Console Tree (the left pane of the MMC); the taskpad view is displayed in the Details Pane. That is, once a shortcut is clicked in the Console Tree, the result is displayed in the Details Pane. Each command is represented as a task that consists of an image, a label, a description, and a mechanism for instructing the snap-in to run the command. Users can run commands by clicking a task.

You can use taskpad views to:

- Include shortcuts to all the tasks a specific user may need to perform.

- Group your tasks by function or user by creating multiple taskpad views in a console.

- Create simplified lists of tasks. For example, you can add tasks to a taskpad view and then hide the Console Tree. This way, users can begin using tools before knowing the location of particular items in the Console Tree or operating system, making it easier for novice users to perform their jobs.

- Simplify complex tasks. For example, if a user frequently performs a given task involving several snap-ins and other tools, you can organize shortcuts to those tasks in a single location that run the appropriate property pages, command lines, dialog boxes, or scripts.

Custom ActiveX Controls

An ActiveX control is a Component Object Model (COM)-based object that can draw itself in its own window, respond to events (such as mouse clicks), and can be managed through an interface that includes properties and methods similar to those in Automation objects. You can insert custom ActiveX controls (objects or components) into a Web page or an application to reuse their functionality. Snap-ins can start an ActiveX control in the Details Pane.

Custom Web Page

The Details Pane of a console can host HTML pages that are on the local computer or hosted on a Web server.

MMC is a point of integration between a Web user interface (UI) and a Win32-based UI. You can display Web pages within a saved console file by clicking **Add/Remove Snap-in** on the **Console** menu, and clicking **Add** in the **Add/Remove Snap-in** dialog box to add a **Link to Web Address**. This permits you to mix and match Web-based administration programs and MMC snap-ins.

Export List

MMC supports exporting the data displayed in all standard list views to a text file. When the user right-clicks the **Export List** context menu item while a Console Tree node with a list view is selected, the visible columns in the list view are exported to a text file in the order in which they appear in the view. You can choose to export only specific rows by selecting them.

MMC Benefits

MMC provides the following key benefits:

- **Task orientation**. The tools being defined to work with MMC are task-oriented in nature. They cater to the task being performed rather than merely displaying the raw objects to be manipulated. Also, because administrators can customize their own tools using pieces from various vendors, they can create tools that contain only the UI they need to complete their tasks.

- **Integration**. The UI for all the management tasks an administrator must perform are collected into a single console. As new applications are added to a computer or network, their administration is integrated into the existing administration common console.

- **Customization of consoles**. Administrators can create custom consoles tailored to their particular management needs. This is useful in enterprise environments that divide administrator groups according to duties. For example, you can create a custom console for software installation and maintenance, another one for scripts administrators, another one for security Group Policy, and so on.

- **Delegation**. Administrators can easily modify existing tools to create new tools with reduced functionality and less complex views of the tool namespace, then give these tools to others. A person who receives such a tool is presented with a simpler, more manageable view of the tasks they are asked to perform.

- **Overall interface simplification**. All tools built for MMC, regardless of whether they are from Microsoft or independent software vendors (ISVs), will have a similar appearance, making it easier for users to use all the tools after learning only one. Because you can mix and match tools from any vendor, you can use the best tool from each management product category. MMC also enables a single piece of software to provide functionality across the interface in a consistent manner.

- **Extensibility**. Developers can extend the base functionality of MMC snap-ins by creating extension snap-ins. This allows software vendors to reuse Microsoft tools without writing a lot of code. Various mechanisms are available for extending snap-ins, including extending the namespace, context menus, toolbars, property pages, and creating Wizard 97-style pages. For more information, refer the Microsoft Platform Software Developer Kit (SDK) available on the Microsoft Developer Network Web site at:
http://msdn.microsoft.com/downloads/sdks/platform/platform.asp

MMC Architecture

The MMC is a Windows-based multiple document interface (MDI) application that makes use of Internet technologies. The console itself has no management behavior; it is a host that contains other software—called snap-ins—that extends the console to offer the actual management capabilities. The MMC model is illustrated in Figure C.4.

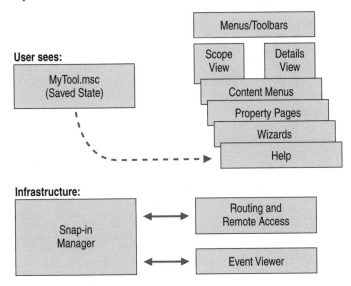

Figure C.4 The MMC model

The UI elements of the tool interact with the MMC Snap-in Manager, which interacts with the various snap-ins. The snap-in Manager also saves settings for you in a document file, known as a management saved console or .msc file. The items at the top of the picture, the .msc file and the UI elements, are all a user interacts with. The items at the bottom of the picture—the Snap-in Manager, the Routing and Remote Access, and Event Viewer snap-ins—are the elements the developers interact with.

To access the Snap-in Manager

- On the MMC **Console** menu, click **Add/Remove Snap-in**.

When an MMC tool is loaded, one or more snap-ins is initialized. These snap-ins are integrated to create the tool's namespace—the hierarchy of objects and containers that are displayed in the Console Tree, and the Details Pane, which displays the view of a selected item in the Console Tree. The namespace is a master tree that represents what the tool can do. It appears similar to a tree view of the files and folders on a hard disk. The namespace can include all manageable aspects of a network—computers, users and groups, and so on. The Details Pane can display information as a list view, taskpad view, ActiveX control, or an HTML page.

The child windows in MMC are views into the master namespace. It is like having multiple instances of Windows Explorer looking at the same hard disk. Each view may be rooted at a different portion of the tree but they all point to the same master data source. If data is currently displayed in multiple child windows, when that data is deleted in one view, it will also disappear from the other views.

MMC Customization

MMC provides a common host environment for snap-ins, from both Microsoft and ISVs. Snap-ins provide the actual management behavior. MMC itself does not provide any management functionality. The MMC environment provides for seamless integration between snap-ins.

Administrators and other users can create custom management tools from snap-ins created by various vendors. Administrators can then save the tools they have created for later use, or for sharing with other administrators and users. This model provides the administrator with efficient tool customization, and the ability to create multiple tools of varying levels of complexity, for task delegation.

MMC is the result of the effort at Microsoft to create better tools to administer Windows-based systems. The Windows administration development team defined a common host for many of its own management tools. The MMC project's goal is to support simplified administration through integration, delegation, task orientation, and overall interface simplification—all key customer requirements.

MMC is a Windows-based MDI application that heavily relies on and uses Internet technologies. Both Microsoft and ISVs extend the console by writing MMC snap-ins that perform management tasks.

The MMC programmatic interfaces permit the snap-ins to integrate with the console. These interfaces deal only with user interface extensions—how each snap-in actually performs tasks is entirely up to the snap-in. The relationship of the snap-in to the console consists of sharing a common hosting environment, and cross-application integration. The console itself offers no management behavior. Snap-ins always reside in a console; they do not run by themselves.

Both Microsoft and ISVs can develop management tools to run in MMC, as well as write applications to be managed by MMC administrative tools. MMC is part of the Microsoft Platform Software Development Kit and is available for general use. More information on the Microsoft Platform SDK is available on the Microsoft Developer Network Web site at: http://msdn.microsoft.com/downloads/sdks/platform/platform.asp.

Small Business Server and MMC Customization

Technology consultants and ISVs have important reasons for modifying MMCs in Small Business Server 2000. For technology consultants, unification is often the goal at each Small Business Server site. The technology consultant may want the Small Business Server 2000 consoles to include a custom snap-in. ISVs typically want to modify the Small Business Server consoles to include items that support the management of their specific third-party application.

Both Small Business Server consoles are run in the User mode-full access as the default console mode. This grants users full access to all windows management commands and to the Console Tree. This mode does, however, prevent users from adding or removing snap-ins or changing console properties. If you want to modify the consoles with a snap-in, you will need to change the console mode to Author mode.

You may modify the Small Business Server consoles in two ways. First, you can display more MMC UI components, which is allowed in the default User mode-full access setting. Second, you can add or remove a snap-in by placing the console in Author mode.

> **Note** The Small Business Server Administrator Console is used in the following examples.

To display MMC UI components

1. Click the **View** menu and then click **Customize View**.

2. The **Customize View** dialog box appears, as shown in Figure C.5. Select the custom view options you want, and then click **OK**.

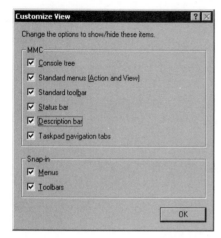

Figure C.5   Making selections on the Customize View dialog box

To modify the Small Business Server Administrator Console

1. Click **Start**, click **Run**, type *mmc*, and then click **OK**.

2. On the MMC **Console** menu, click **Open**. The **Open** dialog box appears.

3. Open the following MMC file to start the Small Business Server Administrator Console:

    %systemroot%\Documents and Settings\All Users\Application Data\
    Microsoft\BackOffice\Management\ITProSBSConsole.msc

4. On the MMC **Console** menu, click **Options**.

5. In the **Options** dialog box, **Console mode** field, select **Author mode**, as shown in Figure C.6.

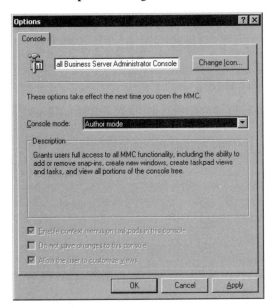

Figure C.6   Selecting Author mode

6. Click **OK**.

7. On the MMC **Console** menu, click **Add/Remove Snap-in**.

8. In the **Add/Remove Snap-in** dialog box, click **Add**.

9. Select a snap-in to add (for example, WINS), click **Add**, and then click **Close**.

10. Click **OK** to close the **Add/Remove Snap-in** dialog box.

11. On the MMC **Console** menu, click **Save and Exit**.

The snap-in you added appears in the Small Business Server Administrator Console, as shown in Figure C.7.

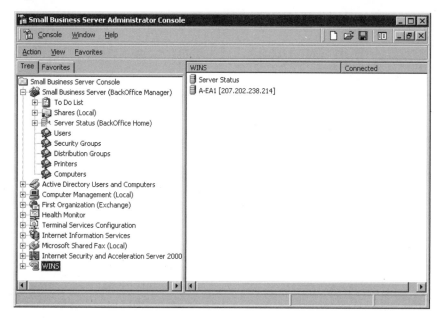

Figure C.7   Modifying the Small Business Server Administrator Console with a snap-in

To modify the Small Business Server Administrator Console

- Edit the following file:

    %systemroot%\Documents and Settings\All Users\Application Data\Microsoft\BackOffice\Management\MySBSConsole.msc

Another customization possibility is to create custom MMCs separate from the Small Business Server consoles. This is a popular solution used with Windows 2000, and its one that provides flexibility in how a management consultant manages their customer sites.

To create a console and add a snap-in, perform the following steps. Snap-ins are discussed in the next section.

To create a new console

1. Click **Start**, click **Run**, and type *mmc* to open a new console.

2. On the **Console** menu, click **Add/Remove Snap-in**.

3. In the **Add/Remove Snap-in** dialog box, click **Add**, select the snap-in you want to use, select either **Local computer** or **Another computer** (for remote management), and then click **Finish**. Note that the choice of a local or remote computer is dependent on the type of snap-in you are using and both selections may not appear in all snap-ins.

    If a wizard appears, follow the on-screen instructions to complete it.

4. To add any available snap-in extensions, click **Extensions**, select the extensions to use from the **Available extensions** list, and then click **OK**.

5. To save a console, on the **Console** menu, click **Save**.

MMC Console Access Mode

Two general access mode options are available when creating custom MMC consoles, Author mode and User mode. To set access mode options, on the MMC **Console** menu, click **Options**, and then select one of the following options:

- **Author mode**. Allows full access to all MMC functionality, including the ability to add or remove snap-ins, create new windows, create taskpad views and tasks, add items to the Favorites list, and view all portions of the Console Tree.

- **User mode**. Provides access to Windows management commands, and defines the level of access to the Console Tree. When you select User mode, users cannot add or remove snap-ins or change the console properties. User mode provides options for defining three levels of access to the Console Tree, including:

    - Full access.

    - Limited access, multiple windows.

    - Limited access, single window.

Group Policy may be used to control access to MMCs. In particular, technology consultants can prevent the use of MMC in Author mode. Technology consultants can enable the **Restrict the user from entering author mode** policy to prevent users from using MMC in Author mode. To do so, in the User Configuration Administrative Templates Windows Components Microsoft Management Console node, click **Group Policy console**.

The available options for the restriction policy are:

- **Enabled**. Click to restrict the user from using Author mode in MMC.

- **Disabled**. Click to allow the user to use Author mode in MMC.

- **Not Configured**. Specifies that no change will be made to the registry for this setting.

Snap-ins

Each MMC tool is built as a collection of instances of smaller tools called MMC snap-ins. One snap-in represents one unit of management behavior. A snap-in is the smallest unit of console extension. Technically, a snap-in is an OLE In Process (InProc) server that runs in the process context of MMC. (An In Process server is server implemented as a dynamic link library (DLL).)

The snap-in may call on other supporting controls and DLLs to accomplish its task.

Snap-ins extend MMC by adding and enabling management behavior. This behavior may be provided in a number of ways. For example, a snap-in might add elements to the viewable node namespace, or it might simply extend a tool by adding context menu items, toolbars, property pages, wizards, or Help to an existing snap-in.

Creating Custom Tools from Snap-ins

MMC provides functionality for creating custom management tools, which allow administrators to create, save, and delegate management tools tailored for specific tasks.

Administrators can assemble multiple snap-ins, from multiple vendors, into a tool (also called a document). An administrator can create multiple tools, and load and unload them when needed. These tools are what the administrator uses to manage the network.

After assembling a tool from various snap-ins, the administrator can save the tool in an .msc file, and then reload the file later to instantly recreate the tool. The .msc file can also be e-mailed to another administrator, who can then load the file and use the custom tool.

> ☑ **Note**   Administrators can also distribute saved consoles and snap-ins to other administrators by using the Group Policy software installation publish and assign capabilities.

Packages are Installable Collections of Snap-ins

To create a tool from snap-ins, a user must get the snap-ins in the first place. Vendors often ship snap-ins in groups called packages. For example, the Windows 2000 operating system includes one or more packages of snap-ins. Additionally, other vendors might ship products composed entirely of packages of snap-ins.

Grouping snap-ins into packages provides convenience and ease when downloading or installing. Autocode download has been added to MMC version 1.2 in the Windows 2000 operating system (and thus Small Business Server 2000); it downloads packages rather than snap-ins. This permits several snap-ins to share core DLLs so that these (possibly sizable) DLLs do not have to be placed in every snap-in.

Types of Snap-ins

Transparent to the administrators, internally each snap-in supports one or both of the following modes:

- **Stand alone snap-in**. Provides management functionality when alone in a console with no other supporting snap-ins. Snap-ins designed for this mode cannot rely on any other snap-ins being present.

- **Extension snap-in**. Provides functionality only when used in conjunction with a parent snap-in. An extension snap-in can extend only given node types. It declares itself as being a subordinate to nodes of certain types, and then for each occurrence of those node types in the console, the console adds the related snap-in extensions below it automatically.

  For example, an extension snap-in might be a Log Pretty Print Snap-in, providing users several ways to print out log files (such as the Windows 2000 Event Viewer log). With this snap-in installed, every log object in the namespace would be extended with the **Pretty Print** context menu item.

  Extension snap-ins can provide a variety of functionality. Some actually extend the console namespace (for example, a snap-in that provides system information about computers would add that system information to the namespace under each computer in the namespace), while others simply extend context menus or specific wizards.

Many snap-ins support both modes of operation, offering some stand-alone functionality, and also extending the functionality of other snap-ins. For example, the Windows 2000 Event Viewer Snap-in reads the event logs of computers. If the Computer Management snap-in object exists in the console, the Event Viewer Snap-in automatically extends each instance of a Computer Management snap-in object and provides the event logs for that computer. Alternatively, the event log can also operate in stand-alone mode, in which case an administrator must manually provide a computer name when the snap-in is opened, and the snap-in provides only the event logs of that computer.

Console Extensibility Modes

Microsoft has defined the following modes of extensibility for snap-ins. Every snap-in must provide at least one of the types of functionality described in Table C.1.

Table C.1 Modes of extensibility for snap-ins

Mechanism	Type	Description
Namespace extension	Per node	The namespace is extended by any snap-in that can be added with the Snap-in Manager. Snap-ins enumerate items in the Details Pane by implementing the IComponent interface.
Context menu extension	Per node	Snap-ins can extend the default menus that MMC creates for items in the Console Tree and Details Pane. To do this, snap-ins must implement the IExtendContextMenu interface.
Toolbar extension	Per view, based on the selection in that view	Snap-ins can extend the toolbar provided by MMC, or they can create a toolbar. Several interfaces can be used for creating toolbars, including Itoolbar, IControlToolbar, IExtendControlbar, and IConsoleVerb.
Property page extension	Per node	Snap-ins can add one or more property pages to a property sheet frame. IPropertySheetProvider, IPropertySheetCallback, and IExtendPropertySheet2 are used to provide Property page extensions. The first two are used by MMC and the third one is used by the snap-in. ☑ **Note** To create Property pages as Wizard 97-style wizards, use the IExtendPropertySheet2 interface and the IExtendPropertySheet2:GetWatermarks method.
Help	Per snap-in	Snap-ins can provide HTML help by using the ISnapinHelp2 interface and the ISnapinHelp2::GetLinkedTopics method.

In all cases, the snap-in has the option of altering the returned enumeration based on the context information passed to it at Open time. This permits snap-ins to register as an extension and offer conditional behavior. For example, the **My Computer** context menu can choose to offer Open Control Panel only when it determines that it is being asked to open Control Panel on a local computer (because Control Panel is not remoteable).

Other than the **Create New** and **Tasks** menu extensions, all others are general user interface extension mechanisms. The **Create New** and **Tasks** menu extensions are used as a mechanism to group operations in a way to permit integrated, task-oriented command structures. Had the console offered only a generic menu extension interface, there would be little consistency in the usage model. In MMC, each node will have a **Create New** and **Tasks** menu. Through this extension registration mechanism, all of these menu items and corresponding functionality are collected into a single UI point of usage.

Using Group Policy to Control the Behavior of Snap-ins

Windows 2000 Group Policy includes several policy settings designed to control the behavior of MMC and snap-ins. This section describes these policy settings.

Controlling Access to a Snap-in

The policy to control access to a snap-in is called the Restricted/Permitted Snap-in.

To access the Restricted/Permitted Snap-in

- In the Group Policy console, expand the User Configuration node, Administrative Templates, Windows Components, Microsoft Management Console Restricted/Permitted snap-ins node.

In the Details Pane, double-click the snap-in you want to permit or restrict, and then select one of the following options:

- **Enabled**. Click this option to explicitly permit the user to access this snap-in.

- **Disabled**. Click this option to prevent the user from accessing this snap-in.

- **Not Configured**. Specifies that no change will be made to the registry for this setting.

If you restrict or explicitly permit access to a particular snap-in, the snap-in is added to a list of restricted or permitted snap-ins. The restricted list takes precedence over the permitted list. This means that if the same snap-in exists on both lists, access to the snap-in is restricted.

Restricting Access to a List of Permitted Snap-ins

Administrators can create a list of permitted snap-ins for users by enabling the Restrict Users to the Explicitly Permitted List of Snap-ins Policy. As a result, only permitted snap-ins are displayed in the list of available snap-ins in the MMC **Add/Remove Snap-in** dialog box.

The Restrict Users to the Explicitly Permitted List of Snap-ins Policy is available in the Group Policy console under the **User Configuration, Administrative Templates, Windows Components, Microsoft Management Console** node.

The available options for the Restrict Users to the Explicitly Permitted List of Snap-ins Policy include:

- **Enabled**. Click to restrict the user from accessing any snap-in that is not explicitly permitted.

- **Disabled**. Click to permit the user to access snap-ins that are not explicitly restricted.

- **Not Configured**. Specifies that no change will be made to the registry for this setting.

BackOffice Home

The BackOffice Home Snap-in is provided by Microsoft as part of Small Business Server 2000. It is the default view of the Small Business Server Administrator Console and provides an at-a-glance view of your server's health.

BackOffice Manager

The BackOffice Manager Snap-in provides quick access to the following administration areas:

- Users
- Security Groups
- Distribution Groups
- Printers
- Computers

The BackOffice Manager's primary benefit is to save or persist queries of Active Directory™ objects in an .msc file for future use. You may define properties on a per-object and per-query basis. This allows you to customize attribute data that is available in column view. You can also customize context menu actions as either Active Directory display-specifiers or command-line tasks. Aggregator nodes can be created to group queries and display concatenated results.

Taskpads and Tasks

Taskpad views are pages to which you can add views of the Details Pane of a console, as well as shortcuts to functions both inside and outside of a console. You can use these shortcuts to run tasks such as starting wizards, opening property pages, performing menu commands, running command lines, and opening Web pages. You can configure a taskpad view so that it contains all the tasks a given user might need. In addition, you can create multiple taskpad views in a console, so that you can group tasks by function or by user.

Taskpad Uses

A taskpad view may make it easier for novice users to perform their jobs. For instance, you can add applicable tasks to a taskpad view and then hide the Console Tree, so that a user can begin using tools before they are familiar with the location of particular items in the Console Tree or operating system.

You may also use taskpad views to make complex tasks easier. For instance, if a user must frequently perform a task that involves multiple snap-ins and other tools, you can present tasks in a single location that open or run the necessary dialog boxes, property pages, command lines, and scripts.

Taskpad Example

This section provides an example for how to create a taskpad and task. The administrator first adds the snap-ins, and then creates separate taskpads and tasks for the Event Viewer, Services, and Shared Folders Snap-ins. Next, the administrator creates a Favorites view that includes these taskpads, hides the Console Tree, and then saves the file in User mode.

To add snap-ins

1. Click **Start**, click **Run**, type *mmc*, and then press **ENTER**.

2. From the MMC **Console** menu, click **Add/Remove Snap-in**.

3. In the **Add/Remove Snap-in** dialog box, click **Add**, and then click **Event Viewer** from the list of **Available Stand-Alone Snap-ins**. Select **Local Computer** and click **Finish**.

4. Click **Close**, and then click **OK**.

To create a taskpad view and tasks for the Application log

1. In the Console Tree, double-click the **Event Viewer Snap-in**, highlight the **Application** node, and then click **New Taskpad View** on the **Action** menu.

2. Follow the on-screen instructions, accepting default settings in the New Taskpad View Wizard.

3. On the **Taskpad Target** page, select the option **Selected tree item only**.

4. To create tasks after you create the Application log taskpad view, select the **Start New Task wizard** checkbox in the final dialog box of the wizard, and then follow the on-screen instructions in the wizard.

5. On the **Command Type** page, select the **Menu** command, and then click **Next**.

   There are three choices on the **Command Type** page, including:

   - **Menu command**. Allows you to run a command from a menu.

   - **Shell command**. Allows you to run a script, start a program, or open a Web page.

   - **Navigation**. Allows you to navigate to a view selected from your **Favorite** tab.

6. In the **Shortcut Menu Command** dialog box, select **List in Details Pane** from the **Command source** drop-down list, click **Properties** from the **Available commands** list, and then click **Next**.

7. In the **Name and Description** dialog box, type a name for the task in the **Task name box**, and then click **Next**.

8. In the **Task Icon** dialog box, select an icon and then click **Next**.

9. On the **Completing the New task Wizard** page, click **Finish**.

   ☑ **Note** To add additional commands to either the Console Tree tasks or Details Pane tasks, click **Run this wizard again** on the **Completing the New Task Wizard** page, click **Finish**, and then follow the on-screen instructions to complete the wizard.

Figure C.8 provides an example of a taskpad view for an Application log.

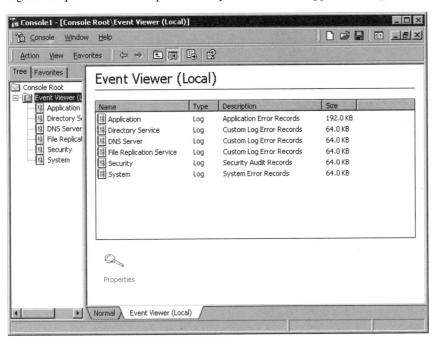

Figure C.8   Creating an MMC Taskpad and Task

Wizards

A wizard is a type of property sheet that is designed to present single property pages in a sequence controlled by the application. To the user, a wizard is a set of windows that present a sequence of steps to complete a particular task. Users can navigate through the sequence by clicking the **Back** and **Next** buttons located at the bottom of each property page.

Some MMC snap-ins use wizards to automate and simplify tasks for users. For example, the Active Directory Users and Computers Snap-in includes the Delegation of Control Wizard that administrators use to delegate control of Active Directory objects. Administrators use this wizard to grant other users permission to manage users, groups, computers, organizational units, and other objects stored in the Active Directory service.

MMC snap-ins can add both standard and Wizard 97 pages; however, the preferred method is to use Wizard 97 pages. For details about Wizard 97 pages, refer to the Microsoft Platform SDK documentation at: http://msdn.microsoft.com/downloads/sdks/platform/platform.asp.

Extending the Set Up Computer Wizard

As an example of extending a wizard, the Small Business Server 2000 Set Up Computer Wizard is presented in this section. The Set Up Computer Wizard can be extended to install ISV applications. To do so, perform the following steps.

To add applications to the Set Up Computer Wizard

1. From the Small Business Server Administrator Console **Favorites** tab, click **Small Business Server Tips**, and then click **Set up Client Computers**.

2. Click **Configure Setup Computer Wizard**. The **Set Up Computer Wizard Properties** dialog box appears.

3. Click **Add** to start the Client Setup Extensibility Wizard.

4. Click **Next**.

5. Type a **Display name** and then click **Next**.

6. Type a path to the setup program for the application and then click **Next**.

7. Click **Finish**. The application has been added to the Applications list in the **Set Up Computer Wizard Properties** dialog box.

8. Click **Close**.

The application you just identified for client installation will appear when you run the Set Up Computer Wizard.

Summary

This appendix focused on the rationale, design, architecture, customization and use of Small Business Server consoles. Several exercises demonstrating how to create management consoles, taskpads and tasks, as well as how to customize Small Business Server consoles were provided.

Office 2000 Deployments

This appendix addresses issues surrounding Microsoft® Office 2000 deployments on a Microsoft Windows® 2000 network. The topics range from basic to advanced deployments. How to customize Office 2000 is also discussed.

Customizing Office 2000 Installations

Office 2000 may be deployed in a customized manner in one of four ways, by using the:

- Office Profile Wizard
- Custom Installation Wizard
- Set Up Computer Wizard
- Group Policy

Office Profile Wizard

Office 2000 is highly customizable. Users can change how Office functions by setting options or adding custom templates or tools. For example, the sales department can create a custom template for invoices or a custom dictionary with industry-specific terms. Users can change everything from the screen resolution to the default file format for saving documents. These user-defined settings can be stored in an Office user profile. Office user profiles contain most of the customizations that users make to the Office 2000 environment.

The Office Profile Wizard stores and retrieves Office 2000 customizations. By using the Office Profile Wizard, you can create and deploy a standard user profile when you deploy Office 2000 so that all of your users start off with the same settings.

When you save an Office user profile, you create an Office profile settings (OPS) file. You can include your OPS file in a Windows installation transform (MST), and the settings are distributed when Office 2000 is deployed. You can also use the Office Profile Wizard to help back up and restore user-defined settings from one computer to another.

> ☑ **Note** If an OPS file contains settings for an application that is not installed, those settings are still written to the registry.

You can customize the Office Profile Wizard to capture only certain user settings and not all Office 2000 settings on the computer, or to run in quiet mode (without user interaction) as part of the Office Custom Installation Wizard. You can also run the Office Profile Wizard from the command line.

When a user receives a new computer, you can use the Office Profile Wizard to preserve user-defined Office 2000 settings from the old computer. Run the wizard on the old computer to create an OPS file, and then store the OPS file on the network. After the new computer arrives, run the wizard again to configure the new computer with the previous settings.

Office Profile Wizard Contents

The Office Profile Wizard consists of three files: Proflwiz.exe, Proflwiz.ini, and Proflwiz.hlp. For information about installing the wizard, refer to the Office 2000 Resource Kit Toolbox on the Web at: http://www.microsoft.com/office/ork/2000/.

Creating Office Profiles

You can distribute different user profiles for different groups when you deploy Microsoft Office 2000. For example, a large corporation with several departments might want each department to specify how Office 2000 is installed on that department's computers. You can configure Office 2000 with the default corporate settings and then have each department update those settings with a unique user profile.

You can approach this task in two ways:

- Create a standard user profile, create separate department profiles, and then substitute the department profiles for the standard profile during deployment.

- Create a standard user profile, create separate department profiles, and distribute both profiles during deployment.

The first approach is simpler, but it requires keeping track of different versions of the customized installation—one customized by the corporate administrator and one customized by each department administrator. The second approach allows the department administrators to deploy Office 2000 without modifying the corporate installation.

Distribute a Department-Specific User Profile

In this scenario, the corporate administrator first creates a default OPS file.

To create a standard corporate user profile

1. Install and configure Office 2000 on a test computer, and then run the Office Profile Wizard to create the default OPS file.

2. Customize the Office 2000 installation to include the default OPS file. In the Office Custom Installation Wizard, the Customize Default Application Settings page includes this option.

Before Office is deployed, the individual department administrators create a new OPS file based on the corporate version.

To create a department-specific user profile

1. Using the corporate transform (MST file), install Office on a test computer.

2. Customize the Office 2000 environment to suit the department needs.

3. Run the Office Profile Wizard to create a new department-specific OPS file.

4. Customize the Office 2000 installation to include the new OPS file.

5. Deploy the customized Office 2000 installation to all department users.

Distribute Both Corporate and Department Settings

In this scenario, the corporate administrator customizes the Office 2000 installation to point to the Office Profile Wizard and OPS file, using a relative path. A relative path allows each department to add the Office Profile Wizard and a departmental OPS file to their administrative installation point.

To customize the Office installation for department-specific user profiles

1. Install and configure Office 2000 on a test computer, and then run the Office Profile Wizard to create a default OPS file.

2. Customize the Office 2000 installation to include the default OPS file. In the Office Custom Installation Wizard, the **Customize Default Application Settings** page includes this option.

3. Customize the Office 2000 installation to include the Office Profile Wizard as an application to be run at the end of the installation, and point to the Office Profile Wizard and OPS file using a relative path. Use the following syntax:
   OPW\Proflwiz.exe /r Department.ops /q

4. Create separate administrative installation points on the network for each department.

5. Create an OPW folder at each administrative installation point, and copy the Office Profile Wizard to that folder.

When Office is deployed, the individual department administrators update the Office installation with their own customized versions.

To install a department-specific user profile

1. By using the corporate transform (MST file), install Office on a test computer. If the corporate administrator included an OPS file, this installation includes those settings.

2. Customize the Office 2000 environment to suit the department needs.

3. Run the Office Profile Wizard to create an OPS file based on the new settings, and name the file Department.ops.

4. Copy the new Department.ops file to the OPW folder on the department administrative installation point.

5. Deploy Office 2000 to department computers.

When Office 2000 is installed, the settings in the corporate OPS file are included. Immediately following the installation, the Office Profile Wizard automatically runs and the corporate settings are updated with the department administrator's changes.

Custom Installation Wizard

The Microsoft Office Custom Installation Wizard allows you to customize the way that all users in your organization install Office on their computers. If you are deploying Microsoft Office 2000 to many computers, it is probably most efficient to first install Office on a network server and then to have users run setup from your administrative installation point.

After you create an administrative installation point, you have many options for managing the deployment of Office. By using the Office Custom Installation Wizard, you can modify the administrative installation point, to control how all the users in your organization install Office on their computers.

By using the Custom Installation Wizard, you can complete the following tasks:

- Define the path where Office is installed on users' computers.

- Define the default installation state for all features of Office applications. For example, you can choose to install Microsoft Word on the user's local hard disk and install Microsoft PowerPoint® to run from the network.

- Add your own files and registry entries to Office Setup so that they are installed along with Office.

- Modify Office application shortcuts, specifying where they are installed and customizing their properties.

- Define a list of network servers for Office to use if the primary server is unavailable.

- Specify other products to install, or other programs to run, on users' computers after setup is completed.

- Configure Microsoft Internet Explorer 5.0 and Microsoft Outlook® 2000 the way you want.

After you fine-tune the options by using the wizard, your modifications become the default settings for anyone who runs setup from your administrative installation point. You can even have users run setup in quiet mode (with no user interaction) so that your modifications define precisely how Office is installed.

Installing Office 2000 from the Set Up Computer Wizard

This section describes how you can install Office 2000 onto the Microsoft Small Business Server computer for deployment on client machines. By doing so, you can make Office 2000 applications available for client setup by using the Set Up Computer Wizard. To enable deployment of Office 2000 applications during client setup, perform the following steps.

To integrate Office 2000 in a Small Business Server installation

1. Insert Compact Disc 1 of Office 2000 into the disc drive.

2. Perform an administrative installation of Office 2000 Compact Disc 1, as follows:

   a. Click **Start**, point to **Programs**, and then click **Command Prompt**. The **Command Prompt** window appears.

   b. At the prompt, type the disc drive letter, for example *E:*.

   c. At the drive letter prompt, for example *E:,* type *Setup/A* to display the **Microsoft Office 2000 Administrative Mode** page (Figure D.1) of the Microsoft Office 2000 Professional Installation Wizard.

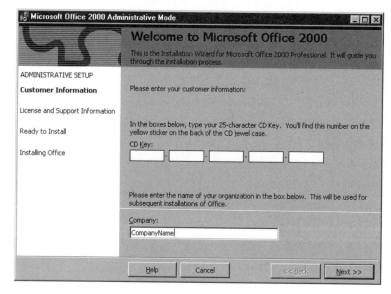

Figure D.1   Office 2000 Administrative Mode Setup

3. Type the **CD Key** numbers in the spaces provided. CD Key numbers are located on the Office 2000 compact disc.

4. In **Company**, type the name of the company, and then click **Next**.

5. Read and accept the terms of the **End User License Agreement**, and then click **Next**.

6. The **Microsoft Office 2000 Location** page appears, as shown in Figure D.2. Type a location for the Office 2000 installation, such as a folder on C: drive of the Small Business Server machine.

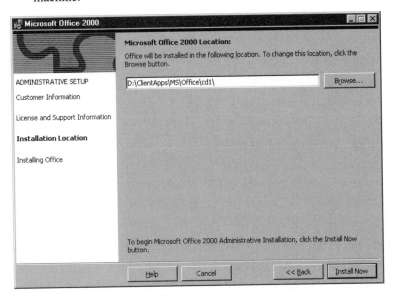

Figure D.2 Providing an installation location for Microsoft Office 2000

7. Click **Install Now** to begin the Office 2000 installation.

8. When the installation is complete, click **OK**, then remove Compact Disc 1 from the disc drive.

After completing these steps, you can then integrate Office 2000 applications into a new client computer setup for use by the Set Up Computer Wizard. The wizard uses these applications to add software to new and existing computers.

To configure Office 2000 for installation from the Set Up Computer Wizard

1. From the Small Business Server Administrator Console **Favorites** tab, click **Small Business Server Tips**, click **Set up Client Computers**, and then click the **Configure Setup Computer Wizard**. The Set Up Computer Wizard Properties dialog box appears.

2. Click **Add** to add an application to the Set Up Computer Wizard.

3. Click **Next** when the Client Setup Extensibility Wizard appears.

4. Type a display name, such as Office 2000, when the **Display Name** page appears, and then click **Next**.

5. Specify the installation path for the application on the **Installation Path and Command**s page. This is typically the path to the setup.exe file.

6. Click **Next** and then click **Finish**.

You can now add Office 2000 applications to new and existing client computers from the Set Up Computer Wizard.

Perform the following steps to remove Outlook 2000 from a client computer.

To remove Outlook 2000 from a client computer

1. Click **Start**, point to **Settings**, and then click **Control Panel**.

2. Double-click **Add/Remove Programs**. The **Add/Remove Program Properties** dialog box appears, as shown in Figure D.3.

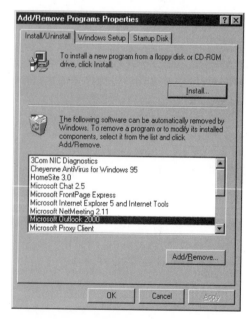

Figure D.3   Add/Remove Programs Properties dialog box

3. Highlight **Microsoft Outlook 2000**, and then click **Add/Remove**. The **Microsoft Outlook 2000 Maintenance Mode** page appears, as shown in Figure D.4.

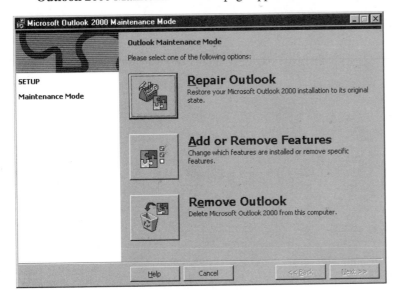

Figure D.4   Microsoft Outlook 2000 Maintenance Mode

4. Click **Remove Outlook** to uninstall Outlook 2000 from the client computer.

5. Click **OK** when the uninstall process is complete.

Group Policy

In a Small Business Server 2000 network that contains Windows 2000 Professional clients, you can use the software installation capabilities of Group Policy to install Office 2000.

To install Office 2000 using Group Policy

1. Click **Start**, point to **Programs**, and then click **Administrative Tools** to start the Microsoft Active Directory™ directory service Users and Computers snap-in.

2. Right-click the **MyBusiness** organizational unit, which is the default organizational unit in Small Business Server 2000.

3. Click **Properties** from the secondary menu.

4. Click the **Group Policy** tab.

5. Click **New** and type a name for the **Group Policy Object Link**.

6. Click **Edit** while the new Group Policy Object Link you just created is highlighted. The Group Policy Microsoft Management Console (MMC) starts.

7. Expand **Computer Configuration**, and then expand **Software Settings**.

8. Right-click **Software Installation**, click **New**, and then click **Package**.

9. Navigate to the .msi file for Office 2000 when the **Open** dialog box appears. This file is located in the folder where you performed the administrative installation of Office 2000. Click **Open**.

10. In the **Display Software** dialog box, select **Published**, **Assigned**, or **Advanced published or assigned**. **Published** means the installation will be optional and **Assigned** means the installation will be mandatory. Click **OK**.

After completing these steps successfully, you have used Group Policy to create a software installation package for installation on a Windows 2000 machine.

Office Server Extensions

An advanced capability of Office 2000 and Windows 2000 Server (the operating system of Small Business Server 2000) is Office Server Extensions. Microsoft Office Server Extensions (OSE) consist of several client and server components that work together to enable OSE features. When you understand the client and server components, it is easier for you to deploy and troubleshoot OSE.

OSEs use several components to provide Microsoft Office 2000 users with Web Discussions, Web Subscriptions, and a secure Web publishing environment. These server-based components are:

* Microsoft Internet Information Server (IIS) (found in Windows 2000 Server) or Personal Web Server (found in Windows 2000 Professional)

* NTFS file system

* Microsoft FrontPage® Server Extensions

* Microsoft Data Engine (MSDE) or Microsoft SQL Server™

* Custom Automation objects

* Active Server Pages (ASP)

* OSE Notification Service and Simple Mail Transfer Protocol (SMTP) mail server

Integrating Office 2000 Applications in Custom Deployments

In Small Business Server 2000, Office 2000 client applications can be integrated with the Set Up Computer Wizard and then rolled out in a standard configuration. If you want to perform a custom deployment of Office 2000 with transforms, client applications cannot be integrated with the wizard. Refer to the *Office 2000 Resource Kit* for details on custom deployment scenarios.

Enhancing Office 2000 Functionality

In direct response to customer feedback, design priorities for Microsoft Office 2000 included reducing the cost of ownership, increasing integration with the Web, and improving support for organizational software. Although Microsoft Office 2000 already offers significant advances, even greater functionality is enabled by combining Microsoft Office 2000 with other Microsoft software—such as FrontPage and Microsoft Internet Explorer. This section addresses Microsoft Office 2000 functionality enhancements.

The sections that follow include descriptions of enhancements to Office 2000 that may be implemented in the small business organization through collaboration with other applications.

File Format Compatibilities

File formats between Microsoft Office 2000 and Microsoft Office 97 are compatible, which means that Office 97 and Office 2000 users can exchange documents natively. Office 97 will be able to open any Office 2000 file without a converter. However, certain formatting options available in Office 2000 will not be compatible, because Office 97 does not recognize the new features. The only exception is Microsoft Access, because of the new support of Unicode (Access did not previously support this file format). Access 2000 now supports downward revision saves to Access 97.

File Error Detection and Fix

Microsoft Office 2000 includes an executable that can be installed on Microsoft Windows operating systems to automatically detect and fix errors to files or registry settings, which is needed for a successful application start. The Microsoft Office Custom Installation Wizard and Microsoft Office Profile Wizard make it simple and efficient to customize how Office 2000 installs in your organization. Better support for roaming profiles makes it possible for Office 2000 users to work using their own preferences and settings, regardless of what computer they are working on, as long as it uses the same operating system.

Reduced Cost of Ownership

One of the most commonly discussed information technology topics today is the overall cost of personal computing ownership and how to reduce it. Reducing the cost of ownership of Microsoft Office is a top priority for Office 2000. It is reflected in new administrative capabilities and in features that make computing with Small Business Server 2000 as easy as possible.

Office 2000 features help reduce the cost of supporting operating system features such as security, customizable Help, and other usability improvements. All of these features are available to all users, regardless of the Microsoft applications in use.

Some capabilities are better implemented at the desktop or server operating system level. If typical system administration problems are fixed at the operating system level, the administrator has an entire desktop that is easier to administer, as opposed to only four or five applications.

The following sections include descriptions of features that enhance Office 2000 functions and also further reduce the cost of ownership when Microsoft Office 2000 is combined with other Microsoft software.

Operating System Shell Update

Windows 2000, Windows 98, Windows Me, and Microsoft Internet Explorer 4.01 or later (Small Business Server 2000 includes Microsoft Internet Explorer 5.0) all include an updated shell that supports additional functionality in Office 2000. A service pack is available for updating the shell in Windows 95 and Microsoft Windows NT® Workstation 4.0. You may download the service pack from Microsoft's download site at: http://www.microsoft.com/downloads.

The functionality enhancements are discussed in the sections that follow.

Install on Demand

Install on Demand automatically installs an Office 2000 feature or application when necessary. For example, if a user has installed some, but not all of the Office components, the missing components will be installed when the user first tries to access them. Install on Demand is activated in the following three ways:

- From within an Office application.
- From the **Start** menu (the shell).
- From within another application, such as a Word document attached to an e-mail message.

The first method works with any operating system on which Office 2000 runs. Both the first and second methods work using any of the following combinations with the shell update:

- Office 2000 and Windows 2000
- Office 2000 and Windows 95, Windows 98, and Windows Me
- Office 2000 and Windows NT 4.0, with Internet Explorer 4.01 or later

The Windows installer service is installed when any one of these products is present. If the Windows installer service is available, it handles the request for installing the application and can install it from a variety of locations, rather than from just one hard-coded location. The last method requires a Windows 2000 Professional client. This improves the resiliency of this feature over the lifetime of the Office 2000 product.

Single Document Interface

With Office 2000 applications, each open document appears on the Windows taskbar. In the past, only the active document appeared. Word for Windows will show individual documents on the taskbar on every operating system on which Office 2000 runs. Microsoft Excel, PowerPoint, and Access make use of the shell update to make this feature possible. This enhancement makes it easier to drag and drop contents from one document to another document by using the taskbar.

Web Folders

Web folders allow you to view Web servers from the Windows Explorer just as you would view network servers or local hard drives. Office 2000 supports the ability to cut, copy, and paste (or drag and drop) documents from a Web server to a network server or local hard drive, or from a local hard drive or network server to a Web server. This makes it easier to use content found on the Internet or an intranet, or to have average users post content to an intranet site or Internet staging server.

Increased Integration with Web

Microsoft Office 2000 increases integration with the Web by providing tools for easy creation of Web content, easy publication to the Web, and simplified retrieval of Web content. Many of these features are enabled entirely by Microsoft Office 2000 and are independent of the browser or server software your organization is using. Some of these features include:

- **HTML file format**. Saving files to the HTML format is as easy as saving to the native application file format. This has greatly improved Web integration. In addition, information is stored in the file for reuse in the original application. For example, if the user creates a spreadsheet and saves it to HTML, all of the elements will appear correctly in a browser. In addition, if the user opens that file again in Microsoft Excel 2000, formulas will recalculate, Microsoft PivotTable® dynamic views will pivot and other features will work as if the file had remained in Excel format. In other words, the Excel spreadsheet will "round-trip" to its binary format (*.xls), to HTML, and back to its binary format with full Web integration.

- **Enhanced application features**. Some applications have added features to support commonly used HTML formats. For example, Word has added support for using frames in creating a table of contents, with a linking table of contents in the left-hand frame rather than embedded within a document as appropriate for a printed document.

- **Save to the Web**. Not only is it easier to save to the HTML format, but it is also easier to save a document as a Web page on a Web server. Simply navigate a Web server as you would a network server, and save your file. This means that Office 2000 users can more easily share documents with people creating Web sites using FrontPage 2000. For example, save a Word document as HTML in a FrontPage-based Internet or intranet site.

Office 2000 Enhanced by Browser and Web Server Functionalities

Some of the new functionality in Microsoft Office 2000 is actually enabled by combining Office with either a specific level of browser functionality, Web server functionality, or both. The following sections describe these features.

Creating and Managing Intranets

Microsoft Office 2000 and FrontPage 2000 together provide organizations with a comprehensive solution for creating and managing workgroup Webs or intranets. FrontPage 2000 lets users create exactly the site they want, which makes updating Web sites easy. It also works great with Office. Office 2000 users can now save HTML documents directly to a FrontPage-based Web site. Features such as shared Office menus and toolbars make Office users feel immediately comfortable using FrontPage 2000.

Robust Web collaboration features such as check-in and check-out, as well as control over security at multiple levels, enable teams to work together with confidence. Because Web sites (both intranet and Internet) are global in nature, FrontPage 2000 integrates with the new worldwide deployment features found in Office 2000, making it easy to deploy throughout your organization.

Features Enabled by Browsers

Some Microsoft Office 2000 functionality is enabled by having an Internet browser view content created by the Office application. Different versions of browsers support different versions of HTML and other Web features. While users with any Netscape or Microsoft browser (version 3.0 or later) will have a good experience with the features described in this section, those with Internet Explorer 5.0 will have the best experience. Internet Explorer 5.0 currently provides the best Web integration—a result of support for more advanced features and layouts of the HTML specification.

Microsoft Internet Explorer 5.0

Users with Internet Explorer 5.0 will have access to all of the features available to users with earlier versions of Internet Explorer, with the following additional features.

Best Viewing of HTML File Format

Users who have Internet Explorer version 5.0 will have the best results viewing Office-generated HTML files. Internet Explorer 5.0 will display and scale vector graphics natively, providing better display and smaller files for Office–generated HTML documents, including PowerPoint presentations. Features such as small caps and vertical text in Word, which will not appear correctly in other browsers, look the same as they would in the Office application that created them.

Solutions with Data Access Pages

Although similar in function to classic Access forms and reports, Data Access Pages are specifically designed to view, edit, and report on data within a browser. Users design pages in much the same way they create forms and reports, yet they can now use new Web-enabled features and easy drag and drop capabilities. The resulting Data Access Pages are essentially HTML pages that have the ability to maintain a live link (are bound) to data that can be in the form of an Access database or even a SQL Server store.

These Data Access Pages are stored as HTML files outside the Access database .mdb file. This allows users to easily send Data Access Pages through e-mail or post them on the Web as HTML pages. The result is that anyone with Internet Explorer 5.0 can now use an Access database without having Access installed on the computer.

Web Features Enabled Through Server Software

Some of the new functionality in Microsoft Office 2000 actually capitalizes on Web server functionality as well as browser functionality. Where existing functionality was available, Microsoft Office 2000 built upon it. If no equivalent server functionality existed, the Microsoft Office group wrote server extensions (known as Microsoft Office Server Extensions) as needed. The enhancements to Office 2000 created by server functionalities are described in the sections that follow.

Windows 2000 Server

The features described in this section are enabled by the functionality of Windows 2000 Server.

PowerPoint Presentation Broadcast Support for Large Audiences

With Microsoft Windows 2000 Server and the Microsoft Windows Media™ Services (formerly Microsoft NetShow® Server) installed, users can deliver a presentation over an intranet, displaying the presentation slides in HTML along with the narration as streaming audio and video. Windows Media Services uses streaming multicast technology to distribute a live or recorded audio and/or video broadcast over an intranet.

PowerPoint 2000 adds ease-of-use to the technology by broadcasting presentations directly from within PowerPoint. A camera is not required but video is supported if used. Because the presentation is sent in HTML format, the audience needs only a compatible browser to view it on PC, Macintosh, or UNIX workstations. For example, this feature may be used for company meetings, presentations to remote groups, or a team meeting at several different locations. No browser is needed by the presenter, but Microsoft Internet Explorer 4.0 or later is required for the audience, with exception of the Macintosh users who will need Internet Explorer 5.0 or later. Windows Media Services are not required for presentations with fewer than 16 viewers and no video.

HTTP 1.1 Servers with PUT Protocol

Web servers that do not have the PUT protocol can only use Hypertext Transfer Protocol (HTTP) to send documents to a client computer. HTTP 1.1 PUT-enabled servers allow Microsoft Office 2000 applications to save files on these servers. This includes any server that can support FrontPage extensions, including the Windows 2000 Server Internet Information Services (IIS), UNIX servers, Apache, Netscape, and Sun Web servers. FrontPage extensions are not required for this feature.

Because most servers today support this, almost everyone can have this additional functionality due to Office 2000.

Save to the Web

Users can publish any HTML content created by an Office 2000 application from within that application. In the past, users needed to use a method outside of Office to publish files to a Web server, but now they can accomplish this using menu commands from within the application.

HTTP-DAV Servers

Distributed authoring and versioning (DAV) is a new, open Internet standard that was created to make two-way communication possible on a Web server. This allows users to send and retrieve or publish documents to a Web server using open Internet standards. DAV will be integrated into future versions of server products.

Web Site Navigation

For any client computer with the operating system shell update mentioned earlier in this appendix (Microsoft Windows 2000, Windows 95, Windows 98, or Windows Me, Internet Explorer 4.01 or later), Microsoft Office 2000 makes it possible to navigate a Web server just as a user would navigate a file server. By clicking **File**, **Open** in Microsoft Word or by using the Windows Explorer, a user can click on a Web server and expand and collapse folders to view their contents, all without having to know the full HTTP path. The difference between this and the Save to the Web defined above is that Save to the Web requires that the user know the fully qualified HTTP path.

Office 2000 Enhanced Web Functionality with Microsoft Internet Information Services

All the features mentioned previously are enabled in addition to those described in the sections that follow.

Remote Data Services

Remote Data Services (RDS) is a way of retrieving data from a Web page supported by Access. There are two main components to RDS. RDS is a client component that is a Microsoft ActiveX® control, and a server component is an ActiveX server component and an RDS application.

Integrated Security

Because IIS runs on Windows 2000 in Small Business Server, the security is integrated with Windows 2000 security. Therefore, any of the Microsoft Office 2000 features implemented from Web functionality will benefit from Windows 2000 security.

IIS with FrontPage Extensions

Organizations using IIS with FrontPage extensions benefit from all the previously mentioned server enhancements and can also utilize the functionality described in the following.

Managing Embedded Files

The HTML format does not actually embed objects within it. Instead, it maintains links to files such as graphics. When users move, delete, or copy HTML files, those other embedded objects normally remain where they are. With Windows 2000, IIS, and FrontPage extensions, the files embedded in the HTML file are moved, copied, or deleted along with it.

IIS with Office Server Extensions

Microsoft Office 2000 ships with server extensions that run only on IIS with Windows 2000. These Office Server Extensions enable new collaboration features that would not otherwise be possible and they leverage the existing functionality in Microsoft Office 2000, as described in the following sections.

AutoNavigation

AutoNavigation is a feature that displays the contents of a Web server, including Office documents, in a Web page. It is a hierarchical view similar to a file directory and allows users to open, print, copy, and paste Web files easily.

Web Discussions with Comments

With the Office Server Extensions, users can have discussions in both native Office 2000 documents and HTML files within the browser. Discussions can be added either through an Office application or through the browser by using a special toolbar supplied by the Office 2000 client. With a level 3 browser (Netscape Navigator 3.0, or Internet Explorer 3.0), the discussions can be incorporated only at the document level, not embedded or integrated into the document, and are viewed in the discussion pane at the bottom of the page. With a level 4 browser or later, the discussions can be made in-line or integrated directly into the document. The toolbar has buttons for inserting new comments, navigating through existing comments, editing and replying to comments, and viewing or hiding the discussion pane.

The comments themselves are actually stored in a database, the Microsoft Data Engine (MSDE), which ships with Office 2000, and has the same architecture as Microsoft SQL Server 2000. In fact, if you expect that the volume of comments will be very large, you can substitute SQL Server 2000 for the MSDE. Because the comments are stored separately, the speed of viewing the document and the size of the document are not affected, and the number and length of the comments can be almost unlimited. Also, users only need permission to write to the server that stores the database, not the actual site itself. This allows users to comment on any site on the Internet because they are not limited to the company's intranet. Users can also choose to subscribe to a document and its discussions so that they can read it offline. New comments, however, cannot be added offline.

The following is an example that illustrates the business benefits of these discussions: Imagine that you have written a new document or proposed a product specification or standard. It's important that users on *any* platform provide feedback, but you don't want anyone else to edit or change the original proposal. With threaded discussions, the size and integrity of the original document are maintained. At the same time, valuable feedback is gathered and concerns are aired.

Web Subscriptions and Notifications

Web Subscriptions and Notifications improve collaboration between people on the Web by keeping users up-to-date. Users subscribe to a particular document or set of documents on a Web server with Microsoft Office Server Extensions, and they are notified by e-mail when the status of any selected document changes. Users can choose to be notified when a document is changed, created, or deleted. Users can be notified of changes immediately or, in the case of a document undergoing frequent revisions, can choose to be notified on a daily or weekly basis.

NetMeeting Conferencing Software

Microsoft NetMeeting® is a collaboration tool that makes it easy to work together without being in the same room. When combined with Office 2000, users are able to consult with co-workers without having to fly across the country or book a large-capacity conference room.

NetMeeting Conferencing and Collaborative Editing

Integration with NetMeeting conferencing software lets users start a conference and share any Office document with others for collaborative editing. With NetMeeting conferencing and collaborative editing, users can use all the creation and editing tools of Microsoft Office together, online and in real-time. For example, an author and a technical expert can review and make changes to a document together at their own desks on opposite ends of the country, or the world.

Microsoft NetMeeting Integration

Users can easily schedule real-time meetings using Outlook 2000 and automatically start the NetMeeting conferencing software with an Office document to share during the NetMeeting-based conference.

Presenters can schedule a broadcast just as they would schedule any other meeting, using Outlook 2000. A "Lobby" page is automatically generated and available when the audience is ready to tune in. When the presenter is ready to start the broadcast, the presentation is saved in HTML format and copied out to the specified server location. If a Windows Media Services server is set up, the pages will be multicast automatically. As the audience tunes in to the Lobby page for the event, the HTML pages will be cached on the machines of each member. When the presenter begins a separate multicast stream with audio and video (if present), the slide navigation commands are sent to the audience. Viewers are also free to join in even after the meeting has started.

Presentation on Demand

PowerPoint 2000 records the live presentation, allowing anyone who missed it to see and hear it later. If the presenter has a microphone, PowerPoint 2000 can even record the audio portion, or the presenter can use the new voice narration feature in PowerPoint 2000 to add the audio portion of the presentation.

Enterprise Integration and Support with Office 2000

Over the years, Microsoft Office has often been first to embrace standards that allow it to be a client in the enterprise and not just a personal productivity tool. Office 4, which shipped in 1993, supported Object Linking and Embedding (OLE), so that it could be programmed by other applications, and also supported other enterprise standards such as Open Database Connectivity (ODBC), Microsoft Mail, and Lotus Notes. Microsoft Office 2000 is continuing the tradition of being an enterprise client by providing enhancements or improvements in the following areas:

- Data access
- Corporate reporting tools
- Ability to create custom solutions with Office 2000

Data Access

All the enterprise support mentioned above is available in Microsoft Office 2000, with additions and improvements for all customers that include improved Excel text import. Many Microsoft BackOffice family customers have requested that Office improve its integration and support for SQL Server, including the improved performance and new capabilities of SQL Server 2000.

OLE DB

Access 2000 supports Object Linking and Embedding Database (OLE DB), a recent standard for data access. By using OLE DB, Access 2000 databases can connect directly to Microsoft SQL Server 2000 instead of going through the Jet engine, the traditional default database engine in Access. Power users and developers can now create solutions that combine the ease-of-use and speedy development of the Access interface (client) with the scalability, performance, and reliability of Microsoft SQL Server 2000. Processing occurs in Microsoft SQL Server for a true client/server solution. Power users and developers appreciate developing using the Access interface, and end users performing data entry find it as easy to use as other Office applications. Support for OLE DB in Microsoft Office has been tested with Microsoft SQL Server, Oracle, Thor, and JOLT.

Microsoft SQL Server OLAP Services Support

Office 2000 provides support for SQL Server Online Analytical Processing (OLAP) Services, a new OLAP capability in SQL Server 2000 that allows users to perform sophisticated analysis on large volumes of data with exceptional performance. Because Office works tightly with SQL Server-based data warehouses, this allows a broader audience of users to access corporate information. For example, users can use a PivotTable dynamic view in Excel 2000 to create persistent local cubes of data from a SQL Server using the SQL Server OLAP Services feature. This provides a new method for high-performance data analysis of large amounts of data, right from the familiar interface of Excel 2000. This eliminates the limitations of working with data in PivotTable dynamic views that existed with the previous version of Excel. The Office Web Components also support OLAP to provide browsing and charting functionality within a browser.

Access 2000 Client Server Tools

Because Access is renowned for its easy-to-use wizards, this functionality has been extended to the client/server realm. A variety of wizards make it easier for Access power users and developers to create a client/server database.

Access users will appreciate the ability to use popular Access wizards, such as the Report Wizard, Form Wizard, Control Wizard, and Button Wizard against a back end in Microsoft SQL Server 2000. These wizards have been updated to support the new client/server architecture.

Client/Server Design Tools

With an Access project, new design tools allow users to create and manage Microsoft SQL Server 2000 objects from the design view, including tables, views, stored procedures, and database diagrams. This makes it easier for current Access power users and developers to extend their database knowledge to the client/server environment.

Microsoft SQL Server-Based Administration Tools

Access 2000 allows users to perform and manage common administration tasks in Microsoft SQL Server 2000, such as replication, backup and restore, and security. This means that users can use Access 2000 on the client to perform SQL Server administrative tasks.

Corporate Reporting

Excel has been a premier corporate reporting tool for years. Its financial analysis capabilities, combined with unique tools such as PivotTable dynamic views, have provided the basis for corporate reporting systems for many organizations. Included in Microsoft Office 2000 are enhancements that make PivotTable dynamic views easier to use and provide Microsoft PivotChart® dynamic views that update each time a PivotTable view is changed. The following section details features that are improved for users who combine Office 2000 with other technologies such as intranets or databases.

Enhanced Web Queries

For those organizations with connectivity to the Web or an intranet, Microsoft has enhanced the Excel Web Queries feature. The new Web Query Wizard makes it much easier to get data from the Web into Excel. This wizard walks users through the process of bringing data from a Web page into Excel 2000, and helps create the query file as they choose the Web page, the desired content for importing, and the type of formatting. Web query pages can be refreshed automatically on a scheduled basis.

Office Web Components

Office 2000 includes three new Office Web Components: a spreadsheet component, a chart component, and a PivotTable component. These new components make corporate data available through any browser.

The spreadsheet component provides basic spreadsheet functionality in the browser, allowing users to enter text and numbers, create formulas, recalculate, sort, filter, and perform basic formatting. It supports frozen panes for keeping header rows and columns visible while scrolling through data, as well as in-cell editing and resizable rows and columns. With the Office Web Components, the Office Spreadsheet component allows users to interact with Excel 2000 data in a browser, as shown in Figure D.5.

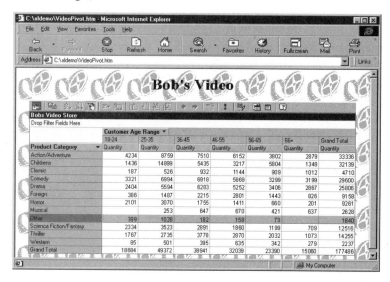

Figure D.5   Presenting spreadsheet information through Office Web Components

The chart component provides interactivity and automatic updates as the underlying data changes.

The PivotTable component is similar to PivotTable views in Excel 2000 and provides a dynamic way to view and analyze database information in the browser. The PivotTable component is created in either Access or Excel and resides on a Data Access Page. This component lets users browse data, dynamically sort and filter it, group it by rows or columns, create totals and focus on the details behind the totals. It helps users work efficiently with large or small amounts of data. Although the author of the Data Access Page determines the initial view, the user can access the Field List Chooser to drag and drop the dynamically linked fields directly onto the page.

More Information

For more information on creating custom Office 2000 solutions using add-ins, templates, wizards, and libraries, refer to Chapter 11 of the *Microsoft Office 2000 Visual Basic Programmer's Guide.* You should also consult the Microsoft Office 2000 Resource Kit located at: http://www.microsoft.com/office/ork/2000/.

This resource kit may also be purchased.

Summary

Microsoft Office 2000 has met its design goals of reducing the cost of ownership, increasing integration with the Web, and improving support for the Web and the enterprise. Users of Office 2000 will benefit from these improvements regardless of what environment they work within. However, users who work in an environment that supports Internet Explorer 5.0, Windows 2000 Professional, IIS, NetMeeting, Windows Media Services, and SQL Server 2000 will find that Office 2000 offers solutions to today's computing problems that are far beyond those of a traditional desktop productivity application suite.

TAPI Solutions for Small Business Server

The Microsoft® Windows® Telephony Applications Programming Interface (TAPI) 2.1, included with Windows 2000 Server, provides a powerful and flexible platform for developing and using computer telephony applications. TAPI 2.1 isolates the hardware layer, which is Layer One in the Open Standards Interconnection (OSI) model, by allowing the Windows telephony API to communicate with any type of telephony hardware device. This frees the developer and user from network and device dependence. The API handles the complex device interaction at a low level that is effectively transparent to the developer and user. TAPI 2.1 is the only platform that enables applications for use on analog telephone, Integrated Services Digital Network (ISDN), Private Branch Exchange (PBX)-based, and Internet Protocol (IP) networks.

Information Sources

For further information on TAPI 2.1, you can download white papers and the TAPI 2.1 Software Developer's Kit from the Microsoft Web site at: http://www.microsoft.com/.

Small Business Server 2000 Resource Kit Tools Installation and Access

This chapter describes how to install and access the tools and utilities supplied on the Microsoft® Small Business Server 2000 Resource Kit Disc, including those specifically developed for Small Business Server 2000. The installation process is automated by the Small Business Server Resource Kit Setup Wizard.

The material for this chapter is presented in the following sections:

- Installing the Small Business Server 2000 Resource Kit.

- Small Business Server 2000 Tool Descriptions

Installing the Small Business Server 2000 Resource Kit

Perform the following steps to install the Small Business Server 2000 Resource Kit on the server computer.

1. Insert the disc in your disc drive.

2. Autorun will commence and the start screen will appear.

3. Click **Install Tools** and follow the on-screen instructions.

Small Business Server 2000 Tool Descriptions

The following section describes select software tools developed for Small Business Server 2000. The remaining tools are described on the disc.

Internet Connection Wizard Webpage Script

This .asp page allows you to configure and run the Small Business Server Internet Connection Wizard. Users can scroll through the Web page, selecting their choices as if they were running through the wizard. Users then type in the path for the location of the script and, when they click "Create Script," a java script file is created. The .asp page will automatically perform the same error checking that the Small Business Server Internet Connection Wizard does.

Users can then take the java script and run it on any server with SBS installed. Simply typing the name of the script will configure the server in exactly the same way as if users had run the Small Business Server Internet Connection Wizard themselves. The script will not perform any action on which Small Business Server is not installed. Users can create a common script and take it with them to another site on a disk or through e-mail, and then run it as part of their normal configuration of a new server.

The .asp page can also accept passed parameters, meaning that users could add the page as part of a series of Web pages and pass user information through to the .asp page, creating the script automatically. The source of the script is provided on the compact disc.

PC Analyzer Tool

This is an application for analyzing the configuration of a server or client computer. More information on this tool is located at: http://www.microsoft.com/piracy/msia/.

Select Tools from the Windows 2000 Server Resource Kit

The compact disc contains select tools from the Microsoft Windows® 2000 Server Resource Kit that are applicable to the Small Business Server 2000 network environment. Tools that do not apply, such as enterprise-level applications, are not provided. The Windows 2000 Server Resource Kit tools that are included are listed in Table F.1.

Table F.1 Windows 2000 Server Resource Kit Tools

File	Tool Name	Description
DELSRV.EXE	Delete Service	Unregisters a service with the service control manager.
DUREG.EXE	DUReg	Shows how much data is stored in the registry, or in any registry subtree, key, or subkey.
INSTSRV.EXE	Service Installer	Installs and uninstalls executable services and assigns names to them.
INUSE.EXE	File In Use Replace Utility	Provides individuals and administrators with the ability to replace files that are currently in use by the operating system.
NETSVC.EXE	Remote Service Controller	Remotely starts, stops, and queries the status of services over a network.
NOW.EXE	Now	Echoes the current date and time plus any arguments passed to it.
PATHMAN.EXE	Path Manager	Adds or removes components of the system or user path.
PATHMAN.EXE	Path Manager	Adds or removes components of the system or user path.
PTREE.MSI	Process Tree	Allows an administrator to query the process inheritance tree and kill processes on local or remote computers.

Table F.1 Windows 2000 Server Resource Kit Tools (continued)

File	Tool Name	Description
PULIST.EXE	PUList	Lists processes running on local or remote computers.
REGBACK.EXE	Registry Backup	Backs up all or part of the Registry.
REGDMP.EXE	Registry Dump	Dumps of all or part of the registry to standard output.
REGFIND.EXE	Registry Search Utility	Searches and optionally replaces registry data.
REGINI.EXE	Registry Change by Script	Modifies registry entries with a batch file.
REGINI.EXE	Registry Change by Script	Modifies registry entries with a batch file.
REGREST.EXE	Registry Restoration	Restores all or part of the Registry.
SC.EXE	Service Controller Query Tool	Retrieves information about services from Service Controller.
SC.EXE	Service Controller Query Tool	Retrieves information about services from Service Controller.
SC.EXE	Service Controller Query Tool	Retrieves information about services from Service Controller.
SCANREG.EXE	Registry Scan	Searches for a string in registry key names, value names and value data.
SCLIST.EXE	Service List	Shows services and their status.
SETX.EXE	SetX	Sets environmental variables in the user or computer environment.
SHOWPRIV.EXE	Show Privileges	Displays the users and groups assigned to a privilege on the local computer.
SLEEP.EXE	Batch File Wait	Causes a computer to wait for a specified amount of time.

Table F.1 Windows 2000 Server Resource Kit Tools *(continued)*

File	Tool Name	Description
SMCONFIG.EXE	Service Monitoring Tool	Monitors services on local or remote computers and notifies the administrator when their status changes.
SOON.EXE	Soon	Schedules commands to run within the next 24 hours.
SRVANY.EXE	Applications as Services Utility	Enables applications to run as services.
SRVINSTW.EXE	Service Installation Wizard	Installs and deletes services and device drivers on a local or remote computer.
TIMETHIS.EXE	Time This	Times how long it takes to execute a given command.
TRACEDMP.EXE	Trace Dump	A command line utility to process a trace log file or real time trace buffers and convert them to CSV file.
TRACEENABLE.EXE	Trace Enable	Displays your current tracing options.
TRACELOG.EXE	Trace Log	A command line utility to start/stop or enable trace logging.
UPTIME.EXE	Uptime	Displays system uptime.
GPOLMIG.EXE	Group Policy Migration Utility	Migrates settings from downlevel policy files to the W2000rk group policy object structure.
Hardware Compatibility List	Hardware Compatibility List	Lists Windows 95, Windows 98, Microsoft Windows NT®, and Windows 2000 compatible hardware.
LBRIDGE.CMD	L-Bridge	Command-line script used to assist in migration from NT4 LMRepl to Windows 2000's File Replication Service (FRS).

Table F.1 Windows 2000 Server Resource Kit Tools *(continued)*

File	Tool Name	Description
SETUPMGR.EXE	Setup Manager	Generates answer files for unattended installations or upgrades on multiple computers.
SETUPMGR.EXE	Setup Manager	Generates answer files for unattended installations or upgrades on multiple computers.
SYSDIFF.EXE	Sysdiff	Pre-installs applications as part of an automated setup.
SYSPREP.EXE	System Preparation Utility	Automates the cloning of a customized configuration of Windows 2000 to multiple computers.
UNATTEND.DOC	Unattended Installation Document	Provides detailed information on how to automate Windows 2000 installation through the use of answer files.
CHKLNKS.EXE	Link Check Wizard	Scans all the shortcut (link) files on a computer and lets user remove dead ones.
CMDHERE.INF	Command Here	Powertoy that adds a "CMD Prompt Here" item to some right-click menus displayed by Windows Explorer.
QUICKRES.EXE	Quick Resolution Changer	Changes display settings without restarting the computer.
RUNEXT.INF	Run Command Shell Extension	This shell extension adds a Run command to the context menu for files that are right-clicked in Windows Explorer
SIPANEL.EXE	Soft Input Panel	Allows computers to use a pen device for input.
WINEXIT.SCR	Windows Exit Screen Saver	Logs off the current user after a specified time has elapsed.

Table F.1 **Windows 2000 Server Resource Kit Tools** *(continued)*

File	Tool Name	Description
APIMON.EXE	API Monitor	Monitors the API calls made by a process.
ATANLYZR.EXE	Apple Talk Network Device Analyzer	Analyzes AppleTalk Devices.
AUDITPOL.EXE	Audit Policy	Enables user to modify the audit policy of local or remote computers.
ENUMPROP.EXE	Enumerate Properties	Dumps all properties set on any directory services object.
GETMAC.EXE	Get MAC Address	Gets a computer's MAC (Ethernet) layer address and binding order.
GUID2OBJ.EXE	GUID to Object	A console program that maps a GUID to a distinguished name.
INSTALER.EXE	Installation Monitor: Monitor Installation	Tracks changes made by setup programs in the Registry, .INI files, and other child processes.
INSTALER.EXE	Installation Monitor: Show Installation	Shows changes made by an applications setup program after having been monitored by INSTALLER.EXE.
INSTALER.EXE	Installation Monitor: Undo Installation	Uninstalls applications originally monitored by INSTALLER.EXE.
LOGANALYST	Cybersafe Log Analyst	A Microsoft Management Console (MMC) snap-in that will assist you in organizing and interpreting security event logs from Windows 2000 by analyzing and generating detailed reports.
LOGEVENT.EXE	Log Event	Logs events to a local or remote computer.

Table F.1 Windows 2000 Server Resource Kit Tools *(continued)*

File	Tool Name	Description
LSREPORT.EXE	License Reporting Tool	Generates TDF of license status for reporting usage and availability.
LSVIEW.EXE	License Service List	Lists available license servers
MSINFOSETUP.EXE	Microsoft System Information Extensions	Extensions used to view System Information Files created as .nfo files or Windows Report Tool-created .cab files within the System Information MMC snap-in.
OLEVIEW.EXE	OLE/COM Object Viewer	Browses, configures, and tests Microsoft Component Object Model classes installed on a computer.
RPCDUMP.EXE	RPCDump	It dumps all of the endpoints in the endpointmapper database, pings each endpoint, gathers some other stats, sorts it a bit, and spits out the data.
SNMPMON.EXE	SNMP Monitor	Monitors Simple Network Management Protocol variables for multiple nodes and logs them to a database.
SNMPUTIL.EXE	SNMP Utility	Queries a Simple Network Management Protocol host or community for Management Information Base values from command prompt.
SRVINFO.EXE	Server Information	Displays network, disk drive, and service information about a local or remote server.

Table F.1 Windows 2000 Server Resource Kit Tools *(continued)*

File	Tool Name	Description
TAPICHECK.EXE	Tapicheck	Indicates whether the specified TAPI server(s) can be contacted and, if there are any errors, it provides first-level diagnostics and offers the user suggested fixes.
WINLOGO LINK	Windows Logo Requirments Documentation	Describes the technical requirements that must be satisfied by an application to receive the Designed for Windows NT and Windows 95 logo.
ASSOCIATE.EXE	Associate	Adds "file extension, executable program" associations to the registry.
COMPRESS.EXE	Compress File(s)	Compresses files.
DIRUSE.EXE	Directory Disk Usage	Scans a directory tree and reports the amount of space used by each user.
DISKMAP.EXE	Diskmap	Displays information about a disk and the contents of its Partition Table.
DISKUSE.EXE	Disk Use	Scans a directory tree and reports the amount of space used by each user.
DMDIAG.EXE	DMDiag	Used to save disk volume configuration to a text file or (over)write a signature to a disk partition.
EXPAND.EXE	Expand File	Expands compressed files.
EXTRACT.EXE	Extract File	Extracts files from cabinet (.cab) files.

Table F.1 Windows 2000 Server Resource Kit Tools *(continued)*

File	Tool Name	Description
FREEDISK.EXE	Free Disk Space	Checks for free disk space, returning a 0 if there is enough space for an operation and a 1 if there isn't.
FTEDIT.EXE	FT Registry Information Editor	Edits the Registry for fault tolerance settings.
LINKD.EXE	Linkd	Links an NTFS file system directory to a target object.
MTFCHECK.EXE	Microsoft Tape Format Check	Verify that tape media is Microsoft tape Format (MTF) compliant.
QGREP.EXE	Qgrep	A tool much like the Posix tool Grep.exe that can perform string search routines on files.
ROBOCOPY.EXE	Robust File Copy Utility	Maintains multiple mirror images of large folder trees on network servers.
RSM_DBIC.EXE	Remote Storage Integrity Checker	Steps through the database and inspects each database object attribute for valid values and referential integrity.
RSM_DBUTIL.EXE	Remote Storage Utility	A graphical user interface (GUI)-based tool used to manually configure libraries that RSM's auto-configuration cannot.
RSMCONFG.EXE	Removable Storage Manual Configuration Wizard	A command line tool used to manually configure libraries that RSM's auto-configuration cannot.
SHOWDISK.EXE	Show Disk Space	Displays configuration and fault-tolerance information for primary partitions and logical drives.
TAKEOWN.EXE	Take Ownership	Allows you to take ownership of a file.

Table F.1 Windows 2000 Server Resource Kit Tools *(continued)*

File	Tool Name	Description
VFI.EXE	Virtual File Information	Retrieves and generates detailed information on files, such as attributes, version, and flags.
IE5NTWA.EXE	Internet Explorer Web Accessories	A selection of useful utilities for Internet Explorer 5.
DESIGN.DOC	Design Template	Design Template.
DESIGN.RTF	Design Template	Design Template.
EXPLORATIONAIR	Exploration Air	A Web application showcase for Microsoft Internet Information Services (IIS) 5.0 and the Windows 2000 Server operating system.
FUNCSPEC.DOC	Functional Specification Template	Functional Specification Template.
FUNCSPEC.RTF	Functional Specification Template	Functional Specification Template
HTTPCMD.EXE	Http Command	Command-line HTTP client.
IFILTTST.EXE	IFilter Test Suite	IFilter Test Suite validates IFilter implementations by calling IFilter methods and checking the returned values for compliance with the IFilter specification.
IISHOSTSVC.EXE	IIS Host Helper Service	Registers host header strings as network basic input/output system (NetBIOS) names allowing intranet users using WINS to access server by host name without Domain Name Service (DNS).
INTERNETSCANNER	Internet Scanner	Network security scanner that generates comprehensive reports detailing security vulnerabilities.

Table F.1 Windows 2000 Server Resource Kit Tools *(continued)*

File	Tool Name	Description
METAEDIT.CAB	Metabase Editor	A tool for checking metabase integrity. Used in conjunction with the Metabase Browser/Editor.
SECTEMPLATES.MSC	Security Configuration Manager Templates	Quickly defines IIS security policies through IIS Security Templates.
STANDARD.DOC	Standards Review Form	Standards Review Form
STANDARD.RTF	Standards Review Form	Standards Review Form
TEMPMAKE.CAB	IIS Permissions Wizard Template Maker	Assist in the creation of new permissions templates for use with IIS version 5.0 and later.
CEPSETUP.EXE	Certificate Enrollment Module for Routers	Windows 2000 will be able to process CEP requests from a Cisco Router. The Cisco router uses CEP to request certificates that it uses for IP Security.
DHCPLOC.EXE	DHCP Server Locator Utility	Locates DHCP servers on a network.
DRMAPSRV.EXE	Drive Share	Automatically Net Share and Net Use client drive for TS access.
FINDGRP.EXE	Find Group	Gets a user's direct and indirect group memberships.
FLOPLOCK.EXE	Lock Floppy Disk Drives	Locks a computer's floppy disks so that only members of the Administrators and Power Users groups can access them.
GLOBAL.EXE	Global Groups	Lists contents of global groups across domains and workstations.
GRPCPY.EXE	Group Copy	Copies the user names in an existing group to another group in the same or a different domain.
IFMEMBER.EXE	IfMember	Checks whether a user is a member of a specified group.

Table F.1 Windows 2000 Server Resource Kit Tools *(continued)*

File	Tool Name	Description
IPSECPOL.EXE	IPSEC Policy Configuration Tool	This tool is used to configure IP Security policies in the Directory Service or in a local or remote registry. It does everything that the IP Security MMC snap-in does and is even modeled after the snap-in.
KERBTRAY.EXE	Kerbtray	Is used to display ticket information for a given computer running the Kerberos protocol.
KLIST.EXE	Klist.exe	View and deleting the Kerberos tickets granted to the current logon session.
LOCAL.EXE	Local Groups	Lists contents of local groups across domains and workstations.
LOGOFF.EXE	Logoff	Logs off a user.
MOVEUSR.EXE	Move Users	
NTRIGHTS.EXE	NTRights	Grants or revokes Windows 2000 rights to or from users or groups.
PASSPROP.EXE	Passprop	Sets domain policy flags for password complexity and whether the administrator account can be locked out.
PERMCOPY.EXE	Permission Copy	Copies file- and share-level permissions from one share to another.
PERMS.EXE	Permissions	Displays a user's access permissions for a file or directory.
PRNADMIN.DLL	Printer Administration Objects	Manages printers, printer drivers, and printer ports on local and remote computers.

Table F.1 Windows 2000 Server Resource Kit Tools *(continued)*

File	Tool Name	Description
RCLIENT.EXE	Remote Console Client	Client tool used to remotely connect to computers running the Remote Console Service.
RCMD.EXE	Remote Command Client	Client tool used to remotely connect to computers running the Remote Command Service.
RCMDSVC.EXE	Remote Command Service	A tool that enables clients using RCMD.EXE to run remote sessions.
RCONSVC.EXE	Remote Console Service	A tool that enables clients using RCLIENT.EXE to run remote sessions.
RDPCLIP.EXE	File Copy	Copy files between TS server and client.
REMOTETAPIMONITOR.EXE	Remote TAPI Monitor	Captures RPC errors and interprets possible TAPI problems.
RKILL.EXE	Remote Process Kill	Enumerates and kills processes on a remote computer.
RMTSHARE.EXE	Remote Share	Set ups and deletes shares remotely.
RSHSVC.EXE	Remote Shell Client	Provides a command-line shell or single command execution service for remote users.
SHOWACLS.EXE	Show ACLS	Enumerates access rights for files, folders, and trees.
SHOWGRPS.EXE	Show Groups	Shows the groups to which a user belongs.
SHOWMBRS.EXE	Show Members	Shows the usernames of members of a group.
SHUTDOWN.EXE	Shutdown	Shuts down or reboots a local or remote computer.

Table F.1 Windows 2000 Server Resource Kit Tools *(continued)*

File	Tool Name	Description
SHUTGUI.EXE	Remote Shutdown GUI	Shuts down or reboots a local or remote computer.
SRVCHECK.EXE	Server Share Check	Lists non-hidden shares on a computer and enumerates the access-control lists for each one.
SU.EXE	SU	Enables a user to run a process in the security context of a different user.
SUBINACL.EXE	SubInACL	Migrates security information between users, groups and domains.
SUBNET_OP.VBS	Subnet Objects	For manipulating subnet objects in the DS.
TAPIDIAG.EXE	TAPI Diagnostics Tool	Captures RPC errors and interprets possible TAPI problems.
TSREG.EXE	TS Registry Editor	Command-line tool to control client-side options.
USRSTAT.EXE	User Statistics	Lists usernames, full names, and last logon date and time for all user accounts in a domain.
USRTOGRP.EXE	User to Group	Adds users to a group from a text file.
WHOAMI.EXE	WhoAmI	Returns the domain or computer name and username of the user who is currently logged on.
WINS.DLL	WINS Replication Network Monitor Parser	An extension DLL used to Parse Wins Data with Network Monitor
WINSCHK.EXE	Winschk	Checks inconsistencies in Windows Internet Name Service databases and verifies replication activity.

Table F.1 Windows 2000 Server Resource Kit Tools *(continued)*

File	Tool Name	Description
WINSTA.EXE	Active Session Tool	Shows active sessions and session count for Remote Admin control.
XCACLS.EXE	Xcacls	Displays and modifies security options for system folders.
CLEARMEM.EXE	Clear Memory	Forces pages out of RAM.
EXCTRLST.EXE	Extensible Performance Counter List	Displays information on extensible performance counter DLLs installed on a computer.
PFMON.EXE	Page Fault Monitor	Lists the source and number of page faults generated by an application's function calls.
SETEDIT.EXE	Setedit	Editing tool for Performance Monitor chart settings files.
TOP.EXE	Top	Lists the processes that are using the most processor time.
VADUMP.EXE	VaDump	Shows the state and size of each segment of virtual address space.
BOOTCONFIG.VBS	Bootconfig	Displays boot configuration information for a computer.
BUS.VBS	Bus	Displays the bus information for a computer.
CACHEINFO.VBS	Cacheinfo	Gets the cache information for a computer.
CDROMDRIVES.VBS	Cdromdrives	Outputs information on CD-ROM drives.
CHECKBIOS.VBS	Checkbios	Displays information on system BIOS.
CODECFILE.VBS	Codecfile	Outputs Information on Codec Files.
COMPSYS.VBS	Compsys	Lists the properties of a computer system.

Table F.1 Windows 2000 Server Resource Kit Tools *(continued)*

File	Tool Name	Description
CREATEUSERS.VBS	Create User	Much like the Addusers tool. However this tool was designed with the Microsoft Active Directory™ directory service capabilities.
DESKTOP.VBS	DeskTops	Lists the desktop properties of a system.
DEVICE.VBS	Device	Controls devices on a computer.
DEVICEMEM.VBS	Devicemem	Outputs information on device memory address ranges.
DISKPARTITION.VBS	Diskpartition	Gets the disk partition information of a computer.
DMACHAN.VBS	Dmachan	Gets the DMA channels on a computer.
DRIVES.VBS	Drives	Outputs information on physical disk drives.
ENABLEDHCP.VBS	Enabledhcp	Enables DHCP protocol on a Computer.
ENUMCLASSES.VBS	Enumclasses	Enumerates Windows Management Instrumentation (WMI) classes within a namespace on a server.
ENUMINSTANCES.VBS	Enuminstances	Enumerates instances of a WMI class within a namespace.
ENUMNAMESPACES.VBS	Enumnamespaces	Enumerates WMI namespaces on a server.
EVENTLOGMON.VBS	Eventlogmon	Monitors event log events.
EXEC.VBS	Exec	Executes a command.
FILEMAN.VBS	Fileman	Performs various simple operations on a file.
GROUP.VBS	Group	Outputs the groups in the specified domain.

Table F.1   Windows 2000 Server Resource Kit Tools *(continued)*

File	Tool Name	Description
IRQRES.VBS	Irqres	Outputs IRQ Information.
KEYBOARD.VBS	Keyboard	Outputs information on the keyboard configuration for a computer.
LDORDERGRP.VBS	Ldordergrp	Lists the service dependency groups on a computer.
LISTADAPTERS.VBS	Listadapters	Lists properties of all network adapters.
LISTDISPLAYCONFIG.VBS	Listdisplayconfig	Obtains the display configuration of a computer.
LISTFREESPACE.VBS	Listfreespace	Lists available disk space on all drives of a computer.
LISTOS.VBS	listos	Lists properties of the operating system on a computer.
LISTPRINTERS.VBS	Listprinters	Lists properties of all printers installed on a computer.
LISTPROPERTIES.VBS	Listproperties	Lists properties of a WMI object or class.
LISTSPACE.VBS	Listspace	Lists the size of each drive on a computer.
LOGMEMINFO.VBS	Logmeminfo	Obtains the logical memory configuration of a computer.
LSTDPCONINFO.VBS	Lstdpconinfo	Obtains the display controller information of a computer.
MOTHERBOARD.VBS	Motherboard	Gets the motherboard information from a computer.
NETCONNECTIONS.VBS	Netconnections	Lists selected properties of network connections.
NETWORKPROTOCOL.VBS	Networkprotocol	Displays network protocol information.
OSRECONFIG.VBS	Osreconfig	Gets or toggles the OS recover configuration for a computer.

Table F.1 Windows 2000 Server Resource Kit Tools *(continued)*

File	Tool Name	Description
PAGEFILE.VBS	Pagefile	Controls pagefiles on a computer.
PARALLELPORT.VBS	Parallelport	Gets the parallel port information for a computer.
POINTDEV.VBS	Pointdev	Gets the pointing device information for a computer.
PROCESSOR.VBS	Processor	Gets the pointing device information for a computer.
PROGRAMGROUP.VBS	PROGRAMGROUP	Gets the pointing device information for a computer.
PROTOCOLBINDING.VBS	PROTOCOLBINDING	Gets the pointing device information for a computer.
PS.VBS	PS	Gets the pointing device information for a computer.
PSTOP.VBS	PSTOP	Gets the pointing device information for a computer.
QUERY.VBS	Query	Performs a General Windows Management Instrumentation (WMI) Query.
REGCONFIG.VBS	Regconfig	Outputs or modifies the registry configuration.
RESTART.VBS	Restart	Shuts down or reboots a local or remote computer.
SCSICONTROLLER.VBS	Scsicontroller	Gets the SCSI controller information for a computer.
SERIALPORT.VBS	Serialport	Outputs the serial port configurations for a computer.
SERVICE.VBS	Service	Controls services on a computer.
SHARE.VBS	Share	Lists, creates, or deletes shares from a computer.
SOUNDDEVICE.VBS	Sounddevice	Lists the sound device properties on a computer.

Table F.1   Windows 2000 Server Resource Kit Tools *(continued)*

File	Tool Name	Description
STARTUP.VBS	Startup	Enumerates the startup programs on a computer.
SYSTEMACCOUNT.VBS	Systemaccount	Displays system account information.
TAPEDRIVE.VBS	Tapedrive	Displays information on tape drives.
THREAD.VBS	Thread	Lists all threads currently running on a computer.
USERACCOUNT.VBS	Useraccount	Displays user account information.
ACTIVEPERL.EXE	Active Perl	The long-awaited "merge" of the two popular Perl ports. ActivePerl includes Perl for Microsoft Win32®, PerlScript, and Perl Package Manager.
AUTOEXNT.EXE	AutoExNT Service	Allows you to start a custom batch file at boot-up without needing to log on to that computer.
CHOICE.EXE	User Input for Batch Files	Prompts user to make a choice in a batch program.
FORFILES.EXE	Forfiles	Enables batch processing of files in a directory or tree.
GETTYPE.EXE	Get Type	Sets the error level to allow you to determine Microsoft Windows NT® workstation, server, or domain.
LOGTIME.EXE	Logtime	Logs start or finish times of programs running in a batch file.
TIMEOUT.EXE	Timeout	Pauses execution of a command for a specified period.
WAITFOR.EXE	Waitfor	Synchronizes a task across multiple computers.

Table F.1   Windows 2000 Server Resource Kit Tools *(continued)*

File	Tool Name	Description
EFSINFO.EXE	Encrypted File Info	Displays information of encrypted files on NTFS partitions.
SYSSCANSETUP.EXE	System Scanner	System security scanner that generates comprehensive report detailing security vulnerabilities.
DNSPROV.DLL	DNS WMI Provider	Allows user to manage DNS zones and records

Summary

This appendix presented installation and content information for the disc that accompanies the Small Business Server 2000 Resource Kit.

Glossary

Symbols

.msc files

Snap-ins can be assembled into a custom console, and then stored as saved console .msc files.

A

Active Directory

The directory service for Windows 2000 Server. It stores information about objects on the network and makes this information available for authorized administrators and users. Active Directory gives network users access to permitted resources anywhere on the network using a single logon process. It provides administrators with an intuitive hierarchical view of the network and a single point of administration for all network objects.

ActiveX

A set of technologies that enables software components to interact with one another in a networked environment, regardless of the language in which the components were created.

ActiveX control

A reusable software component that incorporates ActiveX technology.

administrator account

A specific Windows 2000 user account that has rights and permissions to set up and manage domain controllers or local computers. The administrator account also has permission to manage user and group accounts, assign passwords and permissions, and help users with networking issues.

American National Standards Institute

(ANSI) A quasi-national standards organization that provides area charters for groups that establish standards in specific fields. Standards approved by ANSI are often called ANSI standards. Additionally, ANSI is commonly used to refer to a low-level table of codes used by a computer.

American Standard Code for Information Interchange

(ASCII) A coding scheme using seven or eight bits that assigns numeric values to up to 256 characters, including letters, numerals, punctuation marks, control characters, and other symbols.

ANSI

See definition for: American National Standards Institute

anti-virus software

Anti-virus software is specifically designed for the detection and prevention of virus programs. Because new virus programs are created all the time, many makers of anti-virus products offer periodic updates of their software to customers.

See also: computer virus

argument

A constant, variable, or expression passed to a procedure or subprogram.

ASCII

See definition for: American Standard Code for Information Interchange

attribute

1. Information that indicates that a file is read-only, hidden, system, or compressed, or whether the file has been changed since a backup copy of it was made. 2. In object-oriented software, an individual characteristic of the object.

B

BackOffice Home snap-in

A customized BackOffice Server snap-in that displays Health Monitor alerts, performance counters, and current service status.

BackOffice Manager snap-in

A customized BackOffice Server snap-in that displays and saves customizable queries of Active Directory objects such as users, groups, printers, and computers. The BackOffice Manager snap-in saves customized queries as query nodes and aggregator nodes.

backup

A duplicate copy of a program, a disk, or data, made either for archiving purposes or for safeguarding valuable files from loss should the active copy be damaged or destroyed. Some application programs automatically make backup copies of data files, maintaining both the current version and the previous version.

backup domain controller

(BDC) In a Windows NT Server domain, a computer running Windows NT Server that receives a copy of the domain's directory database, which contains all account and security policy information for the domain. The copy is synchronized periodically and automatically with the copy on the primary domain controller. BDCs also authenticate user logons and can be promoted to function as a primary domain controller as needed. Multiple BDCs can exist in a domain. Windows NT 3.51 and 4.0 BDCs can participate in a Windows 2000 domain when the domain is configured in mixed mode.

See also: primary domain controller

backup operator

A type of local or global group that contains the user rights needed to back up and restore files and folders. Members of the Backup Operators group can back up and restore files and folders, regardless of ownership, access permissions, encryption, or auditing settings.

bandwidth

In communications, the difference between the highest and lowest frequencies in a given range. For example, a telephone line accommodates a bandwidth of 3,000 Hz, the difference between the lowest (300 Hz) and highest (3,300 Hz) frequencies it can carry. In computer networks, greater bandwidth indicates faster data-transfer capability and is expressed in bits per second (bps).

BDC

See definition for: backup domain controller

browser

Software that interprets Hypertext Markup Language (HTML) files posted on the World Wide Web, formats them as Web pages, and displays them.

C

cable modem

A modem that provides broadband Internet access in the range of 10 to 30 megabits per second (Mbps).

cache

A location for frequently accessed files that are read from memory or a local disk for faster access.

child domain

For DNS and Active Directory, a domain located in the namespace tree directly beneath another domain name (its parent domain). For example, example.reskit.com is a child domain of the parent domain, reskit.com. A child domain is also called a subdomain.

See also: parent domain, directory partition, domain

clean installation

Installation of an operating system on a new computer or a computer with a reformatted disk drive.

client computer

On a local area network (LAN) or the Internet, a computer that accesses shared network resources provided by a server computer.

COM

See definition for: Component Object Model

Component Object Model

(COM) A specification developed by Microsoft for building software components that can be assembled into programs, or that add functionality to existing programs running on Microsoft Windows platforms. COM components can be written in a variety of languages.

computer name

A unique name of up to 15 uppercase characters that identifies a computer to the network. The name cannot be the same as any other computer or domain name in the network.

computer virus

A computer virus is an executable file designed to replicate itself while avoiding detection. A virus may disguise itself as a legitimate program. Viruses are often rewritten and adjusted so that they will not be detected. Anti-virus programs must be updated continuously to look for new and modified viruses. Viruses are the number one method of computer vandalism.

See also: anti-virus software

connectivity

1. The nature of the connection between a user's computer and another computer, such as a server or a host computer on the Internet or a network. This may describe the quality of the circuit or telephone line, the degree of freedom from noise, or the bandwidth of the communications devices. 2. The ability of hardware devices and/or software packages to transmit data between other hardware devices and/or software packages. 3. The ability of hardware devices, software packages, or a computer itself to work with network devices or work with other hardware devices, software packages, or a computer over a network connection.

console

A control unit through which a user communicates with a computer via a primary input device (keyboard or mouse) and a primary output device (screen). A console integrates all the tools, information, and Web pages an administrator needs to perform specific tasks.

Console Tree

In MMC, a tree-formatted, ordered listing of all the nodes available in the current console, appearing in the left pane. The display of the Console Tree is similar to a folder and directory structure on a hard disk drive. The items in the Console Tree (for example, Web pages, folders, and controls) and their hierarchical organization determines the management capabilities of a console.

See also: Details Pane

copy backup

A backup that copies all selected files without marking them as having been backed up—the archive bit is not set. A copy backup is useful between normal and incremental backups, as copying does not affect other backup operations.

See also: daily backup, differential backup, incremental backup, normal backup

D

daily backup

A backup that occurs every day, copying all selected modified files the day the backup is performed. These files are not marked as having been backed up—the archive bit is not set.

See also: differential backup, copy backup, incremental backup, normal backup

database

A file composed of records, each containing fields together with a set of operations for searching, sorting, recombining, and other functions.

default gateway

The gateway used to connect to the rest of the network.

See also: gateway

defragmentation

The process of rewriting parts of a file to contiguous sectors on a hard disk drive. Defragmentation is done to increase disk speed access and retrieval. For example, when files are updated, updates are typically saved on the largest continuous space on the hard disk, often on a different sector than other parts of the file. When files are fragmented like this, a computer must search the entire hard disk each time the file is opened to locate all of its parts, which slows down response time considerably. Routine disk defragmentation is recommended.

Details Pane

In MMC, the right pane that displays the results of a selection in the Console Tree.

See also: Console Tree

device driver

A program that allows a specific device, such as a modem, network adapter, or printer, to communicate with Windows 2000. Although a device can be installed on a system, Windows 2000 cannot use the device until the appropriate driver has been installed and configured. If a device is listed in the Hardware Compatibility List, a driver is usually included with Windows 2000. Device drivers are loaded (for all enabled devices) when a computer is started, running transparently thereafter.

DHCP

See definition for: Dynamic Host Configuration Protocol

DHCP-server computer

A server computer running DHCP that allocates IP addresses to the host computers on the network as needed.

dial-up networking

The client version of Windows 2000 Remote Access Service, which enables users to connect to remote networks.

differential backup

A backup that copies files created or changed since the last normal or incremental backup. Files are not marked as having been backed up—the archive bit is not set. If you are performing a combination of normal and differential backups, restoring your files and folders will require you to have the last normal and last differential backup.

See also: normal backup, incremental backup, copy backup, daily backup

digital certificate

An encrypted file containing user or server identification information, which is used to verify identity and to establish a secure link. It is called a client certificate when issued to a server administrator.

digital subscriber line

(DSL) A special communication line that uses modulation technology to maximize the amount of data that can be sent over copper wires. DSL is used for connections from telephone switching stations to a subscriber, rather than between switching stations.

directory partition

A self-contained section of a directory hierarchy that can have its own properties, such as replication configuration. Active Directory includes the domain, configuration, and schema directory partitions.

See also: naming context, child domain

directory replication

The process of updating the directories of all servers within and between sites.

See also: directory replication traffic

directory replication traffic

The network traffic created during the process of updating the directories of all servers within and between domains.

See also: directory replication

Directory Service

A Microsoft Windows NT Server process that manages information in the directory database and handles directory requests from users services and applications. The directory service provides the Microsoft Exchange Server Address Book enforces the rules governing the structure and contents of the directory and sends directory replication notifications to directories on other servers and processes directory replication notifications from other servers.

disk quotas

A Windows 2000 feature for restricting disk space usage on disks formatted for NTFS. Disk quotas can be set on basic or dynamic disks, from the Disk Manager snap-in.

See also: dynamic disks

distribution group

A group of recipients created to expedite mass mailing of messages and other information. When e-mail is sent to a distribution list, all members of that list receive a copy of the message.

See also: group

DNS

See definition for: Domain Name System

domain

A group of computers that are part of a network and share a common directory database. In Windows 2000, a domain is a security boundary and permissions that are granted in one domain are not carried over to other domains.

See also: child domain

domain controller

A computer running Windows 2000 Server that manages user access to a network, which includes logging on, authentication, and access to Active Directory and shared resources.

domain local group

A Windows 2000 group available only in native-mode domains, which can contain members from anywhere in the forest, in trusted forests, or in a trusted pre Windows 2000 domain. Domain local groups can grant permissions only to resources within the domain in which they exist. Typically, domain local groups are used to gather security principals from across the forest to control access to resources within the domain.

See also: universal group

Domain Name System

(DNS) A TCP/IP standard name service that allows clients and servers to resolve names into Internet Protocol (IP) addresses and vice versa. Dynamic DNS in Windows 2000 enables clients and servers to automatically register themselves without the need for administrators to manually define records.

DS

See definition for: Directory Service

DSL

See definition for: digital subscriber line

dual-boot system

A computer that allows a user to start one of two operating systems on a PC.

dynamic

A process occurring immediately and concurrently.

dynamic disks

A portion of a hard drive, called a disk, which is managed by the Disk Management snap-in. Dynamic disks can only contain dynamic volumes, also created and managed by the Disk Management snap-in.

See also: disk quotas, dynamic volumes

Dynamic Host Configuration Protocol

(DHCP) A protocol for assigning Internet Protocol (IP) addresses to computers and other devices on a TCP/IP network. Dynamic addressing permits a computer to have a different address each time it logs on to a network.

dynamic volumes

A logical volume on a hard drive created using the Disk Management snap-in. Dynamic volumes can be formatted in several disk configurations: simple, spanned, striped, mirrored, and RAID-5. Dynamic volumes can only be created on dynamic disks.

See also: dynamic disks

E

ETRN

A type of signal sent from an SMTP e-mail client to the managing e-mail server that initiates e-mail delivery from the STMP server to the SMTP client.

extensibility

The ability to add functionality to an existing application.

Extensible Markup Language

(XML) A meta-markup language that provides a format for describing structured data. This facilitates a more precise declaration of content and more meaningful search results across multiple platforms. In addition, XML will enable a new generation of Web-based data viewing and manipulation of applications.

F

FAT

See definition for: file allocation table

fault tolerance

The ability of a system to respond to an event, such as a power failure, so information is not lost and operations continue without interruption.

file allocation table

(FAT) A table on a disk set aside to reference file locations on that disk. The table is a chain identifying where each part of a file is located. It acts similarly to a table of contents for a book.

file sharing

The use of computer files on networks, wherein files are stored on a central computer or a server and are accessed by more than one user. When a single file is shared by many people, access can be regulated through such means as password protection, security clearances, or file locking to prohibit changes to a file by more than one person at a time.

File Transfer Protocol

(FTP) The protocol used for copying files to and from remote computer systems on a network using TCP/IP, such as the Internet.

filter

A program or set of features within a program that reads its standard or designated input, transforms the input in some desired way, and then writes the output to its standard or designated output destination. A database filter, for example, might flag information of a certain age. Also, a pattern or mask that data is passed through to weed out specified data. For instance, a filter used in e-mail or in retrieving newsgroup messages can allow users to filter out messages from other users. In Internet Information Server (IIS), a feature of ISAPI that allows preprocessing of requests and postprocessing of responses, permitting site-specific handling of HTTP requests and responses.

firewall

A combination of hardware and software that provides a security system, usually to prevent unauthorized access from the Internet to an internal network or intranet.

forest

One or more domain trees that do not form a contiguous namespace. Forests allow organizations to group divisions that operate independently but still need to communicate with one another.

FTP

See definition for: File Transfer Protocol

G

gateway

A device that connects networks using different communications protocols so information can be passed from one network to the other. A gateway transfers information and converts it to a form compatible with the protocols used by the receiving network.

See also: default gateway

global catalog

A server that holds a complete replica of the configuration and schema naming contexts for the forest, a complete replica of the domain naming context in which the server is installed, and a partial replica of all other domains in the forest. The global catalog is the central repository for information about objects in the forest.

global group

For Windows 2000 Server, a group that can be used in its own domain, in member servers and workstations of the domain, and in trusting domains. In all those places a global group can be granted rights and permissions and can become a member of local groups. However, a global group can contain user accounts only from its own domain.

group

A collection of users, computers, contacts, public folders, and other groups. Groups can be used as a security identifier or as a distribution list. Distribution groups are used only for e-mail. Security groups are used to grant access to resources. A group in Windows 2000 is roughly equivalent to a distribution list in Exchange 5.5.

See also: distribution list

Group Policy

An administrator's tool for defining and controlling how programs, network resources, and the operating system operate for users and computers in an organization. In an Active Directory environment, Group Policy is applied to users or computers on the basis of their membership in sites, domains, or organizational units.

Group Policy object

A collection of Group Policy settings. Group Policy objects are essentially the documents created by the Group Policy snap-in, a Windows 2000 utility. Group Policy objects are stored at the domain level, and they affect users and computers contained in sites, domains, and organizational units.

H

hardware

The physical components of a computer system, including any peripheral equipment such as printers, modems, and mouse devices.

host

The main computer in a system of computers or terminals connected by communications links.

HTML

See definition for: Hypertext Markup Language

HTTP

See definition for: Hypertext Transfer Protocol

Hypertext Markup Language

(HTML) A system of marking up or tagging a document so that it can be published on the World Wide Web. Documents prepared in HTML contain reference graphics and formatting tags. You use a Web browser (such as Microsoft Internet Explorer) to view these documents.

Hypertext Transfer Protocol

(HTTP) A client/server protocol used on the Internet for sending and receiving HTML documents. HTTP is based on the TCP/IP protocol.

I

ICANN

See definition for: Internet Corporation for Assigned Names and Numbers

IIS

See definition for: Internet Information Services

IMS

See definition for: Internet Mail Service

incremental backup

A backup that copies only files created or changed since the last normal or incremental backup. Files are marked as having been backed up--the archive bit is set. If a combination of normal and incremental backups is used to restore your data, you need to have the last normal backup and all subsequent incremental backup sets.

See also: normal backup, copy backup, daily backup, differential backup

independent software vendor

(ISV) Also known as a third-party software developer. An individual or an organization that independently creates computer software.

Integrated Services Digital Network

(ISDN) A completely digital telephone/telecommunications network that carries voice, data, and video information over the existing telephone network infrastructure. It is designed to provide a single interface for hooking up a telephone, fax machine, computer, and so on.

Internet Corporation for Assigned Names and Numbers

(ICANN) A corporation that accredits domain name registration companies.

Internet Information Services

(IIS) Microsoft's Web service for publishing information on an intranet or the Internet, and for building server-based Web applications. Upon installation, Exchange 2000 extends the messaging capabilities of IIS and incorporates them into the Exchange message routing architecture.

Internet Mail Service

(IMS) An Exchange component that enables users to exchange messages with Internet users. It can also be used to connect sites over any simple mail transfer protocol backbone.

Internet Packet Exchange

(IPX) The protocol in Novell NetWare that governs addressing and routing of packets within and between LANs.

Internet Protocol

(IP) A network routing protocol used to address, route, and reassemble IP packets.

Internet Server Application Programming Interface

(ISAPI) An easy-to-use, high performance interface for back-end applications using Microsoft's Internet Information Server.

Internet service provider

(ISP) A business that supplies Internet connectivity services to individuals, businesses, and other organizations.

Intranet

A network within an organization that uses Internet technologies and protocols, but is available only to certain people, such as employees of a company. An intranet is also called a private network.

IP

See definition for: Internet Protocol

IP address

A 32-bit address used to identify a node on an IP internetwork. Each node on the IP internetwork must be assigned a unique IP address, which is made up of the network ID and unique host ID. This address is typically represented with the decimal value of each octet separated by a period (for example, 192.168.7.27). In Windows 2000, the IP address can be configured manually or dynamically through DHCP.

IPX

See definition for: Internet Packet Exchange

ISA

See definition for: Microsoft Internet Security and Acceleration Server

ISAPI

See definition for: Internet Server Application Programming Interface

ISDN

See definition for: Integrated Services Digital Network

ISP

See definition for: Internet service provider

ISV

See definition for: independent software vendor

J

There are no glossary terms that begin with this letter.

K

There are no glossary terms that begin with this letter.

L

LAN

See definition for: local area network

LDAP

See definition for: Lightweight Directory Access Protocol

legacy

Pertaining to documents, data, or systems that existed prior to a certain time.

Lightweight Directory Access Protocol

(LDAP) A network protocol designed to work on TCP/IP stacks to extract information from a hierarchical directory such as X.500. It is useful for searching through data to find a particular piece of information.

load balancing

Windows Clustering scales the performance of a server-based program (such as a Web server) by distributing its client requests across multiple servers within the cluster. This is known as load balancing. Each host can specify the load percentage that it will handle, or the load can be equally distributed across all the hosts. If a host fails, Windows Clustering dynamically redistributes the load among the remaining hosts.

local area network

(LAN) A group of computers and other devices dispersed over a relatively limited area and connected by a communications link that enables the devices to interact together.

log file

A file that stores messages generated by an application, service, or operating system. These messages are used to track the operations performed. For example, Web servers maintain log files listing every request made to the server. Log files are usually ASCII files and often have a .log extension. During backup, log files are created to record the date the backup tapes were made and the names of files and directories successfully backed up and restored. The Performance Logs and Alerts service also creates log files.

M

MAPI

See definition for: Messaging Application Programming Interface

message queue

An ordered list of messages awaiting transmission, from which they are taken up on a first in, first out (FIFO) basis.

Messaging Application Programming Interface

A messaging architecture enabling multiple applications to interact with multiple messaging systems across a variety of hardware platforms. MAPI is built on the COM foundation.

MHTML

See definition for: MIME Encapsulation of Aggregate HTML Documents

Microsoft Internet Security and Acceleration Server

(ISA) The BackOffice Server and Small Business Server component that provides network firewall capabilities and local caching of Internet content.

Microsoft Management Console

(MMC) A management display framework that hosts administration tools and applications. Using MMC you can create, save, and open collections of tools and applications. Saved collections of tools and applications are called consoles.

Microsoft Transaction Server

(MTS) A COM-based transaction processing system that provides a run-time environment for objects that perform the business logic of n-tier applications.

migration

The process of moving an existing messaging system to another system by copying the existing mailboxes, messages, and other data, and importing that information into a new messaging system.

MIME

See definition for: Multipurpose Internet Mail Extensions

MIME Encapsulation of Aggregate HTML Documents

An Internet standard for sending HTML documents within (MIME) formatted messages. The HTML documents are included as body parts and are referenced by URLs in the message.

mixed mode

The default mode setting for domains on Windows 2000 domain controllers. Mixed mode allows Windows 2000 domain controllers and Windows NT backup domain controllers to coexist in a domain. Mixed mode does not support the universal and nested group enhancements of Windows 2000. You can change the domain mode setting to Windows 2000 native mode after all Windows NT domain controllers are either removed from the domain, or upgraded to Windows 2000.

See also: native mode

MMC

See definition for: Microsoft Management Console

MMDS

See definition for: Multi-channel Multi-point Distribution Systems

modem

Short for modulator/demodulator, a communications device that enables a computer to transmit information over a standard telephone line.

MTS

See definition for: Microsoft Transaction Server

Multi-channel Multi-point Distribution Systems

A broadband technology for connecting to public networks such as the Internet.

Multipurpose Internet Mail Extensions

(MIME) A standard that enables binary data to be published and read on the Internet. The header of a file with binary data contains the MIME type of the data, which informs client programs (such as Web browsers and mail packages) that they cannot process the data as straight text.

N

namespace

The snap-in UI combination of the Console Tree and the Details Pane.

naming context

A term used in X.500 and LDAP standards.

See also: directory partition

native mode

The condition in which all domain controllers within a domain are Windows 2000 domain controllers, and an administrator has enabled native mode operation (through Active Directory Users and Computers).

See also: mixed mode

NDR

See definition for: non-delivery report

Node

1. A junction of some type. 2. In local area networks (LANs), a device that is connected to the network and is capable of communicating with other network devices. 3. In tree structures, a location on the tree that can have links to one or more nodes below it.

non-delivery report

(NDR) A notice that a message was not delivered to the recipient.

normal backup

A backup that copies all selected files, marking each file as backed up--the archive bit is set. For normal backups, only the most recent copy of the backup file or tape is needed to restore all of the files. A normal backup is usually performed the first time a backup set is created.

See also: copy backup, daily backup, differential backup, incremental backup

NTFS

See definition for: NTFS file system

NTFS file system

The file system designed for use specifically with the Windows NT operating system. NTFS supports file system recovery and extremely large storage media. It also supports object-oriented applications by treating all files as objects with user-defined and system-defined attributes.

NTLM

Name for the protocol formerly known as the Windows NT LAN Manager.

O

object

The basic unit of Active Directory. It is a distinct, named set of attributes that represents something concrete, such as a user, a printer, a computer, or an application.

organizational unit

An Active Directory container into which you can place objects such as user accounts, groups, computers, printers, applications, file shares, and other organizational units. Organizational units can be used to contain and assign specific permissions to groups of objects, such as users and printers. An organizational unit cannot contain objects from other domains. An organizational unit is the smallest unit you can assign or delegate administrative authority to.

Outlook Web Access

Outlook Web Access for Microsoft Exchange 2000 Server provides users access to e-mail, personal calendars, group scheduling, contacts, and collaboration applications using a Web browser. It can be used for UNIX and Macintosh users, users without access to a Microsoft Outlook 2000 client, or users connecting from the Internet. Outlook Web Access offers cross-platform client access for roaming users, users with limited hardware resources, and users who do not have access to their own computers.

OWA

See definition for: Outlook Web Access

P

packet

A transmission unit of fixed maximum size that consists of binary information. This information represents both data and a header containing an ID number, source and destination addresses, and error-control data.

paging file

A hidden file on the hard disk that Windows 2000 uses to hold parts of programs and data files that do not fit in memory. The paging file and physical memory, or RAM, comprise virtual memory. Windows 2000 moves data from the paging file to memory as needed, and moves data from memory to the paging file to make room for new data. Also called a swap file.

parameter

In programming, a value that is given to a variable, either at the beginning of an operation or before an expression is evaluated by a program. Until the operation is completed, a parameter is effectively treated as a constant value by the program. A parameter can be text, a number, or an argument name assigned to a value that is passed from one routine to another. Parameters are used as a means of customizing program operation.

parent domain

For DNS and Active Directory, domains that are located in the namespace tree directly above other derivative domain names (child domains). For example, reskit.com is the parent domain for eu.reskit.com, its child domain.

See also: child domain

partition

A logically distinct portion of memory or a storage device that functions as though it were a physically separate unit. In database programming, a subset of a database table or file.

PDC

See definition for: primary domain controller

Point-to-Point Protocol

(PPP) A data link protocol for dial-up telephone connections, such as between the computer and the Internet.

Point-to-Point Tunneling Protocol

(PPTP) An encryption protocol used for remote computers to securely access other computer networks across an Internet connection. Often used with virtual private networks (VPNs).

POP3

See definition for: Post Office Protocol version 3

POP3 server

A server that provides access to a single Inbox.

Post Office Protocol version 3

(POP3) An Internet protocol that allows a client to download mail from an inbox on a server to the client computer where messages are managed. This protocol works well for computers that are unable to maintain a continuous connection to a server.

PPP

See definition for: Point-to-Point Protocol

PPTP

See definition for: Point-to-Point Tunneling Protocol

primary domain controller

(PDC) A Windows NT 4.0 and 3.51 domain controller that is the first one created in the domain, containing the primary storehouse for domain data. Within the domain, the PDC periodically replicates its data to the other domain controllers, known as backup domain controllers (BDCs).

See also: backup domain controller

protocol

A set of rules and conventions by which two computers pass messages across a network. Networking software usually implements multiple levels of protocols layered one on top of another.

Q

query

A specific set of instructions for extracting data repetitively and presenting it for use.

R

RAID

See definition for: redundant array of independent disks

RAS

See definition for: Remote Access Service

redundant array of independent disks

(RAID) A mechanism for storing identical data on multiple disks for redundancy, improved performance, and increased mean time between failures (MTBF). RAID provides fault tolerance and appears to the operating system as a single logical drive. Windows 2000 provides three RAID levels: Level 0 (striping) which is not fault-tolerant, Level 1 (mirroring), and Level 5 (striped volume with parity).

Remote Access Service

(RAS) On a local area network, a host that is equipped with modems to enable users to connect to the network over telephone lines. Works with dial-up networking to allow one computer to connect to another through a modem to access shared resources, such as drives or files.

remote administration

Administering a computer or network from another computer.

roaming user profile

A server-based user profile that is downloaded to the local computer when a user logs on. It is updated both locally and on the server when the user logs off. A roaming user profile is available from the server when logging on to any computer that is running Windows 2000 Professional or Windows 2000 Server.

robust

Able to function or to continue functioning well in unexpected situations.

S

SCSI

See definition for: Small Computer System Interface

Secure Sockets Layer

(SSL) A protocol designed to establish a secure communications channel to prevent the interception of critical information, such as credit card numbers.

Simple Mail Transfer Protocol

(SMTP) The standard protocol for Internet mail. SMTP transfers mail from server to server and from mail system to mail system. In Exchange 2000 Server, SMTP is the native transport protocol.

Small Computer System Interface

A standard high-speed parallel interface defined by the X3T9.2 committee of the American National Standards Institute (ANSI). A SCSI interface is used for connecting microcomputers to peripheral devices, such as hard disks and printers, and to other computers and local area networks.

SMTP

See definition for: Simple Mail Transfer Protocol

snap-in

Software that makes up the smallest unit of a Microsoft Management Console (MMC) extension. One snap-in represents one unit of management behavior.

SSL

See definition for: Secure Sockets Layer

subnet mask

A 32-bit value expressed as four decimal numbers from 0 to 255, separated by periods (for example, 255.255.0.0.). This number allows TCP/IP to distinguish the network ID portion of the IP address from the host ID portion. The host ID identifies individual computers on the network. TCP/IP hosts use the subnet mask to determine whether a destination host is located on a local or a remote network.

System Monitor

A Windows 2000 tool that allows you to measure the performance of your own computer or other computers on the network in real time or for historical trending. With System Monitor, you can collect and view extensive data about the usage of hardware resources and the activity of system services on computers you administer.

systemroot

The path and folder name where the Windows 2000 system files are located. Typically, this is C:\Winnt, although a different drive or folder can be designated when Windows 2000 is installed. The value %systemroot% can be used to replace the actual location of the folder that contains the Windows 2000 system files. To identify and open your systemroot folder, click Start, click Run, and then type %systemroot%

T

taskpad

A dynamic HTML page that receives information from Microsoft Management Console (MMC) regarding extension tasks, returning actions to the appropriate snap-in.

TCP/IP

See definition for: Transmission Control Protocol/Internet Protocol

Transmission Control Protocol/Internet Protocol

(TCP/IP) A protocol that networks use to communicate with each other. It is the de facto standard for data transmission over networks, including the Internet.

trust relationship

The relationship between two domains that makes it possible for a user in one domain to access resources in another domain.

TURN

A type of signal sent from an SMTP e-mail client to the managing e-mail server that initiates e-mail delivery from the STMP server to the SMTP client.

U

uninterruptible power supply

(UPS) A device, connected between a computer (or other electronic equipment) and a power source (usually an outlet), that ensures that electrical flow to the computer is not interrupted because of a blackout and, in most cases, protects the computer against potentially damaging events, such as power surges and brownouts. All UPS units are equipped with a battery and a loss-of-power sensor; if the sensor detects a loss of power, it switches over to battery so that the user has time to save any work and shut off the computer.

universal group

A Windows 2000 group available only in native mode that is valid anywhere in a forest. A universal group appears in the global catalog but contains primarily global groups from domains in a forest. This is the simplest form of group and can contain other universal groups, global groups, and users.

See also: domain local group

UPS

See definition for: uninterruptible power supply

URL

(Uniform Resource Locator) An address for a resource on the Internet. URLs are used by Web browsers to locate Internet resources.

V

virtual private network

(VPN) Similar to Remote Access Service, this solution provides secure, encrypted access to corporate networks from clients connecting through the Internet.

VPN

See definition for: virtual private network

W

There are no glossary terms that begin with this letter.

X

XML

See definition for: Extensible Markup Language

Y

There are no glossary terms that begin with this letter.

Z

There are no glossary terms that begin with this letter.

Index

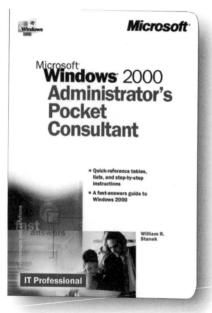

The practical, *portable* *guide*
to Microsoft Exchange 2000 Server

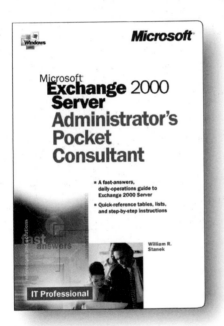

This book is the concise, easy-to-use reference you'll want with you at all times as you support and manage Microsoft® Exchange 2000 Server and Exchange 2000 Enterprise Server. Ideal at the desk or on the go from server to workstation, this hands-on, fast-answers guide focuses on what you need to do to get the job done. With extensive easy-to-read tables, lists, and step-by-step instructions, it's the portable, readable guide that will consistently save you time and effort.

U.S.A.	**$29.99**
U.K.	£20.99
Canada	$43.99

ISBN: 0-7356-0962-4

Microsoft®

mspress.microsoft.com

The *practical,* portable *guide to* Microsoft **SQL Server 2000!**

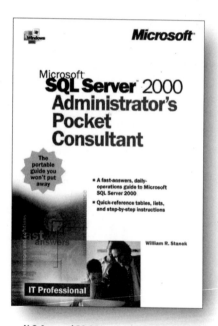

U.S.A. **$29.99**
U.K. £20.99 [V.A.T. included]
Canada $43.99
ISBN: 0-7356-1129-7

MICROSOFT® SQL SERVER™ 2000 ADMINISTRATOR'S POCKET CONSULTANT is the ideal concise, immediate reference you'll want with you at all times as you deal with the details of Microsoft SQL Server 2000 database administration. Whether you handle administration for 50 users or 5000, this hands-on, fast-answers guide focuses on what you need to do to get the job done quickly. With extensive easy-to-read tables, lists, and step-by-step instructions, it's the portable, readable guide that will consistently save you time and minimize system downtime by giving you the right information right now.

Microsoft®

mspress.microsoft.com

Ready
solutions
for the
IT administrator

Keep your IT systems up and running with the ADMINISTRATOR'S COMPANION series from Microsoft. These expert guides serve as both tutorials and references for critical deployment and maintenance of Microsoft products and technologies. Packed with real-world expertise, hands-on numbered procedures, and handy workarounds, ADMINISTRATOR'S COMPANIONS deliver ready answers for on-the-job results.

Microsoft® SQL Server™ 7.0 Administrator's Companion

U.S.A.	$59.99
U.K.	£38.99 [V.A.T. included]
Canada	$89.99
ISBN	1-57231-815-5

Microsoft Exchange Server 5.5 Administrator's Companion

U.S.A.	$59.99
U.K.	£38.99 [V.A.T. included]
Canada	$89.99
ISBN	0-7356-0646-3

Microsoft Windows® 2000 Server Administrator's Companion

U.S.A.	$69.99
U.K.	£45.99 [V.A.T. included]
Canada	$107.99
ISBN	1-57231-819-8

Microsoft Systems Management Server 2.0 Administrator's Companion

U.S.A.	$59.99
U.K.	£38.99 [V.A.T. included]
Canada	$92.99
ISBN	0-7356-0834-2

***Microsoft*®**

mspress.microsoft.com

END-USER LICENSE AGREEMENT FOR MICROSOFT SOFTWARE

Microsoft Small Business Server 2000 RESOURCE KIT

IMPORTANT-READ CAREFULLY: This Microsoft End-User License Agreement ("EULA") is a legal agreement between you (either an individual or a single entity) and Microsoft Corporation for the Microsoft software identified above, which includes computer software and may include associated media, printed materials, additional computer software applications, and "online" or electronic documentation ("SOFTWARE"). By downloading, installing, copying, or otherwise using the SOFTWARE, you agree to be bound by the terms of this EULA. If you do not agree to the terms of this EULA, do not install or use the SOFTWARE.

SOFTWARE LICENSE

The SOFTWARE is protected by copyright laws and international copyright treaties, as well as other intellectual property laws and treaties. **The SOFTWARE is licensed, not sold.**

1. **GRANT OF LICENSE.** This EULA grants you the following rights:

   a. **SOFTWARE.** Except as otherwise provided herein, you, as an individual, may install and use copies of the SOFTWARE on an unlimited number of computers, including workstations, terminals or other digital electronic devices ("COMPUTERS"), provided that you are the only individual using the SOFTWARE. If you are an entity, you may designate one individual within your organization to have the right to use the SOFTWARE in the manner provided above. The SOFTWARE is in "use" on a COMPUTER when it is loaded into temporary memory (i.e., RAM) or installed into permanent memory (e.g., hard disk, CD-ROM, or other storage device) of that COMPUTER.

   b. **Client/Server Software.** The SOFTWARE may contain one or more components which consist of both of the following types of software: "Server Software" that is installed and provides services on a COMPUTER acting as a server ("Server"); and "Client Software" that allows a COMPUTER to access or utilize the services provided by the Server Software. If the component of the SOFTWARE consists of both Server Software and Client Software which are used together, you may also install and use copies of such Client Software on COMPUTERS within your organization and which are connected to your internal network.

   Such COMPUTERS running this Client Software may be used by more than one individual.

2. **DESCRIPTION OF OTHER RIGHTS AND LIMITATIONS.**

   a. **Limitations on Reverse Engineering, Decompilation, and Disassembly.** You may not reverse engineer, decompile, or disassemble the SOFTWARE, except and only to the extent that such activity is expressly permitted by applicable law notwithstanding this limitation.

   b. **Rental.** You may not rent, lease, or lend the SOFTWARE.

   c. **Support Services.** Microsoft does not support the SOFTWARE, however, in the event Microsoft does provide you with support services related to the SOFTWARE ("Support Services"), use of such Support Services is governed by the Microsoft policies and programs described in the user manual, in "online" documentation, and/or in other Microsoft-provided materials. Any supplemental software code provided to you as part of the Support Services shall be considered part of the SOFTWARE and subject to the terms and conditions of this EULA. With respect to technical information you provide to Microsoft as part of the Support Services, Microsoft may use such information for its business purposes, including for product support and development. Microsoft will not utilize such technical information in a form that personally identifies you.

   d. **Software Transfer.** You may permanently transfer of all of your rights under this EULA, provided you retain no copies, you transfer all of the SOFTWARE (including all component parts, the media and printed materials, any upgrades, this EULA, and, if applicable, the Certificate of Authenticity), **and** the recipient agrees to the terms of this EULA. If the SOFTWARE is an upgrade, any transfer must include all prior versions of the SOFTWARE.

   e. **Termination.** Without prejudice to any other rights, Microsoft may terminate this EULA if you fail to comply with the terms and conditions of this EULA. In such event, you must destroy all copies of the SOFTWARE and all of its component parts.

3. **UPGRADES.** If the SOFTWARE is labeled as an upgrade, you must be properly licensed to use a product identified by Microsoft as being eligible for the upgrade in order to use the SOFTWARE. SOFTWARE labeled as an upgrade replaces and/or supplements the product that formed the basis for your eligibility for the upgrade. You may use the resulting upgraded product only in accordance with the terms of this EULA. If the SOFTWARE is an upgrade of a component of a package of software programs that you licensed as a single product, the SOFTWARE may be used and transferred only as part of that single product package and may not be separated for use on more than one computer.

4. **INTELLECTUAL PROPERTY RIGHTS.** All title and intellectual property rights in and to the SOFTWARE (including but not limited to any images, photographs, animations, video, audio, music, text and "applets" incorporated into the SOFTWARE), and any copies you are permitted to make herein are owned by Microsoft or its suppliers. All title and intellectual property rights in and to the content which may be accessed through use of the SOFTWARE is the property of the respective content owner and may be protected by applicable copyright or other intellectual property laws and treaties. This EULA grants you no rights to use such content. If this SOFTWARE contains documentation which is provided only in electronic form, you may print one copy of such electronic documentation. You may not copy the printed materials accompanying the SOFTWARE.

5. **U.S. GOVERNMENT LICENSE RIGHTS.** SOFTWARE provided to the U.S. Government pursuant to solicitations issued on or after December 1, 1995 is provided with the commercial license rights and restrictions described elsewhere herein. SOFTWARE provided to the U.S. Government pursuant to solicitations issued prior to December 1, 1995 is provided with "Restricted Rights" as provided for in FAR, 48 CFR 52.227-14 (JUNE 1987) or DFAR, 48 CFR 252.227-7013 (OCT 1988), as applicable.

6. **EXPORT RESTRICTIONS.** You agree that you will not export or re-export the SOFTWARE (or portions thereof) to any country, person or entity subject to U.S. export restrictions. You specifically agree not to export or re-export the SOFTWARE (or portions thereof): (i) to any country subject to a U.S. embargo or trade restriction; (ii) to any person or entity who you know or have reason to know will utilize the SOFTWARE (or portion thereof) in the production of nuclear, chemical or biological weapons; or (iii) to any person or entity who has been denied export privileges by the U.S. government. For additional information see http://www.microsoft.com/exporting/.

7. **DISCLAIMER OF WARRANTIES. To the maximum extent permitted by applicable law, Microsoft and its suppliers provide the SOFTWARE and any (if any) Support Services *AS IS AND WITH ALL FAULTS,* and hereby disclaim all warranties and conditions, either express, implied or statutory, including, but not limited to, any (if any) implied warranties or conditions of merchantability, of fitness for a particular purpose, of lack of viruses, of accuracy or completeness of responses, of results, and of lack of negligence or lack of workmanlike effort, all with regard to the SOFTWARE, and the provision of or failure to provide Support Services. ALSO, THERE IS NO WARRANTY OR CONDITION OF TITLE, QUIET ENJOYMENT, QUIET POSSESSION, CORRESPONDENCE TO DESCRIPTION OR NON-INFRINGEMENT, WITH REGARD TO THE SOFTWARE. THE ENTIRE RISK AS TO THE QUALITY OF OR ARISING OUT OF USE OR PERFORMANCE OF THE SOFTWARE AND SUPPORT SERVICES, IF ANY, REMAINS WITH YOU.**

8. **EXCLUSION OF INCIDENTAL, CONSEQUENTIAL AND CERTAIN OTHER DAMAGES. TO THE MAXIMUM EXTENT PERMITTED BY APPLICABLE LAW, IN NO EVENT SHALL MICROSOFT OR ITS SUPPLIERS BE LIABLE FOR ANY SPECIAL, INCIDENTAL, INDIRECT, OR CONSEQUENTIAL DAMAGES WHATSOEVER (INCLUDING, BUT NOT LIMITED TO, DAMAGES FOR LOSS OF PROFITS OR CONFIDENTIAL OR OTHER INFORMATION, FOR BUSINESS INTERRUPTION, FOR PERSONAL INJURY, FOR LOSS OF PRIVACY, FOR FAILURE TO MEET ANY DUTY INCLUDING OF GOOD FAITH OR OF REASONABLE CARE, FOR NEGLIGENCE, AND FOR ANY OTHER PECUNIARY OR OTHER LOSS WHATSOEVER) ARISING OUT OF OR IN ANY WAY RELATED TO THE USE OF OR INABILITY TO USE THE SOFTWARE, THE PROVISION OF OR FAILURE TO PROVIDE SUPPORT SERVICES, OR OTHERWISE UNDER OR IN CONNECTION WITH ANY PROVISION OF THIS EULA, EVEN IN THE EVENT OF THE FAULT, TORT (INCLUDING NEGLIGENCE), STRICT LIABILITY, BREACH OF CONTRACT OR BREACH OF WARRANTY OF MICROSOFT OR ANY SUPPLIER, AND EVEN IF MICROSOFT OR ANY SUPPLIER HAS BEEN ADVISED OF THE POSSIBILITY OF SUCH DAMAGES.**

9. **LIMITATION OF LIABILITY AND REMEDIES. Notwithstanding any damages that you might incur for any reason whatsoever (including, without limitation, all damages referenced above and all direct or general damages), the entire liability of Microsoft and any of its suppliers under any provision of this EULA and your exclusive remedy for all of the foregoing shall be limited to the greater of the amount actually paid by you for the SOFTWARE or U.S.\$5.00. The foregoing limitations, exclusions and disclaimers shall apply to the maximum extent permitted by applicable law, even if any remedy fails its essential purpose.**

10. **NOTE ON JAVA SUPPORT.** THE SOFTWARE MAY CONTAIN SUPPORT FOR PROGRAMS WRITTEN IN JAVA. JAVA TECHNOLOGY IS NOT FAULT TOLERANT AND IS NOT DESIGNED, MANUFACTURED, OR INTENDED FOR USE OR RESALE AS ONLINE CONTROL EQUIPMENT IN HAZARDOUS ENVIRONMENTS REQUIRING FAIL-SAFE PERFORMANCE, SUCH AS IN THE OPERATION OF NUCLEAR FACILITIES, AIRCRAFT NAVIGATION OR COMMUNICATION SYSTEMS, AIR TRAFFIC CONTROL, DIRECT LIFE SUPPORT MACHINES, OR WEAPONS SYSTEMS, IN WHICH THE FAILURE OF JAVA TECHNOLOGY COULD LEAD DIRECTLY TO DEATH, PERSONAL INJURY, OR SEVERE PHYSICAL OR ENVIRONMENTAL DAMAGE. Sun Microsystems, Inc. has contractually obligated Microsoft to make this disclaimer.

11. **APPLICABLE LAW.** If you acquired this SOFTWARE in the United States, this EULA is governed by the laws of the State of Washington. If you acquired this SOFTWARE in Canada, unless expressly prohibited by local law, this EULA is governed by the laws in force in the Province of Ontario, Canada; and, in respect of any dispute which may arise

hereunder, you consent to the jurisdiction of the federal and provincial courts sitting in Toronto, Ontario. If this SOFTWARE was acquired outside the United States, then local law may apply.

12. **ENTIRE AGREEMENT.** **This EULA (including any addendum or amendment to this EULA which is included with the SOFTWARE) is the entire agreement between you and Microsoft relating to the SOFTWARE and the Support Services (if any) and it supersedes all prior or contemporaneous oral or written communications, proposals and representations with respect to the SOFTWARE or any other subject matter covered by this EULA. To the extent the terms of any Microsoft policies or programs for Support Services conflict with the terms of this EULA, the terms of this EULA shall control.**

13. **QUESTIONS?** Should you have any questions concerning this EULA, or if you desire to contact Microsoft for any reason, please contact the Microsoft subsidiary serving your country, or write: Microsoft Sales Information Center/One Microsoft Way/Redmond, WA 98052-6399.

SI VOUS AVEZ ACQUIS VOTRE PRODUIT MICROSOFT AU CANADA, LA GARANTIE LIMITÉE SUIVANTE VOUS CONCERNE :

RENONCIATION AUX GARANTIES. Dans toute la mesure permise par la législation en vigueur, Microsoft et ses fournisseurs fournissent le PRODUIT LOGICIEL et tous (selon le cas) Services d'assistance TELS QUELS ET AVEC TOUS LEURS DÉFAUTS, et par les présentes excluent toute garantie ou condition, expresse ou implicite, légale ou conventionnelle, écrite ou verbale, y compris, mais sans limitation, toute (selon le cas) garantie ou condition implicite ou légale de qualité marchande, de conformité à un usage particulier, d'absence de virus, d'exactitude et d'intégralité des réponses, de résultats, d'efforts techniques et professionnels et d'absence de négligence, le tout relativement au PRODUIT LOGICIEL et à la prestation ou à la non-prestation des Services d'assistance. DE PLUS, IL N'Y A AUCUNE GARANTIE ET CONDITION DE TITRE, DE JOUISSANCE PAISIBLE, DE POSSESSION PAISIBLE, DE SIMILARITÉ À LA DESCRIPTION ET D'ABSENCE DE CONTREFAÇON RELATIVEMENT AU PRODUIT LOGICIEL. Vous supportez tous les risques découlant de l'utilisation et de la performance du PRODUIT LOGICIEL et ceux découlant des Services d'assistance (s'il y a lieu).

EXCLUSION DES DOMMAGES INDIRECTS, ACCESSOIRES ET AUTRES. Dans toute la mesure permise par la législation en vigueur, Microsoft et ses fournisseurs ne sont en aucun cas responsables de tout dommage spécial, indirect, accessoire, moral ou exemplaire quel qu'il soit (y compris, mais sans limitation, les dommages entraînés par la perte de bénéfices ou la perte d'information confidentielle ou autre, l'interruption des affaires, les préjudices corporels, la perte de confidentialité, le défaut de remplir toute obligation y compris les obligations de bonne foi et de diligence raisonnable, la négligence et toute autre perte pécuniaire ou autre perte de quelque nature que ce soit) découlant de, ou de toute autre manière lié à, l'utilisation ou l'impossibilité d'utiliser le PRODUIT LOGICIEL, la prestation ou la non-prestation des Services d'assistance ou autrement en vertu de ou relativement à toute disposition de cette convention, que ce soit en cas de faute, de délit (y compris la négligence), de responsabilité stricte, de manquement à un contrat ou de manquement à une garantie de Microsoft ou de l'un de ses fournisseurs, et ce, même si Microsoft ou l'un de ses fournisseurs a été avisé de la possibilité de tels dommages.

LIMITATION DE RESPONSABILITÉ ET RECOURS. Malgré tout dommage que vous pourriez encourir pour quelque raison que ce soit (y compris, mais sans limitation, tous les dommages mentionnés ci-dessus et tous les dommages directs et généraux), la seule responsabilité de Microsoft et de ses fournisseurs en vertu de toute disposition de cette convention et votre unique recours en regard de tout ce qui précède sont limités au plus élevé des montants suivants: soit (a) le montant que vous avez payé pour le PRODUIT LOGICIEL, soit (b) un montant équivalant à cinq dollars U.S. (5,00 $ U.S.). Les limitations, exclusions et renonciations ci-dessus s'appliquent dans toute la mesure permise par la législation en vigueur, et ce même si leur application a pour effet de priver un recours de son essence.

LÉGISLATION APPLICABLE. Sauf lorsqu'expressément prohibé par la législation locale, la présente convention est régie par les lois en vigueur dans la province d'Ontario, Canada. Pour tout différend qui pourrait découler des présentes, vous acceptez la compétence des tribunaux fédéraux et provinciaux siégeant à Toronto, Ontario.

Si vous avez des questions concernant cette convention ou si vous désirez communiquer avec Microsoft pour quelque raison que ce soit, veuillez contacter la succursale Microsoft desservant votre pays, ou écrire à: Microsoft Sales Information Center, One Microsoft Way, Redmond, Washington 98052-6399.

System Requirements

To use the Microsoft Small Business Server 2000 Resource Kit compact disc, you need a computer equipped with the following minimum configuration:

- PC with 300-MHz Pentium II or higher processor

- 128 MB RAM minimum; 256 MB recommended

- Microsoft Windows 2000 Professional or Windows 2000 Server

- 50 MB available hard disk space for minimum tools install; 220 MB recommended for complete tools install with electronic book

- Super VGA monitor; 256-color display card recommended

- CD-ROM or DVD-ROM drive

- Microsoft Mouse or other compatible pointing device

Some of the tools on this CD might have additional system requirements, such as Microsoft Excel.

OWNER REGISTRATION CARD   *Register Today!*   0-7356-1252-8

Return the bottom portion of this card to register today.

Microsoft® Small Business Server 2000
Resource Kit

FIRST NAME   MIDDLE INITIAL   LAST NAME

INSTITUTION OR COMPANY NAME

ADDRESS

CITY   STATE   ZIP

(   )

E-MAIL ADDRESS   PHONE NUMBER

U.S. and Canada addresses only. Fill in information above and mail postage-free.
Please mail only the bottom half of this page.

**For information about Microsoft Press®
products, visit our Web site at
mspress.microsoft.com**

Microsoft